D1046768

The Gate and The Light

By the same author,

"WHAT HATH GOD WROUGHT"

THE GATE AND THE LIGHT

Recollections Of Another Pilgrim

By

Arnold Brown

BOOKWRIGHT PUBLICATIONS
Toronto, Canada

ISBN No. 0-9691772-0-8

Printed in Toronto, Canada, for Bookwright Publications, Suite 900, Continental Bank Building, 130 Adelaide Street West, Toronto, Canada, M5H 3E8

Designed by Fusion Studios, Toronto

THE GATE AND THE LIGHT

is for all who will read it,
but especially for my wife and daughters
who were a more important part of this saga
than they may realize or the book reveal

The man ... looking upon the Evangelist very carefully, said, "Whither must I fly?"

Then said the Evangelist, pointing with his finger over a very wide field, "Do you see yonder wicket gate?"

The man said, "No."

Then said the other, "Do you see yonder shining light?"

He said, "I think I do."

Then said the Evangelist, "Keep that light in your eye, and go up directly thereto, so shalt thou see the gate; at which, when thou knockest, it shall be told thee what thou shalt do."

From "The Pilgrim's Progress"
by John Bunyan 1628-1688

Foreword

In his autobiography General Arnold Brown invites his readers to board the magic carpet and to follow him into the fascinating world of Salvation Army ministry on five continents. We visit evangelical and social centres, hospitals and headquarters, and meet people of deep convictions and total commitment to the service of mankind. We are introduced to the residents in our rehabilitation homes, as well as to royalty, to statesmen and politicians. We meet the young people of The Salvation Army and also some of the veterans of the movement. We meet that "army behind the Army," the advisory boards, with whom the writer is so well acquainted.

But we are invited to visit other worlds as well. We watch the spiritual and intellectual development of a young Canadian salvationist, divinely destined to become the eleventh General of the Salvation Army. We are introduced to natural beauty and cultural accomplishments in many parts of the world. We are reminded of the pre-eminence of spiritual issues over material things.

We are indebted to General Brown for sharing his experiences, his faith and his philosophy in such a captivating way. Conscientious thoroughness has been the hallmark of Arnold Brown's work throughout his Salvation Army ministry. This book is no exception. It meets the criterion expressed in Paul's admonition to Timothy: "Try hard to show yourself worthy of God's approval, as a labourer who need not be ashamed!"

Jarl Wahlström, General
International Headquarters,
London, England.

Acknowledgements

Is it legitimate to describe *The Gate And The Light* as autobiography seeing not everything the writer has experienced, thought or sensed is included?

Confidentiality, modesty and even a vestige of self-protection exact omission. Confidentiality, as any doctor, lawyer or clergyman knows, imprisons in the memory episodes which are the very stuff of "best sellers." Modesty inescapably tempers the style of recording life's highest moments and occasional achievements; it is impossible to avoid Paul's admonition: "Don't cherish exaggerated ideas of yourself or your importance." (Rom. 12: 3, Phillips).

Self-preservation in failing to expose all of one's personal failings springs less from vanity, in my instance, than from the honest hope that nothing recorded should, however slightly, lower the dignity of the office of the General, one which I consider myself to have been especially privileged to occupy.

I found the book difficult to plan. To sketch one's career chronologically makes for easy sequence; but reflection on certain themes continues across the decades. Episodes criss-cross their way to a conclusion regardless of the calendar or changed circumstances. I therefore decided that I would use my personal experiences as "jumping off" points for the expression of views that may not have matured until many years later. With this faltering explanation I can only hope for the reader's indulgence if narrative suddenly becomes observation.

My gratitude is limitless: to the General who willingly provided a Foreword; to my understanding wife, since many of the experiences recorded were hers also (to her I must often have appeared present in body but absent in thought while attempting to relive in a matter of months the interests of a lifetime); to Lieut-Colonel Will Burrows (R) who ferreted out facts when recollection was uncertain; and to the many others whose interest in The Salvation Army and its history persuaded me to undertake the recording of my small contribution to its God-glorifying and humanity-helping ministry.

The Salvation Army has been for me a "gate" of opportunity to an exhilarating and rewarding life. Illuminating that "gate" unfailingly has been "The Light of the World," Christ Himself, in Whose Name and power my nearly half-a-century of officership has been joyfully rendered.

— A.B.

Contents

CHAPTER 1

A Time To Be Born

There seemed to be two Londons. There was the real city, its sombre buildings dripping with rain. And there was the other, an upside-down city, a rippling reflection in the wet road splashed into a thousand distortions by the wheels of huge lorries and explosive gusts of wind. Two Londons. One present, solid, tangible. The other, also present but, like memory, without firm edges, sometimes clear and sometimes tremblingly elusive.

Present and past, one mirrored in the other, were with me as we whisked by "The Angel," one of the city's ancient landmarks, on that drenching December morning in 1981, a few days before my active service as a Salvation Army officer melted into what friends encouragingly termed "active retirement."

I had a strange thought and a stranger feeling. Nearby, White Lion Street shadows a better-known Pentonville Road as it noses its way into Islington High Street. At No. 35, on the 15th of September, 1853, a London *parfumeur* (not by trade, the family said, but by profession!) named George Brown and his wife, Anne Augusta, welcomed a son into the family and gave him the Christian names of Edwin Rees. The infant was to be my paternal grandfather.

My strange thought?

Could this percolator of scents have realized that by his procreation he had moved one generation closer to providing a world leader for a movement which, only a mile or so away, would not come into being until his son was twelve years old? How could he?

The stranger feeling followed.

It was sensuously disturbing; at first a mental shiver, and then a physical trembling. The blood of that perfumer was in my veins. I was part of his posterity. Without ever knowing it, he was substantially to endow the movement known as The Salvation Army. His September child was himself to father five sons and four daughters, seven of whom were to become officers in this as yet unborn battalion of the church militant. One would be my father and, had he lived to see it, Arnold Rees Brown would have been as surprised as his perfumer grandfather that, on the 5th of May, 1977, at historic Sunbury Court on the banks of the Thames where it flows lazily past Hampton Wick, I should be elected as the international leader and eleventh general of The Salvation Army. My own astonishment outclasses that of all my forbears and contemporaries put together.

On Christmas Day, 1873, twenty-year-old Edwin, now a hairdresser (the term then meant a maker of hair-pieces) with a Manchester address, married Lydia Burgess, four years his senior, in the Russell Street Chapel, Liverpool, "according to the rites and ceremonies of the United Methodist Free Church." These were my paternal grandparents, and frequently I was taken from our home in Egremont, Cheshire, by ferry across the Mersey River, for Sunday tea in their Liverpool home.

My bearded grandfather seemed to me to be a man of immense age, a kind of Noah, or at times, I thought, a Methuselah. Only the sweets from his overcoat pocket, dispensed as we walked together to the Sunday evening meeting held in what was then known as the Liverpool VI Corps of The Salvation Army, moderated my fear of him.

If I feared my grandfather, I adored my grandmother. She moved among her family with dignity, authority and a freely-demonstrated affection. She loved and was loved. I know little of her background but, as a child, suspected that she had had a better education than my grandfather or, if not, possessed a higher intelligence. Three books on my shelves are a slight clue. Written by her brother, the Rev. Wm. Burgess, a Chicago clergyman, they display considerable scholarship. One, *The Bible in Shakespeare,* is impressive in its mining of the Bard's plays and poetry to discover the Biblical origins of so much of what he wrote. Another, *Bible Sidelights from Shakespeare,* is described as a compilation of twenty lay homilies from parallel texts of the Bible and of Shakespeare's works. In the preface the author asserts that the greatest of the world's dramatists drew "living waters from exhaustless wells" and that he "gathered his most precious pearls from the deepest depths —the Bible." My great-uncle must also have been a devotee of Oxford's first professor of fine arts since the third title is *The Religion of Ruskin.* All were published by Fleming H. Revell. An accomplished brother does not mean an accomplished sister, but I choose to think that the two were not entirely disparate.

How Edwin and Lydia Brown came to give seven of their nine children to Salvation Army officership was chronicled pseudonymously under the title of "The Simpson Family," the narrative running in serial form for many weeks in the 1922 British edition of *The Young Soldier,* The Salvation Army's paper for children.

I have told the story often and in many parts of the world. Charlie, the eldest of the Brown children, in the company of a group of boys, was seeking to enliven the peaceful calm of an early Sunday evening. A passing procession of Salvationists on their way from an outdoor meeting to an indoor service in their hall provided all and more that mischief and boyish exuberance could hope for. A hard, dirty cabbage stalk lay in the gutter, a perfect missile. Flung forcibly at the marchers by Charlie, it hit a woman on the temple. She fell to the ground, blood spurting from the wound. The march was totally disrupted and, while the marchers attended to the casualty, the boys vanished.

Conscience, however, was sharper than the cabbage stalk. Later in the evening Charlie found his way to the Salvation Army hall and made his apologies to the doorkeeper. This individual obviously felt that the divine intention behind the march had been grossly violated and, grasping Charlie by the lobe of an ear, led him through the worshipping crowd and deposited him at the Mercy-Seat, the altar of the Army, suggesting in forceful tones that the trembling lad should first of all apologize to the Lord and seek His forgiveness. Apologies to the wounded woman could follow.

This strange introduction to the Army was for Charlie a valid introduction to Divine grace. He was soundly converted, the first of the brothers and sisters who were, under their mother's sensitive guidance, to be led first to Christ, then into the movement, and, finally, into Salvation

Army officership. With almost all of one's uncles and aunts on the paternal side of the family, with their spouses, wearing Salvation Army officers' uniforms, it was little wonder that as a boy I thought the world was all Salvation Army and that The Salvation Army dominated the world.

My mother came into this hothouse of uniformed, marching, praying and testifying enthusiasts from an alien realm. She was one of a large family, the fourth of fourteen children, ten boys and four girls. Hardship had knitted the family together. Each was concerned for the other, and if shelter, or meals, or hospitality of any sort were required, it was given as lavishly as resources would permit.

My maternal grandfather had evidently not done as well as some other branches of his family. Because of distant connections he was proud of his family name, Horrocks, and through a long life, matched by that of his wife who also lived to be nearly one hundred years old, he possessed a dignity of person and speech. He was a painter of a kind that required special skills, but in a field where contracts were few. He specialized in the decorating of theatres, cinemas, music halls and those churches that wanted an ornate presentation of Biblical truths or spiritual admonitions. Taken to see him at work I marvelled at how he made the gold, crimson and blue scrolls intertwine with the mocking masks of Greek and Roman actors and invisibly-held musical instruments. But he and his family knew hard times. As unemployment multiplied half an egg per person at the table was regarded as a feast. The welfare state was decades away.

My mother was fortunate enough to secure employment as a waitress in a highly reputable restaurant. All her life she was a perfectionist, and undoubtedly that perfectionism was displayed as she waited on the tables. There she and my father met. It was love at the first meal. My father's intention to become a Salvation Army officer eventually became hers. Annie Horrocks now had two families, the Horrockses and the Browns, to whom she belonged. Both gave her affection and encouragement and, in 1907, she and my father journeyed to London to enter the Training Home as cadets. The strong discipline of the college meant total separation for the period of training. Human love had to take second place to the moulding of character and the inculcation of a fiery passion for the salvation of the world. Commissioned as officers they were sent their separate ways. While divine obligations were discharged, human love, supported by frequent letters and an occasional meeting, survived. They were married at Southend-on-Sea, an attractive, intelligent and eager couple lost in God's will and their devotion to each other.

I was their firstborn. Only one Christian name, Arnold, was given me. My father thought that more than one was an affectation. My surname, Brown, would be the fourth, or even third, most common in the English-speaking world. But at least I acquired the first two letters of the alphabet for my initials, and it meant that often I came off rather well in lists that were carefully alphabetized! My parents were by now the corps officers at Tottenham II, as the group of Salvationists in that part of London was designated. On Saturday, December 13, 1913, I entered the world and a sparsely-furnished Salvation Army officers' quarters. The superstitious may have worried over the frequency of "thirteens." The house in which I was born was No. 13. My mother's birthday was on a 13th. And when, in 1969, General Erik Wickberg handed me my appointment as Chief of the Staff and second-in-command of the worldwide Salvation Army he postscripted his more serious words with the comment that he hoped I did not mind being The Salvation Army's thirteenth Chief of the Staff!

My first clear childhood recollection is one of paralysing terror. It was generated, I now realize, by the panic that gripped my mother and the women from neighbouring houses who stood, grouped on the street in Seacombe where we now lived, watching an enemy zeppelin ominously circling the Liverpool docks. Bombing and gunfire echoed across the Mersey, and the whole frightening scene was canopied by a fiery-red sky. My father was "at the front." I knew the phrase but not its significance, only that it was something which woefully distressed my mother and which was given as the explanation for every baleful happening in the home and in our existence. The aerial attacks on Liverpool meant hours of agonizing apprehension for my mother. Members of the two families to which she was so closely bound were at risk on the other side of the river, and there were no telephones for an early, comforting word that all was well once the attack had ended.

The nearness of enemy action intensified for my mother her worry over the safety of her young husband whose whereabouts, other than that he was "at the front," were unknown. Night after night I heard her praying that he would return safely.

CHAPTER 2

New Life In A New Land

"Brave men, and worthy patriots, dear to God ... " is a Miltonian phrase that describes my father. Little wonder that when a passer-by saw him in his Salvation Army officer's uniform during the early weeks of the First World War and handed him a white feather, the jingoist's symbol of cowardliness, he straight away enlisted in the Royal Warwickshire Light Infantry setting aside, only temporarily he thought, his Salvation Army officership.

In the second bloody battle of Cambrai, one of the war's disasters for the Allied forces, his spinal column was damaged and his body spattered with shrapnel. A long period in military hospital followed. When assisted out of the Red Cross lorry at the front door of his home he was unbelievably doubled over, as though some giant had taken a piece of malleable iron and bent it until the ends met. Continual hospital treatment fortunately had its therapeutic effect and eventually his soldierly bearing was restored, though his medical future remained uncertain.

My father's homecoming began a chapter of delight for his young son. There were increasingly longer walks while he related stories of mud-filled trenches, of danger and heroic deeds, and of unequalled comradeship as men fought side by side to preserve freedom and liberty. He was an excellent raconteur, evoking sharp images and mimicking the characters he described. Nightly he would read aloud from the Bible and Shakespeare, much of the latter being difficult for a child of my age to understand. Sometimes he regaled my mother and me with the tales of

Edgar Allan Poe and other authors. As a reader he could manufacture realism and forge suspense. Characters had their own voices and gesture added a dramatic dimension. I tingled with horror as he described the slowly-descending canopy that would squeeze to death the unsuspecting victim in the bed below. He loved good literature and the best in music, poetry and art. I know now from what he wrote and painted that, had he had a longer and more formal education he could, with the native ability he possessed, have gone far.

The war, however, had put paid to any such possibility. He was disillusioned in respect of most authorities. He was sick of war and its horrors and constantly spoke of "the stricken widow and the orphan's tear." He was desperately sad about the decline of British craftsmanship and pessimistic about any return to a vital Christian society, yet he remained a surprisingly cheerful man and his hearty laughter echoes in the memory. For him, everything of good centred on his wife and children. I had been joined by a brother, Bernard. There had also been a sister, Hilda, who died in her first year. Not until my manhood did I learn of the struggle there was to pay for that funeral. Tearfully, my father told me how it took the family's last coins to buy the half-dozen, half-price daffodils that were laid on the little white coffin, all that my parents could afford as a floral demonstration of their heartbreak.

My mother played an equally influential, though different rôle in my childhood. Often I felt she read my thoughts, so appropriate to them were her responses of praise, guidance or reproof. Before the goodnight kiss she would talk about God in such an intimate way that childishly I thought of Him as a member of the family, always present if never visible. Jesus I came to regard as "a very special Friend" Who, with His angels, watched over me in the soft darkness, and Who was comfortingly near when I dived under the bedclothes in search of warmth. Comprehension at this age was not elastic enough to include the Holy Spirit in the Divine members of our human family.

My first "spiritual experience" was at my mother's knee. After saying my prayers one evening I was reminded very tenderly of some of the day's infractions, a source of unhappiness to her but, more importantly, a matter of grief to a loving Heavenly Father. I burst into tears. If a boy of seven can have "a broken and a contrite heart" this one did. Through the soothing counsel of my mother, I knew for the first time the salve of Divine forgiveness. My "conversion" dates from that night.

The Church of England school to which I was sent had high standards. The religious atmosphere and emphases were totally compatible with my mother's spiritual ministry, and the days passed with extraordinary pleasantness. Nearly sixty years later I visited the school and was given "a hero's welcome." In the main foyer, in full Salvation Army officer's uniform, stood a clothier's dummy holding a welcome sign to the Army's General. Once again I trod the still-familiar corridors to visit each of the classes, one of which gave a vigorous rendition of "Onward, Christian Soldiers" as an appropriate greeting. The headmaster invited me to speak to the pupils. To the wide-eyed surprise of most I said that the saddest experience of my early life was suffered at this very school. I had been given a new, small-size bicycle and was allowed to ride it to school. One day I came out of class to discover that my beautiful bike was nowhere to be seen. I walked home, choking with sobs, and was met by my father who wanted to know the cause of my distress. When I stammered out the tragic reason he roared with laughter. "You silly boy," he said, "you didn't take your bike to school today. It's still in the backyard." Staff and students, the mayor of the borough who was present, and two men who had actually been my fellow students and had been specially invited, joined in the hilarity.

My father's unhappy personal legacy from the war caused him to peer with anxiety into England's unpromising future. The early Twenties were for him a nauseating display of flippancy. The general search for pleasure was wild and feverish. Flappers dancing the black-bottom in the face of seething social disquiet disgusted him. He seemed to know that a paralysing general strike was fast approaching and that it had already thrown its ominous shadow across the mindless gaiety of those whose post-war profits permitted such careless indulgence. His sympathies were totally with the millions drifting towards what, fifty years later, would be referred to as "a cycle of deprivation."

He made a decision that the family would emigrate to Canada. His chief concern, he told his own and my mother's family, was to ensure a good future for his children. (Three of them, Henry, Edwin and Olive would be Canadian born.) For that concern I have in my heart thanked my father a thousand times. How the transfer was financially accomplished I do not know. In those days the resources of parents were part of an unrevealed world of domestic information so far as the children were concerned. "The joys of parents are secret; and so are their griefs and fears," asserted Francis Bacon. In all likelihood my father was helped by an older brother, Bernard, an erstwhile Salvation Army officer then doing well in business in the quiet, conservative town of Belleville, Ontario, a divisional railroad centre whose population comprised working and retired railroaders, retired farmers and those who serviced their needs.

Our family arrived at its new home in April, 1923, accompanied by an unseasonal blizzard, "the winter's last kick," according to the uncle and aunt who received us. Until the day forty years later when I stood in a howling storm, knee-deep in the snow that surrounded the open grave, and conducted his funeral, Uncle Bernard was an exuberant encourager, a generous dispenser of optimism and, on occasions when personal funds were painfully limited, the Lord's way of answering prayer.

Like many migrants of the early Twenties there were for my parents all the difficulties of securing accommodation, getting established in business and of adjusting to new ways of life and even of language, something which my brother and I seemed to accomplish without effort. But my father persisted and built up a reasonable business while my mother worked long hours to make some money in order to save a little against "the rainy day" which, by nature, she feared would someday be a reality.

For me these were golden years. The beauty of the open spaces, the sharp contrast of the seasons, the brisk joy of being part of a young and vigorous country, the national urge to succeed, with the possibility of doing so, seeped into my boyish experience. As I entered my teens, activity in The Salvation Army was providing new and wonderful opportunities. The door to music-making and musical appreciation was opening. If I had not succeeded, as my father had hoped, with the violin, I was beginning to redeem his hopes on the cornet. Something tells me that had the pianoforte, and not the violin, been his choice for me, I might have exceeded his expectations.

A young Welshman, Jack Green, who had fled from the slag heaps of the Rhondda Valley and the hazards of the coal face, became my tutor. I had never heard cornet playing like his. I was swept off my musically adolescent feet by the sweetness of his tone and his dazzling executancy. But he had only one object in tutoring me. My music must be for the service of God. "Music," he often repeated, "is the one art which came from

Heaven to earth, and the only art we will take with us from earth to Heaven." In 1978 I had the privilege, as General, of pinning on his uniform the medal of the Order of the Founder, the Salvation Army's highest honour awarded to a Salvationist. I was only one of the hundreds, if not thousands, he had similarly trained and influenced.

My first Salvation Army bandmaster, an immigrant from Staffordshire, imposed on others the exemplary discipline by which he himself lived, moved and had his being. His passion for punctuality was fanatical. His musical abilities were limited and prophylactically immune to emotion. He was rigid in his conducting. Common time was a calisthenic outlining of "The City Foursquare." Waltz time made him extremely uncomfortable. As our musical knowledge increased, some younger members of the band would feign eagerness for explanations which they felt were beyond the bandmaster's competence to provide. A hand would go up and a question ingenuously posed. One I recall clearly. "Bandmaster, it says here *ben marcato*. What does that mean?" A short silence was followed by a classic answer.

"That, surely, is the name of the man who wrote the melody," he answered unblinkingly.

To this very day I do not know whether the question had floored him and the answer was the best he could give, or whether, very slyly, he had decided to beat us at our own game. Perhaps it was the latter.

Jack Green insisted that nothing could equal the quartette, vocal or instrumental, for emphasizing the integral value of each part and for establishing proper respect for "balance" in the ensemble, seeing the short score, with its four parts, was the basis of all music. For some years the Belleville Quartette played and sang its way through festivals, church teas and lodge dinners and, not ever to be missed, the chicken suppers—a gourmandizer's dream—arranged annually by rural congregations. The food was our only pay, and we saw to it that we were generously reimbursed. Green and Brown comprised the cornet section. Joe Johnson, who returned eventually to his Staffordshire home in Chesterton and to the corps where he served as bandmaster and songster leader for many years, played tenor horn. Stan. Lessels, the euphoniumnist, like Jack Green, remained in Belleville and was the faithful Corps Sergeant-Major until entering a well-deserved retirement. Forty years after I left for the training college we were again together at a Toronto congress and posed for a photograph in the same seating arrangement as for our first picture taken for publicity purposes. Of the four, I alone had long since ceased playing.

Because of the music there were visits to prisons and penitentiaries, hospitals and old people's homes. I was beginning to understand that even in a new land there were age-old ills, sickness and sorrow, crime and baseness and bitter loneliness. The word "penitentiary" bothered me. Many of the inmates seemed anything but penitent! But if I stood nervously before several hundred of them in their drab garb and with shaven heads, I also stood as one whose sympathies were being kindled and whose mind was already asking the question: What can *I* do for people like this?

Music, of course, was not all of life. Attendance at Queen Mary elementary school had been a dreamy experience from which I awoke only at examination time. Schooling in England had begun for me at a younger age than for my Canadian friends, and this made my early educational passage tranquil and almost effortless. One of the teachers carried the military rank of colonel which somehow added to the strong aura of discipline which prevailed. He is recalled because of a disagreeable mannerism which most of the class could imitate to perfection, but only behind his back. Teachers generally, however, were respected, even feared. Inattention was as unthinkable as it was unallowable. A pupil spoke when spoken to. Behaviour on the playground was as controlled as in the classroom. The educationalists had not yet done their imperfect work!

The most daring experimentation of the time was smoking. Those who could not afford to buy cigarettes, or acquire them in some other way, used the summer-ripened leaves of the maple tree. (How could the national emblem be so debased?) My excursion into this forbidden "grove of Academe" was short-lived. With a couple of other offenders I came up from under the arches of a bridge where privacy to indulge blended with a pleasant view of the river. Alternately puffing and coughing, I swaggered along the street until I saw my mother approaching. There was no time either to evade her or to stub out the homemade cigarette, and I stuck it in my trouser pocket. While my mother questioned me, a wisp of smoke and a faint glow of fire appeared as the wretched thing burned a hole through my trousers and told the whole story of my transgression. I have, it should be noted, been a lifelong non-smoker!

One of my most engaging discoveries of this period was the public library. I went as often as I could, poring over the reference books which could not be loaned, and on each visit taking out as many volumes as were allowed. There were fees and fines, but what matter? The shelves were laden with the most entrancing pleasures beckoning me to indulge. If I could not be found by my parents or friends, more often than not the comment was, "He's at the library. He's always there." As I climbed the stone steps to the entrance, the gates of history and the world swung open. Writers and poets of the ages were waiting to talk to me. Scientists eager to share their secrets clamoured for my attention. To the founder of that library I owe an unpayable debt, despite his business. He was a distiller!

Voracious reading habits had one unhappy effect. Ordered to bed at a certain time, I discovered that with my flashlight I could read under the covers, and for hours on end. As the months went by the strain on my eyes began to tell. I had difficulty in focussing. My handwriting, which to me appeared normal, was horribly distorted. Finally, there was an opthalmic examination to assess the damage I had done, and for several months all reading was forbidden. "There should be moderation even in excess," said my father, slightly misquoting Disraeli whose writings he admired. Those were empty, resented weeks, but as the doctor had predicted, "Nature will take care of the situation very nicely, thank you!", and nature did.

Matriculation studies at high school were accompanied by the deafening sounds of demolition and construction. What had begun as a grammar school was to be a collegiate and vocational institute, and only at the end of my time were the new facilities occupied and enjoyed. With the new edifice new types of curricula were introduced, so that while literature, languages and mathematics remained, bookkeeping, typewriting and commercial law were added. Two teachers are particularly remembered. One for the gentle way in which she persuaded me that Meredith's lines, "Lovely are the curves of the white owl sweeping / Wavy in the dusk lit by one large star," are among the most flowingly beautiful in the English language. She was as physically attractive as the other teacher was unbendingly strict. Perhaps one has to be severe to teach the undisciplined fingers of boys and girls the art of touch typing. She took a particular interest in me, I felt, though I was shocked when she revealed that she had entered me in an Underwood typing competition for high-speed accuracy. She was inordinately pleased when I merited the silver cup and my picture appeared in the school's annual magazine as the winner of the year's commercial scholarship. Nevertheless, if my mind drifts back to those formative years, it is the literature teacher who floats most appealingly into focus.

During my school years there were two calamities. The first left me with a nightmarish memory I will never erase. I can still see my distraught mother, coatless and hatless in the winter weather, being physically restrained from leaping into the icy waters of what was called Victoria Harbour, an inlet from the Bay of Quinte with a park on one shore and an assortment of commercial and private wharves running down from warehouses on the opposite shore. Brother Bernard, then seven, had, on that never-to-be-forgotten Saturday morning, run and jumped on the frozen bay with a playmate, a son of the officers then stationed in charge of the Belleville Salvation Army Corps. One fell through the ice. The other tried to save him. Both were drowned and, despite every effort, the two swollen bodies were not recovered for burial until four months had passed and the winter which had gripped the family in grief yielded to the melting days of springtime. David's cry for Absalom, "My son, my son ...," was no more freighted with anguish than my mother's that dire morning. I can still hear her screaming the same words, so overwhelmingly did this family sorrow engulf me.

The second blow, like the first, fell without warning. My father's disability recurred in startling ways. His brain started sending capricious signals to the extremities. Walking briskly, his favourite walking stick pendulating rhythmically, a leg would suddenly lose its power of propulsion and he would fall and remain in a heap until help came. Passing a plateful of food his hand would inexplicably lose its grip. Plate and food would crash on the floor. Permanent invalidism was now the medical verdict. Without him the business could not be sustained, and income, until a war pension could be adjusted and insurance claims proven, lessened appallingly.

The effect on me was crucial. My dream of higher education was fatally ruptured. Now it must be work, work with a salary that would keep the home together and family life in one piece until better days arrived. It was no cross to do this. I respected and loved my parents. I grieved that my father had been denied the opportunities he would have had as a

Salvation Army officer, part of the penalty for his years in the forces, and that now his hope of providing a good life for his children was also under risk. If I regretted not being able to go to university, I came to appreciate the people and business systems to which I was exposed as a clerk and secretary in a divisional office of the railway. Additionally, in the hope of extra earnings, I set myself up as a Public Stenographer, knowing that my salary was "saving the day" for the hard-pressed family.

Better times did follow, and in 1933 I made a journey that was to put into perspective my youthful longings for my native England. Despite all that a new land had given, I yearned to see again the land of my birth. On the last night of the sea voyage from Montreal to Liverpool I got as near to the prow of the liner as was allowed, and stared into the night until the glimmering of the first land-based light was seen. Involuntarily I recited Scott's lines, "Breathes there the man, with soul so dead, Who never to himself hath said, This is my own, my native land!"

The purpose of my visit, in addition to seeing relatives and carrying news of the "colonist" branch of the family, was to hear all the best music I could, so ardent had my love of the art become, one awful, ego-shattering experience notwithstanding. I had been invited to participate as cornet soloist in one of the year's premier festivals in Toronto arranged by the famed Dovercourt Citadel Band. I rehearsed diligently. The air-varié was thoroughly memorized. The lad from the little town was ready to show the metropolites how it should be done. As the performance progressed, I saw out of the corner of my eye that two well-known composers had me under scrutiny. Adjutant Bramwell Coles, already established as the "March King of The Salvation Army," and Major James Merritt, also an outstanding composer and exponent of the concertina, were watching every depression of a valve and, critically, I thought, assessing quality of tone and technique. The thought was unnerving, and stage fright swept over me. Tongue and fingers struggled to sustain coordination, but in the middle of the second variation gave up the struggle. I sensed the crowd's sympathy, but it was a poor substitute for the *bravos* I had anticipated. I stood in front of the silent crowd feeling silly, annoyed and bitterly disappointed. My tongue was still cemented to the roof of my mouth, so ruthlessly can nerves dry up the flow of saliva. I blurted out a sentence which some who were present have never let me forget. "Boy," I said, "am I dry?" The words lacked felicity, but they were aridly truthful. It was my last appearance as a cornet soloist.

As a bandsman, the bands of the United Kingdom were of principal interest, and for some months I travelled about attending contests and festivals, hearing and comparing the best of Salvation Army and competing aggregations. There were also unexpected opportunities for leading meetings and speaking. Sitting on the deck of the ferry crossing the Mersey from Liverpool to Seacombe I saw a young Salvation Army officer. I made myself known to him and he gave me a warm invitation to come to his corps and lead a Sunday's meetings. I accepted with alacrity. Thirty-one years later the same officer, Lieut-Colonel Victor Smith, warmly welcomed me to the International Public Relations Department in which he was serving as a regional officer.

I was to visit families in Chesterton, North Staffordshire, whose relatives had settled in Belleville, and was invited to take part in a young people's anniversary. Following a long tradition, the Sunday afternoon and evening services were to be held in the Wesley Place Church to which children and parents, with the corps' musical sections, paraded in the July sunshine. I was astonished on reaching the town to see posters everywhere indicating that these special gatherings would be "Conducted by Bandsman Arnold Brown, the Boy Preacher of Belleville, Canada." The printed order of services designated me in the same way, rather to my embarrassment on two counts: I was already twenty years of age and, I felt, hardly a "boy"; and, regrettably, I could hardly claim to be a "preacher." I recall the excitement of the march, the church crowded with people, but have no recollection of "the Boy Preacher's" sermons, only that the hospitality of my hosts was as cordial afterwards as before.

A further opportunity permitted me to lead meetings at the corps where the Brown family had its Salvation Army beginnings. Not far from such Liverpool landmarks as Lime Street Station and St. George's Hall, I shared the platform with a candidate for officership who was soon to leave for the training college in London. One of my final appointments as General in office was to visit the social services headquarters in Hackney, London. In the group of officers was Brigadier George Gretton, the erstwhile candidate, now a retired officer. After the farewell meeting we shook hands and together thanked God for the way in which two lads had been allowed to come full circle in a career that had provided innumerable platforms since our nervous start forty-eight years before.

Near the end of the visit I realized that I had spent no time at all in visiting historical Salvation Army locations. I made a hurried pilgrimage to Mile End Waste in the East End of London where William Booth had preached outside the "Blind Beggar" public house. While I stood looking at the bust which marks the place, feelings of admiration for this "prophet to the poor" mingled with dismay that the area around the monument was so poorly kept. The railings were unpainted. Old newspapers and rubbish swirled about an unkempt, drunken man curled up like a pile of rags against the stone work. As I moved away I heard a voice saying, "But who will carry on William Booth's work? His hands are still. His voice is silent. The need continues. Who will ... who ...?"

My years as a young Salvationist had prepared me for this encounter. I knew to Whom the voice belonged. I had wanted to be a Salvation Army officer more than anything else, even more than to be in the diplomatic service of which I was youthfully enamoured. For a time I thought that nothing could equal the dignity and security of embassy service. In 1980, in Kinshasa, Zaire, having breakfast on a sunlit patio with an ambassador who, with his wife, had extended gracious hospitality in the official residence, he spoke of the physical risks to which he and his family were exposed. What had once been a position beyond all ugly interference was now the target of the terrorist. "You chose the better part," he told me. But standing by Booth's monument that afternoon I felt more chosen than choosing.

I turned back to the unfortunate man and offered to help him. The gesture was both honest and symbolic; honest in that I genuinely wanted to do something for him, and symbolic in that I wanted the whole of my life to contribute somehow to the world's betterment. The action marked a decision that was ratified a few days later. In the Royal Albert Hall cadets of the "Torchbearers" session were being commissioned as officers. As I listened to their sessional song with its stirring theme, "Out there, out there, where the darkness reigns out there, Torchbearers are going, faith and love ever glowing ..." I knew what I must do as soon as I returned to Canada—follow in my parent's footsteps and apply for Salvation Army officership.

CHAPTER 3

The Gate And The Light

Many who knew me felt I was well prepared for the life of a cadet. I felt differently. True, attachment to a smaller congregation means increased opportunities for participation and the gaining of leadership experience. At sixteen I was the Young People's Sergeant-Major with not one, but two, Sunday Schools, two miles apart, to manage. That I should at so early an age have been entrusted with such a responsibility reflects either the foresight or foolhardiness of my superiors. The taping of meetings was then unknown, for which Heaven be praised! Had my green efforts at trying to control some hundreds of restless children been recorded, the playbacks, I fear, would be positively unbearable. Thankfully, what is past is past. Let the witches of Endor leave well enough alone.

Too busy to realize it, the task was nevertheless challenging my imagination, enforcing preparation and providing a total immersion course in human relations. And all this at sixteen! But one cannot teach what one does not know. I was expected, above all, to present the facts of the Bible and convincingly convey the great truths it teaches. Of necessity at first, and later with deepening interest as I became more and more fascinated with this "Book of books," I would fill any odd moments by reading from a pocket New Testament which was my constant companion. This habit led to my first soul-winning experience.

Occasionally, my work would include the checking of car numbers in the railway freight yards. One day, as I climbed into a caboose (the name given in North America to the trainman's car which usually travels at the end of a freight or goods train) standing on a spur line, I saw a train conductor pull out of his uniform pocket a New Testament and begin to thumb its pages. I immediately extracted mine and said, "I see we have something in common."

"Not much," the man replied ruefully. "You have everything to live for. I have nothing. He appeared to be the embodiment of the legendary, hard-bitten railroader, and his gruffness was to be expected.

"Then why are you reading the New Testament?" I asked.

"To try and find something, some help, some hope," he commented, especially emphasizing the word, "some." "It's a last resort."

Where the words came from I do not know. I told him there was help and there was hope; that in Christ, approached in contrition and faith, there was not only life, but "life more abundant." The conductor began to share his problems in details and vocabulary so lurid that I begged him to make his confession directly to God, and on his knees.

"I will kneel with you and pray," I heard myself saying.

He was a big man. He lumbered to his feet and then dropped like a stone weight on to his knees. Let those who will deride an incident like this. For me it was a dramatic confirmation of the power of the Gospel. As the man cried and prayed, I stood on the bright edge of Heaven itself. Surely this was the most rewarding ministry that life could offer, that of helping people to find "eternal life." Other vocations might influence the individual or society for good, but only the ministry of the Word could influence beyond the temporai.

When the conductor stood again, he looked at me, shook my hand and said, "I feel like a new man." I had won my first convert for Christ. If there is "rejoicing in Heaven over one sinner that repenteth" my own exhilaration in this moment, and ever since as I have seen people draw nearer to God's will and way for them, is totally explained.

Frequently, my convert, when checking the passengers' tickets on the speeding train for which he was responsible, would bend over a travelling Salvationist and give his testimony, telling how he was led to Christ in the unprepossessing surroundings of an old caboose parked in the Belleville freight yards.

Despite other similar encouragements I greatly needed all the training the college would provide. I was inwardly nervous, rather reticent and somewhat self-demeaning. Not long after my arrival I was sent for by the principal, Colonel (later Commissioner) John S. Bladin, an Australian in whom the qualities of toughness and tenderness seemed to be in perfect balance. Every last ounce of him was organized. When he strode about the college corridors one had the impression that he was invisibly borne along by Authority itself. He was as mature as I was immature, as self-possessed as I was ill-possessed, and I felt it painfully as I sat before him.

"Brown," he said, not unkindly, "why do you always turn in another direction when you see me coming? It gives me the impression that you have just come from doing something you ought not to have done."

I started to stammer out some kind of explanation, but he broke in and said, "This is not a prison. It's not a military camp. There's no need for self-depreciation. Develop what God has given you and use it; there's a world of difference between self-confidence and self-conceit." It was sound advice, and I took it.

"Not a prison," the Colonel had said. But for nine months I shared a narrow cubicle housing bunk beds with a Newfoundlander whose unfailing cheerfulness saved us both from possible claustrophobia. Authorities today would insist on far more cubic content per person in an institution housing rootless men for the odd night or two, let alone for nine months!

Sessions of cadets now bear the same name all around the world, many of the names in recent years being my personal choice. The chooser of our sessional name for 1934-1935, unduplicated elsewhere, fortunately for him or her remains anonymous. We regretted the name. It lacked "class." It was devoid of anything that symbolized our high mission. We were simply, "Toilers." Try as I did to justify the name from Scripture it was impossible. Joseph's naming of his first-born, "For God ... hath made me forget all my toil ..." (Genesis 41: 51) seemed highly inappropriate. The words recorded of Jesus (Mark 6: 48), "And He saw them toiling in rowing ..." had little relevance. Simon's confession (Luke 5: 5), "We have toiled all the night, and have taken nothing," seemed the most despairing of all. One thing was certain, we were not intended by the donor of our sessional designation to be anything like the lilies "which toil not." The training pressures of the months saw to that!

Whatever my private thoughts about the sessional name, they had to be pocketed when the principal instructed me to write the words for the sessional song. They were to be set to music already composed by the then Adjutant (later Colonel) Bramwell Coles, at that time assistant editor of *The War Cry* in Toronto. His skills as a composer were universally acknowledged, and collaboration with such an eminent musical figure was daunting. I did my best, hoping that Coles's music would make such an inspiring impression that the lyrics would pass unnoticed. Worst of all, I had to blank out from my mind the parody sung with abandon, but clandestinely, at least by the men cadets, "We'll be Toilers, oiling boilers ..." and so on. One can only marvel that the official song emerged with the dignity and meaning it did.

The principal was a born thespian. He lived for the platform. He could tell a story as few can, and had an amazing store of them. He loved pageantry, and his annual productions, in which the cadets, under his personal and determined direction worked out his theatrical ideas, were what today's producers call "spectaculars." My own interest in drama came alive when I was ordered to forget my inhibitions and realistically portray the "leaping up" of the lame man healed as a result of his encounter with the Apostles Peter and John at "the gate called Beautiful." For the principal also, in the words of this narrative, it was "such as I have give I unto thee." And what he gave his cadets in this realm was priceless.

I was far less happy about another dramatic part assigned me. Dressed as the devil I was to run through the street crowds hotly pursued by cadets shouting, "Get him! Stop the devil!" After allowing myself to be caught, I was unceremoniously dumped into a trunk. To the crowd captured by these histrionics a cadet would speak from the top of the trunk, stepping off every now and again to allow me to lift the lid and give a fiendish laugh while I switched on a red light intended to create a still more infernal aspect. Once, a voluble cadet, carried away either by his subject or his own eloquence forgot to step off the trunk. There were few air-holes, and in desperate need of oxygen I pounded on the lid. This only encouraged the orator to expatiate on the absolute necessity of keeping the Evil One securely boxed. Not until I virtually toppled him off the lid did I again breathe properly. That afternoon the devil was almost laid to rest!

In retrospect, I can hardly believe that I cavorted in such a garb along Montreal's elegant St. Catharines Street. At one of the main corners the famous Montreal Citadel Band was standing in perfect circular formation and playing to a large crowd. I decided to execute a kind of "in and out the window" manoeuvre and dodged playfully among the bandsmen with zealous cadets on my tail. The positioning and performance of the band was utterly disrupted, not a little to the annoyance of the well-known bandmaster-composer-organist, Norman J. Audoire, F.C.C.O. He did forgive me. It was from his home and my last meal as a single man that I went to my wedding ceremony four years later.

Training, with its glorious fellowship, its hothouse cultivation in Biblical and doctrinal knowledge, its spurring of the reluctant in house-to-house visitation, and the vigorous public meetings in which the cadets were prentice participants, like all good things, came to an end.

I hold the opinion that no administrative activity of the Army more securely links the movement's present to its future and, indeed, determines the quality, competence and passion of that future, than the training of its officers. As General, I reserved to myself the appointment of all senior training personnel, so importantly did I view this work. Our centres of training may be called "colleges," but they are not academic institutions. It is assumed that every entrant already has a certain level of educational achievement. The "college" is really a "battle school."

There are still widely-divergent views as to how long the training period should be. In the earliest days of organized training the period was only a few weeks. In 1904 it was extended from six to nine months. My own residential period, thirty years later, was still nine months. Introduced in 1960, the period in many countries is now two years. In the western world the acceptance of married couples (unthought of in my day), often with children, has greatly altered the schema of training. If a longer period can be afforded by the Army in a particular country, and if the lengthened curriculum does not become a backwater for superfluous activities and fringe subjects, then perhaps it has value. For families, however, two years is a long time to live under regimentation with both parents struggling to qualify without either of them neglecting any familial responsibilities. But short or long, the training period, I believe, should be tough. Cadets should be tested to the extreme. The regiment should be demanding. Granted it is difficult for training staffs not to treat cadets as "pupils," themselves as "faculty," and the college as a centre of higher learning. In reality, cadets should be treated as soldiers taking advanced commando courses in which every ounce of strength, all concentration of mind, and the totality of spirit is directed towards combat fitness. Is it yet fully understood that, without exception during the training course, every standard set, every procedure followed, inevitably has a long-term reaction that consequentially affects the quality and effectiveness of the Army's future leadership?

As Chief of the Staff I secured General Wickberg's permission to convene an international conference of training principals. The aims of training received considerable consideration. Aims, after all, should be decided before methodology is introduced. All agreed that the training of cadets for Salvation Army officership had three main obligations. Firstly, to produce men and women who know God in holiness of heart and purity of life, in prayer, witness, service and sacrifice, and who show that they know by their nobility of character and the quality of life. Secondly, to produce men and women who know themselves, their strengths and how to direct them, their weaknesses and how to overcome them, their possibilities for good and how to develop them. And, thirdly, to produce men and women who know their mission, who understand the implications of God's call to officership, who realize what the Army is and for what it exists, who share the burden of the world's sin and suffering, and who desire, above all else, beyond self, comfort and recognition the glory of God and the salvation of the world.

In military fashion The Salvation Army "commissions" its cadets as officers when the training period is satisfactorily completed. Some, I felt, did not understand that the granting of a commission not only admitted the recipient to officership, but also conveyed all that is commonly drawn from the term, "ordination," only the ceremonial form of conferment being different. As General I had full support in revising the wording of the commissioning statement so that the thought of "ordination" was more explicit:

> *"Cadet_____________ : In accepting these pledges which you have made, I commission you as an officer of The Salvation Army and ordain you as a minister of Christ and His gospel."*

Thanks to those who trained me, and to a gracious Holy Spirit Who helped me to see everything as part of a Divine process preparing me for a lifetime task, I increasingly came to know God, to know myself, and to know the mission to which I had been called. But commissioned as an officer my training had by no means ended. It had, in fact, hardly begun.

CHAPTER 4

Into Battle

The two Lieutenants in yellow-braided uniforms stepped off the train and went to collect their trunks from the baggage office. The June sun shone on a deserted platform. There was no waiting world eager for our arrival. The comforting sounds of college life had evaporated for ever. My first impression of our new appointment was of sunshine and silence. Lieutenant Jas. Sloan and I were beginning careers whose destinations we could not envisage. With our own corps to command and our own community to win, only the present mattered. I thought back to this moment when, as Chief of the Staff, I asked my one-time colleague if he and his wife would take charge of the Army's work in Singapore. With the same willing spirit that possessed him on our arrival in Bowmanville, he packed up and went to the Far East.

The town of Bowmanville, forty miles east of Toronto and hugging the Lake Ontario shoreline, had had an exciting Salvation Army history. In the earliest days the town had accommodated a training college for officers. Most of the leading people of the town were converts and became local officers. They were so influential that, as aldermen and councillors, they passed the strictest of ordinances; even swearing on the streets became an indictable offence.

But times had changed. Nearby Oshawa, where Bowmanville Salvationists had pioneered the Army's work, had thrived while Bowmanville, with severe losses of industry, had become a quiet centre. No town, however, could have had a greater respect for the Army. Many townspeople were descendants of early-day Salvationists and proud of it. There was little money about; income was minimal, and we soon realized that we would have to live a lenten life apart from the hospitality of soldiers and friends which, as time went on, proved to be unfailing.

Here began one's practical lessons in personnel management. The corps sergeant-major, we had been told in college, was responsible for conducting the open-air meetings. On the evening of the day of our arrival a street meeting was scheduled to be held in a rural village close by. The little band was on hand. Other soldiers greeted us and joined the circle. But no sergeant-major. He arrived an hour later and took belated command. Afterwards, I ventured to mention his unpunctuality and, in reply, was treated to a forceful diatribe against the whole concept of daylight saving time. (He obviously did not know that a highly respected English Salvation Army bandmaster, W. Punchard, O.F., in association with Wm. Willetts, the innovator, had had much to do with its introduction!)

"I milk my cows on God's time," he said, "and if you'll dispense the milk of the Word on God's time, I'll never be late."

Lying in bed I pondered the problem. How, I asked myself, could I resolve this confusion in which a local officer's responsibility, the unreadiness of cows to release their milk and the proclamation of the Gospel were horometrically and hopelessly mixed together. After praying about it, and many other subjects, I fell asleep still puzzled as to what could be done with uncooperative cows and a stubborn farmer who considered them more important than a newly-commissioned Salvation Army officer's authority. So ended Day One as a Corps Commanding Officer.

Friendships made during my seventeen-months' stay were to last a lifetime. None could have had a gentler easing into a life of leadership than this corps and this town provided. Pulpits of the local churches were graciously opened to us. Each preaching opportunity bolstered confidence and enlarged our circle of acquaintances. In visitation we discovered needs which two young men had hardly known existed, and did what we could to help.

All Salvationists in Canada were involved at the time in an evangelistic crusade entitled, "The World for God." We were eager participants as the January, 1936, campaign bulletin issued by territorial headquarters reported. Under the title, "How Some are Working at the Campaign," the following appeared: "Lieutenants Brown and Sloan at Bowmanville, Ontario, recently adopted new methods. On Saturday night, in the main street, in the presence of a splendid crowd, they presented 'The Devil on Trial.' On Sunday, unusual tactics such as personal invitations, kneeling on the streets, bombardments and special music and singing, resulted in good crowds and eighteen souls for the day."

It came as a shock whenever we discovered that the Army was not as well known as we thought. On one occasion the then Danforth (now Agincourt) band paid a weekend visit. On the Sunday afternoon an outdoor festival was arranged in a nearby village. The Reeve who officially greeted the band expressed his surprise that William Booth had found time to begin the world-wide Salvation Army while managing his immense lumber interests. (A well-known Ottawa firm carried the name of Booth. We were grateful that the Reeve had not heard of Booth's Gin!)

In an effort to combat the public's lack of knowledge we decided to hold an enormous field day. Bands and songster brigades from several corps were talked into helping us. Never had the town seen so many uniformed Salvationists as on that Labour Day. What if the commissary, in the hands of a small Home League battling with the biggest catering challenge in its history, fell short of the crowd's demands for food; or what if the burning heat exploded the tires of more than a few parked automobiles; or what if the whole undertaking was bathed in perspiration and frustration from an almost too successful event? All was resolved in the cool of the evening when two proud Lieutenants headed the long procession through the town, martial music blanketing all other sounds, and with hundreds of burning torches illuminating the singing, playing, clapping marchers. It was demonstrably, "Onward, Christian soldiers." The town, we felt, had been shaken into a new awareness of the Army and its mission. For the local corps, with its renewed spirit, there was only one way to go—forward. Progress was assured. The God who had blessed the weather and the witness would assuredly prosper our future.

One unique and highly instructive feature of the corps' life was the presence every Sunday morning of about eighty young men from a government detention institution located on the outskirts of the town. Marched in to their places they seemed to crowd the hall to its limits. The soldiery and other worshippers appeared to have been admitted by courtesy. To keep the attention of the youths while attempting to follow as normal a pattern of meeting as possible was a demanding experience. To win the boys' friendship was even harder, since there were strict rules about fraternization. The authorities, fortunately, were not only cooperative but pleased that the lads could come, and every encouragement was given when, now and again, some of them came forward to the Mercy-Seat and sincerely asked God to help them straighten out their so far twisted lives. Would it be fair to say that the meeting leaders learned as much as the youthful hearers? The answer surely is Yes. Sunday morning meetings in the Army are traditionally called Holiness meetings. For us they were "*Practical* Holiness" meetings. The challenge was to get a young man over the line from love of self to love of God. Conversion from sin to righteousness had to precede any enunciation of the doctrine of *Perfect* Love.

A telegram received on a Friday afternoon instructed me to be in the office of the Chief Secretary at territorial headquarters the next morning at 9 o'clock. I had no idea what the interview could be about. Admittedly, I had shown more than a passing interest in a Montreal Citadel songster. On Friday nights, after the treasurer of the corps had counted the income and had pushed to one side of the table the money required to settle any bills, the allowances for the two lieutenants were doled out somewhat grudgingly from what was left. Usually, it was not much. Without an occasional supplement from divisional headquarters it would have been insufficient for basic needs. We had insisted, however, that all liabilities should be met first, despite the outcome for us personally. The distribution made, prayerful thanks were offered by the treasurer for salvation and solvency. My practice was to get as quickly as possible afterwards to the hotel at the corner of the street where there was a public telephone. By long distance I would speak to the young lady who was occupying all of my romantic thoughts and who, after cadetship, I fervently hoped, would become my wife. She was an exceedingly attractive and popular person, and I felt that the regular Friday night calls, however costly, were a form of insurance I could not neglect, though practically all the money the treasurer meted out went into the pay slot. Sometimes the money would miraculously flow back into the return slot, as though a sympathetic operator felt that this particular romance should be encouraged, or the machine itself rejected taking money from someone poorer than itself. The Friday night calls, and the letters now flowing regularly between Bowmanville and Montreal, constituted the only unreported activity for which I might be called to account.

At 9 o'clock the next morning I was admitted to the second-in-command's office. The then Colonel Wm. R. Dalziel, a big, impressive and exceedingly capable leader, barely looked up from his desk.

"Go home, Brown, and pack your bags," he said. "Farewell from your corps tomorrow. Be back here at 9 o'clock on Monday morning to begin work."

I was dumbfounded. What of my corps? What kind of work was I now to do? But the atmosphere did not allow for conversation. It was impregnated with instruction. I did, however, ask about the work. The Colonel, still lost in the more important matters on his desk, indicated that I was to serve in the editorial department for three weeks, three months, or who knows? Everything depends ... Obviously the interview was over. At the door I made an unfortunate gaffe. Out of sheer relief that I now knew the worst, I mentioned how glad I was that I had not been sent for because of some discrepancy or aberration. The Colonel reacted swiftly.

"Come back," he said, wagging a long forefinger, "if you have anything to confess."

I knew I had made a *faux pas* and had no wish to compound it. Mumbling words of thanks I backed out quickly and awkwardly through the baize-covered double doors.

I was not a complete stranger to the location and layout of the editorial department. In 1936, congress gatherings were led in Toronto by General Evangeline Booth. They included a mammoth Sunday afternoon rally for which the massive Maple Leaf Gardens was filled. My duty was to take down in shorthand all this eloquent, commanding daughter of the Founder said in public. Such an assignment put me literally at her feet during all the events. The night hours were spent transcribing her utterances; the typescript had to be ready for the editor-in-chief's surgery the next morning. The General's vocabulary was extensive. My shorthand was suffering from disuse, but the finished product must have satisfied my superiors since it was accepted without comment. I learned afterwards that this assignment had put me under observation as a possible future appointee to the department. The arrangement had also been sympathetically viewed by the chief secretary who, during the brief Saturday morning interview already mentioned, had been so laconic and pre-occupied. During my cadetship he had led a series of sessions at the training college. His theme was "Service." In the course of one of his addresses he stressed the point that "he who leads must serve." The thought caused me to write a poem which found its way to the editor-in-chief. It was my first published contribution to *The War Cry*. After its appearance the Chief Secretary had written saying, "You should cultivate your poetical gift." All these strands had evidently come together.

I was assigned to the chair lately vacated by Adjutant Bramwell Coles and previously occupied by General Clarence Wiseman when a young, single captain. All of the editors under whom I served had high standards. Colonel James Hawkins, a charmingly flamboyant Welshman, could dictate a full-page feature article without stopping to catch a breath. I still regard this as a staggering accomplishment. His English successor, Colonel Ernest Webb, was a "professional." By that I mean he had earned a good livelihood with his editorial qualifications outside The Salvation Army. He had been an editor on *The Brighton Sun*, and while walking on the sands of that English south-coast resort was sold a copy of *The War Cry*. What he read caused him to offer his capabilities and his life to God in the Army. He had an astonishing knowledge of all aspects of publishing which, fortunately for me, he was always ready to share. He knew why the compositor's block was a "stone," and the frame into which the type was placed was "a chase." In my learning period I was disturbed to hear that he violently disliked "widows." The offenders, I came to know, were not those who had unfortunately been bereaved of their husbands, but any short line of type at the top of a column. I quickly learned how to lengthen a widow.

The Colonel was an unrelenting taskmaster. Above his desk hung a motto: "No journal is worth its salt that is edited in the spirit of a tame rabbit." He was no "tame rabbit" in dealing with copy. Once I stood by his roll-top desk and watched him tear my report of a meeting which I had thought was rather well written into confetti. While it fluttered into the oversize wastepaper basket he simply said, "You can do better than that." If, however, a phrase pleased him, or an old idea wore fresh language, he fairly bubbled with compliment. He once gave me a copy of Sir Edmund Gosse's *Father and Son* with the comment that if I could learn to write like this onetime librarian to the House of Lords the literary considerations of the Kingdom of God and the Army would be considerably enriched.

If the Colonel was a taskmaster, he must also have been a romantic at heart. Vicariously, I suspected, he enjoyed the romance that was bringing Cadet Jean Barclay and myself nearer to marriage. He made it possible for us to meet regularly once our engagement was approved, and strongly championed our right to do so in the face of the training principal's objections. But all the "hearts and flowers" were not allowed to outweigh the importance of deadlines and production schedules. My fiancée had been commissioned as an officer and appointed to Hanover, an Ontario town whose foundations had been laid by German immigrants. It was our hope that the wedding would take place in June, 1939, but permission could not be given. The Christmas edition of *The War Cry*, sections of which were printed in four colours on an uncooperative flat-bed press, took months to run. June was no time for a wedding. Romance would have to yield to requirements, and the bride-to-be was sent to an interim appointment in Dundas to await my availability. The one silver lining to this cloud of delay was that we were now only some forty miles apart.

The September wedding took place in Montreal five days after Canada had declared war on Germany. The bride's mother, well-known for her artistic tastes, had transformed the time-worn citadel into a bower of beauty. Captain (later Lieut-Colonel) Ernest Parr, considered by many to be the finest soprano cornet soloist of all time, was the best man. Songster Ruby Ritchie, a lifelong friend of the bride's, was bridesmaid. Forty years later an unbroken wedding party would meet again to celebrate the event. But the perils of the war ahead could not be excluded from the ceremony performed by the chief secretary, Colonel Geo. W. Peacock. He could not refrain from giving the congregation which filled the hall a lengthy address on "The Cross and the Swastika." Honeymooning in New York we were invited to tea by the Army's newly-elected international leader, General Geo. L. Carpenter, and his wife, who were enroute to London. Thirty years later the bride and groom would sail from the same pier for an appointment at International Headquarters and, eventually, follow the Carpenters into ultimate responsibility.

"An intelligent wife," says the Book of Proverbs (19: 14, NEB), "is a gift from the Lord." Intelligence, I soon discovered, was only one of many praiseworthy qualities possessed by my young wife. Were they all to be named, the list would stretch through the forty-two years of shared active service, at the end of which no-one could better merit Stevenson's lines in "A Husband to a Wife": "Teacher tender, comrade, wife, / A fellow-farer through life; / Heart-whole and soul-free, / The august Father / Gave to me." If tribute goes no farther—and it could—it is only that one who has been the acme of fidelity while adding sincerity and elegance to every aspect of our private life should not be subjected to public embarrassment.

The United States quickly reacted to the outbreak of hostilities. All foreign currency was frozen. Our resources were extremely limited and they were in Canadian funds which, overnight, no one wanted. Desperate, we appealed to our own headquarters in New York for help. Help us they did, but we were dismayed at the reduced amount of American money we received for our Canadian funds, and could only comfort ourselves with the thought that we were now able to make the return journey to Montreal and Toronto.

Traditionally, single men officers serving on headquarters were appointed following marriage to command of a corps. We expected a similar move, but it was apparent from the delay in receiving a decision that the matter was one of debate at the administrative level. Finally, we were instructed to find accommodation, and my wife was appointed to secretarial work in the editorial department, an arrangement which added to our overflowing happiness. A rent allowance of $35. per month was agreed. A furniture allowance of $250. was approved, though the financial secretary in conveying the decision added his own view that "the amount approved is really too generous. Surely you can manage with less." A small apartment was found at $38.50 per month. The difference was to be a personal responsibility. Years later, in Los Angeles, I took the same financial secretary to task for his "sanctified niggardliness," amid the good-natured ribbing of his friends.

With the departure of Colonel Webb to become Personal Literary Secretary to General Evangeline Booth, my immediate superior, Major Walter Putt, was made Lieut-Colonel and editor-in-chief. He was a man without the faintest tinge of superiority and treated me as a trusted equal from whom nothing related to the life of the office and the preparation of the periodicals was withheld. He was an esteemed mentor.

Reflection suggests that all officers should have a period in an editorial office. Not all would adapt, but knowledge of the Army, its history, its structure, its personnel around the world and its manifold ramifications would filter into their mind and memory in a way unparalleled by any other sphere of officership. In an editorial department Bacon's assertion that "Reading maketh a full man; conference a ready man and writing an exact man" is totally confirmed, and the more "exact" men we have the better.

By his free admission Colonel Putt was not a writer, though he could put together as clear a paragraph as any. He was an editor whose skills made many a writer's work acceptable for publication. Grammar he knew. Syntax he defended. Etymology he venerated. I recall his returning one morning from prayers almost transported by Charles Wesley's lines, "There let it for Thy glory burn / With inextinguishable blaze." He spent some minutes stressing their apt beauty before vanishing into his office and his more usual silence.

Only the editor-in-chief knew privacy and a degree of quiet. The rest of us were squeezed into an outer office with barely matching square footage. One side of the office was completely fenestrated, with no relief from summer sun or wintry draught. Grimy roofs and neighbouring buildings constituted a cheerless view. The other wall was glass-panelled. Beyond it was a gaggle of tailoresses cutting, sewing and trimming ladies' uniforms. If creative calm tried to exist on our side, it never did on the other. The latest vital statistics of women officers, loudly bandied about with reasons other than fitting the dress to the subject, and occasionally to the accompaniment of jesting laughter, had to be kept out of the prose we wrote by stern mental discipline. Surviving such conditions made more believable the statement that genius can work anywhere, except that we had little genius and the seamstresses could not be silenced.

My appointment to the editorial department had been *pro tempore* ("for the time being"), a useful device which allows an administration time to sift its uncertainties, but which threateningly clouds an appointee's future. Eventually the appointment was confirmed, and for nearly ten years in the confines of what the staff fondly referred to as "the verb foundry," I did work that continually exhilarated me. Editorial perception was sharpened until good copy could be spotted a mile away. Submissions with a deluge of words and a drizzle of thought were recognized before the second paragraph was read. Liquidity, I came to understand, is not only a financial necessity. It is a precious element all too often missing in written communication. Even now I do not find it easy to avoid a stilted, angular sentence, but what a debt I owe to that succession of editors.

My collision with editors of another school lay twenty years ahead.

CHAPTER 5

Meetings And Music

I cannot retrace the early years of officership without feeling like the renowned Dr. Albert Schweitzer. "One other thing that stirs me when I look back at my youthful days," he wrote, "is the fact that so many people gave me something or were something to me without knowing it." Neither can I name all my unsuspecting benefactors. They were legion. One was a corps officer who offered me the leadership of his band. Numerically strong, the Lisgar Street (Toronto) Citadel Band was also musically aspiring.

Rehearsals and engagements involved a long journey from our home to the citadel. On Sundays it meant an early departure in the morning and a return near midnight. The Sunday evening meetings were prolonged but usually spirited. The corps was a pulsating centre of evangelism, and the fire was continually fanned by the prayers of a remarkable group of saintly veterans the like of whom, gathered in one place, I have seldom since encountered. Perhaps more important than conducting the music was the conducting of the prayer meeting, a responsibility I was called upon to assume almost every Sunday night.

The prayer meeting, so called, is actually an extension of the service proper, a period largely devoted to appealing, with songs and prayers interspersing, to the unsaved and unsanctified in the congregation to come forward and kneel at the Mercy-Seat. Here they are exhorted to confess their sin and their need, to exercise faith, and to claim Divine forgiveness and the saving grace of Christ by the regenerating work of the Holy Spirit.

Calling this postlude period a "meeting" meant that some of the congregation, often the very ones for whom it was intended, got up and left, regarding one meeting a night as sufficient. I felt that the transition from proclamation to invitation should be imperceptible. One should flow into the other. I noticed that sometimes when the Bible message ended there was a reverential hush as the congregation realized the immanence of God. It was then relatively easy to invite seekers to come forward, and easy for them to respond. At other times there was no bridge. To generate the right atmosphere of devotional self-examination the prayer period leader had to start from the beginning.

From my boyhood I sensed the importance of "the appeal." The power of the prayer meeting was imprinted on my consciousness when, as a youngster, I watched two veteran Colonels, Adby (a former soloist in many of the Founder's meetings) and Morehen, one short, the other tall, *dually* leading congress prayer meetings in the Massey Hall, Toronto. In their frock coat uniforms, and striding back and forth across the stage, they alternately pleaded with a passion to which my tender heart responded.

I was about to cross the road one day and had just stepped off the pavement when I had what can only be described as a vision. In my mind's eye I saw myself leading a prayer meeting on the stage of the same Massey Hall, the scene of so many large Salvation Army assemblies. There I was, pleading, exhorting, singing, praying and rejoicing as men and women made their way down the aisles to the front. Could such ever be reality? In a children's meeting in the little town of Belleville perhaps. But Toronto, Massey Hall, an adult congregation, a stage from which all The Greats had preached and pleaded? As quickly as it had come the scene vanished and the images dissolved. I continued across the street, having crossed for an instant from the "now" to the "then." Not many years were to elapse, however, before the vision was a realized experience many times over. When, for the first time, I stood at the lectern on the Massey Hall stage, an inner voice whispered, "You have been here before."

The Second World War had a distressing effect on the musicians for whom I was responsible. The younger men had volunteered or had been "called up." As playing members decreased in number, anxiety for the safety of absent members multiplied. I thought long and hard about the causes and consequences of the war. The social upheaval it precipitated was obvious. Many of my young bandsmen were being propelled overnight into responsibility of frightening proportions. Lads who had reluctantly been allowed to drive their father's automobile were piloting multi-million dollar planes with horrific, death-dealing capabilities.

My mind juggled with unanswerable questions. Earl Haig's oft-quoted statement, "It is the business of the church to make my business impossible," condemned me personally. Why had the Gospel message not prevailed? How had the church, of which I was a part, failed so dismally? It seemed ridiculously incongruous to me that the country designated as the chief enemy had been for so long the fount of theological thought. It was harrowing to realize that young Salvation Army bandsmen of other countries, so like the men to whom I had said farewell, were facing each other in combat, perhaps fatally. Bonhoeffer, with his execution at Flossenburg still to come, wrote: "The church knows nothing of a sacredness of war. The church which prays the 'Our Father' asks God only for peace." Pray for peace we did!

While admiring the necessary and often courageous work being accomplished by fellow officers with the Red Shield Auxiliary Services, I felt led to offer myself as a chaplain. There was considerable correspondence with the appropriate military authorities and Salvation Army leaders, but nothing came of it, for two reasons. Chaplains were appointed in ratio to the number of enlisted men designating themselves as Salvationists. On this basis I was not needed, but my editorial and secretarial qualifications, the Ministry of Defence informed me, would ensure an immediate and substantial placement if I wished to follow this course. I had no inclination to do so. The second reason, I assumed, was even stronger. Some officers, I was reminded, were needed on "the home front," a decision that was justified in my instance seeing the editor-in-chief was frequently unwell and my responsibility for the periodicals commensurately increased.

The long journeys from the apartment to the bandroom finally became too inconvenient, and a transfer was made to the North Toronto Corps, only a few streets away. For more than twenty years it was to be not only our centre of worship, but also one of much musical and social activity. The war dragged on, and with an added dimension of family concern. My wife's officer-parents were posted to London, England, to manage a hotel pre-empted by the Canadian government to be operated by The Salvation

Army for Canadian servicemen on leave. Aware that it was late in life for them to be undertaking such a venture, we bade them an emotional farewell as they went aboard a camouflaged vessel moored at a Montreal dock. In the dead of night, lines would be cast off and the ship would head for its rendezvous with an Atlantic convoy. Our apprehension would have been greater still had we known that the Barclays were to be numbered among the heroes and heroines of the London Blitz. For weeks no-one on the hotel staff slept in a bed. At best, with the heavy bombing, sleep was sporadic. Constant fire-watching was vital. While fires blazed all around their West Central Hotel, the officers did their best to provide a "touch of home" for those whose absence from Canada and their loved ones had already been far too long.

My father and mother-in-law returned to Canada badly shaken by the strains they had undergone, but in time to welcome their first grandchild, our long-awaited infant daughter, Heather Jean. Seven years were to pass before her sister, Beverley Ann, equally welcomed, was born. Though we had been spared the physical suffering imposed by the war on so many, we suffered in spirit. One night, as I hummed a lullaby hoping to hasten sleep for the tiny bundle of loveliness in the crib, from the radio in the background came the raucous declamations of Der Führer, punctuated by the frenzied, chilling "Sieg Heils" of an hysterical audience. The peaceful innocence of baby Heather and the mad screaming of the battle-bedevilled were in total contrast. If, as Thornton Wilder said, "The future is the most expensive luxury in the world," I knew in that moment I would give everything I had to buy it for this and every other of the world's infants born to inherit the follies of their elders.

The horses of relief that galloped across the world at war's end were pulling heavy chariots of change. Like others, I was aware that many young men, some still in military uniform, and young women, were at loose ends. War had meant specific duties and stimulating enterprises. Suddenly the young people were "all bemused and bewildered." They were attending the Salvation Army meetings but otherwise living in a vacuum, unsure of the future and uncertain about themselves. Those I knew were talented, but their talent was dormant and I did not want to see it drain away. I brought about forty of them together and they proposed that a youth chorus be formed. The response was startling. In no time the group was supporting intensive rehearsals and an astonishing degree of vocal excellence was reached. Overnight, it seemed, the group was attractively uniformed. Soon there were many invitations to accept, and broadcasts enlarged the group's recognition. Two major festivals, "Radiant Rhapsodies," and "Highlights and Harmonies," presented before large crowds, set remarkable standards. Most gratifying is the reflection that out of the company came eight Salvation Army officers, some of whom are today holding high office. All of the group, as far as can be learned, are active Christians, most of them staunch Salvationists.

With the war's end, the Army's international leaders were able once again to travel overseas. Tremendous expectation greeted the announcement that General and Mrs. Albert Orsborn were to make a tour of Canada, and there was added excitement for me when I was appointed as the General's aide-de-camp for the period of his stay in the Dominion. The tour began in Halifax and ended in Vancouver. At each major city there were public gatherings, officers' council sessions, innumerable private interviews and discussions with government authorities. The strain of the long trip and a crowded itinerary was greatly eased by the mode of travel and the comfort it provided. The coast-to-coast journey was accomplished by rail, the railway company's presidential carriage, staffed with a chef and a valet, having been put at the General's disposal. In addition to ample private quarters for the international leaders, a dining room, a lounge and an office, the coach provided accommodation for the International Secretary, Commissioner Joseph B. Smith, the Territorial Commander, Commissioner Chas. Baugh, Captain (later Colonel) Kenneth Rawlins and myself. One other member of the party, the International Youth Secretary, Colonel (afterwards Commissioner) Edgar Grinsted was accommodated elsewhere on the train. All met for meals in the presidential car when travelling between stops, except for the one occasion when the coach in which Colonel Grinsted lay fast asleep was shunted on to another, and later, train. When I went to fetch him for breakfast (for which, ordinarily, having left the austerity of Britain behind, he was never late!) he had disappeared. For the rest of the party there was great humour in the situation. For the Colonel, minus Canadian funds, it was a hungry experience. The train conductor's signals, however, led to an eventual reunion and a presentation, with mock gravity, of a survival course certificate to the Colonel.

Handling correspondence, sending cables and taking dictation as the four thousand miles were traversed gave me a glimpse of the wide-ranging concerns and the strange problems demanding solutions that were part of life for the Army's head. From the small, mobile office and its incessant claims, I saw the General, time after time, shake himself free and move to platform or pulpit as the dispenser of spiritual truth and the almoner of inspiration. The impression made on me was lasting. Sitting at the type-writer, fingers flying as the miles flew past, glancing occasionally at the flat prairies golden in the late summer sun or at the Rocky Mountain peaks majestic in the moonlight, the thought that there might be future responsibilities beyond these present, secretarial duties never entered my mind. I was lost in the privilege of the moment. And, surely, no-one on that train, least of all myself, could ever have entertained the thought that I would be the fifth successor to the General I was now serving.

By the time I reached International Headquarters in 1964 General Orsborn had retired. Leading meetings at Boscombe, the corps he attended, he sat beside me on the platform. In the quiet preceding the start of the service the General leaned over and said, "You were once my Lieutenant. Today, let me be yours."

At North Toronto I succeeded Colonel Robt. Watt as bandmaster of the corps band which had made a name for itself under the Colonel's tuition. With the fraternal rivalry that existed among the Toronto bands of the time this aggregation was a David among Goliaths. Only modesty forbids relating the number of times the Goliaths were slain. Living again with musical scores reawakened my interest in composition. Prior to officership I had been a correspondence student of strict and free counter-point with the remarkable Bandmaster George Marshall. Disabled by a mining accident while a young man, he became a notable figure in the world of Salvation Army composition. During my 1933 visit to England I paid him a visit, and, while we talked, pushed the wheelchair he occupied around the garden of his home. I regarded him as a "master," but there was nothing overbearing in his manner or speech. He talked more of spiritual truths than of musical form. When I bade him goodbye he took my hand in both of his and said, "Try and preserve the Army spirit in all you do." And, as if asking himself the question, said, "And what is the Army spirit?" After a momentary silence he answered himself: "Surely it must be the Holy Spirit."

Little did he or I on that day think that it would be my future responsi-

put it. But behind the drum, faced with a large poster on the wall headed, "I believe!," and announcing an evangelistic campaign under that title, I wrote the words and music of the song, "I Believe!" In accepting the song for publication, the head of the Music Editorial Department wrote, "Few songs have so encapsulated in a single chorus our Articles of Doctrine."

Though leaving bandmastership, music was not altogether forsaken. Commissioner Chas. Baugh, a former chief of the staff appointed as territorial commander for Canada, shared his hopes for an annual festival of music of the highest calibre. "A showcase night," he called it. He himself had been a member of the renowned International Staff Band and, despite his years in finance and auditing, had not lost his love of music. We stood on the floor of a deserted Varsity Arena, in Toronto.

"Can you fill this place, Brown?" he asked.

Hope rather than confidence answered. "I'll certainly do my best," I replied. In that moment the annual Spring Festival of Music was born. Each time I return to the Varsity Arena I see in memory the impressive figure of the late Sir Ernest MacMillan, then conductor of the Toronto Symphony Orchestra, on the podium and leading the massed bands in the "Hallelujah" Chorus from Handel's immortal "Messiah." MacMillan was one of the world's chief authorities on the interpretation of Handel's music.

Nor had opportunities for conducting entirely disappeared. I was privileged to conduct what was probably the largest convocation of bands ever brought together in Toronto. On the night of September 16, 1949, the pleasure steamer, S.S. "Noronic," while berthed at the city's waterfront, had burst into flames. The luxurious vessel was reduced to a charred hulk. One hundred and eighteen persons perished in the inferno. Others were saved by an heroic Salvationist policeman, Cy. Cole, who dived into the heated waters of the harbour again and again and brought them to safety. Salvationists were recruited to assist in the improvised morgue set up in the horticultural building of the Canadian National Exhibition, meeting relatives and helping in the grim task of identifying the bodies and supportively caring for the bereaved. The assignment was a sensitive one. A few passengers had registered under assumed names or illicitly as married couples.

The city convened an official memorial service in the spacious but unattractive Coliseum on a Sunday afternoon, and asked the Army to supply the music. Relatives and friends came from all parts of North America to join in the mourning. When an immense crowd is silent, the silence is extraordinary—more silent than common silence; almost palpable and somehow gently crushing. It was like that on this occasion, with periods of soundlessness broken only by an ejaculation of sobbing which, in the quiet, seemed like the sobs of many. To wield a baton in such circumstances is to understand the phrase, "deep calleth unto deep." I sought to draw from the several hundred bandsmen the sad sonority required by Chopin's "Funeral March," the "Dead March" in "Saul" and the hymn-tunes that belong to such grieving moments. The dignity and majesty of the sound threading its way through the emotional response of the listening congregation electrified me. What Eliphaz described to Job I experienced: "Fear came upon me, and trembling ... the hair of my flesh stood up."

Other unforgettable musical occasions were to come. While attending the International Staff College (now the International College for Officers) in October, 1951, I was invited to accompany the International Staff Band to Buckingham Palace where music was to be played in the forecourt for King George VI, then seriously ill. The programme included Sir Hubert Parry's "Jerusalem" which, I was told, was a favourite of the monarch's. During its rendition an equerry approached the band and summoned the bandmaster, Major (later Colonel) Bernard Adams, and myself to meet Her Majesty Queen Elizabeth inside the palace. At the time Her Royal Highness the Princess Elizabeth, soon to be Queen, was touring Canada, and the fact of my being from the Dominion, I thought, explained my inclusion. As the two of us marched across the gravelled forecourt to the entrance, the bandmaster was repeating, "What shall I say? What shall I say?" But there was no need for nervousness. Her Majesty, after expressing the thanks of the King and herself to the band, asked the Major if the façade of the palace made an effective sounding board for the crowd listening beyond the palace railings. It was a technical question that the bandmaster was well qualified to answer, and after that the audience proceeded smoothly and delightfully. We were presented to Her Royal Highness the Princess Margaret as she stood near, but behind, her mother. Her girlish beauty quite captivated me. There were questions about Canada and, in particular, about the cities that Princess Elizabeth would be visiting that week.

The audience over, we returned to the band already in marching formation and swung out through the main gates and the crowds of tourists and sightseers. My elation was not in the least dampened by the comment of one of the bandsmen.

"I've lived here all my life," he said in mock irritation, "but this fellow, Brown, is only in the country six weeks and he's inside the blooming palace!"

It was during this association with the International Staff Band that I had the thought that the band should make a tour of Canada. It would be the band's first visit to North America and I could see it as a most successful venture. Commissioner Dalziel, then Canada's territorial commander, leapt on the idea, and in 1952 the tour took place. From the moment of welcome by the Governor-General, the Rt. Hon. Vincent Massey, in the lovely grounds of Rideau Hall, Ottawa, to the festival given in "the hall of mirrors" in Government House, Victoria, B.C., later destroyed by fire, the band received a tumultuous welcome everywhere across the Dominion. In the Corral, at Calgary, the band appeared wearing ten-gallon stetsons. As the march, "Star Lake" (Ball), was played, the conductor suddenly produced a six-shooter and a startled audience heard the drum-beats, a feature of the march, replaced by gun shots. The applause could not be stopped.

Transportation was mainly by air, but as a precautionary measure and because accommodation on the Viscounts of that day was limited, the journeys were made in two groups. It was fortuitous that each group could function on its own as a band. At Halifax, N.S., due to fog, one group was delayed several hours. When the men arrived some of the events were over, the other half having managed most efficiently. This led me to remark that, as organizer and tour manager, I could have obviated many billeting problems, increased the profits and been saved a lot of anxiety about transportation had we brought only a hand-picked half of the band. The playing and singing of the bandsmen set new and exceedingly high standards for their Canadian comrade musicians to reach. For this alone, and had there been no other advantages to the tour (there were many), it would have been eminently worth while. This is corroborated by the fact that the tour was repeated in 1957, but the novelty and impact of the first visit was quite unrepeatable.

Music-making became less possible as the years passed. All I ever owned was a mouthpiece, never an instrument, but when I look at it a host of rewarding memories spring to mind. My final "playing" days were in the company of a congenial group comprised mainly of officers attached to territorial headquarters in Toronto. Calling ourselves the T.H.Q. Musical Party we sought to help the smaller corps by our playing, singing and leadership of meetings. Maintaining the needed instrumentation was not easy. Headquarters officers, like all others, are subject to changes of appointment, and the administration had other objectives than the perpetuation of our well-motivated but less than vitally essential combination.

CHAPTER 6

Waters Of Trepidation

Writing in the December 1981 issue of *The Officer* I confessed that two appointments in particular plunged me into the icy waters of trepidation. On reflection I do not know how I would finally have managed without those two appointments. I had to swim harder, but the frigid waters provided stimulation, and even refreshment.

The first came in an irregular way. With my wife I had been directing a music camp in the United States and returned to Toronto to find myself the centre of questioning. Curious friends wanted to know what my next appointment was to be. I was blissfully unaware that I was being farewelled from my niche, but everyone assured me that my successor had been named and was probably even now on his way from South Africa. The territorial commander, Commissioner Benjamin Orames, with whom I had often travelled, had not mentioned the likelihood of change. I therefore asked to see him. He apologized profusely, something I had not expected, and explained that my successor had indeed received his appointment and, quite naturally, had cabled the news to his children living in Canada. They were under no embargo and freely shared their delight at their father's return to his homeland. Confirmation from International Headquarters, however, had been inexplicably delayed, and this was necessary before any official local announcement could be made.

I was to leave the work in which I had found unlimited satisfaction in order to create a new position and to introduce a new function. A rather impressive title was devised—Territorial Publicity Representative—

which, in one Northern British Columbia town was unfortunately abbreviated to "Pub Representative." Professional journalists had previously done the work I was now to do. Two of them I knew well and had often marvelled at the wide range of contacts which they turned to good account for the Army. To me the appointment was intimidating, the more so because of the talented, experienced people I knew myself to be following. My brief was simply stated—to make the Army as well known and as accurately understood throughout Canada and Bermuda as it ought to be. No small task!

As professional journalists, my predecessors had directed most of their effort towards the press, and, to begin with, I followed in their fourth-estate footsteps. It was "back to school," and to a hard one at that. News has a deathly high mortality rate, according to one wit; today's excitement is interred before tomorrow's sun shines across the city desk. This meant, for example, writing up an evening event and personally delivering the copy to the news editors of the various newspapers the same night, however late the hour. Satisfaction lay in seeing the item in the next day's editions. I quickly learned that an "exclusive" story is more persuasive than a general release. But this meant finding perhaps four different aspects of a single event and writing a story on each. Effort was quadrupled, but so were the rewards. One's stock also went up in the news room, or with the feature editors.

But no matter how adhesive relationships were with reporters and editors, space was always at a premium, and competition for it in the melée of press agents was ruthless. Only the most interesting and best-written pieces ever see the light of day. For the near-best there is only the everlasting darkness of the paper shredder. For ten years everything I had written, subject to the editor-in-chief's approval, hardly ever withheld, was printed. There was no competition. What was composed on the fifth floor was sacrosanct in the basement print shop. Now, critical eyes read the copy. If it survived a first glance, sub-editors might "doctor" the story to give it the "slant" that suited the readers' mood of the moment. In the process a sequence was sometimes altered and, occasionally a fact, to the annoyance of my superiors and my own chagrin.

Picture editors were for me a special specie. Let it now be admitted that my superiors were human enough to appreciate seeing their likeness in a national daily accompanied by some worthy comment, though it was difficult to convince some of them that picture editors have an arithmetic philosophy—that three are better than four, and two are better than three, and that they also have an ingrained preference for pictures of children and animals rather than of adults doing nothing but staring into the lens of the camera.

In the trade there is what is called, "cropping." It is not a disease, but it can have fatal results. Usually it means losing unnecessary background in a photograph so as to bring the main subjects forward. In order to make a picture fit available space cropping can also mean the deletion of individuals who unfortunately are at the extreme sides of a group when photographed. One can only imagine the darker thoughts of those who, after being solely responsible for the success of a reported event, were "cropped" away. A classic example of cropping occurred years later when my wife and I arrived in Lusaka, the capital of Zambia. A photographer caught us at the bottom of the steps from the plane being greeted by the English officer-commanding and his black general secretary. The next morning the excellent photograph, four or five columns wide, appeared on the front page of the leading paper. It had been cropped to show only the black general secretary welcoming "General Jean Brown, international leader of The Salvation Army," according to the cut line. It was three cheers for both feminine and black leadership.

As fascinating and instructive as were my contacts with the press, I was intrigued by another aspect of the mass media—the radio. I knew we would be knocking on radio's door all too late, but I felt the door could be opened if we went about it the right way. Under the broadcasting code stations were obligated to give a percentage of their broadcasting time, free, to charitable and philanthropic causes, and to programmes in the public interest such as safety and community health. Under this provision I envisaged a regular Army programme, interpretive, inspirational and with a spiritual message that would reflect the movement's primary aim. Bound as the station owner was to provide such "sustaining" time, the choice of cause was his. Naturally he would select programmes which, by their high quality, would gain listeners, not lose them. As sympathetic as he might be to a particular interest, he was not in business to see his ratings plummet because a programme was amateurishly put together. He wanted no negative chain reaction; a poor programme affects the one that follows it, and sponsors had to be reckoned with, as did firms paying for "commercials." All wanted the largest possible audience. The manager and programme director of even the smallest station knew this all too well.

How to break through all these barriers was a mind-sharpening challenge. A commission headed by the then Colonel Wiseman recommended that a sum of money be invested in production, in the hope that a quality programme could be prepared and the stations persuaded to air it gratuitously. The recommendation was approved and the project was launched. I was given a free hand. The format, I decided, should include Salvation Army music, a dramatic episode that would emphasize a Biblical truth, a brief homily summarizing the presentation and a distinctive "sign-off" which invited listeners in material or spiritual need to contact their nearest Salvation Army officer. I chose as a title for the series, "This is my Story." I saw the programme as telling the Army's story and the story of individuals whose lives were depicted in the dramatic segments. Fanny Crosby's line, "This is my story, this is my song," with Mrs. Joseph Knapp's tune, gave us our programme signature. Joel Aldred, already a well-known broadcaster, was the first commentator, and this heightened acceptance by both stations and listeners.

Public Relations officers competently laid the groundwork, and I personally canvassed the management of every station in Canada and Bermuda. Soon we were "on the air" from scores of originations. The impact of the early programmes was astonishing. Some officers, beleaguered by responding individuals in a way that they had not formerly known, were critical of the "wide open" invitation to "contact your nearest Salvation Army officer." Most found that the programme brought their community nearer to the officers' quarters and to the Army hall, and encouraged us to continue production. Enquiries began to arrive from Salvation Army leaders in the United States as to whether the project could be developed continentally. For many years this was to be the salvation of the project. American funds ensured the best production, and talent from the States added to the variety of the format.

Negotiations with unions were tangled and often frustrating. A religious movement moving into the professional radio production field was not common. Union leaders were caught between sympathy and the immutability of their rule books. The leader of the musicians' union in Canada had been a Salvation Army bandsman during his youth in England. For him, decisions were doubly difficult. Professional actors and actresses were hired for the dramatic episodes. Some of them have since become universally known and their voices and faces are familiar to millions. Others did not make it. When, in 1974, I returned to Canada as Territorial Commander, many of those who had brought "This is my Story" to a high level of acceptance by some hundreds of radio stations in a number of countries, and had later participated in "The Living Word" television series, entertained my wife and myself to dinner and to an evening filled with reminiscence and laughter as the "fluffs" of the recording sessions, never heard by the public, were recalled. The many talented Salvationists who spent innumerable hours in rehearsing and recording deserve a "distinguished service" medal.

Wide coverage meant both favourable comment and some criticism. The critics usually failed to recognize that the budget was abysmally small and that the audience was a widely diversified one. More than once I thanked Sibelius for his advice: "Pay no attention to what the critics say; no statue has ever been put up to a critic." Criticism or not, the series produced unexpected results. Men in prisons listened regularly to the programme and asked for the free Bible courses which were offered from time to time. More than one would-be suicide changed his intention after listening to an episode. Small groups of religiously-minded people in remote areas sought the Army's spiritual leadership. Men and women found Christ and reported their conversion to the first Salvationist they met. Young people, moved by the dramatic force of certain episodes, felt led to become Salvation Army officers. On the material side, the number revealing their needs greatly increased.

If we were late in grasping the potential of radio, we were not too late for television. Stations were springing up across the country and were looking for material to fill out their schedules. Local production was costly, often beyond the means of community stations in their earliest days. This also was in our favour. The advice given us was the same as for radio: produce a worthwhile programme and there would then be every possibility of it being aired. Experience in radio production was a direct corridor to achievement in the realm of television, and many of the problems were the same. One in particular was magnified. If radio production had been expensive, television production costs were formidable. Again, unless the project could be undertaken continentally there could be no series. Army leaders in Canada and the United States were certainly cognizant of the power of this audio-visual medium of mass communication. The hesitation that had delayed the use of radio did not exist with this newer medium. The only constraint was financial.

I undertook a successful but wearying six-weeks' tour across Canada visiting all television stations, projecting a print of the pilot film and soliciting free air-time for the anticipated series. The journey included a visit to Whitehorse, in the Yukon, a town founded during the Klondike gold rush of 1898 on the banks of the Lewes River, more than a thousand miles north of Vancouver. The long winter night had already set in, and in the eerie darkness I trudged through the snow to a warm reception by the station staff who persuaded me to participate in the longest radio interview of my career. It lasted the entire morning. But any preening of myself would have been fatuous. As I left, the interviewer-producer-disc jockey said, "Nice having you. In this unreal town it's a relief to have somebody—anybody!—to talk to on the air."

The new territorial commander for Canada was Commissioner W. Wycliffe Booth. Powers of administration, refined artistic competence, particularly in music and painting, and the drive of a locomotive at full throttle blended in the personality of this grandson of the Army's founder. In his time he had staged many dramatic presentations, notably in the Palais de Chaillot in Paris, and he was determined that a television series should blanket Canada with the Army's message. He packed me off with the pilot film to the Army's four administrative centres in the States to secure each territory's financial support on a formula basis. The name of the programme, "The Living Word," and the proposed format, already had the recommendation of the creative Continental Film, Radio and Television Commission of which I was a member.

With funds promised, production promises had to be fulfilled. The aim was to create thirteen half-hour programmes a year. The lower basement of the Toronto headquarters was transformed into a film studio and sound stage. The physical hurdles were high. Filming could only take place when there was absolute quiet on the building, as well as on the set. Total sound-proofing of the studio was impossible. If someone unthinkingly used the elevator the sound track of the scene being shot was ruined. It soon became evident that all filming would have to be done through the night hours. Crews and participants would assemble at 11 p.m. and leave exhausted at 3 a.m. or 4 a.m. This meant overtime rates for the professionals, so that we took a lean view of mechanical failures or forgotten lines. Some of the dramatic episodes were shot "on location"—on a freighter sailing down the St. Lawrence River, in a bell foundry where this ancient craft had not been forgotten, or in the famous organ factory at St. Hyacinthe, Quebec. These were fascinating expeditions that compensated for the midnight tedium and the claustrophobic suroundings of the studio. A Canadian officer, Leslie Pindred, who was later to serve in the Netherlands and Australia as a commissioner, was the first "host" on the programme. He was succeeded by an American officer, Captain (now Lieut-Colonel) Ernest Miller, whose vocal solos were an added inspiration.

The production team, headed by an award-winning cinematographer, Leslie P. Thatcher, was amazing in its dedication. All credit for achievement belongs to them; they earned it. The sets for all the dramas were created in the studio, and the discovering and borrowing of needed set-pieces or artifacts seemed to be accomplished miraculously. What we lacked in money had to be balanced out by resourcefulness.

As time went on it was necessary to move farther afield in our search for suitable Salvation Army music. One of our chief successes was the enlisting of the International Staff Band's help. The bandmaster and the bandsmen themselves entered enthusiastically into the long and demanding filming sessions in the Merton Park Studios in South London, and provided the series with a reservoir of excellence from which items could be drawn as required. Members of the Music Editorial Department and composer-bandsmen assisted with special musical arrangements, lengthening the list of those who had contributed to the series in this way—a list that began with Territorial Bandmaster Percy Merritt and Colonel Bramwell Coles, the latter once again living in Toronto in retirement. My visits to London to supervise production served to link me closely with the men of the "I.S.B." Neither I nor they could have had any thought that within a decade, as Chief of the Staff, I would be directly responsible for the band's existence and wellbeing. Three attractive young women Salvationists in Atlanta, Georgia, possessing excellent voices, became known as "The Living Word Trio," and by their participation added another visual and vocal dimension. All three are today Salvation Army officers.

Every production decision was important, but one had far-reaching, beneficial results. With the spectre of the budget always haunting us there was raised the serious question as to whether the series should be filmed in black and white or in colour. Aesthetically there could be no debate. Colour was far more desirable, but not its cost. Still, we argued, it was the film of the future, and eventually the decision was taken. Had we not so decided, the films would have had a short life. Though at the start our colour prints were occasionally broadcast in monochrome, it was not long before all stations were airing in colour. We were "ahead of the market," and many of the films still belie their vintage.

In retrospect I see that several people paid a high price for this successful venture. Through these years I missed much of the "imperceptible, lovely growth" of our children due to so much travelling and the long days that ran into longer nights of production activity. I was dismayed to discover that I had missed many of a father's unrepeatable joys in the childhood of his offspring, so swiftly did these busy years pass by, and I was doubly grateful for one who succeeded in being both father and mother to two near-fatherless girls.

One jarring incident marred the production success of the series, at least for me. I was not a member of the Central Finance Council, as it was then called, but I knew that annually the allocation of funds for television production sparked spirited debate. After one such session, figures were provided to the territorial commander which seemed to indicate that as a department we had considerably overspent the continental budget. I did not know about the figures until I was instructed to meet the commissioner outside the North Toronto hall prior to his presiding over a meeting. He was so distressed that he could not wait until the next morning for a conference. In his car he gave me a raking over the like of which I had never experienced. I had, he said in the strongest of language, plunged him into unconsciable, irremediable disgrace with his American fellow commissioners. He was so upset that he came close to accusing my staff of misappropriation, at which point I could contain myself no longer. We were not responsible for the accounting, and I knew that my colleagues were impeccable in the matter of receipts and vouchers. Deeply hurt, I said that I could not tolerate the imputation and that there should be an independent enquiry. There was. Assigned to the task was Lieut-

Commissioner Llewellyn Cowan, of New York, a highly-competent accountant, and all was found to be completely in order. More than once through succeeding years Commissioner Cowan and I have smiled over Commissioner Booth's immediate penitence. It was demonstrated in a way that revealed the Commissioner's greatness of spirit. Unexpectedly, he landed at our home, the trunk of his car filled with plants. "I'll put these in your garden for you," he said, "and whenever you look at the flowers you'll be reminded of my appreciation and not my allegations!"

CHAPTER 7

Armour Bearer

The arrival of Commissioner and Mrs. Wycliffe Booth in command of the work in Canada ushered in for me a nine-year period of frenzy, flounce and fulfilment. Unexpectedly, I was assigned to accompany the bilingual arrivals on their welcome tours across the Dominion, to introduce them to Canadian Salvationists and to present them suitably to the authorities in the various provincial capital cities. The first tour completed I was dubbed *le petit copain* and became, in the Commissioner's somewhat feudal terminology, his "armour bearer." I had nothing to do with armour, as such, but I did have to be "armoured" at all times against the eventualities that might arise, and they frequently did!

One Easter Monday evening, for example, we were entering the Hamilton Temple for a united meeting that the Commissioner had not wanted, but which the divisional commander had made up his mind to have. It had been a long series of Good Friday and Easter meetings, and the Commissioner was certain that a Monday night gathering would be disappointingly anti-climactic. It was obvious as we marched in that the immense crowd, which not only filled the auditorium but also blocked the foyer and the aisles, caught him off guard. As we neared the platform he turned and whispered hoarsely, "Brown, did I remember to tell you that you are giving the main Bible address tonight?" There was no time for protest. We were already in our places and the crowd was giving the Commissioner and his wife a prolonged, rousing welcome. The meeting proceeded. I gave the address. The Commissioner's thanks in no way betrayed what I suspected was the fact, that having decided in his mind that the Monday night event would be a non-starter, he had not prepared himself for it. Years later there were occasions when I myself did not feel as well prepared as I should have done for a big event, but with my memories I could not bring myself to impose in the same way on any of my own "armour bearers."

I also discovered that an "armour bearer" was one who, never having before sung a solo in public, was expected to do so without hesitation when announced. Usually I did not even need to exercise any powers of choice. The song was chosen for me, and the key in which it was to be rendered was authoritatively signalled from the piano by the Commissioner himself who would then provide a highly competent accompaniment.

This close association with a grandson of the Army's founder made me the fortunate recipient of many anecdotes relating to William Booth and, perhaps more particularly, to his father, Bramwell Booth, for whom he had been a devoted and conscientious aide-de-camp, managing the General's day to day routines with diligence and no little authority. Not only by inheritance, but by total personal commitment, the Commissioner was the epitome of the Blood and Fire soldier. For him it was a divine obligation to emphasize the "Salvation" which was at the centre of The Salvation Army's name. This drove him to seek out "the lost" with such energy that new forms of social service sprang into being, or established ones were enlarged, more rapidly than many believed possible. "Impossible," was not a word in his vocabulary, English or French. He simply took it for granted that "with God all things are possible." Permeating all that he and his wife sought to do among the prostitutes, the homeless, the alcoholics, the forgotten and the sick, was what he called "my passion for souls." He expected seekers in every meeting, even meetings of the most formal kind when the general feeling was that to press an appeal was not quite suitable.

One Sunday afternoon in a crowded United Church he had lectured on the history of the Army that was already written, and the history that should be created. He had warmed to his theme and, still holding the people's interest, had gone very much over time. Late as it was, he felt there should be an appeal and instructed me to make it. He himself, and his wife, were extraordinarily faithful in moving about a building during the prayer period and personally counselling any who appeared to be debating their spiritual future. As the Commissioner moved off to speak to someone in the congregation he passed a headquarters officer and emphatically said to him, "Get off the platform and speak to someone about their soul. Get them to the Mercy-Seat."

"I have no direction from the Holy Spirit that I should do it," said the surprised, discomfited officer.

"Direction?" echoed the Commissioner. "I've given you all the direction you need. Now do it!"

It is necessary to say that on several occasions when one would have thought a response improbable, there were seekers. I had to admit to myself that the Commissioner was sometimes stronger in faith than his armour-bearer. But not always. He delighted to tell this story against himself. My wife and I had accompanied him to Old Orchard, Maine, where traditionally every summer Salvation Army camp meetings bring outstanding speakers and eager congregations together. The Commissioner was the speaker, and had confided to me that he was troubled about the matter of "fishing" (a reference to the words of Jesus: "Follow Me, and I will make you fishers of men.") while I led the prayer meeting. He thought that some of the senior officers might think he was doing it "for effect," and, if they did, it would be counter-productive. He was unusually sensitive to the views of his American counterparts. He wrote me a note during the meeting saying, "Carry on with the meeting, and pray for me while I do what I must."

When the moment came, he stepped off the high stage and made his way immediately to a well-dressed man in a grey suit seated near the front. Afterwards, the Commissioner said, the conversation went something like this:

"Have you enjoyed the meeting?"

"Very much," the man replied, his head still bowed in prayer.

"Have you felt that God has been speaking to you during the meeting?"

"Yes," said the man.

"Then supposing you and I together kneel at the Mercy-Seat," said the Commissioner, wanting to make sure of his "catch."

"Perhaps I should have made myself known," said the man. "I'm a Salvation Army officer and the Divisional Commander from Buffalo." At this point in the recital the Commissioner would burst into laughter. "Serves me right," he would say, "for trifling with what is my duty."

The Commissioner's tenure was longer than that of any other occupying the same position to date. His nearest rival was his aunt, the redoubtable Evangeline Booth, whose term as Commissioner for Canada ran from 1896 to 1904, since referred to as "the golden decade" in Canada's Salvation Army history. (Did she accomplish in eight years what might have taken others ten?) She was the third member of the Booth family to be general and international leader of the Army. Despite Commander Eva's daring sortie into the hazards of the Yukon Gold Rush, and other attention-attracting enterprises, it is safe to say that her nephew left behind him a far more impressive list of achievements. From the Atlantic to the Pacific, in buildings and services, the mark of his hand can still be seen.

Le petit copain found himself loaded with duties well outside the brief of his appointment, but the journeys, while time-consuming, were invaluable learning experiences. The opportunities for leading great gatherings encouraged confidence, and a growing expertise in revising failed travel arrangements was perfect training for those future days when journeys would be on a global scale and involving every form of transportation from jeep to jumbo jet. Booth would have expected the former to travel as fast as the latter.

He and I were worlds apart in temperament, but I appropriated from him all I could by way of Army history, administrative procedure, and methods of dealing with difficult people and situations, something at which he was impressively adept.

My service in Canada, like his, was drawing to a close, and in a way this took me by surprise. Not in the slightest did the Commissioner reveal that International Headquarters had periodically requested my transfer, and that consistently he had advanced strong reasons why the transfer was "not possible at this time" ... "should possibly be considered at a future date" ... "would be difficult to arrange just now ..." The correspondence, when it happened to cross my desk as Chief of the Staff some years later, made fascinating reading.

Booth's initiative led to the establishing of a general hospital in Labrador City, a mining settlement on the mainland portion of the Province of Newfoundland. Because of permafrost, construction was unique and difficult, and the Commissioner took immense satisfaction in its achievement. With this in mind, he named his English retirement home on the outskirts of Wokingham, "Happy Valley," a reminder of the Labrador community where Salvationists perpetuate the preaching of the Gospel first introduced by the Moravians in 1771. The Commissioner found himself residing in his "Happy Valley" before he wished, since his health gave way while leading congress meetings in New Zealand. On one of our last visits to "Happy Valley," having been received by the Commissioner in full uniform though now seriously ill, he said: "I suppose, Chief, you will one day write and tell all sorts of stories about me."

"Possibly, Commissioner," I said, "but none will be unkind."

"Those were the days," he said wistfully, and launched into a recital of incidents over which we had laughed many times before, and of others which had led us both to tears. No-one in forty-seven years of active officership provided me with more good stories. His unpredictability spawned them. His sudden impulses made them inevitable. In a little prairie town I was awakened one night to hear the Commissioner and his wife, who were occupying the next hotel room, in loud discussion. The Commissioner's wife, troubled by deafness, was patently not wearing her hearing aid. The Commissioner had been disturbed by the noise of a drunken party in one of the rooms along the hall, and was setting out to put the lid on it. At the door, he knocked imperiously and announced who he was, though his dishevelled appearance, which I could see through my partly opened door, totally belied his rank and station. He wore no dressing-gown. His pyjama jacket was open and fluttering. His hair dribbled about his head. His cultivated voice, invested with aristocratic annoyance, rang out loud and clear. From inside, a drunken shout suggested that the caller should "Get lost!" The Commissioner now threatened to call the police, and a chorus of woolly voices dared him to do it. Disregarding his appearance he went downstairs to the reception desk, but it was deserted. This was not the Dorchester or Claridges. The night watchman was probably among the celebrants. Fuming, the Commissioner returned to the floor and challenged the occupants of the room once more. But to no avail. He would have to return to his own room, regroup his thoughts, quieten his feelings and devise some new strategy. At his own door, alas, he discovered that he had locked himself out, and a deaf wife had no idea that he was demanding entrance. His pounding seemed louder than the bibulous revelry, and at this point the "armour bearer" took over. I invited the harassed protestor into my room and with a "I hope you will sleep, Commissioner," returned him to his destination via a connecting door.

Few could be more sympathetic to the plight of the poor, or more practical in trying to alleviate it. He once decided to do a microscopic inspection of all the men's hostels. I was to accompany him and make notes of everything that transpired. We arrived in Winnipeg where an old building, named after Earl Haig, had served tremendous needs for many years. He inspected every room and flushed every toilet. The superintendent was in close attendance making explanations when necessary. We came finally to a large dormitory, outmoded, but of necessity fully used. In a dramatic gesture, the Commissioner went down the rows of beds pulling linen and covers on to the floor. What was revealed here and there aroused the Commissioner's indignation and devastated the superintendent who sought to justify the shortcomings on the basis of inadequate cleaning staff, many of whom were subnormal and were being helped by having a small job to do. When a further, helpful explanation occurred to the brigadier in charge, the Commissioner could not be found. Minutes later he was spotted dangerously high up on the roof examining the eavestroughing and the skylights.

The next morning we flew to Edmonton, and the operation was repeated. The building was relatively new, the superintendent very alert. But off came the bedclothes in the same theatrical way. Happily, all the linen was antiseptically fresh, and the Commissioner apologized profusely for disturbing the dormitory's hygienic neatness. In a burst of gratitude he asked for all the cleaning staff to be assembled and gave them a "Montgomery at Alamein" speech. Honesty and humbleness then took hold of one slightly disordered mind. Mop in hand the cleaner stepped forward and thanked the Commissioner for his words, concluding his rambling effort with the comment, "We generally change the beds once a fortnight, Commissioner, but when they telephoned last night from Winnipeg we changed them all this morning, ten days early!" No-one enjoyed the revelation more than the Commissioner.

Underneath the demand and drive there was in the Commissioner and his wife a pool of pity which frequently welled up in compassionate action that ignored convention. In their own home a party for prostitutes meant a welcoming kiss from Mrs. Booth for each of the women. Young women officers were instructed to wait on these *filles de joies* as welcome guests of honour and not in any way as members of a sad sisterhood that lived in a twilight world of exploitation. I marvelled that these women would respond to such an invitation, but their hostess knew most of them by name and many of them by their story. The party was not a passing gesture; rather was it another point of contact in a continuing, persistent concern.

A moment of high drama occurred during a visit to a maximum security prison approached by a winding road through a great forest. The warden and his staff were seated behind the Commissioner and his party, and armed guards stood in the aisles facing us. The Commissioner had spoken to the large assembly of prisoners in a simple and deeply-moving way about home, children, love, disappointment, sin and a forgiving Christ. He then suggested that all present should bow in prayer. At this point a man broke the rules and rushed forward towards the Commissioner. He fell on his knees and threw his arms around the Commissioner's legs. Looking up, he shouted through his sobbing and tears, "Help me! Save me! My God, I'm going to die ... my family, my family ..." The guards moved forward to remove the man, but the Commissioner's authoritative gesture waved them away and, strangely I thought, they obeyed. "Let him pray," the Commissioner said, "and we'll pray with him and for him, and for all others who need what only Divine grace can supply."

I went on with the meeting, and many of the men raised their hands requesting prayer for themselves or their families. Meanwhile, the Commissioner soothed the distraught man back to composure and then led him back to his place. The screams of the man, a suspected murderer, echoing around the steel and stone are not forgotten, nor is the hubbub of reaction as the prisoners noisily shuffled their feet, their only form of response seeing conversation was forbidden. But clearest of all is the memory of two men kneeling on a prison floor, arms around each other, both in uniform, one in prison grey, the other in Salvation Army navy blue, while prisoners and their keepers all appeared transfixed by an intervention more Divine than human.

Possibly the most widely-quoted definition of The Salvation Army originated in Canada and came spontaneously from the lips of the Rt. Hon. Arthur Meighen, P.C., an erstwhile prime minister. He was reckoned to be one of the Dominion's golden-tongued orators, a devastating opponent in debate and, in repartee, a combination of forked lightning and a razor's edge. I had accompanied Commissioner Booth to a luncheon meeting of the Toronto Board of Trade, a prestigious occasion that brought together several hundred businessmen, at which he was to be the guest speaker. The chairman, recognizing the former prime minister's presence and aware of his presidency of the Army's national advisory board, turned to him and asked if, before the Commissioner spoke, he would care to say in a few words what he saw The Salvation Army to be. Mr. Meighen, in appearance a distinguished figure, rose at once. As though they had been carefully crafted and perfectly polished, his impromptu words fell extemporaneously into place without the slightest hesitation. "Some say The Salvation Army is a welfare agency," he said. "That is a mistake. The Salvation Army is a vital spiritual force with an acute social conscience." Fortunately, I had the wit to write the statement down; it could so easily have been lost for ever. After the meeting I repeated the statement to the Commissioner and suggested that it should find its way into the Army's *Year Book*. Once published, it took seven league boots and raced around the world, and I was to hear it quoted, not always accurately, innumerable times in my travels. Whenever I heard it, I would see the impressive form of an aging statesman whose name, support and generosity are memorialized in the Army's beautiful "Isabel and Arthur Meighen Lodge" for senior citizens in Toronto, slowly rising to his feet, and hear again his voice as, with masterly succinctness, he placed the emphasis where every Salvationist would wish it to be put in respect of the movement's meaning and mission.

In age I was now nearly at the half-century mark, and having received a new appointment, prepared myself for another leap into unknown waters. Unfamiliar they certainly were, but, once submerged, I found them tropically pleasant and landing me on some favoured and fascinating shores. Appointed as the national youth secretary, I was told that the burdens of television production were still to be mine. I also had the uncomfortable feeling, soon proved prescient, that I had not been released from my undefined and unlimited responsibilities as an "armour bearer."

In a hand-written letter the Commissioner wrote: "So far as your new task is concerned I have very *great* hopes. In fact, the Army is only *growing* through its young people. I look to you to make that growth go into top gear. The job is A.O.K., the opportunities limitless. Now, the command is Go, Go, Go!"

It remains arguable whether a youth worker needs the physical fitness of youth or the wisdom of advancing years. The ideal, probably, is to have "the heart of a boy and the mind of a man." For instance, at fifty it seemed rather late for ski weekends. I could revel in the crystal air, enjoy the chatter of the young people as they challenged each other to still faster runs down the mountainside, bask in the afterglow around the blazing log fire and breathe freely in the atmosphere of high devotion pervading the Bible study sessions that crowned the excursion. But to be on skis for the first time in one's life, facing a gently deceiving slope, with a large gallery of young people expecting to see a finished demonstration of "how it should be done" was petrifying. The "finished" demonstration was soon finished—a dizzying take-off, a brief thrusting through the mountain air at ever-gathering speed and then an unplanned somersault ending with head and shoulders buried in the snow and two untrustworthy legs signalling frantically for help. O, youth leadership, I thought while interred in the freezing snow, what imbecilities are commited in thy name.

The young people were frequently my teachers. I was struck by the rapidity of their maturation. Mid-teen youngsters were suddenly men and women with opinions of their own, opinions that hardened into convictions that could determine a life's direction. I saw involvement not only as a key-word, but as a vital necessity. "Use me or lose me," was more than a slogan, though a good one that I quoted often. The intense involvement of my own teen-age had held me firmly to God and the Army; there was never time for plotting other pastures or scanning the green of other hills.

It is my considered evaluation that the youth programme of The Salvation Army cannot be bettered. It meets every inclination of the young, from skilfully planned Bible studies to adventuring in the great outdoors and to making music under expert tuition, all permeated with character-building emphases that make for good citizenship in two countries, one earthly and the other heavenly. In this programme the child can have the happiness it deserves, and meet the hopes of "The Preacher": "Young people, enjoy your youth. Be happy while you are still young. Do what you want to do, and follow your heart's desire. But remember that God is going to judge you for whatever you do. Don't let anything worry you or cause you pain. You aren't going to be young very long.

So remember your Creator while you are still young, before those dismal days and years come when you will say, 'I don't enjoy life.' " (Ecclesiastes 11: 9,10; 12: 1. TEV) If dismal years are ahead then childhood and youth, I firmly believed, should be laced with laughter. I have always agreed with Heinrich Heine that "laughter is wholesome. God is not so dull as some of the parsons make out. Did he not make the kitten to chase its tail?"

I took office when youth around the world was stepping over the threshold of rebellion. In the Strange Sixties, as someone has said, next to "new" and "now" the most powerful word in advertising language was the word "young." "Our youth do not need to be patronized, petted or pilloried," said Leighton Ford. "What they do need is those who will try to listen, to understand and to have something real to share in terms of a genuine experience of the power of God." This was the message I carried across Canada to the devoted men and women who, through their work with youth, were seeking to safeguard the future of the Kingdom of Heaven on earth. At the end of the Sorry Sixties, Miss Elizabeth Manners, a highly-respected English headmistress, summed up the effect of the decade on youth in her book, *The Vulnerable Generation*. She noted with distaste the clothes, the music, the easy morals and the rebellious attitudes of many young people, but felt that the young were not all to blame. She castigated silly parents who say, "I shan't send him to church. It's up to him"; the hopelessness of the slums, political disillusionment, and so forth. What she wrote as a solution I had stressed. The attitude of elders to the young people ought to be, she said, "rooted and grounded in love." That, I had discovered, was easier stated than realized, since many parents were prisoners of the double standard and could hardly deserve being designated as parents. A British peeress, hauled into court because of the drug-taking and drug-pushing offences of her daughter, when slated by the judge for defaulting in parental responsibility, said, "I can't do anything about her; after all, I'm only her mother!" It was a ringing signal to the church that if parents were abdicating, as had the schools, even more was expected from it in moral guidance and character-developing leadership.

Within the Army's ranks parental standards generally were high, and Salvation Army young people did have the noblest of luminous examples to follow in Jesus. As long as their sense of purpose could be aroused and sustained all would be well. About the young people outside of our ranks I was gravely perturbed. Where was the sense of purpose to come from for them? On the Isle of Wight, off the south coast of England, a hundred and fifty thousand young people would shortly come together in an omnibus sharing of emptiness. No politician, no statesman, no cleric, no scientist, no economist, no technologist could draw a crowd like that. It puzzled me, and finally overwhelmed me, that a song could, a poem could, a seeking after "something" could. Not until these young people were caught up in an overmastering purpose would their potential be realized. It was just such a purpose—the defense of their land, the protection of their loved ones and their nation's survival—that turned the R.A.F. pilots of the Thirties, with their long hair and defiantly-casual dress and attitudes into disciplined, motivated, spirited men to whom, for the preservation of a decent civilization, so much is owed. If only young people could be stirred like this by the love of God to give their allegiance to Christ and His cause.

While national youth secretary I learned the necessity for seeking to understand young people. A new uniform was being considered by the Boy Scouts Association. By virtue of my appointment I was a scout commissioner and a member of the association's national council. At a special meeting a number of boys had been selected to "model" different kinds of uniform being proposed by professional scouters. I watched the faces of the boys as they came in, one by one, and paraded before the members of the council whose word, like supreme court judges, would be final. Invariably, the look on the lads' faces reflected their own judgement on the outfit they had been asked to wear. Some looked embarrassed. One or two were cynical. One obviously thought his gear was unbelievably ridiculous and showed it in his prancing and laughter. When the "mannequins" had retired someone asked, "Has anyone questioned the scouts themselves about which uniform they prefer?" There was stony silence. That boys have likes and dislikes had been forgotten, but, be it said to the council's credit, the decision was postponed until a wide canvass had been made.

It was not only a matter of understanding the likes and dislikes of young people (these have to be balanced against the experience and wisdom of their elders), but also of understanding the spiritual stirrings of young hearts and the, as yet, untarnished hopes of impressionable minds.

I was keen that our divisional youth secretaries who had direct responsibility for the scouts, among the several youth organizations claiming their supervision, should be fully equipped for their rôle. Some said they were too busy to take the courses offered which would lead to proper qualification, qualification which was all-important in view of the extensive camping programme. I felt I had no option but to take the time, which I could ill afford, to take the courses. Included was a week in the toughest of outdoor circumstances and under the most demanding of instructors. I was probably the oldest on the course, and a matter of curiosity to the others, especially when provincial police cars came swirling into the camp, sirens screeching, with officers demanding to know the whereabouts of one Arnold Brown. Without telephone access, Commissioner Booth had found another way to contact his "armour bearer," every call being an emergency of one sort or another!

The night I had to follow the stars, make my own bivouac and cook my own food with the barest of aids and supplies was among the wettest I can remember. All night long it poured with rain. There was not a star to be seen. Map and compass played disconcerting tricks. We were due back at base at 3 o'clock the next afternoon after hacking our way, at the end of the ramble, through a quarter-mile of thick brush and crossing a stream on a bridge consisting of a solitary log. To heighten the hazard, the log had been debarked. With the long rain it was greased to slimy perfection. Tired beyond description, soaked to the skin, bitten by flies and mosquitoes and sore from axing my way through resisting underbrush, I started across the log. Midway, I pirouetted gracelessly and slid into the river, face up, with the weight of the rucksack frustrating all efforts to assume a breast-stroke position. My shout for help was instinctive and belittling, but no-one came and I finally struggled to the bank. In the words of Coleridge's *The Ancient Mariner* "So lonely 'twas, that God himself / Scarce seemed there to be." The most pitiable aspirant ever for Gilwell beads marched back into camp. As I sat shivering beside an uncooperative fire, drying out my uniform, I could not help rubbing my hands with glee. I had proved the point. The course *could* be encompassed by busy officers. I had done it, and now the colleagues who had said they were too occupied would have no excuse. "The race is not to the swift, nor the battle to the strong." The slow and the weak and the fifty-year-olds can gain "the victor's palm and a joy untold."

At some of the splendid scout functions I attended in later years I wore my Gilwell beads with pride. The agony with which they were won was kept a dark secret!

Not only the "armour bearer" but the knight he served were both to be called to London and International Headquarters, the Commissioner to be the General's travelling representative and myself to serve in the International Public Relations Department where other things than armour were awaiting to be borne. Leaving the young people's work with no little regret, I found that one axiomatic truth at least had been engraved on my mind: the child is not only the father of the man, but the man must be the father of the child.

CHAPTER 8

A Green And Pleasant Land

Robert Browning's "Oh, to be in England / Now that April's there" was probably not in mind when I was instructed to attend a conference at International Headquarters in the Spring of 1964 for the purpose of reviewing the English-language teaching literature being used in Salvation Army Sunday schools. There was considerable criticism of the manuals being issued from London, certainly not of their literary style which was excellent, or of the background information which was extensive and accurately researched. The difficulty sprang from the fact that lessons graded to the children's academic and psychological levels were easily available in the United States and Canada, with attractively printed handbooks in colour for use by the children themselves. Large firms in North America were offering their materials to The Salvation Army at discount prices and were willing to arrange for them to carry a Salvation Army imprint and have editorial scrutiny prior to printing.

There were drawbacks. The language of the lessons lacked the Army's distinctive terminology. Illustrations featured a Roman collar where a Major's uniform would have been desirable. It was church steeple versus a marching band. And while Salvation Army terminology of an earlier generation was softening to meet contemporary understanding, there was a reluctance to lose certain characteristic references and to orientate a child to a church-related vocabulary that would be missing later on. The firms bidding for the Army's business employed highly competent religious educationalists and Christian psychologists, and though our participation would be relatively small compared with their massive output, there was a strong attempt to secure the Army's custom.

My counterparts in the United States and I were of one view. If International Headquarters could produce the kind of graded lessons now proving so successful in the teaching of children and in the expansion of Sunday schools, this would be the best of all developments. There was a good deal to be said for all English-speaking Company Meetings—the Army's term for Sunday schools—teaching the same lesson and using the same materials on the same Sunday. Only International Headquarters could bring this about.

The conference proved to be fascinating and broadening. For the first time, I think, I began to comprehend the limitations under which International Headquarters functioned. There was a financial problem. It would be costly, formidably so, to enter the field of multi-coloured, multi-level materials for both teachers and children. As it was, Canada and the United States were the most substantial purchasers of the manual currently being produced. Without their participation the cost to the remainder of the English language territories would be prohibitive.

Another problem was that of translation. International Headquarters-prepared materials could not easily be translated into the many languages used in the Army world. The non-English regions had been fending for themselves for many years, either adapting the London materials (exceedingly difficult because of the erudite language used and the scholarly explanations provided), often beyond the skill of available translators, or using local language materials which, while not wholly suitable (again because of the lack of Salvation Army essence, terminology, illustration and aim) was the best answer possible.

Commissioner Albert E. Mingay was the appointed chairman and under his presidency the group worked hard and cooperatively to find an answer. The answer was a compromise. The teacher's manual, the one and only production, would henceforth recognize at least two age-levels, and the conference ended in the hope that competent writers would be found in various parts of the English-speaking world to assist the editor. The new scheme was short-lived. North America subsequently went its own way, and International Headquarters later introduced a teaching cycle, "Living and Believing," which found acceptance far beyond the Salvation Army's borders.

The conference over, I went to pay a visit to my mother and sister in Southbourne. I was about to return to Canada when a telephone call made it plain that on no account was I to leave England without first seeing the General. The time of interview would be communicated to me. I notified my wife and headquarters in Toronto of my delayed return, but could not enjoy the extended stay because of the one question that, like an unbanishable banshee, kept haunting me. Why did General Coutts want to see me? Had our attention to the religious education dilemma been found wanting? Were our findings so unacceptable that we would, as a group, be asked to reconvene?

Eventually the call came, and I took a train to London, little thinking that in a matter of weeks I would again be in Southbourne accompanied by my wife and our younger daughter. As the train ran past the Southhampton docks it did not occur to me that aboard the *S.S. Queen Mary* we would soon be berthing at one of those selfsame quays. In London, I discovered that I was the only one of the conference delegates to be summoned to the General's office, and my bewilderment multiplied. I had no presentiment of what was to come. I did think, when I was received, that the General was uncommonly forthcoming to an overseas, and junior, officer when he spoke frankly of the serious need for more modern social service buildings in the United Kingdom and sketched requirements so immense that his concern was visible. The General was well-known for his quintessential courtesy, but I was taken aback when he left his chair, came around the desk, and, with a typewritten brief in his hand, sat beside me.

"Could we, please, go through this together?" he began. All who have known General Coutts will recall the special inflection with which he could invest the word, "please." It made the one addressed feel larger than life ("imagine the General asking me ...!"). His plan was an ambitious but timely one, twenty-four new or modernized institutions, the whole project to be related to the centenary of the Army's beginnings in 1865. The financial objective was a staggering three-million pounds sterling. The General then got down to details. Would this work? How should one go about that aspect? Primed by such questioning the stream of suggestion began to flow. When the subject had been examined fully and my diagnoses respectfully heard, there remained the matter of prognosis.

"Ah," said the General, "a very good point. We want you to come to International Headquarters and bring the plan, with the alterations you have mentioned, to fruition." He named a date, and I remember mentally calculating the number of days before the consultant, which I had thought myself to be, would become the responsible director. Certainty and uncertainty churned almost nauseously inside me—certainty that the biggest challenge of my career so far would shortly be mine, and uncertainty that I could justify the General's expectations.

I would, of course, be returning to my birthplace, but in the United Kingdom there were relatively few people I knew. In Canada I had boasted that I knew every officer and his or her family relationships. In England I would be "an innocent abroad." An immediate consideration outlawed such speculations. How would the news be received by the family? What arrangements could possibly be made for our elder daughter, now a nurse in training and without income? Our younger daughter would accompany us, but what of her schooling? I walked the streets of London that balmy Spring night until the early hours of the morning before returning to the hotel where I was staying. As soon as my flight could be arranged I would telephone Canada with my arrival time and word of our transfer. To my infinite relief my wife seemed less shocked by the news than I had been. Her commitment to officership had, from the outset, embraced every eventuality. Ifs and buts were not in her vocabulary of dedication.

My territorial commander's reaction was different. On the first Sunday back in Toronto, my wife and I were invited to spend the afternoon with his wife and himself. On arrival it was suggested that the Commissioner would like to have some private conversation with me in his upstairs study. He wanted to know the details of the work I was to do; nothing about the appointment had been communicated to him. Was it not all a mistake? Could the General's plan possibly succeed? Had I said I would go? Did I realize what awaited the family? The questions came thick and fast, and I was at a loss to know how far my answers should go. It seemed unthinkable to the Commissioner that the long arm of the administration could reach across the Atlantic and snatch his "armour bearer" away. Nor was it a congenial thought that the "armour bearer" could possibly know more about the arrangements than the Commissioner! I was afterwards to learn that a last-ditch protest had been fired off to London, but that later a brief cabled answer, "Decision taken. Brown proceeds to London," defused every possibility of postponement or cancellation. Within weeks the Commissioner received his own farewell orders. The Booths would actually be in London before the Browns.

I stood in the early autumn sunshine at Trafalgar Square. To my left was Admiralty Arch and beyond it the Mall with Buckingham Palace distantly in view. Across the Square stood Canada House. Streams of traffic uncoiled themselves past the Nelson monument, thinning and thickening like a cobra lithely thrusting itself forward. Each change of traffic lights unleashed new waves of pedestrians, each of whom appeared to have a destination, and, in their anxiety to reach it quickly, nudged their way along the crowded pavement. I seemed to be the only individual standing still, the only one uncertain about a goal. Nervousness was turning me into another of the Square's monuments without any of the lion-like features of those I was facing. In my briefcase I had some hundreds of letters of introduction written by friends of the Army in Canada and the United States to their British counterparts or friends in business, or to their dealers or suppliers. I had armed myself with every possible encouragement before leaving Canada. The letter I held in my hand, the first to be presented, was addressed to the occupant of an office whose windows looked out on the maëlstrom around me. It was a now-or-never moment and, stifling my reserve, I made for the interview.

The reception was cordial beyond my extremest expectations and profitable beyond my most ardent hopes. The vice-president of the international company to whom I had presented myself, Mr. George Baillie, of the Canadian Pacific System, had been a member of Salvation Army advisory boards in other parts of the world. He would willingly lead me to the "right" person to be chairman of a London advisory board, the formation of which was my first objective. He promised to telephone me when a contact had been made. In leaving, I almost floated across the deep pile carpet. The apprehension of an hour before was replaced by the exhilaration of a work now launched, a work that might after all be successful.

I turned at the office door to say a parting, "Thank you!" and my new collaborator replied saying, "I'm glad to do it for the Army." Then pointing upwards, he added with simple sincerity, "Surely this is the

Father's business." On his part it was a spiritual commitment. For me, it was the augury I needed.

The next time we met, Mr. Baillie introduced me to a big, ruddy-faced man whose words, gestures and, indeed, his whole body, twinkled with good nature. Sir Nutcombe Hume, KCB., MC., then chairman of the Charterhouse Group, had forgotten more about high finance than I could ever know. He knew, and this was important to us, more financiers than most of his colleagues in "the City." Mr. Baillie was certain that Sir Nutcombe was "our man," but "our man" was not to be easily persuaded. He listened carefully to Mr. Baillie's, and my own, pleas but made no commitment. We parted on the understanding that if I provided him with all the printed material I could about the Army he would read it, and, in three months, give his decision as to whether he would become chairman of the London advisory board and secure its membership.

Though I had more work than hours in which to do it, particularly with laying the groundwork for the imminent capital appeal and with those preparations for the forthcoming International Congress for which my department was responsible, it seemed as if Sir Nutcombe's reply would never come. Perhaps I had provided too much reading matter, everything from the volumes of Army history to the latest statements of account, more than most eager researchers could plough through without some kind of sabbatical. But one day the call came, and the caller as well. Sir Nutcombe's chauffeur deposited him and the load of books at the front door of our headquarters. His cryptic observation was that, having read all the material, he had no option but to meet our request. At the time I did not know that incognito he had visited several institutions and had sat, unrecognized, in Salvation Army meetings to get, as he said, "the feel of things."

Sir Nutcombe's decision set in motion a remarkable process of enlistment in the Army's cause. It also initiated for me an enriching personal friendship. To his intimates this burly financier with the quicksilver mind was known as "Nut." As such he always introduced himself on the telephone, and though he asked me many times so to address him, I simply could not bring myself to do it. I rejoiced in his friendship, but respect curbed any use of his nickname. Before long he had surrounded himself with leading personalities representative of most of the professions who could aid the Army in its immediate need for a "face lift" of the social services and in its longer-term development. From the corridors of Whitehall came Sir Maurice Dean, KCB., KCMG., whose last appointment had been Permanent Secretary of State for Energy, a quality he eminently reflected in his own personality. After Sir Nutcombe's death he became chairman of the board. With the Army's medical work in mind, Sir Arthur Porritt, serjeant-surgeon to Her Majesty The Queen, and eventually Governor-General of New Zealand, joined the group. A younger man, David Nicolson, later knighted, who successfully master-minded the amalgamation of British Overseas Airways Corportion and British European Airways to form British Airways, had been born in the same Canadian town as my wife, Amherst, Nova Scotia. This made an interesting link with an organization and management expert whose subordinates aided the Army in streamlining methods in several headquarters departments. From the insurance world came Sir John Benn, Bt., whose forbears had instituted homes for working boys in London, housing the news vendors and barrow-boys of an earlier generation. Sir Hilary Scott, a one-time president of the Law Society, brought expert counsel in legal matters. These, and a number of other equally influential and dedicated men and women, responded to Sir Nutcombe's call.

The first meeting of the advisory board was memorable. I had briefed Sir Nutcombe that every Salvation Army event, including its business meetings, began with prayer. The agenda, approved by him, therefore had as its first item, "Prayer." Three leading Salvation Army officers were among the group and, as the arrivals were being seated, one sent me a telegraphic note, "Prayer. Who?" I scribbled back, "I have no idea. The chairman will decide." But it was to my own amazement, as well as to the surprise of the nervous commissioner who thought he should perhaps be prepared, that when the meeting was called to order the chairman said, "We are now associating ourselves with The Salvation Army. All of their meetings, I understand, are prefaced by prayer, and we must follow their example. Will you, Lord Balerno," he said, addressing one of the new members, "offer prayer." The petition was an eloquent expression from someone used to communing with the Divine. "O, Jesus," he began, "help us as we put our shoulder to the wheel of hope and help, and as we seek to assist The Salvation Army in moving its ministry of mercy nearer to those who need spiritual and material aid." And so on. The Salvationists present were delighted. Business and prayer were not, after all, polarized. The man in the pin-stripe suit might have budgets on his mind, but he had the spirit of intercession in his heart. Perhaps the petition should not have elicited such surprise seeing the petitioner was a descendant of the compiler of a well-known Bible commentary.

That first meeting held another surprise for the Salvationists present. When the last published statements of account were under discussion, the chairman looked to a responsible officer and questioned an item on page fourteen of the printed accounts. The officer immediately began to leaf through his papers to find the entry to which reference was being made, only to hear Sir Nutcombe say, "Don't bother turning it up. It says ..." He then proceeded to give a flawless recitation of the entire page from memory. Not only had he read our accounts but had memorized them, a demonstration of his own commitment to our cause, and a slightly embarrassing reproach to ours.

William Booth moved about the world involving men and women of influence, of authority and wealth, of public spirit and community compassion, in the work to which he had given himself. A hand on the shoulder, a challenging word, a strong letter, all were used by him to generate understanding and sympathy, to create positive help for the great Cause. I was convinced that the advisory board concept was a recapturing of the genius of the movement's founder, that it was an organized attempt to link on to the practical service of the Army that expertise which is waiting to serve, that influence which needs only a worthy purpose to set it to work. If earlier years had a Rider Haggard, a W. T. Stead, a George Bernard Shaw, the Crossleys of Manchester, the Billups and the Corys of Cardiff, Bishop Taylor of California, William Gooderham of Toronto, Mary Fowler of Liverpool, Samuel Morley of Nottingham and Cecil Rhodes of Africa, to list only a few, there is today no less significant a succession in the membership of Salvation Army advisory boards in several lands and many cities.

Inaugurating boards throughout the United Kingdom I pointed out that Salvation Army officers are not primarily businessmen or masters of either logic or logistics. They are, first and foremost, people who are dedicated to that spiritual and practical ministry desired by our Lord Himself: "Inasmuch as ye have done it unto one of the least of these My brethren, ye have done it unto Me." This means that for Salvation Army officers, time-and-motion studies, the niceties of law, the intricacies of property acquisition and management, the multiplied complexities of welfare administration and the philosophic content of certain of the social sciences must, by pressure of the paramount work to which they are called, follow secondarily. But in all of these fields the advisory board member can competently act. He can often cause the Army's extended hand of help to reach farther and to function faster.

The standards of membership in an advisory board are high. There must be a respect for Christian ethics. Members are drawn from various communions and denominations, usually forming shining examples of a working ecumenism. There must be personal integrity and an absence of vested interests, and the individual must be highly respected in the community. He will also possess expertise in some field that will be useful to the Army. The Army is not so much interested in the use of a man's or woman's name as it is in his flesh-and-blood support. I say, "woman's," because it is important that boards should have the benefit of those intuitive and compassionate qualities that are part of the female member. There should be that perception in all the members which, while noting the necessities of the community, also acknowledges the national, and indeed the international, nature of the Army. The effective board member will always sense those basic religious impulses that stimulate and nourish the Army's ministry in service. Advisory boards, understanding the nuances that make each community distinctive, can strengthen the links between the Army and the people at large. They can forge priceless understanding between the movement and government authorities at all levels. How well was spectacularly demonstrated by Sir Nutcombe Hume and his associates.

The inception of advisory boards in the United Kingdom happened with lightning speed and surprising success. In this I had the experienced help of a Canadian officer, Lieut-Colonel John Steele. His Scottish burr and New World capability in public relations worked wonders. Perhaps all that was needed was the sowing of the idea; certainly the soil was receptive. The seed itself germinated swiftly and strongly. The first board to be completely formed and inaugurated in the United Kingdom was in the warmhearted industrial area of Rochdale, Lancs., whose famous daughter, the internationally respected singer and entertainer, Gracie Fields, quickly sent her good wishes from her retirement home in Capri.

Working against a fatal illness unsuspected by many of his associates, Lord Fraser of Allander, DL., LL.D., brought into being the Glasgow Advisory Board (later renamed the Strathclyde Advisory Board) which for calibre of membership could uphold Scotland's reputation against all others. Among the many interests of the House of Fraser was the famous London departmental store, Harrods, and Sir John Henderson, closely associated with its management, was recruited by Lord Fraser to be the first chairman. Sir John liked nothing better than to testify to his Christian experience in a Salvation Army meeting.

In Birmingham, where a massive men's hostel was among the centenary projects, Francis B. Willmott, a prominent industrialist, and the members of his board opened the doors for my appeal to the corporation for substantial financial help. It meant twenty-one visits for discussion with local authority officials, but the elation of a particular return journey is remembered. In my briefcase I had the firm promise of a grant of more than a quarter-million pounds, something certain of my superiors found difficult to believe. The building was graciously and officially opened by Her Royal Highness the Princess Alexandra whose remarks I have quoted a sufficient number of times in various parts of the world to have them memorized. "The Salvation Army," she said, "does not erect an edifice merely for the sake of its architectural beauty. Its buildings are dedicated to the glory of God so that that glory might find its way into human lives. Salvation Army buildings are functional buildings, and that function is the instilling of spiritual hope and the infilling of human courage."

Sitting at lunch with a group of leading Nottingham citizens, I proposed that the house in which William Booth was born should be the centre of a living memorial, an imaginative social services complex. Charles M. Boak, elected as chairman of the advisory board, saw the dream realized. The Founder's birthplace was completely renovated in the best Georgian style and, around it, was built a charming home for senior citizens and a goodwill centre to meet emergency needs and situations. Tourists coming from every part of the earth would not only visit a museum but an uptodate manifestation of service, something of which Nottingham's famous son would have enthusiastically approved. Few who were present for the opening of the complex at Nottintone Place will forget the powerful words of Commissioner Catherine Bramwell-Booth as she stood in front of the slightly larger than life statue of William Booth, in the centre of the courtyard, and reminded her hearers of her grandfather's dedication. Among the most impressed was Sir Keith Joseph, then the minister responsible for social services, who invariably recalled the occasion whenever he met a Salvationist or addressed a Salvation Army gathering.

During these years the Duke and Duchess of Rutland, who preside over what is the smallest county in England, became hard-working friends of the Army through the good offices of an untiring advisory board member, Mrs. Edna Crawley. Among many events, they sponsored a gala Salvation Army Night at the University of Nottingham which began with a torchlight procession of the musical sections from the gates to the great hall. It was a glorious summer night and, from the tessellated balcony, Their Graces were as eager as any to catch a first sight of the march. The county town in Rutlandshire is Oakham where members of the council presented me with a large donation for the campaign and, afterwards, with tremendous pride, showed me the Norman banquet hall in the local castle which has a unique collection of horseshoes presented by the kings, queens and nobles who had passed through the town.

As we went up and down Great Britain, bringing new boards into existence, nurturing the nascent groups, stimulating action, there were satisfactions and surprises. I recall going to Plymouth on one occasion, the Plymouth made famous by Sir Francis Drake, and by the Pilgrims for whom it was the last port touched on their historic voyage to the New World. An attractive city had risen phoenix-like from the ashes left by the merciless bombing during the Second World War. I enquired which of the eminent, most respected citizens might be most likely to help me set up an advisory board. I was directed to a solicitor by the name of Mr. David Foot Nash whose answer, when I asked if he would bring such a board into being, fascinated me. He told me that years before the Founder of The Salvation Army, William Booth, had called on his grandfather who was a prominent builder.

"I want," said William Booth, "a building that will seat two thousand people every night, and I want it at once."

"That is quite possible," said the builder.

"The only problem is," said Booth, "that I haven't got a penny towards paying for it."

"Never mind that," said the contractor, "I'll put up the building, and whenever you have a hundred pounds that you don't know what to do with, send it to me on account."

"And," said Mr. David Foot Nash to me, "the building was erected, and the crowds filled it, but there is no record of how the account was settled." Happily, he went on to say that if his grandfather had thought it an honour to help William Booth then he, too, in his generation, would do all he possibly could. That he did so I can vouch for from my own experience of his generosity and organizing ability.

I was seated next to the chairman of a new advisory board who had accepted my invitation to attend a musical festival presented by the local band and songster brigade, both highly competent aggregations. That our new friend was impressed was evident. He applauded the items long and loud. When a collection was taken, I could not help noticing that he had put a one-hundred pound note on the plate. At the end of the festival I delicately enquired if this had been his intention.

"It was no mistake," he said. "My factory is nearby, but until tonight I didn't know such indescribable gladness existed just around the corner. Not until tonight have I ever been asked to contribute to the Army's work, so you see I have a lot of catching up to do."

The International Congress celebrations in the midsummer of 1965 provided several opportunities for members of newly-formed advisory boards to see The Salvation Army in its strength. With large numbers of delegates from every corner of the earth, board members began to sense the magnitude and influence of the movement to which they had allied themselves. Quite soon after the congress a collection of the addresses given by Her Majesty The Queen, the Archbishop of Canterbury, the Rt. Rev. Dr. Michael Ramsay; the Home Secretary, the Rt. Hon. Sir Frank Soskice, QC., MP.; and General Frederick Coutts, the congress leader, was published under the title, *Into the Second Century.* I felt it would interest advisory board members to have a copy, and a distribution was made. Shortly afterwards, Sir Nutcombe Hume called me to his office. The little book lay on his desk, opened at page fifty-two.

Pointing to a paragraph describing the Royal Albert Hall gathering on Friday evening, July 2, he asked, "What does this reference mean? It says here, 'Within minutes of the appeal there were queues in the three aisles leading to the Mercy-Seat of those who quietly waited an opportunity to renew their vows in public. It was a stirring sight ... Whole families, officer couples, innumerable overseas delegates, veterans, scouts, guides and songsters from the centenary chorus made their personal offering.' "

I explained the purpose of the Mercy-Seat as a place where confession of wrong, or of need, or of love for Christ, could be made; a place where the consecration of one's being to God could be made publicly. I quoted the words of the Psalmist: "I will pay my vows unto the Lord now in the presence of all His people," and told him what the Mercy-Seat had meant in my own life and experience. There was a long silence.

"The next time I come to a Salvation Army gathering could I kneel at the Mercy-Seat?" he asked.

I explained that there was "the Mercy-Seat of the heart," an ever-present place of meeting with the Christ, and that one need not wait for a public gathering. He thanked me, and, at his request, I prayed with him and for him.

"It may not be long before they find this old bag of bones in a heap on the pavement," he said. The "twinkle" was there, but so also was a hint of seriousness. His forecast was accurate. Not far from his home, and very near to the Royal Albert Hall where the congress Mercy-Seat had aroused his curiosity, he was found dead. To him, and scores like him to whom I found myself bound in gratitude, The Salvation Army owes an unpayable debt.

CHAPTER 9

"For God's Sake, Care!"

In 1964 when the development of the national appeal for 3-million pounds was testing the creative capabilities of my colleagues and myself to the limit, Richard Usborne had written a letter to editors in which he said, "Definition of a slogan: a form of words for which memorability has been *bought* (the italics are his)." To find the form of words which, as a fund-raising theme, would strike the right note and, by its originality, imprint itself on the national mind, was an unusually difficult exercise. I must have written out hundreds of attempts, shaping them into innumerable permutations, and then, with an unsatisfied stroke of the pen, sent them into oblivion.

The power of a slogan to alter history or to make it is well known. Votes can be won or lost, as every politician realizes, by the aptness or otherwise of an election cry. We desperately wanted an appeal that would "buy memorability," one that, once heard or read, would bore into the mind and defy expulsion. How much did Franklin D. Roosevelt owe to his early presidential slogan: "A chicken in every pot, two cars in every garage"? Extravagant perhaps, but arresting. The slogan we wanted, however, could not cater to self-interest. The chicken had to be provided for the other man's pot. Sympathy had to be aroused for those who would never own one car, let alone two.

The kind of creative assistance we needed was discovered in a small but imaginative agency, and into our discussions came an exceedingly able account executive, David Kingsley. To him and Major (now Commissioner) Will Pratt belong the credit for the seed-ideas which were ploughed into the appeal slogan. The first proposal both attracted and repelled me. Something was right about it, and something was wrong with it. The words laid on my desk were, "For God's sake give a pound."

"For God's sake," was daringly right. Everything we were doing was for "His" sake. Our use of the phrase could possibly lift it from the level of common expletive to a recognition of its highest and best meaning. People *should* help their more unfortunate brother and sister "for God's sake." But, "for God's sake" should they give a pound? Was the phrase not being shifted from the altruistic to the mercenary by linking it with a specific amount of money? I knew the reasoning behind the suggestion. The British public's contributions to the Army had not increased commensurately with its increased standard of income and life-style, and the slogan was a blunt indication of what, it was thought, should be an "average" donation. Too blunt, I felt. More thought, more scribblings and more discussion led to the final determination when I changed the theme to, "For God's sake, care!" Any mention of money, and specific amounts of it, I decided, should stand away from the main slogan. In order to forestall criticism from any who might think our use of the phrase, "For God's sake," scandalous, I insisted that the word, *"God's,"* be underlined. This emphasizing, it was thought, would indicate our respectful, and even reverential, use of the term. The word, "care," was always to be followed by an exclamation mark. More important than contributions would be the stirring of a wider spirit of caring on the part of the general public.

Suddenly, the entire United Kingdom was aware of our appeal as the slogan shot its way into every aspect of the mass media. The visual impact of the slogan, with its jagged, uneven lettering, was magnified, creating a "style" that others quickly copied, one church body in another part of the world plagiarizing not only the artform but the slogan itself, without modification or alteration. A left-handed compliment.

The slogan aroused contrasting reactions. I was challenged by certain well-intentioned Salvationists as to its suitability, but discovered that asking the challenger to create something better was a quick way of ending complaint or criticism. Most Salvationists and the general public stood with Raymond Baxter. "Think for a moment," he wrote, "of the wealth of creative effort which lies behind every successful slogan, catch-phrase and gimmick of contemporary commerce. Think, if you will, that it could have been put to more beneficial purpose. Then think of The Salvation Army's stark and brilliant appeal, 'For God's sake, care!'—and thank God for whoever thought of it." The slogan also impressed the noted writer, Brigid Brophy. "The Salvation Army," she wrote, "is one of the few organizations that actually gets a move on and does something to help. Indeed, it does a vast deal. That it chooses to do so 'For God's sake' humanists should swallow with Shavian panache, continuing to support the world's only totally non-aggressive army with fervour and gratitude for man's sake." Editorially, the *Daily Mirror* declared: "The spirit of General Booth lives on. Using the techniques of the modern world The Salvation Army now demands: 'For God's sake, care!' It deserves every penny it gets."

Thinking retrospectively, I am of the opinion that the centenary appeal would have been even more successful and would have imposed less strain on the organizers if there had not been the rush to capitalize on the goodwill which the centenary celebrations and the international congress aroused. Public appreciation of the Army was high. But no public appeal for funds can successfully mature without two highly-organized and closely-related elements, and these in some measure we lacked. There must be effective publicity so that the public is aware of the appeal, and there must also be an enthusiastic, informed field force to harvest the public's generosity.

To spearhead the publicity a brochure, *Tragedies Of Affluence,* was put together in the hope that it would be, in intention at least, a worthy successor to William Booth's *Darkest England And The Way Out.* It was designed to make the average citizen, and those who had responsibility for the national good, conscious of the social problems that existed, what was being done about them, and what more needed to be done. Getting the factual material required for such a survey, if the document were to be taken seriously, was difficult. The compilers wrote to some twenty-one welfare agencies and societies asking for specific information. The agencies were unaware of who had requested the information and for what purpose it was required. An astonishing number, sixteen, replied that the enquirers would be better helped if they wrote to The Salvation Army in view of that organization's extensive welfare work and the fact that its thousands of officers were deployed in almost all the towns and cities of the United Kingdom! Their response reinforced my own, long-held belief that the Army is not only competent to comment authoritatively on many aspects of social service, but should, indeed, be doing so. This was confirmed many times in successive years when in conversation with ministers of the crown or members of parliament. "You are much nearer the human situation than my best advisors," one minister said to me. "The modesty which restrains you should be balanced against the fact that what you say could effectively help to shape legislation. You owe it to us."

Tragedies Of Affluence created something of a sensation. Copies were to be seen on all the newsstands. On the day that a press conference learned of the social needs of the country as seen through the eyes of The Salvation Army, a copy of the brochure lay on the desk of every member of parliament, the editors of leading newspapers and other periodicals and all the notable shapers of public opinion that research could list. The brochure, its attractive printing thwarting any thought of early discard, drew the attention of its readers to the vast problems with which the Army and others were wrestling. It revealed the numbers and needs of homeless men and women, the shocking increases in unmarried motherhood, the plight of half-a-million children in fatherless families, and the needs of six hundred thousand housebound and needy aged.

Looking back, one is reminded that change is really the only constant factor in the structure of society. In 1965 more accommodation for unmarried mothers was needed, but within five years there was an amazing decline in this type of work. In so short a period the stigma which formerly had attached to the unmarried mother had disappeared. There were as many illegitimate births, indeed more, but young unmarried mothers no longer sought asylum in some distant hideaway, nor did parents who, a few years before, would have been terribly embarrassed by the stares and stories of neighbours, refuse to have their daughter and grandchild in the home. The new requirement was for more accommodation for the single parent and her child. Fortunately, those unmarried mothers' homes that benefited from the capital appeal were easily transformed into suitable accommodation for the single parent who would leave her infant in care during the working day and return to assume her rôle of mother in the evening and through the night. Still further adjustments have been required. Today's single parent may be male as well as female. Changing norms produce new needs.

Flowing out of *Tragedies Of Affluence* came innumerable press, radio and television interviews, panel discussions and feature articles. The publicity gathered a momentum which almost overwhelmed us. "The public's awareness of The Salvation Army," said one journalist, "has been improved. Few before the campaign realized the amazing extent of the Army's social service work. Doors of hope have been opened to many distressed people who had never before realized that The Salvation Army could help them with their problem." Newspapers and magazine publishers gave free advertising space. Disc jockeys and recording stars helped with radio and telephone campaigns. Salvation Army bands and singers were introduced into commercials. The now-famous slogan materialized on billboards throughout the country, sometimes placed next to other advertisements in such a way as to provide great humour, media comments about which multiplied the effect. People in underground trains sat staring at the slogan and the telling photographs which illustrated it. "By the time you've finished your journey, The Salvation Army will have opened its arms to another child. We're father, mother, aunt, uncle, brother, sister and two cousins to thousands of deprived children. Who cares?", the advertisement asked.

Seventeen of the world's best-known photographers volunteered their talents to the Army absolutely free. John Street, who visited the Army's home for children in Liverpool called "Strawberry Fields" (immortalized for many in the Beatles' song of that name), and who photographed a child mercifully brought from a cruel situation, wrote: "It was pretty much a job like any other. Depressing, but not too upsetting if you don't think hard. But I can't forget Raymond who is four and can run faster backwards than he can forwards. You go near him and he backs instantly against a wall. His father bashed him every time he caught a glimpse of him." Raymond's hounded look, caught by the camera in the hands of a sensitive artist, haunted thousands of people. A later photograph showing an entirely changed Raymond provided a happy ending to a sad story, but fell far behind the first photograph in impact.

For the photographers themselves the experience was catalytic. The only instruction given them was that they should go where an Army officer goes, see what he sees of deprivation, and try to capture it on film. Peter Atherton, a master among fashion and still-life photographers, ventured into what was for him an unreal and unrealized world. "I spent three days in Bath and Bristol taking photographs for the Army. I sat up all night, absolutely unable to sleep. I had gone into a room crawling with what couldn't be flies—they were like flies, but five times bigger. No lavatory—just buckets. People had to sleep here." The photographs were exhibited in London and other major cities and drew scores of thousands of viewers. It is doubtful if a more electrifying visual commentary on the social scene had ever been brought together in such a form before. Later, Constable & Company Ltd., published a collection of the photographs, beautifully printed by The Curwin Press Ltd., under the title, "For God's sake, care!" In a foreword, General Coutts said, "What a solitary artist like Hogarth did for the eighteenth century, this group of artists has done for the second half of the twentieth. Preferring directness of vision to any beauty of line, they have demonstrated the presence of continued poverty in the midst of comparative plenty. For this rude reminder we owe them our thanks."

In undertaking what was for the Army in Britain its largest ever capital appeal there had to be positive attitudes. One of the chief tasks of the organizers was to stimulate optimism, to encourage the workers to regard the campaign as an adventure, a battle, an initiative that had noble substance. Salvationists themselves were more apologetic about making the Army's needs known than were those who viewed our services from the outside. Some officers had come reluctantly to the conclusion that physical improvement of the social service buildings was a most remote possibility. Conservative estimates at the time placed the amount required for replacing or refurbishing all the institutions at something near thirty-five million pounds. Undeniably, there were evidences of dilapidation and, in one or two instances, near-dereliction, but many social welfare services now taken for granted in Great Britain had been pioneered by the Army, and the price of that pioneering had eventually to be paid. The disused warehouses, the converted mills, the adapted factories, all of which served helpfully in early days when bitter need made improvisation acceptable, were now in disrepair, if not in decrepitude. The standards for both buildings and services demanded by the authorities had risen, and no-one could quarrel with that. An increasing number of Salvation Army officers had added certification to compassion, and they also knew what modern standards should be.

Prior to the appeal launching I visited every institution. I saw wash basins hewn from stone so old that the washing of a million hands had worn them until they would hardly hold water, and the water, running about the wooden floors, had produced a rot so extensive that men got their boots caught between the boards.

But in all this I saw no reason for negativism. The wear and tear were proud service medals. The buildings had, in their latter years, served the finest purposes of their existence. The institutions were old because no-one had contributed new ones. I was far more impressed with the dedication I saw demonstrated within the tired buildings than with the deteriorations that admittedly were eye-sores. Officers working in these depressing surroundings were, without knowing it, writing glowing entries on the pages of sacrificial service. I remember the Major who had to carry his tall, gangling teenage son with the mind of an infant, a lad who could speak only the garbled language of the seriously afflicted, going out from his own sorrow to wash the latest, stinking arrival at the hostel and help him with his meal. The Army, I found, still had its Angel Adjutants, one of whom, Martha Field, was as familiar among the roughs of Nottingham's back alleyways as she was in the corridors of the magnificent city hall. I was convinced that if the dedication were preserved the decrepitude would go, and clean, bright, highly-functional buildings would eventually replace them. I served long enough to see it happen.

With the elaboration of the welfare state it was imperative that government authorities be made fully cognizant of the scope and effectiveness of the services which, as a voluntary society, the Army had contributed for so long without any demand whatever on the local or national treasury for capital aid. In this area, the newly-formed advisory boards moved with speed. Where large grants were being sought, either from the authorities or private foundations, doors were unlatched and distances between canvasser and contributor shrank unbelievably. Negotiations with local authorities were sometimes drawn-out affairs. Briefs had to be prepared and submitted. Councillors had to be thoroughly informed and, in some instances, won to the view that the voluntary society could perform more efficiently and cheaper than the authority-run facility. I, personally, encountered none who had to be convinced that the spiritual dimension of the Army was a detriment. In point of fact, no beneficiary of the Army's help was forced to attend meetings or have anything to do with its religious aspects unless he voluntarily wished to do so. A generous city council in one of the large conurbations put itself on record that whatever spiritual help the Army could give, and a client wished to take, could only be regarded as "a plus." The Founder's axiom that it is no use taking a man from the slum and putting him into a palace until you take the slum out of the man, or he will quickly turn the palace into a slum, was regarded as sound philosophy and sounder social service.

But strong publicity, even if outdistanced by performance, needed something else—a strong field force. No matter how alive a person became to the human needs about him, and to a movement that had dedicated itself to meeting them as far as it could, that awareness was hardly likely to convince that person to sit down, write out a cheque, put it in an envelope and stamp it, and then go with it to the nearest post-office or postbox. To bring the donor from vague sympathy to specific action someone had to knock on the door of the home, or call on the telephone. That the Army can mobilize its people so quickly is a continuing wonder. From Weymouth to Wick Salvationists flew in on the widespread wings of national publicity to link donor with need.

In 1965 the Charity Commissioners had already given some forty-five thousand bodies permission to appeal for funds, and one suspects that the number has grown considerably since then. Traditionally, the Britisher is a generous supporter of good causes even though, unlike many other countries, donations to charity are not deductible for tax relief. Contributors can, however, enter into a Deed of Covenant with the government for a specified number of years, and this entitles the charity to whom a donation is made also to receive the refund of tax, a procedure which materially increases the amount received by the charity. In the instance of death the deed would fall away and the estate would not be required to continue the obligation. Nor did I ever hear of the government taking legal action in case of default. In my opinion such cases would be few since, generally speaking, a Britisher's word is his bond.

To have realized the appeal's objective immediately would have been a happy situation. This was impossible seeing many contributors had pledged their gifts over a three to five year period. Notwithstanding, work on the social service projects had to proceed, not only because of the urgent need, but also as evidence of good faith with the donating public. This threw additional, and occasionally worrying, burdens on the Army's chancellor, Commissioner Frank Fairbank, who had to find bridging monies; this, fortunately, he managed to do.

A closing-off of the appeal finally had to be faced, and the thought occurred to me that if a fund-raising appeal required dramatic introduction, why should it not have a dramatic conclusion? So was born the "Centenary Climax" with its unique feature, the sale of "Salvation Bonds." The "bond" was designed and printed in different denominations by the famous printers of English banknotes. The "bond" was simply a receipt lifted to an intriguing level which read: "We, The Salvation Army, pledge ourselves to use this donation in its entirety in the fight to improve the lot of 400,000 children in want, 675,000 elderly neglected and 1,000,000 social misfits in Britain today. We thank you most sincerely for your donation of ..." It was signed by Frederick Coutts, International Leader of The Salvation Army.

Not everyone understood the idea. There were enquiries as to what rate of interest would be paid and the date on which the bonds would mature! Salvation Army officers who were the "bond salesmen" good-humouredly lifted two lines from Anna L. Waring's hymn: "In service which Thy love appoints / There are no bonds for me."

One of the hoped-for outcomes of an appeal for capital funds is a greatly increased number of regular donors towards maintenance requirements. This was abundantly achieved by the "For God's sake, care!" appeal, and the organizing team felt that such a long-term benefit was a crowning of their strenuous endeavours. Only fund-raisers know the bittersweet mixture of disappointment and elation, unexpected resistance and glad surprise that is implicit in the mounting and conducting of such an appeal. For them there is both the agony and the ecstasy.

The appeal years were marked by many memorable events, most important being the official opening of the new Booth House for homeless men in London's east end and within a stone's throw of where William Booth's consequential ministry began. It was my first association with a royal occasion and I was infinitely grateful to Mr. Frank Douglas, vice-chairman of the London advisory board, whose links with the Palace were such that we had an early, favourable word concerning Her Majesty The Queen's presence. Any event involving a royal personage is an exercise in precise and detailed planning. None could have been more helpful than the Rt. Hon. Sir Philip Moore. He was then the assistant private secretary to Her Majesty, and received me most cordially in his office at Buckingham Palace when I presented a brief of proposed arrangements. Later, we met at Booth House with the security officers. Every step to be taken was reconnoitered. Who would stand where was carefully noted, and the number of minutes to be devoted to each group was calculated for recommendation to Her Majesty. As we were parting in the parking lot I observed that Sir Philip was driving a Renault. Smilingly, I expressed surprise that a French-made car would have a place in the royal fleet. "We have three," he replied good-naturedly. "We want the Common Market to succeed!"

I was concerned that there would not be a big enough crowd of people outside the building to make the ribbon-cutting ceremony an impressive moment. To ensure that there would be, I asked for groups of Salvationists from all the nearby corps to attend. The request was unnecessary, and to a ludicrous degree. Returning to Booth House on the day of the opening some two hours before The Queen was due to arrive, I reached the parking area with immense difficulty. The wide street was blocked by dense crowds and the police were doing their best to bring organization out of confusion. I had had my own last-minute confusions. A telephone call from the Palace indicated that Her Majesty had learned that a certain woman was on the staff of Booth House. Some time before there had been a disastrous fire in the home in which she lived, and her daughter had been frightfully burned. The Queen had asked if the daughter, whom she had visited after the fire, could be with her mother when the tour of the new building was made. With time running out, I discovered that the daughter was at work. I contacted the head of her firm and passed on the royal request. The girl was put into a taxi and taken home where she changed her clothes. She was then brought to Booth House where the opening exercises were already in progress. When Her Majesty greeted the mother, the daughter was standing with her. For them, the Queen's interest and sympathy made the day unforgettable. For us, it was a demonstration of The Queen's willingness to go compassion's extra mile.

Booth House is located in the Borough of Tower Hamlets which is politically as different from its neighbour, the City of London, as the merchandising methods of Mile End and Cheapside. The top floor of the new Booth House had been allocated to the City of London as an aged men's residence to be known as the Rawson Home. Christopher Rawson, a personal friend, was at that time chairman of the city's social services committee. The Queen had agreed to unveil a commemorative plaque and declare the Rawson Home officially opened, as well as unveiling the large and beautiful plaque in the main entrance of Booth House. Protocol therefore demanded the presence of both the Worshipful the Mayor of Tower Hamlets and the Rt. Hon. the Rt. Worshipful the Lord Mayor of London. In the circumstances the Mayor of Tower Hamlets would take precedence. I was called to the office of the Remembrancer of the City of London who wished to know the details of the Lord Mayor's participation. He asked me to discover discreetly whether the Mayor of Tower Hamlets would be wearing robes. In my next visit to the Tower Hamlets city hall I brought up the matter of dress and heard one of the mayor's aides say, "Tell the Lord Mayor to do what he wants, and that you will do what you want. This is our show, not his." I called up all my reserves of tact and succeeded in securing a diplomatic answer to take back to the Remembrancer. A traditionally robed Mayor was present to greet Her Majesty as she stepped from her limousine, and a traditionally robed Lord Mayor was inside in the foyer awaiting her arrival.

Processing from the car to the main entrance I noted the unbounded respect and affection of the East Enders for their monarch. The air was alive with cheers and applause. As The Queen moved forward the loyalists were reaching out to touch her, murmuring in a vivid Cockney accent enriched by esteem, "Gawd luv yer, Ma'am! Gawd luv yer!"

The 1965 international congress to which allusion has already been made, indelibly emphasized for me, a Canadian serving for the first time outside of his own country, the internationality of the Army and the universality of Divine love. Inspiring gathering after inspiring gathering united Salvationists in a more passionate desire to bring the good News of the Gospel to the whole world. Any who debated the necessity for such a congress must have been effectively silenced by its spiritual success. More than fifty years had passed since London had witnessed such a multi-racial, multilingual convocation of Salvationists, and the enthusiasm of the delegates caught the imagination of both the general public and the media.

I was asked to conduct a take-off of an extremely popular radio programme, "In Town Tonight," during one of the congress gatherings, a missionary rally in the Royal Albert Hall. For the information and enjoyment of the congregation I interviewed delegates from various lands, including a black officer from Rhodesia who was, in his own right, an hereditary chief. He came on to the stage dressed in skins and feathers, brandishing weapons of war and leaping about while he uttered blood-curdling cries. I complimented him on his "well-ventilated festival uniform" which, to the delight of the crowd, he offered to exchange for mine. The difference in our sizes would have produced an unthinkable result. He answered my questions fluently about African life and, among other aspects, that of food. He said that his people did not eat fish, and this led me to ask, "Then what is your favourite dish?" He was momentarily quiet, and then said, most decisively, "A clay pot." I was nonplussed, and the merriment of the congregation can easily be imagined. I had been "hoist by my own petard."

Little did I think that thirteen years later, on that same stage, I would be presiding over meetings of the next international congress celebrating the centenary of the birth of The Salvation Army and its name. For my immediate colleagues and myself the joy of the 1965 congress was extended while production of a commemorative film was completed. A talented Indian woman officer, Ruby Manuel (now Mrs. Commissioner Mannam Samuel), was the "symbolic" delegate through whose eyes and background the congress was viewed. One has to be barren of emotion not to be deeply moved, even today, by the closing scenes of the gathering in Trafalgar Square as, with Army flags waving, the huge crowd from all corners of the earth united to sing William Booth's own song, "O Boundless Salvation."

There was a brief respite from the incessant pressures of the public relations department when a friend offered to sponsor a visit to the Holy Land. This benefactor's intention was to see that as many of the clergy as possible should "walk where Jesus walked." For her, clergy included Salvation Army officers. I found myself part of a group led by the Rev. James Currie, a much loved Scottish minister who had visited the Holy Land regularly for many years. It was said of him that in Israel he knew every pebble worth knowing. He had a most engaging personality and kept the spirits of his charges at a high level despite transportation problems or alterations in the schedule. From a small, well-worn black book he shortened many a bus journey with hilarious jokes told in a choice Scottish accent. When the bus stopped at a significant location, however, seriousness would take over and the atmosphere would become completely devotional. As an appropriate portion from the Bible was read the centuries receded, and a fuller meaning of the passage would emerge. Our leader's familiarity with the Holy Land led him to preface the tour with advice that all who visit Israel should carefully note. Some sites, he maintained, were "authentic," and should be so regarded. Others were "traditional," invested with a degree of authenticity by the passing centuries. Still others were "alleged to be" on the assumptions of historians, archaeologists and others. The "traditional" sites should be viewed with respect on the basis that, for example, had not a church been erected commemoratively at a certain place, all indications of the original location of the event might perhaps have been lost for ever.

Certain points visited in Jerusalem itself were so crudely commercialized that sensitive pilgrims, myself among them, were left with feelings of revulsion. For me, in Jerusalem, only the Garden of Gethsemane with its aged and gnarled olive trees, a "traditional" site which came into the possession of the Franciscan Fathers in 1681, evoked the mystery and sorrow of Christ's person and passion. Tiberias, on the other hand, made it easy for the mind to recapture the earthly presence of the Lord and to reconstruct His ministry. Through the years Jerusalem has modernized, but the Sea of Genessaret is still as Jesus saw it and sailed on it.

Our party "went down from Jerusalem to Jericho," winding lower through the sandy hills to 1296-feet below sea-level to bathe in the Dead Sea. I had a dramatic illustration of the healing powers of its saline waters. The vaccination given me in London had left a nasty scab with an angry-red swollen arm and a certain amount of discomfort which I had tried to forget. I stepped ashore after floating about for three-quarters of an hour. Gratified, I saw that the swelling had gone, the redness had disappeared, and so had the scab. This most minor miracle gave me an added understanding of how those who, at the word or touch of Jesus, experienced an instantaneous cure of the most dreadful or debilitating of illnesses, must have felt. Ascending to Jerusalem on the return journey we saw the Holy City silhouetted against a cerulean sky still warmed by a sun that had dropped beyond our sight. A few twinkling lights presaged the darkness to come. Walls, domes and minarets beckoned us as they had the pilgrims of the Psalmist's day. Small wonder that, as the breathtaking sight was first glimpsed, they sang, "Jerusalem is builded as a city that is compact together." I have not seen a painting or photograph since that comes close to catching the twilight glory of that ravishing vista.

We were unfortunate enough to be in Jerusalem immediately prior to the Six Days' War and could not help but sense the gathering tempest. Just before the conflict erupted we passed through the Mandelbaum Gate into Jordan. As the one Canadian in the group, my passport had been stamped by Israeli officials when entering their country. Jordanian authorities immediately confiscated the passport and held me incommunicado for some hours before allowing me, without a passport, to rejoin the party. Only when leaving was it returned, one page of it having been saturated with purple indelible ink. I asked the immigration officer what had happened, and he replied, "There is no such state as Israel, and we have obliterated the reference to it in your passport."

That night we saw Jordanian soldiers with their red and white chequered headgear crouching along the walls, guns at the ready. On the Israeli side there was loudly amplified music, dancing in the streets and searchlights criss-crossing the night skies while fireworks blazed in vari-coloured patterns. More than one in our party expressed the thought that perhaps we were on the wrong side of the wall. We were, however, generously treated, and through one of the Rev. Mr. Currie's innumerable "friendly contacts" we were taken to Amman, Jordan's capital city. Few cities in the world, I thought, could match this desert port for unnerving noise. The shouting in the bazaars, the untuneful wailing of the muezzins and blaring, deafening music loaded the hot night air with continuous din. The streets were thronged with pilgrims on their way to Mecca or returning from it.

A look at the beautiful royal palace did nothing to increase any desire for a longer stay, and I was relieved when, finally, we crowded on to a plane bound for Beirut, Lebanon. On arrival, I could hardly believe the contrasts; peace instead of war, quiet instead of uproar, refinement instead of primitive custom. French style and elegance marked the cuisine and service at our hotel. There was nothing to make us think that Lebanon's own holocaust was in the not-too-distant future. From

Beirut to London was an uneventful flight. The pilgrimage was over. We had "walked where Jesus walked," but in view of all we had seen and heard a disturbing question lingered: what would be His reactions were He to tread the same paths again?

As an appreciated afterglow I had the privilege, morning and evening, of addressing the Rev. Mr. Currie's large Sunday congregations in St. James Pollocks Church, Glasgow. A Salvationist songster was the vocal soloist and must surely have made a better impression on the members of the tour party who shared the day than I had when attempting, during the Israeli evenings, to teach them Salvation Army choruses to the accompaniment of handclapping which, I soon understood, was not a regular feature of worship in the Church of Scotland!

CHAPTER 10

"Service Above Self"

Unsure of myself and of the situation, I stood outside a door in an office block in the heart of London. On it were displayed the words: *No Admittance.* Inside, a group of influential men were discussing my suitability for membership in the Rotary Club of London. I wondered if the words on the door were an unhappy omen but, after knocking, a cheerful voice invited me to enter. That afternoon I began, through this international service movement, an association with a million public-spirited men around the world and an experience that served to strengthen the already strong bond between Rotary International and The Salvation Army.

The Rotary movement, with its succint motto, "Service Above Self," was begun by a Chicago lawyer, Paul Harris, in 1906 to encourage fellowship between men of goodwill and to foster the idea of service to others. Its growth has been phenomenal, and the movement has certain striking similarities to The Salvation Army. Both are non-political. Both are open to men of every race, colour and language. Both seek to help the needy by personal involvement. Both have known proscription in countries where altruism is thought to be incongruous and compassion unnecessary. The relationship is further enhanced by the fact that the wife of Paul Harris, a charming Scottish lady was, it is understood, a Salvationist when a girl in her homeland.

Membership in Rotary widened my world. Not in any geographical sense; the Army assuredly did that for me!, but by the countless opportunities it provided for meeting with community leaders engaged in professions and occupations spanning the whole gamut of human activity and achievement. These contacts helped me to move in understanding beyond the boundaries of Salvation Army involvement which ordinarily dominated my life. Conversely, every contact was an opportunity for explaining the Army and interpreting its mission. From my induction in 1964 onwards, I found the doors of Rotary clubs around the world open to hear what I had to say. I have no record of the number of clubs I addressed during my worldwide tours, but the *London Rotarian* paid me high tribute after one of our journeys: "During his recent visit to India and Pakistan, Past President Arnold Brown also visited several Rotary clubs and was invited to address them. One asks oneself how does he find the time? But he does, the finest ambassador of Rotary goodwill we have ever had." The writer unquestionably over-extended himself in praise, but embarrassment is eased by recollecting that always the address had to do with the Army, its spirit, its mission and its message.

My contacts with Rotarians and their clubs were pleasantly varied and often uniquely coloured by local custom. Late one evening in Trivandrum in the lovely state of Kerala at the south-west tip of the Indian subcontinent, I was given a ceremonial welcome that could hardly be surpassed. Some distance from the scene of the meeting I was met by the officers of the club, their ladies, a group of musicians and beautifully-costumed youngsters laden with baskets of rose petals. Greeted by the men, the ladies anointed my forehead and escorted me, the flute band preceding us, up the road now strewn with fragrant petals. Following the business of the club I was invited to speak. Afterwards, all retired to a dining hall where each was provided with a large banana leaf on which, one after another, various delicacies were served.

In Kandy, Sri Lanka, I was still answering questions, following my speech, until nearly midnight. When a visit to Seoul, Korea, was being developed, I was invited by the main club to be the luncheon speaker. On arrival in the city, I was told that the day of the event had been changed. I was now to speak on the Saturday afternoon, a strange time, I thought, for a club meeting. Having visited the notorious 38th Parallel and met some of the American troops at Panmunjong, I arrived at the So Jong Cultural Centre, an attractive auditorium, where I discovered not a club luncheon group, but some thousands of Rotarians and wives attending a district assembly. I had an expert translator, Major Peter Chang, and he and I tried to rise to the unexpected and remarkable occasion. A beautifully engraved plaque records the appreciation of Korean Rotarians, and I keep it among my treasures.

During the week before the Six Days' War in the Middle East I attended a Rotary meeting in Jerusalem. The Holy City was not without its forebodings, but at that luncheon Israelis and Arabs, Jews and Moslems and Christians met in perfect fellowship on the highest level of mutual trust, bound together by something that would remain even though the Holy City was soon to be torn by the unholiness of war.

A fraternal visit to the celebrated Rotary club of New York reinforced long-held links with the London club. I spoke from a rostrum described as "New York Rotary's greatest treasure." The ornate lectern is equipped with a bell taken from the British auxiliary warship, "Patrol No. 20," and presented by the London club in 1922. The wood on which the bell is mounted is oak timber from Admiral Nelson's famous flagship, "Victory." With Nelson's challenge, "England expects every man to do his duty," evoked in the mind by the historic piece of timber before me, I dutifully tried to maintain England's Rotary reputation.

Rotary clubs meet in all sorts of accommodations. My memory of the Sao Paulo, Brazil, club's locale is of an old auditorium filled with nearly six hundred members seated at long tables, an inordinately high stage accommodating the head table. Many meet in modern hotels; others in time-worn parish halls. Some enjoy the finest food and most elegant service. Other clubs must serve themselves. Still others take little or no food and put the cost of a good meal to good causes. Several times while crossing the Atlantic I attended meetings on board the *S.S. France* and the *QE 11*, meetings which did not count for attendance but which were always photographically recorded by courtesy of the purser.

When I crossed from Lahore, in Pakistan, to Amritsar, in India, there were border tensions. Some awkwardness in entering India was forecast. Deplaning, I was met at the airport not only by a strong delegation of Salvation Army officers and bedecked with garlands, but also by a large number of Rotarians headed by the club president. Generously, the Rotarians had arranged to entertain the Salvationists to refreshments in the airport lounge. While welcome speeches were being exchanged, the Rotary president arranged for our passports to be examined and our luggage to go through customs. Brief minutes later, our passports were returned, duly stamped, and the president indicated that our luggage had been cleared and was already in the car. I ventured to say that the reception in no way matched the fears of my advisors, to which the president replied that seeing he was the airport controller things had possibly moved more easily!

An after-dinner speaker, I learned, should dine wisely but not too well, and should speak well but not too wisely, a reminder that a certain amount of humour can make the more serious elements of an address palatable. "I make them laugh," the Army's founder is reputed to have said, "and while their mouths are open I ram the Gospel down their throats." But humour is not easy to convey when one is speaking through a translator. It was always a relief to be able to speak to a club in English. I sat beside H.R.H. Prince Fleming when he was president of the Copenhagen central club and told him I had brought a translator with me. "No need for translation," he said. "Everyone here will understand if you speak in English. If you speak in Canadian," he added smilingly, "it might be a bit more difficult." The same experience was repeated with the Brussels club, and it was evident from the response that the members had much more than a superficial knowledge of the English/Canadian language.

Invited to stand for election as vice-president of the London club I sought the agreement of the Chief of the Staff and the General. Permission was given and I was elected. I was fortunate to serve my apprenticeship under President Gordon Crawford, an executive of a multi-national firm, who had already been president of the Liverpool club and was quite at home in chairing proceedings. From vice-president to president was an almost automatic move, and on the first Wednesday in July, 1970, at the Café Royale, where the meetings were held, I took the chair.

The story behind this famous Picadilly restaurant fascinated me. It was founded by a Monsieur Nicole who had fled from France to escape the consequences of his debts. He began business in a modest way but, little by little, acquired the adjacent properties so that in larger surroundings he could cater to the French exiles and to the aristocracy who were devotees of *haute cuisine française*. The man who married his daughter was a rabid Bonapartist, an annoying disappointment to the old man. Yet despite the son-in-law's opposite political sympathies,

M. Nicole took him into the business. When the premises needed refurbishing the son-in-law was given the responsibility and, in M. Nicole's absence his initial "N" was used to adorn the walls, the cutlery and the napery. Maliciously, however, each "N" was surrounded by a laurel wreath and crown so that it matched the Napoleonic emblem. It was a fiercely angry proprieter who returned to his restaurant, and it was a castigated son-in-law who hurriedly left it.

I was anxious to do well in the new rôle. As a wearer of Salvation Army uniform I did not want to lower the club's estimation of the Army. Their respect had been demonstrated in several sensitive ways. For example, the club council had arranged that their Salvation Army president should have no responsibility whatever in respect of entertaining guest speakers to drinks, a striking break with tradition. The same thoughtful respect obtained at the annual dinner held at the Savoy Hotel when my wife and I were hosts. After a magnificent meal, toasts were proposed in brilliant terms by some of the club's natural orators. The evening's chairman then explained that while there would now be dancing, the president and his wife would be leaving. The dance band struck up, "Onward, Christian soldiers," and my wife and I, spared the necessity of "leading the dance," marched out of the ballroom to the accompaniment of the members' singing and clapping. There was another reason for my desire to excel. I was, as far as I could discover, the first president holding other than a British passport. True, I had been born in London, but by citizenship I was a Canadian. It was a splendid opportunity to demonstrate that "we colonials" had not done badly after all!

During my presidency, and whenever during my travels I addressed a Rotary meeting, I wore the collar and pendant of office. It made a colourful, impressive addition to my uniform. Arriving at a hotel in Cologne near that city's famous cathedral, and descending from the taxi, I was surprised to see the staff of the hotel lined up in a corridor of welcome, everyone from manager to porter standing at attention. I thought this was a particularly cordial gesture and made my way through the guard of honour feigning a nonchalance that hopefully would convey the impression that I was quite used to this sort of thing. At the entrance, however, the mistake was realized. I was not the oberbürgermeister of a neighbouring city who was expected at precisely the same moment. My presidential trappings had been mistaken for a mayoral chain of office!

In the world of Rotary, the Rotary Club of London has at least two claims to international fame, and these I would often refer to with considerable pride. Two outstanding members of the club, while walking over the Surrey hills one sunny morning in 1926, had directed their thoughts into four channels: club service, community service, vocational service and international service. This new idea was discussed far and wide and was presented to an international convention at Ostend in 1927. It was agreed to, and so became a part of the international constitution operating today wherever Rotary functions. The other cause for pride arose out of a visit to the Rotary Club of London in 1921 by the world-famous Scottish entertainer and Rotarian, Sir Harry Lauder. During his speech he asked, "Shall London ever have a thousand Rotarians?" To answer the question a committee was formed, but it was soon realized that it would be impossible to have a thousand members in one club, and that other clubs would need to be formed. At a conference of British Rotarians held at Scarborough in 1933 the idea of allowing a new club to be formed within the territory of an existing club was ventilated, and at an international convention in St. Louis, U.S.A., an enactment amending the constitution was passed making it possible. Due to a London Rotarian's grasp of the movement's true meaning the joy of Rotary fellowship has come to many thousands of men. One man's vision made it real. When I left the United Kingdom at the time of retirement there were one hundred and six clubs within the boundaries of the Greater London Council comprising the largest district in Rotary, District 113.

The London club, perhaps because of the convenience of its meeting place, as well as its eminence, has attracted Great Britain's finest speakers and most colourful personalities. As president I attempted to be exact in fact and as effusive as good taste would allow in introducing the guest speakers. I recall confiding to Madame Ninette de Valois, founder of the Royal Ballet, before she spoke, that I had been practising hard the proper pronunciation of her name. She burst into laughter and said, "But that's only a stage name. At heart I'm a simple girl from the Welsh valleys with a very ordinary name. Welsh girl or not, I had not practised for nothing, and I called her to her feet in the best Gallic accent of which I was capable.

Among the visiting speakers was Sir William Armstrong, later Lord Armstrong of Stanstead, then Head of the Home Civil Service and Permanent Secretary to the Civil Service Department, a position of immense influence which he occupied with distinction. After retirement he became chairman of the Midland Bank and, as such, a member of our Salvation Army London advisory board. It was a double pleasure to have him address the club seeing this brilliant public servant, like myself, had been born to Salvation Army officer parents.

Head table contacts with notable visiting speakers produced some surprises. The Rt. Hon. Sir Edward Boyle, PC., MP., respected patron and critic of the arts, told me during the luncheon that he not only like Bach but also Moody and Sankey. *Sotto voce* he sang in my ear, "Ask the Saviour to help you,/ Comfort, strengthen and keep you;/ He is willing to aid you,/ He will carry you through." "That," he said, "is a good song—useful and encouraging."

The Dean of Westminster Abbey, the Very Rev. Dr. Edward Carpenter, was a frequent and welcome speaker. His eloquent address on the "Royal Peculiar"—a designation given to the historic abbey—revealed this distinguished churchman's ability to clothe erudition in the choice garment of simplicity. This particular occasion led to a personal friendship which made access to Westminster Abbey for significant Salvation Army occasions delightfully easy. I was deeply moved to find the Dean at the head table on the day of my last club attendance prior to retirement when I, and the club in which I had found rich friendship and from which I had drawn incalculable inspiration, exchanged farewells.

My first of several meetings with Mrs. Margaret Thatcher was when she came to address the club as minister of education. She was passing through a rigorous period and was the object of bitter criticism in respect of certain of her policies. Seated beside her I was aware of her attractive femininity and the impression she gave of having just stepped out of the proverbial band-box, the stepping out not having in any perceptible degree disarranged her person, her dress or her composure. When she spoke, the femininity remained. At the appropriate moment there was the beguiling pout or the quietly confidential smile. But the defence of her policies was delivered with more than masculine strength. Lamb and lion had decided to co-exist in the guise of a minister of the crown. The prime ministerial rôle was obviously not beyond her capabilities.

The name, Jack Davis, bespeaks to both Rotarians and Salvationists the highest kind of dedication to good causes and kind deeds. At precisely the time I took office as General and international leader he became the world president of Rotary International. As boys, he and I had attended the same schools in Belleville, Canada, moving together from grade to grade. Education completed, he moved to Bermuda where he made his home and his career. His delight at my involvement in Rotary was expressed periodically in letters which unfailingly reflected the spiritual dimensions of his life. The Phillips pocket New Testament he gave me, with its meaningful inscription, accompanied me everywhere. To know the Christian hospitality extended by Jack and his gracious wife, Doris, at lovely "Coolshannah" on the shore of Hamilton Bay was to know the sweetest perfume of solicitude. Strangely, as my term of leadership was ending, so were Jack's earthly days. With his passing Rotary lost one of its foremost champions, The Salvation Army lost one of its most ardent advisory board members, and I lost a great and good lifetime friend. When the high school we had both attended held its golden jubilee celebrations notice was given to the fact that, on the international scene, the school had produced at least one president and at least one general.

Salvationists in Great Britain gave quick response to my request that they should team up with the Rotary club of London to bring out of the scarred areas of Northern Ireland hundreds of children upon whose lives deeper scars were already forming; to bring them to quiet countryside and to cheerful seaside, to streets without barricades, and to towns without sound of bullet and bomb. What greater reward than to receive a letter from a ten-year-old which said: "I want to thank you for my holiday. It was wonderful, all of it. The difference, I guess, was the peace of it all. And if what we had was peace, then that's what we need a lot more of here in Ulster."

The men who inhabit Booth House in London's east end will have seen a plaque on the door of one of the rooms they gratefully use. The room was a gift from the Rotary Club of London. As a further and farewell act of admiration for the Army's work, a substantial amount was handed to me before leaving England "to be used at the General's discretion." During the last week in office I directed that a trust fund be established, the earnings of which would assist young men and women of limited resources to meet the costs of training as Salvation Army officers in order to engage in a lifetime of "Service above self."

In 1973, and again in 1975, I had the privilege of addressing international conventions of Rotary in Lausanne, Switzerland, and in Montreal, Canada. I arrived in Lausanne the evening before I was scheduled to speak, and was sumptuously accommodated in the Lausanne Palace Hotel. The ornate surroundings and the splendid cuisine did little to allay my nervous anticipation. Through a restless night I must have delivered the address twenty times, with the catastrophic results that nightmares can induce. In the morning I was not certain that the real world would be any less menacing than the dream world. A waiter laid breakfast on the balcony and, in the sunshine of a perfect May morning, with Lac Léman glittering peacefully beyond the city buildings, needed tranquillity came. I reported to the Palais de Beaulieu for the plenary session and met R.I. President Roy Hickman by whose arrangement I was to address the more than seventeen thousand delegates. Only three persons were on the vast stage when the meeting came to order, the president, a past international president and now chairman of the Rotary Foundation trustees, Kiyoshi Togosaki, and myself. The introduction was fulsome and complimentary to a degree that came near to re-igniting my fears. The president's theme for the convention was, "A new look at world peace," and this was my appointed topic.

"Those of us who live where law and order is preserved are grateful," I said. "The law, as we know, helps civilization to survive anarchy and barbarism, but it is spiritual faith which is the living, moving power that constantly urges men on to higher and better things. We live in a clever, sophisticated age. But are men and women any wiser? Has man found a cure for his fears, either real or imaginary? Man, if he is going to bring the world into peace, cannot live without faith. Otherwise, he becomes static, fossilized." I wanted my hearers to grasp the highly personal element in what I was saying. "Peace begins in the individual spirit. Thereafter, its concentric rings widen to include those in the home and the family, the neighbours across the road or across an ocean."

Assuming that my listeners sincerely wanted to know how world peace could come, I made bold to say, "To understand is the first step. To show interest and friendship on a personal level is the next step. To inculcate hope and courage follows. And, eventually, and hopefully, the armistice takes place within the man, and the inner struggle gives way to lasting peace. World peace begins when we succeed in bringing the spirit of peace to one man or woman who is without it."

Just before I rose to speak, Togosaki reached over and tapped me, saying, "Don't be nervous. Everything will be fine." He spoke in English without a trace of Japanese accent. After the event I thanked him for his encouragement. In return, he told me what an effective influence one of our greatest Japanese Salvation Army leaders, Commissioner Gunpei Yamamuro, had had on his life when a young man. He referred appreciatively to "The Common People's Gospel," produced by the Commissioner which, through the years has had a circulation of many millions.

Two years later I tried desperately to convince R.I. President Bill Robbins that it was too soon to appear again as an international convention speaker. He was not to be dissuaded, and since I was, at the time, territorial commander for Canada and Bermuda, the convention venue, Montreal, was close at hand. This time the address was to be given on the Sunday evening in Montreal's massive Forum. From the lectern it was a sight to be remembered, so huge was the crowd. To hear one's own voice penetrating such a vast arena of silence was awesome. The theme chosen was, "Renew the spirit of Rotary," and I suggested that a renewal of the spirit of true fellowship and selfless service could be, as the ancient Chinese proverb has it, "The spark that lights the flame that lights the fires on ten thousand hills."

Rotary's concern with ethics led me to say, "I know as well as any man that there are problems in ethics; that there are border-line cases; that there are innumerable greys between black and white. But the spirit of Rotary confirms that when due allowance has been made for these, men and women know, through all the earth, the difference between right and wrong, between good and bad, even as they know the difference between night and day, wet and dry, cold and heat."

Admittedly, I was speaking as a Rotarian, but I was also under Divine obligation to point to the One who is Way, Truth and Life. "The life that wants the deepest satisfaction must sail with the greatest Captain. What is determined is that the sea of life is filled with hidden and jagged shoals. There are rough waters and tearing gales to be faced. Who is it that will bring us into our desired haven—not having avoided life, but having conquered it? For myself, belonging to God, I am part of His eternal certainty. How much better is this than being fettered by pagan, anarchistic, nihilistic ideologies that seek to manipulate man's individuality into plastic subservience! The spirit of Rotary insists that injustice is always and everywhere wrong. Fraud and ingratitude, dishonesty and dishonour can never be justified. To steal another man's wife, to ill-treat a child, to be cruel to a dumb animal, to return evil for good, to betray a trust, to save oneself at the expense of another—these are not relative ethics. They do not change with changing times nor vary from one generation to another."

What exaltation of spirit reposes in a kind word after such a speaking ordeal. The number who came to me afterwards and said that my words were "for them" wiped away the doubts about the content of the speech that had plagued me before delivering it, and cancelled out my uneasiness that I had been too sermonic.

What began in my vice-presidential year became a tradition in the Rotary club of London. For the Christmas luncheon meeting talented Salvation Army musicians were in welcome attendance, and the International Staff Band provided strong accompaniment to the hearty singing of carols. Underneath the rich music and party gladness I never failed to sense the mysterious pervasiveness of what we call "the Christmas spirit" with its transmuting ability to make children of all types of men. To add to the festivity, I contributed for several years "A Curious Christmas Carol" in which the foibles of certain members and the pecadilloes of club officers were recounted in wastepaper doggerel and sung lustily and laughingly to a well-known seasonal tune.

My presidential year was enormously rewarding but complicated. Early in my term, appointment as the Army's Chief of the Staff brought me global concerns and demanded much travelling. The club's tolerance whenever I was unexpectedly absent was incredibly generous. Every suggestion I made of resignation was resisted. In my heart of hearts I was glad. Had my resignation been accepted I would have lost far more than the club would ever have known.

The championing of high ethical standards in business is part of Rotary's idealism. A vocational service assembly was organized annually by one of the New York club's directors and past presidents, John Ellis. If he has been an indefatigable and notable servant of Rotary, he has also been an unflagging supporter of The Salvation Army. These twin interests have made him and his delightful wife, Laurel, familiar figures at special events of both movements in many parts of the world. I could not refuse, despite an overloaded schedule, when he asked me to give the address at one of his remarkable seminars. For it, the opulent ballroom of the Waldorf-Astoria hotel was crowded. Rotary's four-way test has as its first question: "Is it the truth?" It was to this fundamentally necessary element in the realms of business and commerce that I chose to speak.

Frequently, I was expected to be more Salvation Army officer than Rotarian and to participate as "father in God" at district and national divine services. What clergyman would not rejoice at being confronted with a Sunday morning congregation of several thousand crowding the Empire Ballroom of Blackpool's famed Winter Gardens? And what cleric would not be challenged when observing that the congregation included many of the United Kingdom's finest speakers and finest spirits? In 1981 the Rotary movement celebrated its 75th anniversary, not only with special projects but with special thanksgiving. For Rotarians of London's District 113 praise and prayer mingled in a crowded gathering in the House of Commons' church, historic St. Margarets, which stands, like an attentive server at the altar, alongside Westminster Abbey. To preach from this most historic pulpit, where for such a stretch of years great men have uttered great thoughts, permitted me to urge my fellow Rotarians to find a future in which they would "do justly, love mercy, and walk humbly with their God."

I rejoice in honorary membership of the two Rotary clubs with which I have had such fulfilling affiliation, the Rotary Club of London and the Rotary Club of Toronto. My international leadership of the Army completed, and with a happy entry into retirement, the Rotary Club of Toronto not only welcomed me "home" in a style suited to "kings and conquerors," but conferred on me Rotary's highest honour by making me a Paul Harris fellow. In accepting the award I publicly rededicated myself to those principles and practices that have brought the recognition of greatness to both Paul Harris and William Booth and to many of their spiritual heirs.

CHAPTER 11

Second In Command

My wife and I were furloughing in the Swiss village of Leysin, a steep climb from the town of Aigle after one leaves Lausanne, Vevey and Montreux while following the northern shore of Lac Léman. We were resting at the Army's small hotel, once a clinic and purchased by a far-seeing Commissioner Henri Bequet who had also pioneered the Army's work in what was then the Belgian Congo, now Zaire. The hotel is located in an idyllic setting. From a front balcony one can glimpse a town almost lost in the valley a mile below and, across the green chasm, the Dents du Midi, their snow-capped peaks nibbling the clouds that float about them. On a clear day the queen of pinnacles, Mont Blanc, comes into view, majestically dwarfing all the mountains that stand on sentry duty in front of her. Here, in this favourite retreat, we found refreshment of mind, body and spirit, and an opportunity to practice our limited French. The wooded hillsides, the sharp mountain air, the serenity at the top of the nearby *telesiege* with silence rising like pine-scented fragrance from below, were a healing balm. One could sit for hours simply dreaming, forgetting, remembering, emptying the tiredness and imbibing vitality, all in a stillness broken only by the far-off carillon of cow-bells.

It was here that General Coutts reached me by telephone to say that I was promoted to the rank of Lieutenant-Commissioner, a notification received with serious thought. But how the news came caused many a smile. At the hotel the schedule included a mandatory rest period following *le dejeuner*. It was not accidental that the annexe was named,

"Mon Repos," and the woman brigadier supervising the establishment expected the rules to be respected—all of them! Regrettably, the rest-period rule was being doubly broken; activity was replacing somnolence and, worse still, I was doing *au chambre* what was permitted only in a part of the building set aside for such sartorial purposes. I was pressing a pair of trousers. From the other side of the door a voice was calling, "Pour vous, Colonel. Le téléphone! C'est Londres. C'est le Général!" Opening the door, I did my best to hide my confusion as well as my twin misdemeanours.

The rank of Commissioner has particular significance for the average Salvationist and engages high respect. Legally, the rank *is* important. Only two conferred ranks are mentioned in the Army's constitution. They are Colonel and Commissioner. In respect of the latter, however, there is a stipulation in The Salvation Army Act 1981 that applies to no other rank. It is a legal obligation upon a General to keep in office a Chief of the Staff and no fewer than twenty-one other commissioners. The number usually is larger, but it can never be fewer. Twenty-two commissioners out of some 25,000 commissioned officers—one out of every thousand, approximately—bespeaks selectivity and implies consequence. To this must be added the dignity, competence, achievement and high degree of spirituality which, through the years, officers have conferred upon the rank, rather than the reverse. Returning to the hotel room, my wife and I stood looking out at the exquisite Alpine scene. In a new way we realized that rank, like clothes, never make the man or woman, and that only totally sanctified service justifies there being such a rank at all.

I had been asked on our return to London not to be out of the city on October 16th, 1969, in order to be available for an interview with the newly-installed international leader, General Erik Wickberg. I was sent for on that Thursday morning and found the General sitting at his desk and indicating that he was awaiting a telephone call. Moments later the phone rang. There was a brief exchange of words. I was still in the dark as to the purpose of the interview, but sensed that something important was afoot. The receiver replaced, the General, who for all of the five years I had served in the public relations department had, as the Chief of the Staff, been the superior to whom I had been responsible, looked directly at me and said, "They have all agreed, and I am appointing you as the Chief of the Staff."

In answering the questions put to nominees at the High Council the General had promised that he would have the approval of five senior commissioners in respect of the appointment of his successor as second-in-command.

"You will be glad to know that the vote is unanimous," the General said. "But we must wait a moment longer."

We sat virtually in silence, the General drumming softly with his long fingers on the glass-topped desk, and I, my mind reeling under waves of unbelievability, wondering what second surprise could emerge from a further telephone call. Another ring. Another short conversation and a firm "Thank you!"

"That call was from the Advisory Council," the General said. "They have unanimously recommended your promotion to full rank." (It would not be long before the rank of Lieutenant-Commissioner would be abolished. I had managed to carry it for a full nine weeks!)

The General expressed some of his hopes and I expressed some of my fears. Both hopes and fears were laid before the Lord in prayer, and I stumbled out into the corridor towards my basement office. I had just welcomed Colonel (later Commissioner) Lawrence Smith from San Francisco who, I had anticipated, would be a most productive assistant in public relations leadership. Now he was to succeed me. Without my realizing it, but in the careful planning of the administration, "the pieces had come together."

In the Regent Hall, near Oxford Circus, and with General Wickberg presiding, I was publicly welcomed as Chief of the Staff and my wife as World President of Salvation Army Guides and World President of The Salvation Army Nurses' Fellowship. It was a lively occasion, made light-hearted at one point by the remarks of a close friend, Colonel Harold Orton, who was later to become commissioner and chancellor of the Army's exchequer. He and I had sat beside each other as delegates to the Staff College under the fatherly direction of Commissioner Fred Hammond, eighteen years before. He told the crowd how faithfully he had remonstrated with me for appearing not to give the various lecturers full attention, but rather occupying myself in sketching them and their gestures, or turning their lecture material into humorous verse. He had warned me by saying, "Brown, unless you learn to pay attention, you'll never amount to anything in this Army."

The office of the Chief of the Staff into which I moved is large enough to serve also as a board room and to accommodate the innumerable conferences which are outside the function of established boards and councils. It is located on "the cold side of the building." The room is seldom penetrated by sunshine, and it is impossible to leave a window open for more than a minute or two because of the noisy tides of traffic roaring along Queen Victoria Street. The layout of the office, when I moved in, was awkward. Callers entered by a door from the private secretary's tiny office, their first glimpse of the Army's second-in-command being the back of his right shoulder and head, while the Chief saw nothing of the visitor until he had rounded the desk, or the Chief had wheeled about to greet him. I discovered that it would be possible to completely reverse the office, and thus give both visitor and visited the advantage of a face-to-face greeting. It was perhaps to be expected that the wits put it about that the new Chief of the Staff was "turning the office of the Chief of the Staff in a completely new direction—mostly the furniture!"

The working relationship of a General and his Chief should set the standard for all similar combinations of leadership. The harmony need not restrict frank discussion or the ventilation of opposing views. A dual searching for the best course of action is, when found, dually supported. If a General, after hearing his Chief's observations still feels that his own plans should be implemented, the Chief's responsibility is to promulgate the decision as though it were his own, yielding to the ultimate powers given to the General by the constitution, by orders and regulations and also by the rank system, all of which combine to make his word final.

For the entire five years I served as Chief, General Wickberg was the Army's international leader. His Swedish courtliness had been polished by the manners of Switzerland and Germany and shaped in dignity by long residence in the United Kingdom. He was multi-lingual and took boundless pains to ensure accuracy and acceptance when writing or speaking in any of the languages with which he was familiar. Unknown to most, and to the surprise of some, the General was, in his scarce free time, an expert at chess and in his youth had played against chess-masters. His administration reflected the elements of the game—concentration, the ability to think several moves ahead without being distracted by an immediate situation, and the indomitable will to succeed.

Most important to me was the fact that the General had been Chief of the Staff for the previous nine years. His long knowledge of people, situations and procedures was always at my disposal, though never forced on me. I would have been content to have been "the General's lieutenant," but he expected me to be what he had appointed me to be. The Army has only one Chief at a time, and he had no intention of being an *eminence grise*. I was to find my own way.

Prior to the General's retirement I was joint-editor with Professor J. W. Winterhager, PhD., DD., the well-informed principal of a Berlin seminary, in the preparation of a festschrift, *Vocation and Victory,* honouring the General's Christian service. In it, tribute was paid to the General's evangelical spirit—his "vital thrust"—and to his theological stature admired by church leaders, eminent writers on religion, and by the notable preachers who contributed to the symposium. My own contribution included the following: "I write as the servant who has been, during the whole of Wickberg's generalship, his right-hand man. I testify that there has been no contradiction between what has been said behind the double doors of his office (to which comes all the major problems of a big movement, and from which flows out that leadership which inspires Salvationists all over the world) and what has been said from the public platform and pulpit. Erik Wickberg is the constant evangelist!" In the saddle of administration General Wickberg's control was firm and steady. If the steed he rode were occasionally restive, and on rare occasions rebellious, the reins were held tightly by sensitive hands.

There is no Memorandum of Appointment for a Chief of the Staff. He is actually the business administrator of the entire international Army, responsible directly to the General and speaking authoritatively for him. His letter of appointment makes it clear that his position is interchangeable with any other should the General feel it necessary to make a change. For seven of the twelve who had occupied the chair before me it had been a terminal appointment. Three of the twelve had become General. Two had moved to other appointments. I would be the third.

The Chief of the Staff is immediately supported by a Chief Secretary who heads what is known as the Secretary's Department to which flows all consequential matters from International Headquarters' departments, the associated headquarters and from national headquarters. Additionally from the overseas territories and commands come matters which do not reach the Chief (as he is commonly addressed) through the International Secretaries, each of whom has a close relationship with a designated area of the world. Every Wednesday is set aside for what is called, "Chief's business." All International Secretaries are in attendance, and the Chief is in the chair. The presence of officers representing all parts of the Army world ensures a global balance of administration. One after another the Under Secretaries present various items, giving the views of those boards and councils which have already studied the details. The Chief, after hearing any further comments from the International Secretaries, makes his decision. Certain matters may be taken under advisement pending the Chief's discussion with the General; others go to the General at once in the form of recommendation.

Though the powers of the Chief appear to be almost unlimited there are checks and balances. As an extension of the mind of the international leader there is the Advisory Council to the General, a selected group of leaders to whom the General can refer any subject he wishes and to whom he *must* refer for recommendation a number of specified matters. The Chief of the Staff, while he can ask the General to put items on the council's agenda, is not a member of that body. This allows the General to have opinion from other than his second-in-command, opinion that is uninfluenced by the Chief's nearness to a problem or proposal.

The appointment as Chief thrust me on to a world stage. Suddenly I had global concerns and was faced with extensive travelling that meant the management of two offices, one looking out on a busy Queen Victoria Street and beyond it to the dome of St. Paul's, and the other a mobile office functioning inconspicuously in the plane, train, ship or automobile in which the miles were being covered.

I had to shape my own philosophy of leadership, and quickly. I had always felt that command could not be isolated from communication. If one were body, the other were breath. Orders might flow down the chain of command, but communication must answer the Why? aroused by the orders. Out of this communication there should be feedback. Intuitively I understood that feedback would be a sign of life. Without it something would be vitally missing.

Reading the memoirs of Viscount Montgomery I had been gripped by the chapter on "My Doctrine of Command," and, in particular, by a paragraph which, while written about a military army, was no less apropos for The Salvation Army: "An army is a most sensitive instrument; its basic ingredient is men and, to handle an army well, it is essential to understand human nature. Bottled up in men are great emotional forces which have got to be given an outlet in a way which is positive and constructive, and which warms the heart and excites the imagination. If the approach to the human factor is cold and impersonal, then you achieve nothing. But if you can gain the confidence and trust of your men, and they feel their best interests are safe in your hands, then you have in your possession a priceless asset and the greatest achievements become possible." If the "basic ingredient" is men, as Montgomery says, the proper, respectful, considerate handling of the officers for whom I now had a close and inescapable responsibility was all-important. Such concern, however, must be impartial. To advantage one to the disadvantage of another would be to the hurt of both. I determined to follow Hutcheson's advice: "That action," he says, "is best which procures the greatest happiness for the greatest numbers."

All-embracing as the Chief's powers might have seemed to me to be in the early occupancy of the office, I realized that I was still "a man under authority." Perhaps the General aided perspective by sending me a copy of *The Readers' Digest* open at the feature, "Humour in Uniform." The first story concerned a chief of the staff of the armed forces who had on the wall behind his desk a framed motto which read: "Administrative Rules for a Chief of the Staff. No. 1: The General is always right. No. 2: When the General is wrong, rule No. 1 will apply." Point taken!

To be "a man under authority" is not to be a man *without* authority. But I quickly saw that much of that authority must of necessity be delegated. Without proper delegation no movement can function effectively. Lack of courage to delegate wisely, and of knowledge how to do it, is one of the most general causes of failure in organization. It is a problem older than history. When Jethro visited Moses, Moses was staggering under the same problem that has killed many a modern businessman. But he was sensible enough to take his father-in-law's advice, and "he chose able men out of all Israel ... and they judged the people at all seasons; the hard cases they brought unto Moses, but every small matter they judged themselves." I had to shake myself loose from my own father's repeated observation that "If you want something done, do it yourself!" There was now far too much for one person to do, and increasingly I delegated responsibilities, reserving always the right to "double check" and, sometimes necessarily, to "triple check." Whether I could claim Andrew Carnegie's epitaph as my own remains a hope: "Here lies a man who knew how to enlist in his service better men than himself."

Scores of times in scores of places I have been asked to say what task I found most onerous in the ten years of leadership spent in the Chief's and General's positions. In answer I invariably quoted the American president, Thomas Jefferson: "No duty the Executive had to perform was so trying as to put the right man in the right place." And, I could add, "at the right time."

I could never approve an appointment, particularly if it involved moving an officer from his homeland to another country, without prayerfully attempting to make myself part of his domestic situation and seeking to understand what penalties within the family the move would exact; or without imagining the most private feelings of the officer himself. The appointment could so easily affect the life-pattern of a family, not only in the acquisition of national customs and language, but in eventual, long separations should a son or daughter marry and adopt the country of the parents' appointment as a homeland. If I sometimes appeared dilatory in announcing an appointment it was usually because I was waiting for some Divine or human reassurance to unknot my concerns about the outcome. When asking officers of senior rank to go to a land whose language they did not know and to an alien way of life, and perhaps at a time when family considerations could make understandable demands on the heart, I was inwardly strengthened by the knowledge that I, myself, had never queried any appointment. My full salute had never been wrapped in a question mark.

I was now faced with more business than ever before, but also with the necessity of giving the strongest possible spiritual leadership. I had often to remind myself, and occasionally others, that mission and administration are not necessarily mutually exclusive. The Army is both a "communion of saints" and big business, but it is of supreme importance to remember that the administration must always be spiritually motivated. The interest is more in souls than in structures.

My first predecessor in the rôle of Chief of the Staff, Bramwell Booth, who occupied the office for thirty-one years, saw this clearly. One of his biographers wrote of him that "he believed the Army was called into being by the will of God, and all he did in it was done on that assumption, and with a determination to set up a standard of service which should be as truly inspired and devoted when its outward form was secular as when it was spiritual." It was a worthy pattern to follow, but I had for my guidance what Bramwell Booth lacked and had to create—Orders and Regulations covering all aspects of Army activity. These are the embodiment of the principles and procedures whereby the movement can pursue an orderly and intelligent life, designed, as William Booth declared, "to ensure the continuity of our best methods." And what chaos there would be without them! Pity any Chief of the Staff who had to manage the affairs of the Army without Orders and Regulations to guide him!

An eminent solicitor once told me, after studying all our regulations in preparation for expected litigation, that he had not seen in any of the many societies he represented such a compilation of "clear and wise" guidance. Because these guidelines are committed to print and expressed in quasi-legal language, some, I discovered, thought of them as rock-hewn immutabilities brought down the mountainside by one man, either the General himself or his Chief of the Staff. The fact is that the process of examination is as continuous as new human situations, changed norms in society, or fresh insights accepted as valid and valuable, make amendment or alteration necessary. It is, however, this written, though changing, corpus that gives foundation to the remarkable discipline of the Army, admired everywhere and hopefully always to be maintained.

Orders and Regulations, then, provide a basis for sound administration and wise governance, and one of the major tasks I envisaged was to see revised and reprinted those Orders and Regulations that were out of date. It was a mammoth undertaking covering several years to which many keen minds gave many wearying hours. I was particularly anxious that once revisions were issued they should immediately be translated so that a language barrier should not be cause for any Salvationist's ignorance of what is the final distillation of that "clear and wise" thought which is called "the Army mind."

As the global nature of the Army was increasingly understood, equally I had to recognize that administration based on international concepts, or fundamental principles, must be capable of adaptation to territorial practicability. What was right for New York may need shading for New Delhi. Both could subscribe to a principle, but the procedure might be slightly different. But New York or New Delhi, the only force which can give Orders and Regulations the authority required to make them effective is the personal loyalty of all who subscribe to them. There is no other way. Loyalty is the only answer, and the extent to which I saw it demonstrated and sensed its reality left me, in the words of Proust, "full of confidence and attachment."

It falls to the lot of the Chief of the Staff to enforce the principles of government, as Bramwell Booth ruefully admitted. For him it was not always smooth sailing. Men in high command needed teaching and convincing and restraining from assuming too pontifical an attitude. In a letter to one errant he wrote: "A very much larger question underlies all this than you seem to realize. To put it in familiar language, it may be stated thus—is this animal to wag its tail and move its own extremities, or are those extremities and that tail to wag the animal? I am speaking out of my inmost soul ... For heaven's sake, don't let us drift into clouds and misunderstanding. I stand exactly where I stood. I have struggled hard to hold on in the line of unity and liberty. I am confronted with some ghastly examples of letting people, *with the best of hearts,* go their own way when it is not ours."

It must be remembered that more than half-a-century has passed since then, and the Army's systems have moved from the experimental to the established. One cannot imagine the necessity for such a letter today. Certainly I was never called upon to write in such a vein. If anything, one hopes that the establishing has not completely cancelled out the experimental! At the end of the day, however, the Chief is referee and umpire. He must see that the rules are kept, irrespective of the team or the star. Infractions occasionally occur. That they should be dealt with is taken for granted. Not only because Orders and Regulations plainly say so, but because the leader must be true to his own responsibility. To evade an issue reveals a weakness within the leader himself. To evade many issues means that weakness seeps into the very structure of administration, and the ultimate end is the disintegration of both the leader and those who have a right to be led. For me, these were always sobering reflections.

I found I was "touchy" on another fundamental aspect of leadership, that of accountability. When serving with the public relations wing of the Army I had maintained that total accountability, and nothing less, was the responsibility of the Army and all who were part of it. As Chief, the necessity loomed more demandingly. The higher an officer rises in administration the more accountable he should feel himself to be. Investigative reporting by the media was invading what had heretofore been the inviolable preserves of church and charity. Few scandals are as sensationally titillating as those surrounding priest or parson or the mismanagement of publicly-contributed funds for alleged good causes. For the Army, I felt, accountability should rest on the highest level. God's people are accountable to God as well as to the general public, and always the purity of their practices will reflect the measure of their love for Christ.

General Wickberg was anxious that all the undertakings given to the High Council which had elected him should be discharged as quickly as possible. He had agreed to convene a conference of international leaders within three years, and planning had to start at once. All such conferences had previously been held in London, and there were many features favouring this venue. I suggested, however, that new benefits might result if the conference moved away from England. To do so would emphasize the internationality of the Army, as well as giving another country the pleasure of hosting the deliberations. The General was animated by the proposal, and it was decided that the event would take place in the United States. The American leaders selected Ocean City as the meeting-place.

Prior to the conference, delegates were taken to the towering United Nations building in New York. The General and myself, with Commissioners Edward Carey, Paul F. Carlson, Joseph Dahya and Jacobus Corputty, were received by the Secretary-General, Mr. U. Thant. Whether or not he felt we were people in whom he could confide he spoke, I thought, with surprising frankness. His comments were tinged with disillusionment, yet not altogether devoid of hope. In quiet voice he said he had anticipated, when assuming his position, leading the nations into a progressive and fruitful cooperation. Instead, he found himself burdened with the raising of funds to underwrite undertakings voted for by the general assembly, the majority of whose member countries were unable to contribute anything at all towards the cost of implementation.

Out of the conference, convened in September, 1971, came several important recommendations. One which was to affect all officers had to do with a revision of the ranks system. In dealing with such a subject there is always the faint fear that some may reckon that time and thought have been given disproportionately to a secondary matter at the expense of those more urgent considerations which should always occupy the attention of Army leaders. The conference, however, gave most of its thought to those spiritual pursuits which are of primary concern—how better to proclaim the living gospel of Christ; how to encourage more ardent personal evangelism; how more effectively to mobilize the Army's international forces in challenging increasing evil. But the things of time also require intelligent and conscientious review, and since all officers are designated by one rank or another, any change in the system would be of particular interest to all.

The sequence and significance of the various ranks has puzzled many non-Salvationists, though most understand that a quasi-military structure requires them. Those who have seen service in the military forces note a certain but imprecise parallelism in the scale of ranks. Strangely, the six volumes of Salvation Army history contain no description of the evolution of the ranks system, other than scattered references to ranks taken or conferred. George Scott Railton, the first to be designated "Commissioner," wrote to William Booth in 1873, addressing him as "My dear General," and signing as "Your ever-to-be-faithful Lieutenant." "General," it is thought was at the first a handy abbreviation of "General Secretary," the official title carried by William Booth at the time. In 1877, when Elijah Cadman "opened fire" on Whitby, he announced that "the attack would be led by Captain Cadman," and had posters printed stating that "The General of the Hallelujah Army" would be participating. Nervous of Booth's reaction to such terminology, he hid a poster in his home, but somehow it was discovered by the General Superintendent who, to Cadman's relief, applauded his initiative and, in so doing, began the perpetuation of his own designation as "General." A sheet of early letterhead bears William Booth's proof marks indicating that the title should follow, not precede, his name. Beside it, he wrote, "It looks pretentious." Certain designations, unrelated to seniority, were appropriated by members of the Booth family, and restricted to them: Catherine,

La Maréchale; Herbert and Ballington, Commandant; Evangeline, Commander; and Emma, Consul.

To military ranks was added extraneously the naval rank of Ensign which perhaps is not so curious when it is known that in the 1800's several vessels were serving the Army's evangelistic purposes in coastal ports or on the canals. Where two or more Salvationist seamen comprised a "brigade" (a further mixture of terms) a "Bo'sun" was appointed to see that meetings were regularly held. In military parlance, adjutancy is a function. The Salvation Army made it a rank, and placed it between that of Captain and Major. In later years there were variations such as Senior Captain and Senior Major, both of which ranks I personally held. For a time Commandant was a popular rank, considerably more so than that of Field Major for which rank the insignia trimmings were bright green, contrasting violently with the navy blue of the uniform.

The objective of the Ocean City conference was simplification, and its desire was to do away with rank preferment in one area of officership as against another. That anomalies did exist was freely acknowledged. That all such anomalies could be eliminated might be wishful thinking; but it was accepted unanimously that, as far as possible, any uneven application of the ranks system should be obviated. Writing on the subject at the time I expressed my conviction that having seen officers at work in many parts of the world, virtually all of them were far more concerned about the work they were doing than the designation they carried while doing it. As a result of the deliberations two ranks were dropped: Brigadier, on account of its ex-sequential placing in the rank structure and the misunderstanding that the use of so prestigious a military designation had caused in the mind of the public; and Lieutenant-Commissioner, a strange marriage of military and civil designations. The deletion of this latter rank was related to the decision to lower the retirement age of commissioners and was intended concomitantly to enhance the rank of colonel. The adjusted scale of ranks now includes lieutenant, captain, major, lieutenant-colonel, colonel and commissioner, a gradation that appears to meet present needs and for the shaping of which I must take some responsibility. It was with reservation that the General agreed to discard the rank of lieutenant-commissioner, and I have myself had some second thoughts about it, though the new constitution does not now recognize such a rank.

Perhaps there will be further simplifications in the future since the term "captain" appears to come more easily to most—a form of address from which all those holding higher rank, including the General, are not exempted. If there is, the rank of lieutenant-colonel could be the next to be abandoned. Most importantly, the revisions mentioned liberated the administration from having to make appointments on the basis of rank related to years of service. Doors of significant responsibility were now flung open to younger officers holding junior ranks.

At this conference, influenced by the current national mood, pressures were exerted by the American leaders for a lowering of the age of retirement for commissioners which, at the time, was seventy for men and sixty-five for women, all other men officers retiring at sixty-five and women at sixty. The General agreed to review the subject and reluctantly, I suspected, decided that the retirement age for men commissioners would be sixty-eight and that over a twelve-year period there would be a gradual descent to sixty-five as the normal age of retirement, a plan that met with general acceptance.

As General, I found it necessary to reintroduce this matter at an international conference of leaders in Toronto in 1979. The descending scale had already reduced the retirement age to sixty-seven, and we were on the threshold of the next reduction to age sixty-six. This would have meant the loss of a number of experienced leaders in the same period—leaders who could not at the time easily be replaced—and I hoped that a new way of avoiding such a situation might be found. The plan which emerged made sixty-seven the "normal" retirement age for men commissioners, with the proviso that retirement could be taken from sixty-five on if application were made one full year in advance. I later came to the conclusion that the regulation was poorly drafted, something for which I must bear full onus. The prerogative of earlier retirement should have been made conditional on the needs of the Army, rather than it being a prescriptive right of the officer. It became disturbingly clear that an officer could be promoted to the ultimate conferred rank at, say, sixty-three, and after one year could then announce his intention of retiring at age sixty-five, despite the fact that his promotion and appointment had been predicated on a four-year period of service. It now meant that before promoting an officer to the rank of commissioner I was compromised to the extent of asking him if he would give an undertaking to serve until age sixty-seven, a procedure beyond the expressed intent of the regulation, and one which could be embarrassing to both parties. I hope that a more satisfactory regulation will spring from the contemplations of my successors.

Such are life's unpredictabilities that, as I left office, American legislators were championing the worker's right to continue working until age seventy, should he so wish. Earlier retirement could mean the loss of vital experience to the economy and an unnecessary hastening of the individual's decline. So much for any attempt to follow the fluctuating theories of the body politic! Though the views of legislators in a matter of this kind are of interest to Army leaders, the Army is not bound to follow them. An officer's commitment to the Army places him outside such considerations. Directives of government which benefit the public weal have the Army's full support, but these, traditionally, do not supersede ecclesiastical arrangements.

At the Ocean City conference I introduced a subject on which I felt strongly, a no-smoking requirement for all Salvationists. Officers and local officers (which term includes bandsmen and songsters) came under regulation that forbade smoking. Additionally, young people who became junior soldiers, in many parts of the world signed a pledge which included a specific promise to abstain. But, strangely, when a junior soldier was transferred to senior soldiership he was not bound by any similar undertaking. To me this was an unfortunate omission, the more so in view of the convincing evidence presented by the medical profession as to smoking's harm and the insistence of government that such harmfulness should be indicated in all advertising having to do with the use of tobacco. Among uniform-wearing soldiers the incidence of use was infinitesimal. The uniform and a dangling cigarette seem totally incongruous to Salvationists, and the combination of the two, if ever seen, would shock many non-Salvationists. Debate, however, centred on those converts who, after a lifetime of using tobacco, had become Salvation Army soldiers but did not wear uniform. There were pleas for tolerance that they should not, on this one account, be denied the privilege of soldiership. I argued that if we believe Divine grace can instantaneously liberate a man from alcoholism, something frequently and joyfully observed in our Harbour Light centres with their alcoholic treatment programmes, then, surely, the same Divine grace could vanquish the habit of smoking. If doctors and others by sheer will-power could abstain, then those who acknowledged the body as "the temple of the living God," would have the highest possible motivation for desisting. Opposition to my proposal was eloquently presented and quite vigorously supported. The conference recommended that the matter be dropped. I was disappointed, but the decision in no way lessened my feelings. When agenda items for the international leaders' conference of 1975 were sought, I submitted the proposal again. Four years more of anti-smoking propaganda and an ever-widening acknowledgement of the dangers of the habit strengthened the submission. The conference, under the leadership of General Clarence Wiseman, passed the recommendation unanimously. Salvationists who were smokers were not to be proscribed by any new regulation. Rather, they were to be given helpful counsel and literature and led understandingly to see the physical and spiritual advantages of abstinence. Today, all who seek soldiership (membership) in the Army must promise not to smoke.

Fairly late in his term of office General Wickberg was hard pressed to hold a conference that would bring together leaders from the whole of North, Central and South America, in the hope that more means of benefiting the Latin American work might be discovered and implemented. I was given the responsibility of organizing the sessions, and in 1973 at Miama, Florida, the Pan-American Conference was convened. Its membership was extended beyond territorial leaders to include chief, field, financial and staff secretaries from all the territories. In degree, the intention of the conference was achieved. Leaders from the north were profoundly moved by the sacrificial service given in circumstances of hardship and occasional hostility by their counterparts from the south. A new hemispheric perception was stimulated, the far-ranging beneficial results of which continue.

Evangelism, always to the fore in the mind of General Wickberg, was the dominant conference theme. He made a positive statement rejecting the views of certain contemporary theologians which "cast a kind of spell over some of our preaching." He warned against "a sort of Christian humanism" that preaches the second commandment and forgets the first. Internationally reputable newspapers such as the *New York Times, The Atlanta Constitution,* the United Kingdom's *Daily Telegraph* and *The Guardian,* and others, were at the time devoting large space to the charismatic revival which was leaping across the boundaries of faiths and denominations, and it was appropriate that the charismatic movement and its effects on the Army should be discussed. Biblical references to glossolalia were carefully examined, and it became evident that the Army should avoid emphasizing the gift of tongues as a necessity, but should recognize that God and man can always communicate privately in a mysterious way.

In its practical aim the conference was successful. There was a closer binding of the Americas with a sharpened conception of each other's differences, not only of language but of culture, forms of government and national characteristics, all of which affected the evangelistic thrust. The conference had, as far as I could discern, only one disadvantage. It occurred too late in General Wickberg's tenure. The High Council that would elect his successor was imminent.

Major conferences involving all leaders could not happen often, yet the discussion of problems and the sharing of solutions was indispensable. "Zonal" conferences appeared to be the answer and these, based on the European Zonal Conference which for some time had been held biennially, were instituted. The first of these over which, at the General's direction, I presided, was held at Limuru, an attractive location not far from Nairobi, Kenya, which, with its higher altitude, was climatically pleasant. Here, black and white leaders from all parts of Africa met to devise ways of working more effectively throughout the continent. Among the delegates was Colonel Zulu, whose name indicates his nation. Huge in build, he was big of heart and his participation, in which wisdom and wit winsomely blended, impressed me. "Every piano I've ever seen that makes good music has both black and white keys," he said, stressing the need for harmonious relationships. He gripped the heart of the conference when he commented, "Sometimes it is necessary to reprove an erring brother. When it is, the episode should be a clean one, and after it is over we should take our brother aside and wash his wounds."

Equally impressive was the then Colonel (later Commissioner) Joshua Ngugi, of Kenya. His knowledge of the Bible was almost startling. I was told that as a young man he had read it through in order to find a Christian name for himself. He had selected Joshua because he felt that this leader's character and fidelity to God were eminently worthy of emulation. His answer to almost every question in conference began with a Biblical quotation: "The Bible says ... and from this we are led to think ..."

At this conference I felt I must urge certain of the delegates to learn English; not that English is thought by Salvationists to be a better language than all others, since the Gospel is preached by them in some one hundred and ten languages. But in order to be able to communicate intelligently and, as need arose, privately, with International Headquarters and its leaders, some knowledge of English would be essential. Because of its birthplace the language spoken by the infant Salvation Army was English and, as the movement grew and spread, English became its *lingua franca.* Not long after the Limuru conference sharp nationalistic feelings on the part of one government demanded the earlier-than-anticipated appointment of one of the delegates as territorial commander. It was gratifying to know that the advice gently given had been taken seriously and that an honest start had been made by him in learning "one more" language—English.

I was privileged to preside over a conference of quite another kind, authorized by the General and organized by the late Commissioner Ernest Fewster. It was held in August, 1972 in the canal-threaded city of Amsterdam. To one of the city's choice suburbs, Amstelveen, came fifty-seven delegates from twenty-six countries, all of them experts in Salvation Army social service. It was only the fourth such international social conference in the Army's history. The first was held in 1897, only thirteen years after the women's social work began, but in those first thirteen years a great deal had happened. There had been the Purity Agitation and the famous "Maiden Tribute" case in 1885—a reflection of the Army's determination to take immense risks in challenging social evils. The disclosure, based on an actual transaction, that young girls could be bought for immoral purposes landed Bramwell Booth in the dock and his champion, W. T. Stead, editor of the Pall Mall Gazette, who published the facts, in jail for three months. The beneficial outcome was that by law the age of consent was raised from thirteen to sixteen years. Slum corps and food depots had been opened. William Booth's "Darkest England Scheme" with its far-sighted, far-ranging syllabus for human betterment had been published in 1890. It had evoked mass support, but also merited vitriolic criticism from the famous Professor Thomas Huxley, as well as from *The Times* of London. This led to the establishing of the Social Trust which still operates in the United Kingdom, separating donations given for social service purposes from all other monies. In 1892 a new, benign form of social service known as the League of Mercy had come into being in Canada. Through it the lonely and forgotten in institutions were regularly visited and helped. All this in thirteen years!

Before the second conference was held, in 1911, there had been further, highly-significant occurrences such as the social agitation in Japan (when asylum was provided for many prostitutes); the establishing of the first missionary hospital at Nagercoil, India; the chartering of the first emigrant ship to launch the Army's resettlement project; the forming of an anti-tobacco legion and the beginning of leprosy work in Java.

Ten years later, in 1921, the third social conference was held; but fifty years were then to pass before the present event could be arranged. That intervening period probably saw the greatest technological development and social change in the history of mankind. Into that half-century was telescoped scientific progress equal in dimension and importance to that of several previous centuries and, consequently, social norms and needs had been drastically affected. The necessity for the 1972 conference was self-evident.

There was no question as to the need for, or the relevance of, social work in the Army's programme. That the end-objective of all such social service is the redemption of the total man was unarguably accepted. The ability of the Holy Spirit to use both the evangelical and social activity of Salvationists to God's glory was repeatedly emphasized as delegates participated in discussion and offered comment. Among them were a medical doctor, a solicitor, case-workers, managers of specialist institutions and services, as well as community workers. All felt that the burgemeester who extended official greeting showed discernment in his understanding of such officers' motivation. "Whenever I see a Salvationist," he said, "I seem to see a sash worn across the uniform on which are the words of Jesus: 'Without Me ye can do nothing.' "

It was my privilege to remind the delegates that the Army's social endeavours are based not only on the programme of the Early Church out of which flowed so many varied "works of mercy," but on the ministry and word of Jesus Himself. "The sight of the people moved Him to pity ... they were harassed and helpless" (Matthew 9: 36 NEB). In our Lord, Salvationist social workers have the incomparable example of One who identified Himself with the deprivations of people. A woman with haemorrhage is deprived of health. A man possessed by a legion of devils is deprived of his senses. A hungry multitude is deprived of bread. A dead daughter is deprived of life. Our Lord's ministry reveals His love, His care, His deep and practical concern over such deprivations. To the deprived He gave healing, sanity, satisfaction, even life itself. It is interesting to note that it is immediately after Matthew's comment concerning the compassion of Jesus, "The sight of the people moved Him to pity," that Jesus made His plea for labourers to work in the fields that were already "white unto harvest." The work done is therefore at the direct call of Christ.

Officers responsible for the Army's extensive medical work throughout South Asia met in Bombay in 1973 under the presidency of the late Colonel Daniel Andersen, MD (Lon.), FRCS (Eng.), DTM&H (Liv.) for crucial discussions about the future of the work. I arrived at the end of a tour in India in time to declare this conference officially convened and to wish the delegates success in their deliberations. On the medical and nursing horizons hovered clouds of uncertainty and perplexity. The day was approaching when some of our hospitals would have to rely on Indian doctors as chief medical officers; not that this was at all undesirable except in one aspect—such CMO's might not be Christian, and without the Christian influence, even though there would be no shortage of skill or compassion, one of the main purposes in operating such hospitals would be negated.

Colonel (Dr.) Andersen, while medical advisor at International Headquarters, and I had had many long conversations as to how best public health nursing in the areas surrounding our hospitals could be developed, a service for which there was desperate demand. It was also felt that our general hospitals could serve as supply bases for a number of satellite hospitals, clinics and dispensaries, thus extending their usefulness in a badly-needed outreach. On a later visit to India I saw this idea maturing successfully in Trivandrum and its surrounding villages. The Army's hospital work appears small in contrast to the nearly half-million active beds serving the sick in the sub-continent. I made this comment to the lady governor of Kerala and observed that our contribution was "only a drop in an ocean of need."

"Only a drop," she replied, "but it shines like a pearl."

CHAPTER 12

Pathway Of Duty

Not all projects begun in General Wickberg's term of leadership, and my own as Chief of the Staff, came quickly to realization. The desirability of amalgamating the social services of The Salvation Army in the United Kingdom led to serious discussions from the end of 1969 to February, 1971 with Commissioners Ernest Fewster, Governor of the Men's Social Services, and Julia Tickner, Leader of the Women's Social Services. Both arms of the social work were approaching the same authorities in the matter of per diem fees and capital grants, but on differing bases and often to the confusion of the deciding bodies. Standardization of the services being rendered was patently necessary, as was the closest possible relationship of all aspects of social endeavour in order to avoid either overlapping or omission. The progressive ideas of these leaders, and of certain of those who succeeded them, did not, however, mature until April, 1978, some months after I had returned to International Headquarters. The process of amalgamation will not, unfortunately, be complete until a way is found to bring in the Goodwill department. Administratively under the direction of the British Commissioner, it is essentially social work of a most direct person-to-person kind, but traditionally has operated under its own trust, inspired by its patron, Hugh Redwood, for many years Fleet Street's most eminent religious journalist.

Another illustration of early sowing and delayed reaping had to do with a revision of The Salvation Army's song book. Experts in this field say that a denomination's hymnary requires revision and re-issue at least every twenty-five years. In a quarter of a century styles change. Certain hymns fall into disuse. New ones catch the imagination and effectively enhance the spirit of worship. With this in mind, in 1974 I asked that a Song Book Council be instituted and be given ten years in which to prepare and release a new edition. To this the General gave ready assent. Returning to International Headquarters in 1977 I found that the council had been working seduously at what is an immense task. The necessity for balancing gospel-style songs against time-honoured, stately hymns led to an extensive canvass of the English-speaking areas of the world so that any greatly-loved and much-used congregational songs that were local favourites would not be omitted. My travels had made me aware of the rich compilations produced in languages other than English. From these, it was my hope, some of the choicest songs might be translated and used to stimulate spiritual blessing as powerfully as when sung in the language originally used by the poet.

*   *   *

General Wickberg's congress in Tokyo afforded me the privilege in May, 1970, of presiding over an historic valedictory meeting marking the end of the Army's use of its well-known Clapton Congress Hall in London. Formerly a children's orphanage, the spacious buildings, with their splendidly-columned entrance, had been the main venue for great meetings for eighty-eight years. At one period it had also housed a cadets' training centre. More significant Army events had taken place within its aging walls than in any other part of the world. Here Catherine Booth, William Booth, and their son Bramwell, the trio usually considered as "the founders" of the movement, had lain "in state." Delegates to the first international congress in 1886 had overflowed its precincts. Here also the Army's "Articles of Marriage" were pronounced for the first time. Massive musical festivals had been held in the arena-like hall attended by the Duke and Duchess of York, later Their Majesties King George VI and Queen Elizabeth; and, as music critic, by George Bernard Shaw. Here, too, the second High Council, weighted with the solemn responsibility of selecting General Edward Higgins's successor, held its sober deliberations.

For the veterans in attendance there was a tinge of sadness to the proceedings. With the expropriation of the property the visible reminder of a thousand lively memories would disappear. Some of those memories were graphically recalled by retired General Coutts, others by General Kitching, retired, who gave the main address. The crowd which filled the huge hall for the "leave-taking" may not have noticed when entering the building for the last time that the clock over the portico had stopped. Symbolically, both hands pointed heavenwards.

* * *

When William Booth died in 1912 the Army's flag had been unfurled in fifty-one countries. That number had greatly increased due to continuous pioneering and also to the growing number of sovereign states resulting from wars, secessions and political bargainings. The Great Commission, "Go ye into all the world and preach the Gospel to every creature," remains both a beacon and a challenge. There are still areas where Salvation Army service is needed. In early 1970 a Portuguese evangelist in the city of Porto made representations to International Headquarters asking that he and the company of people who looked to him for spiritual guidance might be recognized as a branch of The Salvation Army. He had come across a book, printed in Portuguese, dealing with William Booth and his work, and had first written to the Army in Brazil asking for information.

Investigation confirmed the group's sincerity and, with help provided by retired Portuguese-speaking officers who had served faithfully in Brazil and who were now living in Switzerland, the work began. It appeared to flourish. Uniformed Salvationists appeared on the streets and people were attracted to the meetings. The future looked promising. I invited the leader to London and in a Westminister Central Hall gathering he made a profound impression with his personal testimony and his glowing report of the work's development.

Few pioneering efforts in the Army's history, however, have had an unruffled career, and this was to be no exception. The Germans have a phrase for it: *"Aller Anfang ist schwer"*—"Every beginning is difficult." When consolidation of the work was thought necessary, I asked Major (now Colonel) and Mrs. Carl Eliasen if they would leave Brazil and direct the work in Portugal. They responded gladly. The evangelist, now an Envoy, resented the move and eventually withdrew. Not all who had been drawn to the Army followed him; though the sapling lost a number of its branches, the root had already gone deep into the soil of Portugal.

With the appointment of Lieut-Colonel and Mrs. Hubert Boardman the spiritual work was augmented by a strong social outreach that greatly interested the wife of the president of the republic, Donna Maria Manuela Ramatho Eanes, who gave it all possible support. When the president paid a state visit to the United Kingdom his wife, to the confusion of some Foreign Office officials, asked that her itinerary be altered in order to include a visit to our International Headquarters where she was suitably welcomed. At her request, my wife and I were among those invited to the glittering banquet tendered the president that evening in the Guildhall.

When leading congress meetings in Lisbon in 1980 I was able to see for myself the expansion of the work. Due to a strike by air traffic controllers I arrived from Madrid by train after an excruciating all-night journey seated bolt upright in a crowded compartment. For most of the tiring hours my left shoulder supported the lolling head of a drunken workman returning to his native city from employment in Saudi Arabia. I was enthusiastically welcomed by newly-uniformed Salvationists and warm-hearted supporters. In one of the gatherings I commissioned the first Portuguese-trained officer, a significant and emotional happening for the devoted band of pioneers. Madame Eanes invited me to take lunch with her at the presidential residence in the Palácio de Belém, after which we were joined by the president who proffered his thanks to the Army for becoming part of Portuguese life, and asked that he and his family might be included in the prayers of Salvationists.

If the whole of the Iberian Peninsula were to come under the Army's flag it meant pioneering the work also in Spain. "I wish they would let me open Madrid," George Scott Railton, William Booth's first lieutenant, said to his wife, Marianne, on his return from the Argentine in the mid-1890's. He spoke Spanish, and his opinion of the language was very high. He considered it well adapted for religious use—"the finest known to the lips of man, stately, dignified, with unparalleled scope for eloquence." These and other facts we learn from Bernard Watson's book, "Soldier Saint," a graphic biography of Railton's life. Far from well, but restless to obey the Great Commission, Railton went to Madrid. He was no stranger to Spain having visited the country as a youth enroute to Morocco and, later on, while doing business for a shipping firm. When good Spanish people were converted and social service began for the unemployed, the suspicion of the authorities was aroused. But it was, says Watson, the character and method of Railton himself which disarmed official hostility. Railton's major problem at the time was his anguished relationship with his superiors, and the period was described by his wife as "five months' utter loneliness in Madrid pioneering slumming work." In midsummer 1895 Railton was recalled to England, arriving in a serious condition of health. His final comment from Spain—"The great thing is to provide immediately for the future of Madrid"—was written from Barcelona where he was prospecting possibilities for expansion of the work.

Seventy-six years were to pass before another incursion was made into Spain to "provide for the future of Madrid." It came about in an interesting way. A member of one of Spain's fervent Protestant families, and his wife, had become Salvationists and were serving as envoys in Geneva, Switzerland. The territorial commander, Commissioner Francis Evans, suggested that if ever anyone was wanted for Spain this couple might be suitable. The thought took root. The proposal that Envoy and Mrs. Enrique Rey should be sent to Spain was approved by the Advisory Council to the General. Political changes had occurred in the country, and freedom of religion was to be part of the charter of human rights. On Ascension Day, 1971, during a large afternoon meeting in Zurich, the Reys knelt as the Army flag was lifted above them and were dedicated to their pioneering task. I appointed them to La Coruna, Spain, where they were known and where it had been decided the work would begin. I instructed them to go with the Bible in one hand and an Army flag in the other.

On the 24th of December, 1971, The Salvation Army was granted the status of a Legal Person enjoying full legal rights in the country with permission to carry on its work without let or hindrance, though, unhappily, certain difficulties in respect of the constitution arose later. Flowing from all parts of the world, financial support made possible the acquisition of properties in Coruna, Madrid and Barcelona. But the development of the work has been slow and, according to the 1982 Year Book, "severely hampered by a shortage of officers." If reckoned numerically the gains of a decade are few, but for every person brought to a new life in Christ or compassionately aided in His Name there can only be thanksgiving. In my final months as international leader I approved the appointment of Major and Mrs. Siegfried Clausen, who had served successfully in Chile, as joint leaders with the Reys in the hope that work could be developed in Barcelona, the city where Railton had completed his valiant but impermanent efforts in historic and lovely Spain.

When a meat exporter in the Argentine transferred his business to the Island of Tenerife, off the north-west coast of Africa, he carried his Salvationism with him and began the work in Santa Cruz. I was anxious that there should be an evaluation of it seeing official recognition was being requested. Coincidentally, while I was wishing Lieut-Colonel Cyril Barnes, the Army's archivist at International Headquarters, godspeed as he entered honourable retirement, he revealed that he and his wife were to celebrate the event with a short holiday in, of all places, Tenerife. I immediately appointed him as my "ambassador," and we sealed the "appointment" with prayer. When the Colonel contacted the Argentinian Salvationist he and his wife were given a demonstrative welcome and spent most of their vacation leading meetings and planning future outreach.

Tenerife is a volcanic peak, the highest of the Canary archipelago, and the volcano is not extinct. Had the environment, I sometimes pondered, anything to do with the eruption of feelings that came later? As in Portugal, the consolidation was temporarily hindered by the lava of misunderstanding that flowed over the little congregation when officers were appointed to advance the cause. Happily, the unrest subsided and, according to latest reports, "many young people have been attracted through the faithful service of the corps officers, and are now joining the ranks of the Army as fully-uniformed Salvationists. Some of them are already preparing themselves for future service as officers."

Other pioneering ventures requiring administrative attention, if not personal involvement, included Venezuela where the work began in 1972. True to pioneering tradition a number of problems arose, mostly in relation to the children's homes operated in cooperation with various authorities. Work in this country is now classified as a "region" under the direction of headquarters in Mexico City.

In 1973 a successful beginning was made in Fiji by New Zealand officers. Not long after their arrival they wished to send a message to headquarters in Wellington to say that all was well and that their reception had been cordial. There were difficulties of transmission, but, eventually, their message was picked up by a ham radio operator in Calgary, Alberta, and relayed from Canada back to New Zealand. As a Canadian I applauded this bit of Canadian helpfulness. The Fiji endeavour prospered and, in addition to the aggressive spiritual work there is now a farm and a rural youth hostel, a rehabilitation hostel for ex-offenders and a school for officers' training.

These were outreach developments that lustred the years spent as Chief of the Staff. But the period also held its fair share of distress. The fiery trials of Northern Ireland, Southern Africa and other strife-torn areas also affected the Army. All too many Salvationists were among those who experienced the pain of bitter conflict. Administratively there were the frustrations of refused or long-delayed entry permits regrettably confusing the inter-territorial movement of officers. Wildly fluctuating currency exchange rates and rampaging inflation worried those responsible for our financial equilibrium. There were, alas, more calls for service than our stretched resources could muster. Proposed legislation in various countries that could limit open-air meeting activity, affect the making of converts and the publishing of Army literature, caused anxiety. One might be tempted to ask if the period was one of singular perplexity or did it only seem so because we lived in it? It requires little beachcombing on history's sands to learn that each generation has its problems. They differ only in kind and intensity.

In the spiritual conflict not all battles are overwhelmingly victorious. There are retreats as well as advances. In late 1970 The Salvation Army was forced to withdraw from Algeria. Left behind were premises from which the Gospel had been faithfully preached and from which, in Annaba for example, food was distributed to the hungry until the last moment. The ministry of social action rejected all approaches seeking discussion and negotiation. Christian missionaries were asked to leave the country, and a number were expelled under a forty-eight hour time limit. The retreat was not accepted placidly by our administrators in France under whose supervision the work had been carried on. But protests were completely ignored. The work had officially begun in Algiers in 1934, though holidaying Salvationists nearly half a century earlier had devoted their vacation to evangelistic endeavour.

But the Salvation Army flag is a restless banner. Furled in Algeria it took flight to the moon. The wife of an advisory board member in Philadelphia, Pennsylvania, Mrs. John W. Chatley, Jr., asked Colonel John Young, commander of the Apollo 16 mission, if he would take three miniature Salvation Army flags to the moon. He agreed, and the venture was approved. While the flag was not actually "planted" on the moon, it has certainly preceded any future inhabitants who might require its message of hope. Visitors to the Franklin Institute can see one of the flags, permanently preserved, on display.

* * *

Early in General Wickberg's term of office, he and I were invited to No. 10 Downing Street by the Prime Minister, the Rt. Hon. Harold Wilson, MP., who by this time had been in office for a full five years. It was early evening and it was obvious that for Mr. Wilson it had been a gruelling day. He looked tired, and one could only speculate as to the kind of demanding decision-making conferences and interviews that had preceded our arrival. He was nevertheless patiently courteous and offered us both a "genuine Havana cigar," forgetting, or perhaps not knowing, that Salvation Army officers are non-smokers. He recalled that an art master who had made a great impression on him when a student, and with whom he had kept contact through the years, was now a Salvation Army officer, Lieut-Colonel George Carpenter (R), son of the Army's fifth general. The prime minister was keen to hear from General Wickberg his views about life in his native Sweden and the success of the Riksdag's expanding social security schemes. The conversation thereafter became a conspectus of the most important social welfare provisions in Sweden and the United Kingdom.

I had opportunity of asking the Prime Minister if, in view of the continuing refinement and elaboration of state-administered welfare services, he thought there would be a future for The Salvation Army and other voluntary societies in the field of social amelioration. His thoughtful answer was enlightening, and I have quoted it on many occasions. There would always be a need for the Army and other voluntary bodies, he said, for three chief reasons. Firstly, no matter how far-reaching are the state's benefits there would always be those who would "slip through the net," and someone would have to pick them up. Secondly, he regretted that the state does not usually discover human need. That is done by men and women of goodwill who bring the need to the attention of the authorities. They then, if they can, try to do something about it. He enlarged on this point by referring to the innovative expressions of social service accomplished by various humanitarian and philanthropic groups, something for which state budgets cannot make accommodation. His third reason was the most telling. The state, he said, administers social aid by the head; but people are human and they need the ministry of the heart. If the Army can function intelligently with the head, and compassionately with the heart, he emphasized, there would always be a place for its spiritual and social ministry. For those observations alone the call on the prime minister was exceedingly valuable.

* * *

The years following the Second World War had witnessed in the western world a distressing decline in Sunday School attendance. For this, many reasons were advanced. An increasing number of parents were now peripatetic during week-ends. Better times meant more automobiles and more mobility for the family. Perhaps nearer the real reason, dismayingly, was the disinclination of parents themselves towards church attendance, and the sad fact that teachers of capability and dedication had been in short supply. The importance of the Sunday school had been overshadowed by the demands of other interests, in the Army notably those of the musical sections.

The United Nations secretariat had announced that 1971 would be known as "The Year of the Child," and this made particularly germane the Army's organization of a global crusade under the simple but telling slogan, "Every Child Matters." So successfully did this campaign arouse concern for the child, his needs, his future and his spiritual education that in several parts of the Army world the effort, under the enthusiastic direction of Colonel Wm. Larson, was extended through the following year. It marked a definite turning point, not only with a welcome upsurge in Sunday School attendance, but with an increased sense of responsibility among adults for the child, "the fountain of the future" for society, the Christian church and The Salvation Army. Years later, when moving through the refugee camps in Thailand where scores of thousands of Kampucheans were being cared for, I saw hundreds of "children of misery," saved from the bullet, starvation or deadly disease, wearing T-shirts distributed by Salvationist nurses and relief workers bearing the words, "Every Child Matters." In those grim surroundings, and with the sound of gunfire only kilometres away, the validity of the slogan took on an ironical and disturbing meaning.

* * *

While numerous items of business engaged my mind, my heart kept turning to India and to a particular lack in our structure. The geographical layout of our territories in India had failed to recognize the importance of New Delhi's establishment as the federal capital when India, in 1950, became a republic. The Army's presence in this great city was insignificant, forestalling any close relationship with government ministries and ministers. Required was a strong presence in this centre of government and city of numerous embassies. Commissioner Arthur Hook, who knew India well and was responsible for the South Asia section of the overseas department at International Headquarters, became an enthusiastic collaborator. Together, but not easily, we found monies for the purchase of a property; but no property acquisition could possibly have engendered greater frustration. When premises appeared to be right for location, price, and with enough land for future development, the purchase, for one reason or another, could not be completed.

Photographs, architect's drawings, financial statements and property proposal forms flowed across our desks with mocking regularity, but the suitable site remained elusive. The matter was unresolved when I left the office of the Chief of the Staff to return to Canada. Though the search went on, not until I was once again in London did the miracle happen. As a first move the audit office was transferred from Pune (formerly Poona), and a children's home was also opened. With a redeployment of headquarters staffs New Delhi became the control centre for the newly-formed Northern India territory, Calcutta remaining the headquarters city for the Eastern Indian territory which would also embrace Bangladesh and Burma. Nowhere else had the Army been so meagrely represented in a national capital; to know that now the Army in India was at last as well placed administratively as in any other country was cause for immense satisfaction.

* * *

Invited to join him for lunch, I met the late Mr. Garfield Weston, a fellow-Canadian and one of the Army's most generous benefactors, in his private rooms at Fortnum and Mason's exclusive Picadilly store, in London. He was the founder of a successful family business with multinational interests, but possessed a simplicity of manner and a directness of speech. His interest in The Salvation Army was the result of a Salvationist nanny's care of him during his earliest years. While his parents worked long hours in the bakery below the Toronto apartment in which they lived, this unknown Salvationist filled his life with activity and affection. Often she took him to what was then known as magic-lantern displays at a nearby Salvation Army corps hall. One of them, he told me, was the melodramatic story of a young and lovely girl lying helplessly on the railway tracks while a death-dealing train raced towards her. He was gripped by the pathos of the scene and remembered that, at the moment of disaster, recorded angelic voices sang softly, "Safe in the arms of Jesus." He had had a rich family life, with nine children of whom he was tremendously proud, and a gracious, devoted wife. "When she was being buried," said Mr. Weston, "all I could think of in that moment of infinite loss were those angelic voices and the hymn, 'Safe in the arms of Jesus.'"

During lunch he intimated that it was his wish to give the Army a large tract of unbroken land adjoining Ontario's Algonquin Provincial Park. The area was rich in natural beauty with lovely lakes, quiet waterways and heavy forests, and with buildings that would accommodate some of the young people he wanted to enjoy seeing the pristine loveliness of Canada. Could we use it for this purpose? I assured him that we could, and would give an undertaking to so use it for at least ten years. To this he agreed.

I was overwhelmed by this act of generosity and the intention that had spurred it, and said so. He laughed, and told me that one of my predecessors, General Kitching, had been to see him in the hope of a donation that would clear the debt on the new International Headquarters building. Mr. Weston evidently told the General that he did not contribute to the cost of administrative buildings, but gave only to projects which directly served the needs of people. "The General was disappointed," said Mr. Weston, "but I comforted him by saying that it was my intention, if I lived until October of that year, to make a substantial settlement on the Army. I then asked the General if he would pray and, when he did," said Mr. Weston, "he fervently, but reverently, asked that I might live beyond October and, indeed, for many years." The simplicity and humour of it pleased Mr. Weston. As I was leaving, he asked smilingly if I would pray and, if I wished, petition that still more time might be granted him! I prayed that within the will of God it might be so.

Within days, General Clarence Wiseman, the Commissioner and territorial commander for Canada, was flown over to London by Mr. Weston and, together with his legal advisors we again met in the private dining room where papers concluding the arrangement were exchanged. Thanks to Mr.Weston's vision and magnanimity thousands of young people have delighted in the surroundings at Madawaska and have learned the enchantment of "the common sun, the air, the skies," amid the incomparable beauty of undisturbed land and timeless waters.

* * *

Those who ascribe a Victorianism to Salvation Army uniform would be surprised to learn how often through a century it has been modified to maintain a relationship with current modes of dress or to suit climatic conditions. As Chief of the Staff I was requested by leaders in the more western parts of the world to abandon the high-collar tunic in favour of the lapel jacket worn with collar and tie by the men, and with blouse and brooch by the women, until now used only as summer apparel. The bonnet, long an expressive symbol of the Army, was now costly to produce due to the problem of securing the right kind of straw and the expensiveness of silk ribbon. A modish hat had been designed which was cheaper, easy to care for and to carry; it was intended to be worn with the lapel uniform. The "new look" proved to be a newsworthy item, and was featured in everything from village weeklies to the world's leading fashion magazines. While the bonnet had never been seen, let alone worn, in many of the countries in which the Army operates, it was sacrosanct in others; no-one wanted to be responsible for its demise. If the "new look" was referred to approvingly by the media or the public, the historic symbolism of the bonnet was unfailingly mentioned with affection.

What was officially desired was the maintaining of recognizability and uniformity, so that whether with bonnet or hat, one style is now the set standard throughout a country or group of adjacent countries. Not long after the burst of publicity concerning the "new look" my wife and I were invited to a garden party at Buckingham Palace. Our daughter, Beverley, accompanied us, she in lapel uniform and hat and my wife in the traditional bonnet and high-collar uniform. Both, in my masculine estimation, wore the differing uniforms attractively. Literally, a score of people, undoubtedly with recent press comments in mind, stopped us in order to compare the two. Younger observers voted wholeheartedly for for the "new look." Older commentators whispered, "Whatever you do, don't do away with that beautiful bonnet." Almost the same words were addressed to Mrs. General Wickberg and my wife as, on another occasion, we sat at tea with the Queen Mother in St. James's Palace. At the garden party nothing at all was said about the uniform I or the other male Salvationists wore. It was obvious, however, that I had been accompanied not only by a wife and daughter, but by two keenly-observed mannequins!

Whatever the variations in Salvation Army uniform, and I once counted fourteen differing forms of it, I found in my journeys that it was in itself a passport into places of both high and low estate. It took me past guards and sentries into the company of monarchs and heads of state. It also permitted me to walk safely through the busties of Calcutta, the barracas of Lisbon and the shanty-towns of many great cities. It made me the recipient of numerous confidences and the repository of the secret anxieties of tycoons and statesmen. To the lonely and friendless the uniform bespeaks friendship and sympathy and, for what it represents, and for what it has allowed me to represent, I can only hope that the uniform will continue to be the "livery of the Lord's own."

* * *

Official duties left little time for personal excursions. I wanted, however, to pay a visit to the North Tottenham corps where my parents had been stationed at the time of my birth. The corps officer was equally desirous that I should. On arrival I was shown into the office where, thoughtfully, the dedication register had been laid on the desk. I immediately recognized my father's handwriting and read the entry concerning my own dedication. I noted with surprise that the ceremony had been conducted by my father himself, and that during the same ceremony two other infants had been given back to God, also by my father. I looked at the name of one and wondered out loud where he might be now. To my amazement, the officer said, "He's right here beside you." He was the corps sergeant-major. "And where," I queried, "might this other child be today?" Almost unbelievably the officer said, "He's playing in the band that you hear".

The divergent ways in which life can be cast was vividly illustrated by this incident. I had visited so many parts of the world and had experienced so much of the variety of life; the other two had remained faithful to God and the Army within a limited sphere, and inwardly I saluted them for it. It was a moment to remember when I called the two to my side and, as an unrehearsed trio, on the same platform where we had been given back to God fifty-six years before, we sang, "All through the years His providence has led me,/ His abounding goodness has been all my song ..."

* * *

A Sunday morning experience of another kind came on July 12, 1970. The date is specified because it was the occasion of the first colour telecast in the United Kingdom of a complete Salvation Army meeting. It originated, appropriately, from the William Booth Memorial Halls corps in Nottingham, the Founder's city, and I had been invited to lead the gathering and to give the address. With only three television channels available to British viewers, any appearance is seen and heard by an audience numbering millions. The post-telecast comments were encouraging. The intrusion of brilliant lighting, moving cameras and silent but observable signals from the production crew did not lessen a wholesome spirit of worship for those present, or diminish an earnest proclamation in music, song and word of the Good News of the Gospel for those of the television audience.

It has been said that "freedom is opportunity to make decisions and character is the ability to make right decisions." Of the making of decisions as Chief of the Staff there was no end; they could not be avoided. One could not simply put on one's cap and go home. If one did this, the unresolved matter remained, lurking on the desk until the moment of return. A decision which was received with more than ordinary interest by many, since it appeared to erode a time-honoured regulation and run counter to a long-standing principle of officership, had to do with permitting the marriage of a retired officer to a non-officer. Journalists writing about the Army seemed always to be fascinated by the fact—which they considered curious, or an invasion of privacy—that a Salvation Army officer was permitted to marry only another officer. In numerous interviews around the world I was asked why this should be so. Usually accepted was the explanation that with the changes of location and kinds of work that frequently affect an officer's life, a mutuality of commitment is essential. Spouses have to be ready to accompany their partner anywhere at any time. Only if both are fully-persuaded officers can the system function successfully and happily. Such requirements, however, are obviated once an officer has retired from active service. In the South Asian and African countries, generally speaking, only married couples had been accepted as officers. The possibility of an officer widow or widower finding an unmarried officer of the opposite sex was limited, if not remote. It was thought by many to be unfair to deny such retired officers the companionship they might desire, or even need, in their declining years.

The matter went to a study group which recommended that provided a retired officer's choice of partner was a uniform-wearing Salvationist in good standing, such a marriage should be allowed. The non-officer partner would not take the rank of the marrying officer or be regarded in any way as an officer. In preparing the draft minute I was surprised to discover that the proposal was not new. It had indeed been recommended nearly thirty years before and had actually been approved. For some mysterious reason, unrevealed by the files, the approval had been withdrawn.

* * *

When appointed Chief of the Staff I had telephoned my mother, widowed for many years and living with my sister in Southbourne, to give her the news. She startled me by commenting, "I wondered if something like this might happen," adding with maternal concern, "but, Arnold, do you really think you can do it?" Her apprehension was understandable. Her memory embraced all of my predecessors. For her, they were holders of high office, "distant and dignified," and it was doubtless difficult for her to accept that one of her own sons was to follow in their formidable footsteps. Her satisfaction, regrettably, was short-lived. Well into her "eighties," and a remarkably active woman, she donned her Salvation Army uniform and on Sundays climbed the steep streets to the Pokesdown Salvation Army corps hall in order to worship with her comrades and friends until, with increasing illness, she could do it no longer. With failing strength she continued to encourage my wife and me with letters that grew shorter as the springtime of 1970 lengthened. The handwriting, once attractively meticulous, reflected a diminishing control of the pen. Her last letter dealt far more with the seriousness of our responsibilities than with her own life's ebbing tide. In April, having just passed her eighty-fourth birthday, she donned her "heavenly uniform" and entered into that unknown land where she was confident she would know and be known by the husband whose spirited and loving presence she, and we, had sorely missed for so long.

The simple Salvation Army funeral service and the quiet interment in a peaceful Dorset cemetery at Lilliput, brought together for the first time in thirty-six years all of her four children, two Salvation Army officers, a naval officer, and a devoted church-worker sister for whose unfailing care of their mother her brothers can never be grateful enough.

What, I wondered as I conducted the commital ceremony, would have been my path through life had not the angelic little woman whose remains were being lowered reverently into the earth, led me, as a child kneeling beside her, into an intimate relationship with Christ as Saviour, Lord and Friend?

CHAPTER 13

Troubled Seas

The General's intimation, when appointing me as his Chief of the Staff, that there were some hard decisions to be made was accepted simply as conversational comment—until I had been at the new desk for a few minutes. On it, was a large file concerning an officer's alleged insubordination about which I had heard nothing, so confidential are such matters kept by responsible officers. The problem concerned a man I knew well, and one who was greatly respected by his colleagues. This made the reading of the correspondence all the more depressing. There is no value in rehearsing the details. All the chief participants concluded their active officership honourably, and, if the episode is mentioned at all, it is because, from adjudicating the issues, my own administrative knowledge was considerably extended.

A court-martial had already been conducted and the officer had been found guilty on several counts of "conduct unbecoming an officer," and approval for his dismissal had been requested. The defendant had exercised his right of appeal and the case, with all the papers, had come to International Headquarters. The appeal was based on the invalidity of the court and its procedures according to the defendant's interpretation of the *Orders and Regulations Governing Courts of Investigation* (revised and re-issued in 1976 under the title, *Commissions of Enquiry*). In asking for an appeal to be recognized the officer had the sympathetic support of a number of his peers, themselves appreciated officers. To overturn the court's proceedings would have meant a new trial by officers previously uninvolved and unaware of the case. This would entail a different, and perhaps distant, location, and the participation of members senior to those who had participated in the original proceedings.

I foresaw the case lengthening into infinity and escalating in bitterness and decided, with some nagging reservations, not to overturn the court-martial, but to assume the powers vested in me by virtue of the office held, and personally to adjudicate on each of the counts on which the court had found the defendant guilty. The way in which the case was handled revealed the extreme and costly lengths to which the administration will go in order to bring such undesirable combat to an armistice. Twice I set up a Panel of Guidance to examine and re-examine all the evidence with total objectivity, seeing I wanted to avoid being the victim of either too much or too little sympathy when rendering judgement. A special envoy was despatched to the country in which the officer was serving, and a meeting was held with him in a secret location in order to preserve confidentiality. Twice the territorial leader came to International Headquarters in an effort to resolve a matter which had caused pain far beyond its importance and the hardening of attitudes which, it was feared, might move the matter into the civil courts or result in a "trial by media."

According to Volume IV of the Army's official history, "scarcely a week went by in the movement's early days when William Booth was not the subject of libel or slander by those who had once fought under his flag, and these last caused him the deepest grief." That such problems are now rare perhaps explains why a leader's spirit can be so disproportionately disturbed when a case occurs requiring only internal discipline and quite without the litigation that so often plagued the Founder.

I am strongly of the opinion that the court-martial is a procedure to be avoided if at all possible. It is worth noting that in a case in which an officer had sued for wrongful dismissal, a Manchester assize court had entered judgement for William Booth, revealing the important fact that a Salvation Army court-martial's decision cannot well be disputed in law by a person who had submitted to appear before such a tribunal. But rather than a court-martial, I feel, each of the several rungs of the administrative ladder should be allowed to provide a step towards the reconciling of differences. Only when the charges are of the gravest and most deplorable nature, and only when a defendant is so sure of his innocence that he is willing for all the details to be aired, does a court-martial appear to be justified. There are not many such instances. If there has been a serious misdemeanour there is usually a resignation. Few offenders want indictment and dismissal.

Only moments of the reader's time will have been occupied in noting the previous paragraphs, but the unhappy case dragged on for months with wearying intransigence. It was nearly three years before a final administrative act closed the file and complete reconciliation was gratifyingly achieved. I had been saddened, as were many others, but was considerably wiser.

More turbulent waters swirled ahead with what came to be referred to euphemistically as "the censorship issue." Officers engaged in editorial work voluntarily assign all rights in respect of their writings to the Army. Like all journalists or editors they are responsible to a publisher, and must accept his scrutiny in the interests of accuracy, appropriateness and conformity to the purpose of the periodical. Through the Army's history and a long line of eminent editors this has been clearly understood, and one can only marvel at the editorial and journalistic talent that has come the Army's way as a result of an officer's dedication of his gifts. It was, therefore, surprising that a small group of officer-editors at the international centre felt that they were writing with "a restrictive eye constantly peering over the shoulder." Nothing could have been farther from reality. Galley and page proofs of periodicals issued in the United Kingdom are customarily seen by the General, the Chief of the Staff and the British Commissioner. Any of the three has the right to question an item on the basis of some particular information he might have, but the questioning has always been minimal, and then only with the thought of saving an editor from himself. Style was never questioned; there was no need. Any comment usually had to do with fact.

Beneath the unrest of the group was the desire for freedom to report critically on public meetings conducted by leaders and upon organizational procedures and structures—a dangerous path to follow since the group's members were not, in my estimation, suitable candidates to stand as "the corporate conscience," or to represent "the public mind." Also subsumed, it was suspected, was an aspiration to parade as "the opposition" to the administration on any point the group wished, though without wide administrative experience and, in some respects, without the capability for it. Salvation Army periodicals do not exist in order to arouse controversy, except perhaps in the challenging of evil. They exist as aids to evangelism in the cause of Christ. The Army requires in its writers the ability to shed new light on old truths, to use their pens so that believers may be strengthened in their faith and inspired in their witness, and in so vivid a way that unbelievers might be persuaded for Christ. To do this in these times calls for the highest of skills. What the Army does not need are writers who bemuse the very people who should be helped; writers given to brilliant denigration of the very things for which the movement stands, and of the movement itself. It is far easier to write a column of criticism which ends as scintillating sawdust than to grip the mind of a reader with a simple truth so engagingly written that it cannot be left unread.

It was against this kind of background that international notoriety surrounded the termination of a well-known and highly-talented officer's service. He had been, it was thought, greatly influenced by Bishop John Robinson's theological expositions at the time of the "Honest to God" furore, and felt that the new, exciting insights that had come to him must be shared in book form. A sabbatical with allowances and the provision of accommodation was granted, a novel departure from traditional Army procedure, on the understanding that the manuscript would be submitted before publication, as all manuscripts are, for approval. Alas, the promise was not kept. When the manuscript was eventually seen, final arrangements with a publisher had already been sealed.

The officer was dealt with on the basis of his broken promise, but, having decided that nothing in the manuscript would be altered or deleted, he turned to the media for support. A campaign was instituted attacking the Army for its "unwarranted censorship" against which, I insisted, the Army's only retaliation would be "no comment." For the publishers of the book it was free publicity beyond the wildest of hopes, and letter-editors of the national newspapers were provided with a flood of material, pro and con. Three church leaders called on the General suggesting that the matter should be placed on the agenda of the next meeting of the British Council of Churches when the Army could then explain its position. They were forthrightly reminded that none of them would appreciate the Army's interference in a matter which was of their own private, denominational concern, and the proposal was quickly dropped.

The author finally permitted his superior to see a copy of the manuscript "as a courtesy." Greatly distressed, the superior remarked on several passages that evoked uneasiness, and brought them to my attention. It was my desire to discuss the content of the manuscript with the writer in the hope that any questionable passages might somehow be rephrased, since no-one in the administration wished to lose the services of this officer for whom I, personally, had great regard. Much of the manuscript, indeed most of it, was excellent, and was written with the literary quality we had come to expect from this journalist's pen. The special work he had initiated among the young, and his compassionate contacts with the spiritually abandoned in the core of the city, made inspiring reading. There were, unfortunately, theological assertions that went far beyond Salvation Army orthodoxy.

I noted with regret in one of my reports that "this officer feels that the Army 'system' has, in his word, 'corrupted' those who have not been free to express themselves honestly in their writing. He feels strongly that Salvation Army authority has no right to claim a greater degree of infallibility than they possess. I questioned his use of the word, 'censorship.' He would not accept that those who would rule on his manuscript would only try to be helpful. He is convinced that we are only interested in 'protecting the establishment'; that we cannot face any truth that is 'controversial,' and that we do not want 'dialogue.' He rejected the thought that any emendations suggested would be 'for the greatest good of the greatest number' within an Army context. He wants 'self-imposed discipline' in the Army, and I asked where this would lead us in music, platform utterance, programme and function."

It was sickening to read, day after day, one-sided comments in the press, even though the "no comment" stance was of our own making. It was equally dismaying to hear the matter discussed by radio panels whose participants completely ignored the fact that a promise made at the start of one's officership is a promise to be kept; or to see television interviews, from which we deliberately excluded ourselves, conveniently forgetting that a dissident officer has two courses of action before him: he can by proper means seek the review of any regulation by which he is bound, or he can resign his commission. A number of those who had valued the author's leadership as their corps officer realized that an officer who flouts a regulation immediately forfeits the right to expect that those in his charge will abide by *their* promises. He completely loses the authority and integrity of personal example, and the use of the mass media to justify repudiation of his commitments can only put his leaders, and his followers, in an impossible position.

The ill-balanced reporting of certain newspapers inflamed the situation. Naturally, many journalists have no conception of an officer's pledges, nor any understanding of the Army's aims and international responsibilities. One national newspaper found it necessary to publish two half-hearted corrections of glaring inaccuracies. A sensational press is not a trustworthy medium of debate on a matter affecting the service and conscience of Salvation Army officers. Yet some assumed that our repeated refusal to discuss the issue with media people indicated that we had no logical position to state, failing to realize that the Army will never resort to an expression of its position through the media, even to its own cost, while there remains hope of reconciling a situation within the Army fellowship.

The unhappy conflict continued throughout the first half of 1970, and in writing to territorial commanders I quoted the New English Bible's rendering of Paul's words to the Philippians, "I have been very thoroughly initiated into the human lot with all its ups and downs. But it was kind of you to share the burden of my troubles." Following a final and inconclusive interview with the author, I wrote to him pointing out that the fact he was determined not to submit his manuscript for discussion, even though this was a condition of the special arrangements made for his extended furlough, was deeply regretted. That he should have taken to the radio, television and the press to denigrate the Army's recognized procedures was a breach of his commission and must call into question his loyalty to the movement. I stated my objection to the way in which the term "censorship" (which does not appear anywhere in any of our regulations) was continually being invested with a despotic and negative meaning. I stressed the fact that our periodicals are "official organs." Those entrusted with final responsibility for the Army are also responsible to see that these further the end-aims of the movement.

Though the manuscript had not been officially submitted, I later asked the author if I might comment upon certain passages in it, and to this he agreed. I expressed disappointment that, as often as not, the words "evangelist" and "evangelism" were used in ways that could hardly be equated with the spirit that would supposedly animate his concept of a "community of loving tolerance." His argument that people can, and do, find in the field of their own non-religious commitment an experience of reality which is as valid as the believer's awareness of God in Christ could not be, as he wished, accepted by us as the equivalent of an "orthodox" Christian experience. His thesis that God is present "somehow" in persons and in their mutual relationships, particularly their "loving relationships," and that Christ is "somehow" personified, or shines forth in these, implied a kind of generalized incarnation which, if it did not explicitly deny it, at least rendered unnecessary, so far as such persons are concerned, the Divine incarnation uniquely present in the historic Jesus of Nazareth.

At the risk of being dubbed conservative or reactionary, I reminded the author that The Salvation Army is composed of men and women who believe that "God was in Christ reconciling the world unto Himself"; that forgiveness of sin is possible only through the redemptive act of Calvary and the regenerative work of the Holy Spirit, and that by these means alone can man be made "a new creature." It was therefore obvious that blessing could not be given to the publication of a book which rendered this basic Christian message in any degree superfluous.

I set up, with the General's agreement, a Panel of Guidance comprised of the author's peers, all of whom would claim to be not only his colleagues but his friends. As a result, one of the group was selected to visit the author and his wife and to offer them goodwill and persuasion. The visit was made, but without any notable result, and the episode moved on to its unsatisfactory conclusion with the loss of the officer and his wife. Others who had raised strident anti-"censorship" voices left for other reasons. For the Army's leaders it was a matter of sorrow that they had failed to persuade a respected officer to drop his arbitrary demand for an immediate end to a regulation which requires all officers to secure an imprimateur on material intended for publication, a demand which he had not previously made through official channels. The loss was costly and hurtful, as is the loss of any officer of the author's calibre.

More than a decade has since passed, and one cannot help wondering what are the present thoughts of those who were the principal participants. For me, it is as Ovid says, "part of grief to remember."

If the two preceding episodes sprang from misguided intention, another which aroused a good deal of public comment arose from a most laudable motive. A former French artillery officer, Commissioner Gilbert Abadie, when a brigadier and the training principal in Paris, was shocked by the pornography being flaunted on every hand and against which the police could not, or would not, take action. He made a vow that he would, at a Divinely-provided moment, make a determined protest that would call the people of France to rise up in protection of "the dignity of man."

That moment came when the production, "Hair," arrived in Paris. Planned with the precision of a military action, and with every element of surprise, Salvation Army officers in the audience suddenly rose and interrupted the performance. The Commissioner, now in charge of the Army's work in France, with tremendous courage, and using a loudhailer, rebuked the "nudity, obscenities and eroticism" with which the play was loaded. In the theatre the reaction was one of amusement. According to one leading newspaper, "the cast good-naturedly allowed Abadie to have his say, then went on with the show to the applause of a packed house." Beyond the theatre, however, public reaction was widespread in favour of the Commissioner's action. He was interviewed many times, and his strong views, articulately presented, were heard in most French-speaking parts of the world. Numerous articles in newspapers and magazines appeared throughout all of the European countries. Following an ecumenical week of prayer, a mass rally, asserting that man's self-respect and dignity were being seriously endangered, was held in the Palais de Mutualité, in Paris. News teams from half-a-dozen French and European television companies covered the event which, while organized by the Army, was presided over by the Auxiliary Bishop of Paris, with clergy and members of parliament participating.

Not all of the French public supported the campaign, *"Pour la Dignité de l'Homme."* At Lyons the Commissioner had to escape through a window because of a tempestuous crowd. The riot squad's intervention resulted in some two hundred persons being detained by the police. Nor did all officers agree with the tactics that had been employed. When a silent march of some hundreds of protesting Salvationists and friends approached the Théatre de la Porte Saint-Martin where the offensive show was playing, they were met by a small group who felt that the public rallies had gone too far in castigating the very youth towards whom they were carefully building bridges of understanding and friendship. Carrying placards bearing such slogans as, "No! to insults to young people. Yes! to The Salvation Army," the group of young *contestataires* collided with the main march. The outcome was general confusion and a spate of media reports which threatened to nullify the thrust of the original protest.

Employees and residents of homes managed by certain of the young officers took their side, and another protest took place outside of the National Headquarters, again with the press "just happening" to be present. This further disturbed Salvationists throughout the country who, unaware of all the circumstances, found themselves the objects of commendation or criticism. They were the recipients of questions for which they did not have the answers. What had begun as an heroic act of a strong-minded leader now seemed to generate uncertainty and unrest among the officers, some of whom, unwittingly, were exploited by the press which obviously wanted every minor misunderstanding to be fanned into headlines, and as sensationally as possible.

My wife and I have a special affection for France and the French people. French Salvationists are unquestionably among the most devoted in the world. Monsieur le Senator Chérioux, in welcoming us to the Hôtel de Ville in Paris, said he "saluted the sublime courage of those French men and women who wear the uniform of the Salvationist." While the Army's social work in that country is large and impressive, its evangelical work, pursued with prayerful tenacity, is not as rewarding as the dedicated officers and soldiers would wish. Faith persists nevertheless, and one has only to spend time with one of the congregations to sense the earnestness in prayer, the vitality of testimony and the responsiveness to Biblical teaching.

For these reasons, as well as the desire to prevent a most worthy enterprise from backfiring into disagreement and disunity, I asked a capable officer to go from International Headquarters as an intermediary and to do everything necessary to effect a *rapprochement.* Feelings had been wounded, unfortunately. Misunderstanding had multiplied, and inflammatory words had been said that threatened polarization. The report brought back by the negotiating officer was unsettling, and I asked the General if I might myself go to Paris and make whatever helpful intervention I could.

My arrival was timely. Two groups of officers, one from the north and one from the south got to Paris about the same time as I did. Their mission was to register criticism that International Headquarters had not acted quicker and more forcefully in settling what had become an unwanted division among the officers. I agreed to see them, and, one by one, they presented their views. I, on my part, tried to make it clear that International Headquarters had done, and was doing, everything possible to ensure that unity of purpose and service on the part of the French officers would be maintained. For me personally, it was an ordeal that stretched throughout the whole of a day and into the hours of the next morning, without cessation. Translation was necessary so that everything said was clearly understood, and this greatly lengthened the proceedings. I sought to draw from each officer a pledge of unqualified loyalty to his calling and to the Army. The sincerity of response moved me deeply. With each officer there was a period of prayer and, while at the end I felt drained of spirit and weary in body, I was convinced that in the long term the crusade which had rocked France had not capsized the Army ship.

Ten years later, attending the Army's centenary and facing the immense crowd which filled the Salle de Pleyel, in Paris, I rejoiced that the dramatic protest against pornography had been made. The French public's admiration for *L'Armée du Salut* had not in any way diminished but, it seemed to me, had increased. The strains of 1970 were lost in the congress triumphs of 1980!

CHAPTER 14

Time For Change

It is the Chief of the Staff's responsibility to call together the High Council, that body which, by Act of the British Parliament, elects the General. With the retirement of General Wickberg I would not only attend my first High Council but would also be legally accountable for its proper convening. What I expected to be a fascinating but routine procedure, there being full information on file for guidance, became instead a hard lesson in legality.

Some months before the Qualifying Date (a date specified in the constitution on which, by reason of rank or appointment held, members "qualify" to receive a summons to attend a High Council) certain officers raised the question in both correspondence and interview of their eligibility for membership of the High Council due to meet in May, 1974. My response was that their rank and status at the Qualifying Date, March 6, 1974, would determine their presence or absence. If they qualified, it would be my duty to call them. If they did not qualify, it was not within my power to summon them. I knew that it would be my obligation to explain to the satisfaction of the High Council the absence of any officer who, it was thought, should have attended; and, equally, to justify the presence of any officer who, it was considered, should not have attended. Within my personal understanding of the constitution the officers in question did not presently qualify. My views, while appearing to be accepted in discussion, were not found convincing by the appellants, and I therefore decided that the matter should be referred to the Army's solicitors. They stated their belief that the officers would not qualify unless promoted to the rank of Commissioner before the Qualifying Date, since they could not, in their present appointments, be considered as "territorial commanders" within the meaning of the constitution.

One of the officers asked if he could seek an independent legal opinion. I said that, to my mind, he had the right to take such action. By this time I had concluded that the matter should be referred to Learned Counsel, the highest possible adjudication outside a court of law, for two reasons: (1) in order that the claimants themselves might be totally satisfied that the High Council membership was scrupulously determined, and (2) that I personally had done all possible to ensure that this was so.

I arrived at the Inns of Court and made my way up a winding staircase to the office of the Learned Counsel whose opinion on this sensitive issue would be our source of legal guidance. A strike by electric power workers had blacked out London and reduced industry to a three-day working week. I groped my way in the half-light of the late afternoon past offices that appeared to be quite uninhabited, and speculated as to whether this was what Wordsworth had in mind with his "purlieus of the law." There was no need to knock on the door of the eminent solicitor's office. It was wide open, and I was immediately invited in. Behind the desk, gowned and heavily bespectacled, sat my advisor. On the desk burned a common white candle embedded in its own melted wax in the centre of a large ashtray. On all the walls, floor to ceiling, were shelves lined with leather-bound volumes. They enshrined, I supposed, the judgements of the courts in cases celebrated or unrenowned, all waiting possible recall to serve as precedents in future cases, celebrated or unrenowned. The flickering candlelight did little to illuminate "the majesty of the law."

Learned Counsel leaned across the desk and handed me a ten-page Opinion. I read: "This is not a matter which the court (if the matter were ever unhappily to come before a court) would be able to decide by inspection of the constitutional documents alone; for these contain neither a definition of a territorial command, nor an exposition of the functions performed by the officers in question. The court would therefore have to seek enlightenment elsewhere. I have no doubt that it would without hesitation turn first to the orders and regulations. These are not part of the constitution, but they do contain an elaborate, formal exposition of the structure, organization and methods of The Salvation Army; and, as such, they provide by far the most weighty evidence as to the meaning of the words used in the constitutional documents."

There followed numerous specific references from our orders and regulations on which Counsel—beside whom, piled on the desk, were copies of all of the Army's regulations, minutes and memoranda—had based his conclusion: "It is my opinion that the officers in question are not qualified to receive summonses for, or to participate in, the meeting of the High Council."

I found it extremely disconcerting to pass on this decision, but I was legally and morally bound to do so. The officers concerned were both colleagues and friends. So far as I personally was involved their presence at the High Council would only have enlarged the fellowship and added to the Council's wisdom. But I was bound by the law, and the very letter of it. I was reminded how much can turn on a single word, a phrase or a sentence, and in order to obviate future misinterpretation, the Memoranda of Appointment in respect of the two positions under review were subsequently altered. With the revision and re-issue of *Orders and Regulations for Officers* there was further clarification. A similar situation is unlikely ever to recur. The subject was briefly raised while the High Council was being formally convened, but the Army's solicitor gave explanations that clearly satisfied the questioners.

The day before the High Council began its work, members were entertained at a reception in St. James's Palace graced by the radiant presence of Her Majesty, Queen Elizabeth the Queen Mother. I was privileged to escort her and present the delegates, a number of whom she had met before in her travels. When introducing Mr. F. Cox, then chairman of the Army's Southampton advisory board, the Queen Mother enquired about the medal he was wearing. "It's an Order I can't quite place," she commented. I explained that it was the medal of the Order of Distinguished Auxiliary Service, given to those friends of the Army who had made a significant contribution to the progress of the Army's work. "Then it's one of the best of all recognitions," said Her Majesty.

With General and Mrs. Wickberg my wife and I were honoured to take tea with Her Majesty. Suddenly, our table became the focus of attention with the excited arrival of the Royal Corgies and their loudly-barked thanks for the under-the-table bits of pastry surreptitiously provided by their Royal owner. As I accompanied the Queen Mother back to her apartments she said how inspiring she always found the company of Salvationists to be, a compliment I found it easy to return on behalf of the High Council members. One of them, commenting on the Queen Mother's regality and friendliness, declared wistfully, "I wish we had her, or one like her, in our country!" Where he was serving there had just been a violent *coup d'état!*

Council members also viewed one of London's private and architecturally elegant venues in the heart of the City of London when entertained to dinner by the London advisory board in the Hall of the Haberdashers' Company. Talented Salvationist-musicians added their festival greetings. This relaxation, together with a Rotary luncheon in the famed Café Royale, during which General Wickberg was the speaker, and a public welcome salute in the Westminster Central Hall, "the cathedral of Methodism," were the only absences from Sunbury Court which for ten days held the members, with their solemn purpose, within its Georgian confines. For those new to Sunbury court, the mansion held historical and aesthetic interest. It was acquired in 1925 by General Bramwell Booth at a very reasonable figure, the intention being to use it as a staff college. Tradition has it that in the time of the Plantagenets it was used as an annexe by courtiers and counsellors visiting the nearby Hampton Court or the royal Windsor Castle a few miles upstream. The grandeur of the crystal chandelier in the lounge is matched by the beauty of the murals painted in oil on to the plaster by the Swedish artist, Elias Martin, between 1768 and 1780 for the 2nd Earl of Pomfret.

Others have written of their High Council participation, though for every member, I suspect, there are personal and private memories. All agree, however, that the procedures of the High Council in selecting an international leader for the Army are more a spiritual exercise than the employment of ordinary electoral processes. The incomparable fellowship, heightened by much prayer and reading of the Scriptures, has all the features of a highly devotional spiritual retreat. Imperceptibly, appraisals of possible nominees are shaped and, as voting time draws nearer, a sense of guidance, flowing from the Holy Spirit's presence, possesses the delegates' minds and hearts. My feelings as a first-time attendant were sharply intensified when I was nominated as a candidate for the generalship. Though I occupied the No. 1 seat in the council chamber by virtue of being the Chief of the Staff I was, like the other thirty-nine present, simply a member. Other Chiefs of the Staff had passed this way, and I wondered if they had had feelings similar to my own. One occasionally had to suppress the urge to comment out of one's closer "official" knowledge on some of the subjects discussed when the Council went into "committee of the whole." To have spoken "officially," unless requested to do so, could have limited the free exchange of comment and lessened the opportunity for evaluating the speakers and their handling of the matter in hand.

It is the elected president who governs all that happens in a High Council, within, of course, the terms of the constitution and the orders of procedure that are adopted. The president was Commissioner Clarence D. Wiseman, then territorial commander for Canada and Bermuda. Later in the proceedings he was nominated for the generalship and decided to stand. Other nominees were Commissioners Geoffrey Dalziel, Paul Kaiser, Leslie Pindred and Bramwell Tripp. Commissioners Pindred and Tripp declined to stand, and Commissioners Dalziel and Kaiser withdrew following the first ballot. A new president had then to be elected. In none of the preceding seven High Councils had a president been nominated.

The balloting is pursued in utter silence. In order of seniority members proceed to the president's desk, receive a ballot, walk to an ante-room, mark the ballot and deposit it in a locked box. There is no hurry. Those who follow may equally want time for prayerful reflection in the solitude that the voting room affords. But by the time the total membership has followed this routine, the silence is throttling and the suspense suffocating. For the nominees, with a lengthy period of interrogation and their nomination speech behind them, the president's announcement of the results comes as a restorative. Whatever the outcome, the ordeal is over and the air of normalcy may be breathed again. Voting took place on May 13 (another thirteen!). With the dawn, my tremblings had been calmed while pondering the prayers for "Day 13" in a book given me for use during the High Council period. Some of the meditations were singularly appropriate: "Help me to act on what I know is Thy will and not to react as circumstances try to impose." "All that is required by Thee is faithfulness in the hour that now is." "Not in vision, nor in voice, but in a mind that is serene, a heart that is filled with joy, and a will that is undaunted, prove that Thou hast been very near to me, even to me." Before the day was out I had leaned heavily on that Divine proximity.

In the 1969 High Council the two nominees who finally stood for election were Scandinavians. They did not, however, originate from the same country. In this 1974 election both major candidates were Canadian. The first vote was indecisive (a clear two-thirds majority is required), though Commissioner Wiseman was leading in the number of votes polled. I had then to decide whether to concede or go through with a second ballot. Out of respect for those who had voted for me I decided to let the Council proceed with a second ballot, the result of which made Commissioner Wiseman the General-elect.

Scant minutes later the High Council was dissolved. As members streamed out of the council chamber and into the lounge a group of commissioners were called to a meeting for the purpose of discussing the choice of a new Chief of the Staff. Obviously, it would be less than representative for a world-wide movement to have its two top leaders from the same country, and the next day, in order to facilitate matters, I asked General Wickberg to give me farewell orders. This he did, and appointed me to succeed the General-elect as leader for Canada and Bermuda. A ten-year period at International Headquarters had come to an end, a decade of burden and blessing. Now, our faces were towards our homeland.

One of the unsought reasons given by "the inevitable analysts" for my not being elected was the fact that I had never been a territorial commander, a position held by the majority of the members of the High Council. This was a fact, but not one of my own making. Officers go where they are appointed; they cannot, and should not, chart a course that leads by specified channels to a specific harbour. But now I was to be a territorial commander and, joy of joys, in a country that my wife and I knew well and with Salvationists whom we respected and loved. From many parts of the world came messages of regret at my leaving the Chief's chair, but if any thought I would be unhappy about the change, they were disappointed. I was not the first Chief of the Staff to leave the office and, incidentally, not the first to proceed from it to command of the Army's forces in Canada. I had no intention of demonstrating anything less than a soldier's ready acceptance of a superior's decision. That I would miss life at "101" was an expected corollary of the move, but so was the anticipation of succeeding the General-elect in a command to which he had given himself totally for seven productive years.

Two months later, on July 13 (those thirteens!) my wife and I were sped on our way by a crowd that filled the Camberwell Hall. On the back page of the printed programme were the words, "Au revoir, but not goodbye."

CHAPTER 15

"God Keep Our Land"

The return to Canada and to new duties was blessedly free of apprehension. I had acquired a knowledge of the Army, its internationality, its systems and its personnel that I had lacked when leaving a decade earlier, and within myself I was more confident due to the shaping and sharpening experiences through which I had passed. I was also more sensitive to the spiritual purposes of the Army, and because of this, welcomed the chance to join with those nearer the front line of battle against secularism, materialism and all the other "isms" which are the adversaries of Salvation-ism.

Canada is a sibling in the world's family of nations, a gangling youngster that seems to be everywhere at once. No wonder! One leg dangles in the Atlantic; the other paddles in the Pacific. One arm almost touches Greenland; the other wags a finger at Russia. In between are 3,845,144 square miles of "vital earth between two furious oceans." This country has often been called "Miss Canada" and "Our Lady of the Snows." Personally, I sense nothing feminine about Canada, except the natural beauty of its lakes and rivers, its mountains and meadows. The land seems to be more of a bumptious boy, irrepressible and sometimes unpredictable, but with those sweet touches of immature grace that make a parent proud, and those flashes of prescient genius that make the aged teacher feel unworthy of his hire.

The youthfulness of this nation is amazing; it is actually two years younger than the international Salvation Army! William Booth had just begun to discover the dimensions of his destiny when the Fathers of Confederation helped to bring this baby nation into being. And yet, as young as Canada is, it is so old that no one knows who named it. Was it the early Iroquois? "Kanata," they said—a cabin, a lodge. Or was it the Algonquins who gave the white man a name for his newly-discovered land? "Odanah," they exclaimed—a settlement. Some say it was the Spaniards who, thirsting for gold and failing to find it (though the hills are fabulously rich with it) stigmatized the land with a cry of disgust: "Acanada!," or "Nothing here!" How wrong, how utterly and gloriously wrong they were!

One cannot write about the country without sounding extravagant. Scenically, the land overflows with beauty. There are the majestic Rockies, the quieter Laurentians, and those flat worlds called the Prairies. There are the Niagara Falls and a thousand and one etceteras. Physically, the country is immensely rich. It is the prospector's dream come true. It is the farmer's wildest hope surpassed. It is the industrialist's super-blueprint in real life. And the end is not yet! No wonder Canadians have an almost fierce love for their country:

From our wild and wind-swept Mother we
have travailèd in pain,
She hath haltered us and bridled us and
broken us in twain;
Yet she holds her children strangely in a
passion never done,
And our hearts are bound for ever in the
spell that she hath spun.

To understand the Canadian people it is necessary to know something of their antecedents. The embryo sprang from two seminal streams of culture, French and English. Canada today has both a London and a Paris. It has its Trois Rivières, its Rivière du Loup, its Dauphin, soft names that speak of France. It also has its Stratford, Liverpool, Halifax, Edmonton, its Windsor and Victoria and Chatham, names that speak volumes in the nostalgic story of mass immigration. The fusion of these two traditions reveals itself in a large bilingual population. Canadian paper currency states its terms of reference in both languages. Though the country is a senior sister in the British Commonwealth of Nations, French-Canadian government ministers, and even prime ministers, are an unexceptional part of the political scene. It is also important, in understanding the Canadian people, to remember the country's one next-door neighbour and friend. As elders will, the United States of America exerts a strong influence upon the impressionable youngster to the north whose affectionate hug is more than four thousand miles long! The waves of a mighty ocean separate Canada from the two lands that gave it a tradition and a heritage, but there is nothing to stop other kinds of waves from billowing over the 49th Parallel with regular flow and seldom an ebb.

Salvationists in Canada appreciate their land as much as their fellows, but their interest is not so much in the country as in the citizens. The man, more than the land, counts. As illimitable as the nation's resources seem to be, they are for time only, and eternity will demand not natural, but spiritual, resources. It was quite appropriate that in such a young country young men should have begun the Army's work. Jack Addie and Joe Ludgate, both near the twenty-year mark, and both English immigrants, started the movement in London, Ontario, in 1882, only fifteen years after Confederation. The thrilling story of that beginning is more completely told elsewhere. As in other parts of the world, the incipient Army had its struggles. Some were vicious and left scars. A "split" in 1892 caused almost a decade of difficulty, but by the turn of the century the flag was flying from coast to coast, and most forms of Army endeavour had been instituted. Within twenty years, at the most, opposition had turned to understanding and appreciation. As Canada grew, so did The Salvation Army. It became woven into the fibre of the national life, an accepted part of things Canadian.

Canada has been a training ground for international Salvation Army leadership. Commissioner George Lyndon Carpenter was territorial commander in Canada in 1939 when elected General, as was Clarence Wiseman in 1974. I was to succeed from this same appointment in 1977, and the officer who greeted my wife and me on arrival back in Canada, the then Colonel Jarl Wahlström, was to be my successor as international leader seven years later. I had first met the Colonel at a European zonal conference and had suggested to General Wickberg that this promising officer should have experience outside his own country. The General agreed and suggested the long jump from Helsinki to Toronto. I was now the beneficiary of that transfer, and a fruitful partnership lasted until the colonel returned to take charge of the work in his native Finland. Two other officers had become Chief of the Staff from Canada, Commissioners John McMillan and Wm. Dray.

As the reins of leadership were taken up I became conscious of the almost unbelievable changes that had taken place in the ten years of our absence from Canada. The city of Toronto, where the territorial headquarters are situated, had pushed its borders north, east and west to such dimensions that I, who had been domiciled in the Ontario capital for some thirty years, had to fall back on maps and guide-books for directions. Montreal to me was a new metropolis, so completely had its central areas been transformed. As we renewed our contacts with other cities, the same progressive expansion appeared to have taken place. Historic Halifax had come into the present and was pushing into the future. Beautiful Vancouver was more beautiful than ever. Nowhere was change so apparent as in Newfoundland, the Dominion's tenth province. To its rugged loveliness had been added all the amenities of modern living, giving it, in a sense, the best of both worlds. Bermuda, which for The Salvation Army falls under the direction of Canada's territorial commander, had thankfully changed least of all. Change in this pin-point paradise was unnecessary and unwanted. The shattering of its peacefulness by the brutal assassination of the Governor was still in the future.

If appointments in Britain had been learning experiences, leadership in Canada was a re-learning experience. When leaving the Dominion in 1964 I prided myself on knowing all of the officers and a good deal about each of them, their point of origination, whom they had married, their family connection, and so on. But in our absence there had been ten commissionings, which meant that there were actually hundreds of new officers unknown to my wife (whose knowledge and memory of people continually impressed me) and myself. Some of them had moved quickly to leading appointments, and I, who had once been a referral point for others, was now the one to ask: "Who is he?"; "Where did she come from?"

There was the expected, sad aspect to our return. Many of the officers whom we had served, and with whom we had served, had gone from the scene—"promoted to Glory" in the language of the Salvationist. Others, active when we left, were now retired. They provided a revealing side-light on "the seven ages of man" and their progression. For some, a decade had made no difference in their physical appearance; time for them had stood motionless. Others had changed so greatly that they were unrecognized at the first meeting, with consequent embarrassment and fulsome apologies. They were illustrations of Spenser's "ever whirling wheele of change." Those who had seen our friends day after day, or even periodically, were oblivious to the change and were astonished at our surprise. Change, admittedly, is not always sudden and violent; it can be imperceptible to those who live with it, and evident only to those who come unexpectedly upon the evolution it has accomplished.

The next three years passed with incredible speed—so quickly that in the memory events can hardly be disengaged one from the other. In view of the enormous distances to be travelled one was in a plane far oftener than in a bus or train. Not infrequently business was transacted in the Toronto office through a morning and a public meeting conducted the same evening in Vancouver, a mere 3,000-miles plus westward! The crossing of three time zones meant that the Benediction would be pronounced at 1 a.m. or 1:30 a.m. Toronto time. This long-distance, high-speed travelling, from which there was no escaping, accelerated the number and sequence of events and inevitably quickened the rapid passage of the months.

Some undertakings, however, were notable enough to resist any blurring in the memory. Arriving from London, my wife and I learned that two major congresses were envisaged to be held in Toronto in 1975, one a women's congress, the other a continental youth congress. My wife (who would be responsible for the women's congress) and I decided that one congress a year would allow for better preparation and more efficient management. Plans for the youth congress, which was to draw young people from all parts of North America, were already far advanced. It, we decided, would be the 1975 event, and the women's congress would take place the following year. Both were memorable. The thousands of Salvationist young people who filled Toronto's Massey Hall were as heartening a confirmation of the movement's promise for the future as one could hope for. The National Commander for the United States, the late Commissioner Wm. Chamberlain, shared the leadership of the gatherings in which effervescence of spirit and seriousness in worship alternated. The climax came when hundreds of the young people moved forward in dedication during the closing minutes of the Sunday morning meeting. Large congregations of active, thoughtful and eager young men and women are an awesome challenge to the preacher. But the free flow of speech for which I had fervently prayed was granted, and the response, reproachfully beyond expectation, left me speechless, wet-eyed and, to use a favourite word of the French-Canadians present, *boulversé*.

The national women's congress in 1976 drew delegates from Bermuda and Newfoundland in the east and from Northern British Columbia in the far north-west, as well as from every part of the country in between. Colonel (now Commissioner) Eva Burrows, at the time principal of the International College for Officers in London, England, was the special speaker. She, with an enchanting troupe of little girls from a Salvation Army Home in Seoul, Korea, together with women representatives of all the Canadian provinces, was welcomed by my wife as they descended the steps from an immense and amazingly realistic representation of a 747 jet on to the stage of the Massey Hall. If the visiting speaker's words tremendously inspired the crowds, the singing of the youngsters from Korea charmed them. Much tact, unlimited patience and the backing of influential friends had been required to negotiate their visit. By this time Colonel Wahlström had been succeeded by the then Colonel (afterwards Commissioner) John Waldron, from the U.S.A., who, with his wife, would assume leadership of the Army in Canada when my wife and I were called again to International Headquarters. At two of the congress gatherings the Colonel and I were the only males present. Facing the thousands of women in attendance was a pleasantly daunting experience. The excellence of the congress arrangements underlined the truth of the phrase, "Never underestimate the power of a woman." But the strong spiritual influences and the deeply-religious feelings that were stirred left the delegates with the uplifting thought, "Never underestimate the power of the Holy Spirit."

In the middle Seventies the terms "Quebecois" and "séparatiste" were becoming increasingly familiar. The election of René Lévesque as premier of Quebec was followed by a Bill which set a time limit on describing all activities in the province in English alone. No longer in the one language only would a letterhead or business sign or the wording on the side of a van be acceptable. The aim was to Francicize life in *la belle province,* and another, later, controversial Bill would seek to further the intention. Rather than wait for the Act's period of grace to run out and put us under penalty, I felt we should quickly indicate our willingness to conform. The procedure, in any event, would bring us nearer the people we wished to reach. French nomenclature was given to our corps and social services, the terminology taking into account the differences between the language of Paris and that of Quebec. As Mark M. Orkin has written: "The French language spoken in Canada is not, contrary to widespread belief, pure seventeenth-century Norman French, nor is it a debased *patois* unworthy to be classed with the noble Gallic tongue, nor yet a pidginized mixture of English, French and Indian, a kind of *petit négre* of the snows. Despite its contemners, it is a vigorous and expressive popular speech, authentically French, archaistic and yet rich in native coinages and idioms, remarkably homogeneous as opposed to the dialects found in France, and firmly established—more than two hundred years after the capitulation of Quebec—as the daily language of approximately six million Canadians."

What we call "the French work" has been surrounded by difficulty from its beginning. Nowhere in Canada had opposition been more violent than in Quebec in the 1800's. "The persecution suffered in this region was equal in severity to that endured by Salvationists in any part of the world. A number of the advance party were permanently injured by the brutal reception they were given by mobsters. Girl officers were stoned and dreadfully beaten." So reads the history of The Salvation Army in Canada. The newspapers, contrary to expectation, blazed forth with denunciations of the Army's persecutors. French and English, Protestant and Roman Catholic journals alike deplored the "most revolting sallies of profanity and obscenity made while those on the platform were engaged in prayer."

As understanding grew persecution diminished, but while the social services expanded evangelical work continued to be laboriously uphill. Francophones among Canadian officers were a rarity, so much so that those appointed to work among French-Canadians had to begin at the beginning with the language. One such was Senior-Major Nora Brokenshire who for decades taught in the Montreal day-school operated by the Army for French-speaking children who did not, or could not, attend a Catholic separate school. For her lifelong commitment to this work the Major was admitted to the Order of the Founder. From this schoo, Salvationists and some officers were produced, but eventually it was forced to close.

The appointment of English-speaking officers to French-speaking communities, or to institutions where those served were predominantly French-speaking, worked a particular hardship on their children. They found themselves either in French-speaking schools or facing extraordinary costs for a place in a school where teaching was in English. But need for the Army's presence was continually enlarging. Greater numbers of French-speaking persons were being helped through the family services, the correctional services, the senior citizens' services, the hospital work as well as in adult rehabilitation and alcoholic treatment centres. To do the work properly a degree of fluency in the language is all-important. Happily, among younger Canadian officers there is a better knowledge of the French language and, with the language now being learned from an early age in the schools, the future should yield a more sufficient number of officers qualified to serve the French-Canadian population.

Many French-Canadians, like English- and other Canadians, needed the message of the Gospel. Unlike those requiring some form of social assistance, they would not come to us. We would have to go to them. At some expense and much preparation *une expédition d'évangélization* was mounted by officer-cadets during the summer. It centred on the city of Sherbrooke where a once-thriving English-speaking corps had long since been closed. The demographic change had been dramatic. Once 85% English and 15% French, the ratio was now completely reversed. While the effort succeeded in renewing interest in the Army's mission, regrettably it had no permanent outcome.

As the voice of separatism grew louder so did the challenge to relate the Army's work to the needs of the province. I determined to pay a goodwill visit to Quebec City, and His Worship, Mayor Gilles Lamontagne, afterwards a member of the federal cabinet, undertook to arrange a reception at the Hôtel de Ville. An accomplished group of bi-lingual Salvationists sang, and I was invited to address the large crowd. As an acknowledgement of the province's aspirations I felt I should speak in French, though until the last minute, in case my nerve failed, I kept the English outline of the talk in my hand. Nothing can be so ruinous to one's composure as the realization that, having pursued perfection in one's own language, one's imperfections in another are being smilingly tolerated or exasperatingly suffered. My attempt appeared to please the crowd. The strain I had experienced melted in the warmth of my listeners' goodwill.

Later I was privately, and almost covertly, entertained at dinner by a group of prominent bi-lingual Quebecois of English background. For them, Quebec was home. Into the city's progress had been poured their talents, their wealth and their hopes. They were, they emphasized, Canadians, and separation from the rest of Canada was a tragedy to be thwarted. They pleaded with me to stress the necessity for "one Canada" wherever I travelled across the Dominion, and to tell people that there were those whose loyalty embraced both the Province of Quebec and the Dominion of Canada. I explained that the matter being so hotly political was one on which I could not publicly comment, but I left them in no doubt as to my personal feelings and those of all Salvationists, as far as I could judge them. Quebec and its people were as important to the Army as any and all throughout Canada. Not "separation" but "reconciliation" was in the Army's bloodstream.

One thing that might relate us more to the French-Canadian population, I thought, would be the provision of some printed matter. To issue a French-language *War Cry* would not be an innovation. Through several of the earlier years of the Army in Canada an *En Avant* was published, but in latter years only copies of the *En Avant* printed in France had been distributed. It was hardly what was wanted. The French edition had no Canadian content. Its Parisian idioms were sometimes meaningless, and certain turns of phrase were puzzling to the French-Canadian reader. My puzzle was how to finance the publishing of an acceptable periodical. In all likelihood that same puzzle continues to restrict the size of today's *En Avant,* a paper of limited dimension and simple layout, but containing some inspiring reading in terms acceptable to *les canayens.* It is gratifying to understand that under the hand of my successors the Army's concern for French-speaking Canada—and that means parts of the Dominion other than Quebec—has materially enlarged. *Tant mieux!*

Many young French-Canadians were enlisted men, and the well-being of the serviceman, and the family from whom he was often separated, has been a concern of the Army since the days of its forerunner, the Christian Mission. More than three hundred men of the 42nd Highlanders about to embark for the Ashanti war in 1874 knew the ministrations of Evangelist (later Commissioner) James Dowdle. Twelve years later the Naval and Military League was established, one of its objectives being the provision of homes where soldiers and sailors, and later airmen, could share some home comforts and hold meetings. The first centre was opened in Gibraltar in 1895, rapidly followed by others in the United Kingdom, Japan, Hong Kong and Barbados.

The first Salvation Army "hut" for soldiers on the field of battle was a rough canvas structure put up during the Boer War at the Estcourt camp, Natal, in February, 1900, according to Volume III of *The History of the Salvation Army*. The intrepid ministering angel behind its erection and function was a Staff-Captain Mary Murray whose father, General Sir John Murray, KCB., had served in India during the mutiny. Following the trail she blazed has been a veritable army of Salvationists rendering whatever service the propitious or unpropitious circumstances would permit, and always as near the front line of battle as the authorities would allow. This was particularly so in the First and Second World Wars and, it should be noted, on both sides of the struggle. In World War I American troops beatified the Salvation Army's "doughnut girls." To the battle-weary soldier "egg and chips" was a splendid feast whenever he managed to reach a Red Shield centre. Commonwealth fighting men sang the praises of "the Army cup of tea" long after the cessation of both Great Wars. During World War II the distribution of comforts reached staggering proportions. The literature of the war was scrawled on millions of sheets of Red Shield notepaper bearing the gentle admonition, "Keep in touch with the folks at home!" while the heartbeat of war was conveyed in the hundreds of letters written by Auxiliary supervisors to the lonely, the bereaved and the abandoned.

As national publicity officer I was asked to assist the author and broadcaster, Scott Young, in the preparation of his book, *The Red Shield in Action*. It relates in detail the magnificent work done by the Army's Canadian Red Shield Auxiliary Services with all branches of the armed forces during the Second World War, and by those officers who served as chaplains. Such service ensured for the Army in Canada an imperishable place in the affection of the returned serviceman and, as time proved, in the appreciation of his children and grandchildren.

Not nearly so well known, but unquestionably a by-product of that earlier ministry, is the present-day work of the Red Shield Services with the Canadian Forces based in Germany as part of the NATO presence. Nearby, British Red Shield workers similarly serve the troops comprising the British Army of the Rhine. As detachments have come and gone, the Red Shield centres, first in Soëst, Hemer and Herne, and currently in Lahr, Baden-Soellingen and Geilenkirchen have helpfully provided in peacetime what was desperately needed in wartime.

It was a mark of the military authorities' appreciation that annually the territorial commander and his wife could inspect the work. Twice my wife and I were flown by the Royal Canadian Air Force from the Trenton air base to Lahr and housed in an officers' club set in beautiful grounds, a retreat, we were told, once used by Hitler. Each time we were entertained in highly hospitable fashion, taking lunch with the staff officers and wives, with the opportunity of speaking to them about the Army's work. Lahr, designated as "The City between the Black Forest and the Rhine" has two city halls. The "old" dates back to 1608. The "new," built in classical style, was erected in 1808. The bürgermeister received me with exceptional cordiality, for a reason he was bursting to impart. Lahr was "twinned" with Belleville, my own Canadian city, which he had visited. He felt he had come to know the city well, its people, and certainly the mayor who, it happened, was a longtime friend of mine. He showed me the Citizens' Civic Register begun by the town clerk in 1356 with the dedicatory phrase: "Unser herre Got ist burger an der stat zuo [*sic*] Lare." ("Our Lord God Himself is a citizen of Lahr.")

There was time enough from the duties that took us to Lahr to allow for a breathtaking expedition by RCAF helicopter down the Rhine Valley. With the ease of a great bird we fluttered about the idyllic castles that nestled on the high hills, swooped down into the valley to glimpse the market gardens of Seelbach where every window carries its own array of flowers, and hovered over the steep, cobbled streets that lead from the Rathaus to a towering church in picturesque Etterheim.

At Baden-Soellingen, not far from Baden-Baden (its double name distinguishes it from spas with similar names in Austria and Switzerland), the Red Shield service centre was actually located on the military base. We had hardly arrived when I was asked by an anxious military colonel if an extension to our facilities could possibly be provided so that younger servicemen, overseas for the first time without the stabilizing influence of a wife and family, could have ample recreation and entertainment without having to resort to the "wet" canteen with its attendant problems. It was something the Army was more than ready to undertake. Baden-

Baden, which lies in the Oos River valley, in the well-wooded Black Forest, is a most attractive city combining beauty and luxury. But more impressive still was a simple happening at the start of our second busy day spent on the base. At 6.30 a.m. there was a knock on the door of the guest house in which we were staying. As I opened the door, the officer commanding, with his escort, came smartly to attention and saluted. He had come personally to march me to a prayer breakfast arranged by the Red Shield supervisor to which military men were bringing those of their sons who were old enough to understand the proceedings and to benefit from them. This, and the Divine services conducted with the troops, emphasized for me the spiritual value, as well as the practical value, of the work. An unpayable debt is owed to all who have, behind the Red Shield, served the forces through the lengthening years of occupation.

During one of the two visits to Germany I was taken to a command bunker from which, in the event of enemy action, the war effort would be directed. It is not for me to relate in detail what I saw. What I did observe and was told left me overwhelmed by the lethal power of the instruments of war which exist, and fearful lest the fatal "strike" should ever occur.

One of Canada's great champions of national and international peace was the late Rt. Hon. John G. Diefenbaker, PC., former prime minister and, at the time of my appointment to Canada, leader of the Progressive Conservative opposition in parliament. His admission to the Order of Distinguished Auxiliary Service in April, 1975, brought together a widely-representative assemblage of leaders in the national life. Described as "an orator of the old school," Mr. Diefenbaker was an outspoken Royalist, and to his immense gratification had been named by Her Majesty The Queen to membership in the august Order of Merit, the only Canadian ever to have been so recognized by the Sovereign. All Canadians felt it was a fitting tribute to a public figure truly described as "an elder statesman" who had long stood for "the better way" in the realms of morality and standards of life and behaviour.

Throughout his distinguished career he had been a vigorous and practical supporter of the Army. In his own city of Prince Albert, Saskatchewan, where he had been the mayor, and later as provincial leader, he had been associated with the annual Red Shield appeal for over thirty years. I wrote asking if he would accept the honour and gave details as to the kind of occasion we planned. There was no answer, and days lengthened into weeks. In no way could one assume with this independently-minded parliamentarian that "silence gives consent." Without his agreement we could not proceed. Just as we began to consider postponing the event, he called me on the telephone.

"I've only now received your generous letter, Commissioner," he said apologetically, "and I will consider it one of the great honours of my long life if The Salvation Army sees fit to acknowledge my small contribution in this way."

And then the incurable politician came to the surface. "By the way, Brown," he bristled, "two hundred years ago your invitation would have reached me faster by smoke signals than by the post-office (at the time much in the news because of its deteriorating service) under this incumbent, incompetent, indescribable government!"

To the delight of all present at the luncheon in the Chateau Laurier, in Ottawa, I related Diefenbaker's comment. None seemed to enjoy it more than the postmaster-general himself who was in the audience. Mr. Diefenbaker's scintillating speech ended on an unexpected, emotional note. His wife had been gravely ill, and he himself had been far from well. Both, he wished to confess, had been unusually sustained by the knowledge that many had remembered them in prayer. The voice of the great debater faltered, and for some moments, which can only be characterized as hallowed, he led his hearers into the realm of the spirit, concluding with an expression of profound faith in the "ever-following goodness and mercy" of God.

The years in London brought me, as one of several lecturers, into close contact with delegates attending the International College for Officers. Lectures were usually followed by a period of questions and answers, an exercise which I found especially stimulating. The questions, it must be said, often revealed the character as well as the concerns of the delegate. In each session an entire period was set aside in the curriculum for delegates to question the General, by the majority regarded as a unique privilege. I believed the period to be not only informative for the delegates, but also therapeutic. Any who had long nursed a cherished notion in the hope of one day being able to put it to "the highest authority" had their chance. I asked that the period be extended to either a whole morning or afternoon. In my opinion it was time well invested.

It was to be expected that some fields would be tilled again and again.

One question regularly posed had to do with the possibility of younger officers serving outside their own country, not only to broaden their own experience, but to cross-fertilize ideas that might be beneficial to the Army's work. Missionary service, as such, was not in the questioners' minds; that was related to a special call. What was envisaged was an opportunity to do the same kind of work as that in which they were already engaged, but in another setting, against the background of another lifestyle and under somewhat different forms of administration. I saw value in some form of exchange, despite the obvious problems such as the securing of visas and entry permits, the availability of suitable educational facilities for the children, and not a few others. And looking back, I would judge that my own transfer from Canada to the United Kingdom would have been easier, and perhaps more productive, had I been in my "forties" rather than my "fifties."

Returning to Canada the chance for experimentation was, so to speak, "on my doorstep." To the south were four American territories with almost 3,500 active officers, some of whom might be eager to serve in Canada. A number of Canadian officers, I knew, would be ready to spend a part of their career in the United States. The adjustments would be relatively easy, the two neighbouring countries having a great deal in common. As negotiations began, it became evident that the choice of officer could not be haphazard. Only those who could suitably represent their homeland, and whose competence and consecration would raise high standards worthy of emulation, should be proposed. The first exchanges were arranged, and in most instances were successful. The terms on which such moves will be made in the future have been codified in the light of experience.

I cannot help feeling that the perimeters of the system should be stretched. Having visited Australia and New Zealand I can foresee the mutual benefit that would result from an exchange of officers from these antipodal lands with officers from Canada. No Salvationist could accept many of Ingersoll's beliefs, but all would agree with his assertion that "We exchange ideas when we exchange fabrics." Nor should younger officers in those European countries where English is a used second language be deprived of a term in an English-speaking territory other than the United Kingdom where such appointments have been consistently made through the years. And, but for the language barrier, many a younger Canadian officer, and the work, would benefit from a period spent in a European country. The Old World has many things still to teach the New.

In Canada, an aspect of administration which was always rewarding but frequently problematic concerned the chain of twelve general and maternity hospitals operated by the Army, a network unmatched in any other Salvation Army territory. By government requirement and Salvation Army standard they operate at the highest levels of professional medical and nursing care, a tree of healing that grew from the unlikeliest kind of seed. The seed was unknowingly planted when General Bramwell Booth, the Army's second international leader, visited a dying woman in whom his wife had taken a sympathetic interest. She asked the General if he would see that her only son, Harry, was cared for after her passing. The General gave his word, and kept it by taking the boy into his own home and family.

Later, the lad accompanied Bramwell Booth's sister, Emma, and her husband, Commissioner Frederick de Latour Booth-Tucker, to India where, already a Salvation Army officer at seventeen years of age, he manifested special interest in caring for the sick; so much so that he was returned to England to qualify as a doctor. Again in India, and under his guidance, the Army began a medical work which expanded rapidly and fruitfully. In wartime, the Army's Thomas Emery Hospital at Moradabad, which Harry Andrews had founded, with its doctors and nursing staff, was put at the disposal of the military forces. But troubles persisted on the North-West Frontier after the war's end, and Dr. Andrews's help was again requisitioned. As senior officer he was in charge of the Khajuri post when word was received that a convoy was being attacked. He went at once to the scene of action and, under heavy fire, established an aid post. He had just completed the task of collecting the wounded and placing them in a van when he was killed by an enemy bullet.

Posthumously, he was awarded the Victoria Cross, the Empire's highest recognition for gallantry in action. He was the first medical doctor ever to be so honoured, and it was my privilege to be present in the V.C.'s room of the headquarters mess of the RAMC., Millbank, London, for the unveiling of a superb painting portraying the action in which Harry Andrews showed such heroism but lost his life.

If the worldwide medical work of the Army sprang from small beginnings, so did the Army's hospital work in Canada. Two of the five young officers who journeyed from Toronto to Winnipeg in 1886 to pioneer the work were faithfully serving six years later when, one bitter winter night, there was a knock on the door of the women officers' quarters. A pregnant girl, with nowhere to go, made a tearful plea for help. Accommodated and cared for, she was the first of a long queue of deserted wives, homeless women and unmarried mothers that came for aid. The rescue home which was established led to the founding of a hospital, incorporated in 1904, and given the name, "The Grace." No-one knows where the name came from, though it has been suggested that "grace" being a theological term meaning, "unmerited love," it would contrast appropriately with "Mercy," the name borne by some Roman Catholic hospitals. A less elevating explanation is that it was named after the wife or daughter of an early benefactor. But the mystery remains.

Other hospitals followed, each deserving of mention for its own accomplishments in service. The Halifax, Nova Scotia, "Grace," affiliated with Dalhousie University, today leads the entire Dominion in its number of births, some five thousand being registered annually. In this city, noted for its several "firsts" in the history of Canada—the first Anglican church, the first newspaper, the first post-office, the first elected public assembly in British North America—the "Grace" has also had its impressive "firsts." Here, for the first time in North America, the "early rising" technique, by which new mothers left their bed the day after the baby was born and started exercises, was introduced. The technique is now universally followed. It was also the first hospital in Canada to introduce natural childbirth, and with considerable success. The chief medical officer of the time reported that "it at least lowered the decibel rate of moaning and shrieking in the delivery room."

In recent times, however, the hospital scene in Canada has been a turbulent one. Health care is a responsibility of the provincial governments, and changes of government sometimes mean new views concerning management and function. The need to reduce costs may mean the centralization of certain types of treatment, or the reduction in the number of active beds or, most distressing of all, closure. One or another of the foregoing nettled our hospital work in Montreal, Toronto, Halifax, St. John's, Nfld., Calgary and Vancouver during my short three-year term as leader in Canada, but without affecting the quality of service.

For several years there had been tedious negotiations with Ontario's ministry of health concerning the possible relocation of the Toronto "Grace" hospital. Not long after I returned the negotiations took another, and mordant, turn; the "Grace" was listed as one of the hospitals likely to be closed as an economic measure. Citizens who had benefited by the high standards of the hospital raised indignant protests, while I and my colleagues feared that the Army's equity in the valuable property might be in jeopardy. It could not be forgotten that the hospitals had been kept functioning through the Great Depression of the Thirties with funds that might well have eased the hardship of other branches of work.

In London, England, I had become acquainted with the magnificent work done by the St. Christopher's hospice in Sydenham, a terminal care institution begun by a skilled and compassionate woman doctor, Dr. Cicely Saunders. Here, a patient's last days were made as happy as possible, and the passing as peaceful as medical skill could ensure. In the hope of avoiding the closure of "Grace," and with the support of all associated administratively with its work, I submitted a brief to the minister of health proposing that the "Grace" should become a St. Christopher's, it being known that beds for the terminally ill were in short supply. I advanced the idea that Army personnel would be able also to surround the patients with the spiritual influences vitally needed by those on the edge of eternity.

To my gratification, in the conference which followed, the minister informed me that the proposal for Grace Hospital's change of use was accepted. He then added the overwhelming news that the long-sought relocation was also approved, and that a general hospital was to be erected in the suburbs with a starting accommodation of 350 beds and an eventual optimum of 650 beds. I could hardly believe what I was hearing, and hurried back to headquarters to tell the chief secretary that instead of losing our one hospital, we were now to have two.

The changeover at "Grace," and the complicated planning for the additional "Grace," had to be left for my successor. It was no small joy when retiring in Toronto to find that the original "Grace" was already, to quote a government minister, a "beacon" attracting the representatives of several Canadian cities which wished to emulate its methods, and that the sod was turned for the new Scarborough "Grace."

Less welcome was the public attention focussed on our hospitals because of the crusade for "abortion on demand" noisily claimed by certain factions of the women's liberation movement. In 1975, 48,000 abortions were performed by doctors in Canada, a few of them in our own hospitals, but usually on the grounds of medical unavoidability. With our pro-life attitude, asserting that the law and moral law are two distinct entities, there were some emotional clashes internally among medical and nursing staffs. On few subjects did I try to read so much and to so fully inform myself as on this complicated subject. With great tact a proposed positional statement was put before the medical chiefs of all our hospitals and, in the end, with minor alterations, it became a guide for procedure. Conforming to the criminal code of Canada, therapeutic abortion committees were set up at each hospital. These, under their terms of reference, could decide whether or not an abortion was a necessity. There was strong feeling, however, that Salvation Army hospitals should not be any less opposed to abortion than the Roman Catholic hospitals where no abortions whatever were performed. In recent times that stronger stand has been taken. I cannot claim any credit for this, but offer full praise to those who succeeded in establishing such a position.

As General, I was frequently asked whether The Salvation Army should be in the general hospital field at all. For the Third World my answer was always a confident, "Yes!" For the western world, I am much less certain. Hospital services are costly and competitive. Medical equipment has an early obsolescence, and the medical staff cannot be blamed for bringing pressure to bear on an administrator to secure "the latest" in everything if it will enhance the healing process. As hospitals have multiplied, Salvation Army officer staff in them has diminished. Today, it is left largely to the administrator and a chaplain to maintain what is referred to as "the Army atmosphere," but this is no small task with hundreds of patients lying-in or attending as out-patients. That the "hospice" care of the terminally ill should be high on our list of priorities is undeniable. Here, full scope is available for the lavishing of spiritually-motivated care. Equally, hospitals for the palliative care of the chronically ill, the handicapped and the dependent geriatric should be within the purview of the Army's healing ministry. If pressed to answer concerning the Army's place in the modern, general hospital field, I would have to admit that I do not favour any more new erections; but, in the same breath, I would have to emphasize that I would not want to see any of the hospitals we are presently operating pass from the scene.

A Salvation Army leader is both legatee and legator. He inherits the accomplishments of his predecessor and, as well, those projects well begun but whose completion outspan his term of office. It was so for me in Canada. While my name may appear on various plaques, the vision and effort belonged to an earlier regime. Perhaps new forms of commemorative expression need to be devised. But, equally, the leader is legator. Turning our faces towards London and international headquarters we bequeathed to our successor nearly eighty property projects, all *en train,* to which his own active vision would add many more. Has anyone left an appointment confident that there is no "unfinished business"? He would be a rare specie. Any officer who pleads for an extension of his stay on the grounds that this or that must be finished is forgetting the legatee-legator reality that affects commissioners as well as captains and, as I would later discover, generals as well.

Leaving Canada for a second time, thirteen years after our first departure (one more thirteen!), my wife and I would carry memories not not only of the significant issues already recorded, but of the several seasons of spiritual refreshment spent with officers in annual retreats; of the powerful congress meetings led by General and Mrs. Wiseman in Toronto, for which their comrades of the years crowded the spacious Varsity Arena, and in Bermuda, where spiritual joy was unbounded; of the privilege of addressing the National Christian Holiness Convention in Rochester, N.Y., and the National Social Conference in Cincinnati, Ohio; of leading the prayer breakfast for hundreds of delegates to the International Convention of City Managers, and of addressing a luncheon meeting of the National Conference on Alcohol and Drug Addiction when my thesis, stressing the virtue of total abstinence and the spiritual elements of rehabilitation, was less appreciated by the "professionals"; of the appointing of pioneers to open the work in the sub-Arctic where a new world was burgeoning; of discussions with the contrasting famous—the Rt. Rev. Dr. Donald Coggan, then Archbishop of Canterbury, and Mr. Jerome Himes, the extraordinarily tall Metropolitan Opera basso, both of whom were fully pledged to the cause of Christ; of unforgettable sessions with cadets, with Salvationist-musicians, and with local officers; and of productive conferences with government agencies in order that more funds might flow to the developing but necessitous countries of the Third World.

For one of my printed farewell messages I borrowed some words of the Apostle Paul recorded in Acts 20: 31, 32: "... by the space of three years I ceased not to warn every one ... And now, brethren, I commend you to God, and to the word of His grace ..." Typographical errors do occur, and the recipients read: "... by the space of three years I ceased not to *warm* every one ..." If our leadership had *warmed* the hearts of those we had been privileged to serve, and had *warmed* their love for Christ, there was cause for abounding gratitude.

But perhaps Galatians 1: 18 might have been a more appropriate parting salutation: "Then after three years I went up to Jerusalem ..."

CHAPTER 16

"A Hundred Anthems Rise"

The retirement of General Wiseman necessitated the calling together of the High Council for the purpose of electing his successor. Answering the summons, I made my way from Toronto to London and Sunbury Court via Bermuda where a new alcoholic treatment centre, the gift of Mr. Dudley Butterfield, chairman of the Bermuda advisory board and a strong supporter, was officially opened. At 9:30 o'clock on the morning of April 29, 1977, the Chief of the Staff, Commissioner Arthur Carr, formally instituted the ninth High Council which, this time, I was attending as the senior commissioner. There were forty-one members, three of whom were women leaders. Commissioner Bramwell Tripp, of New York, was elected president, and under his able direction the work of the council proceeded smoothly and swiftly.

All of the feelings experienced during the High Council of 1974 reasserted themselves—the joy of a fellowship that literally brought the whole world into one's conversation; the inner stirrings when prayer was offered in languages that seemed more intensely expressive than one's own; and the enrichment provided by the devotional gatherings in which reports of heroic Christian witness in distant places were recounted.

On the morning of May 4, four delegates were nominated: Commissioners W. Stan. Cottrill, Geoffrey Dalziel, Harry Williams and myself. Two declined, leaving Commissioner Williams and myself as candidates. We both now faced the trial of answering the forty questions collated by the appointed question committee, and, late in the afternoon, this responsibility was discharged. I spent the evening in A-28 (my assigned room in the Sunbury Court Annex) preparing a nomination speech, with two Scriptural verses typed out and lying on the table before me: "Anxious thoughts may fill my heart, but Thy presence is my joy and consolation." (Psalm 94: 19 NEB); and Proverbs 16: 33 (NEB), "The lots may be cast into the lap, but the issue depends wholly on the Lord." The latter provided perspective as I worked over my script.

The next morning, Thursday, the weather had deteriorated. Chill winds had blown the blossoms from the trees and the paths around the conference centre were carpeted as with confetti. On this final day of the High Council the deliberations were calm but purposeful. By lot, Commissioner Williams gave his nomination speech first, and between the two adresses there was a prayerful five minutes of silence. I began to speak at 9.44 a.m., and finished, according to the official record, at 9.59 a.m. A few minutes later the council adjourned, reassembling at 11 o'clock for a period of prayer and the singing of a song written for the High Council and its task by Commissioner Arthur Pitcher.

At 2.30 p.m. the council came together for the final, decisive act for which the members had been summoned—to cast their vote. The president of the council, in accordance with the order of procedure, read the declaration:

> "As we, the Members of the High Council, approach the momentous task of electing a General of The Salvation Army, we do with one accord render glory to the Triune God, Father, Son and Holy Spirit, and in the name of Jesus Christ our Saviour invoke the guidance and aid of the Holy Spirit in the discharge of our solemn responsibility, desiring only that the will of God shall be done."

I have already described the taut atmosphere during the balloting at the previous High Council, but on this occasion the tension lasted only twenty-eight minutes, and the issue was decided on the first voting. At 3.08 p.m. the president announced, "We have chosen a General-elect." I thanked those who had voted for me and expressed the hope that I would merit the support of those who had voted otherwise, and assured the council that the friendship between the two candidates was as strong after the election as before it. Leaders from South Asia colourfully garlanded me, and all members, in turn, shook my hand and pledged their loyalty. In these moments composure deserted me; it was impossible to hide the deep emotion I was experiencing.

Within minutes of signing the Deed of Acceptance I was in front of television and film cameras which were probing not only the shape of a General-elect's face but, hopefully, the shape of his mind. I had the discomfiting sensation of having been catapulted from a joyous equality shared around the green, baize-covered tables by all the councillors into an almost frightening "alone-ness," somewhere beyond the state of *primus inter pares.* While my mind struggled to grasp the full significance of the ballot's outcome, my inner turmoil (a General-elect being as human as other men!) was increased by anxiety as to how "the news" could be conveyed to my wife, at that moment 37,000-feet in the air flying back from women's rallies held farther away from Toronto —yet still in our own command—than Toronto is from London!

To the media men and women I made a general statement and, thinking of my predecessors, said in part: "I think of the Founder and General Bramwell Booth, and can only pray that a portion of their spirit might be given to me. I think of Higgins with his dignity and his presence. I think of Evangeline Booth and her eloquence and forceful personality. I think of Carpenter with his saintly faithfulness; of Orsborn with his inspirational poetry; of Kitching with his ardent Salvationism; of Coutts with his scholarly use of the spoken and written word. I think of the steady statesmanship of Wickberg, and of Wiseman with his fervant evangelism. All I can say is, 'Who is sufficient for these things?' But all that I have, and all that I hope to have; and all that I am, and all that I hope to be, is totally dedicated to God in the Army."

After that, the interviewers had their individual turn. One reporter who, I suspected, wanted to make my statements fit his pre-written feature bandied terms like "flattened hierarchies," tempting me to say, even before I reached International Headquarters how my "democratizations" would affect the Army's autocracy. Another challenged the "ivory tower control" he believed the generalship implied. I pointed out that an officer of any rank is first and foremost a soldier; he is on "the ground floor"; he is where the action is. Still another wanted to know if I would be "bland or brutal" in my leadership. He was thoroughly confused when I said, "Both. I am made 'all things to all men, that I might by all means save some.'" At this point he began to understand that I was not thinking organizationally. Interviews over, members of the now dissolved High Council had a farewell meal together and, with surprising speed, departed for their appointments. For the General-elect, before he can return, there are still more radio and television interviews, as well as an important briefing session with the General and the Chief of the Staff.

In the serious hours immediately following the High Council's conclusion there was a moment of relieving humour when it was learned that the Chief of the Staff's cabled notification to territories and commands around the world had suffered a distortion in transmission. The message as released read: "Brown elected. God bless the General." Alas, a full stop was misplaced, so that one leading officer read with understandable incredulity: "Brown elected God. Bless the General."

Two months is not a long time in which to attend a succession of farewell gatherings in a country as widespread as Canada, and to pack one's belongings for shipment overseas. Somehow it was accomplished, and, according to *The War Cry* a "standing room only" crowd overflowed the Toronto Temple for the final meeting. Good wishes from the Governor-General and the Prime Minister were read, and representatives of the federal, provincial and municipal governments, the clergy and the Toronto advisory board spoke encouragingly. There was a moment of surprise when Mr. Clate Raymond, North America's most dynamic champion of the Sunday school, made a lively speech and presented me with the National Achievement Award on behalf of the four hundred churches which comprise the Christian Education Association. After the meeting he begged me to be the principal speaker at one of his continental conferences attended by some thousands of Sunday school workers, but it was not to be. My appointments diary was uncooperative in respect of every date proposed, and, sadder still, the very last letter this likeable crusader dictated was sent to me by his secretary, unsigned. Quite unexpectedly he had been called to his heavenly reward.

Saying farewell, my wife and I were aware that when Canada again became our domicile, our active service would be over. The page was turning and the last, momentous chapter was beginning. There were contrasts with our earlier departure for London, thirteen years before. Previously, we had left behind our elder daughter, in training as a nurse, and our younger daughter, then thirteen, had accompanied us. This time we bade goodbye not only to a daughter, but also to a son-in-law and two grandsons whose joint conclusion was that either their grandparents should not go to London, or that they both should travel with us.

The voyage from New York to Southampton aboard the "QE II" allowed my wife and I to "catch our breath" and prepare for the many appointments immediately ahead. But to be incognito was impossible; the New York newspapers had seen to that. So it was not altogether surprising to be told by a faultless waiter for whom table service was an art, that he and his brother had been evacuated from London during the war and had been placed with two Salvation Army ladies in Reading "who were kindness itself." Enroute, a lasting friendship was established with a publisher of horological journals and his wife who told us that her father had drowned when a Stranraer ferry sank. "The first person to come to our house," she said, "was the Army officer. He prayed a little prayer, and no one in our family will ever forget that prayer, or the sincerity of it." How astonishingly large are the outcomes of small deeds!

As the "Queen" docked at Southampton my wife and I donned for the first time uniforms bearing the insignia of our new office. I, however, was without a General's cap. But not for long. While a press conference proceeded in one of the ship's salons, I was handed a brown paper bag. In it was the required headgear. Still answering questions, I opened two envelopes which were inside the cap. One was from the maker asking me to accept the cap with his firm's compliments. The other was an invoice from our own trade department billing me for the cost! Properly attired, we went down the gangway to meet the welcoming delegation from International Headquarters led by the Chief of the Staff and Mrs. Commissioner Carr. Neighbourly welcomes followed as we arrived at the Beckenham house in which we had lived when serving as the Chief of the Staff. The rose bushes I had regularly pruned were in full and brilliant bloom, a magnificent bouquet of greeting.

The office of the General is on the "warm" side of International Headquarters. Facing south it catches and holds whatever sunshine there is. Through the large bay window one can see the marine traffic on the Thames, and, on the opposite bank, the house where Sir Christopher Wren worked while watching his "monument," St. Paul's Cathedral, climb into the sky. In the period away from London there had been improvements. Upper Thames Street, flanking the river, was now a covered artery diverting some of the traffic from Queen Victoria Street. Above it, were indications of a City of London school to come in that future when there would be money enough to proceed with construction. For the nearly five years that I occupied the office there were no signs of development, and the charming view remained unobstructed. The mooring of a helipad, and the aerial activity that followed, only added novelty and movement to the scene.

Alone in the office, and at the desk for the first time, I dwelt inwardly on the course that the years had taken. I thanked God for the front-line service from which I was able to return to International Headquarters with a fresh outlook, and for the years as Chief of the Staff which, in this moment, I realized was a second-to-none preparation for the duties to come. Ahead lay a lengthy round of welcome events, each different, but all fortifying one's confidence and providing assurance of loyal support. There was one all-important decision to be made at once. Commissioner Carr, with his unrivalled knowledge of headquarters procedures, would finish his active service in a matter of weeks, and to any nomination I would make the assent of five senior commissioners would be required. The words spoken under Divine impulsion by the prophet Ezekiel were in my mind: "And I sought for a man among them, that should ... stand in the gap." Happily, I did not have to add, "but I found none." My nominee was Commissioner W. Stan. Cottrill who had served as my chief secretary when Chief of the Staff. Few officers could match the internationality of his service—in Great Britain, Manchuria, Malaysia, Rhodesia, Japan and Korea—and he was no stranger to International Headquarters, its routines and its lines of communication. I was to have total agreement from the recommending commissioners and, for the whole of my tenure, there was with Commissioner Cottrill the kind of relationship that should exist in every Christian leadership situation. His integrity and spirituality commended him to all.

That first day at the office ended with a visit to the Mermaid Theatre, under the shadow of Blackfriars Bridge, where Sir Bernard Miles (now Lord Miles) greeted us. He pointed proudly to his Salvation Army lapel badge, informing me that he was an "adherent" of the Regent Hall corps. By his courtesy the theatre was often at the Army's disposal, and here we previewed the newest musical prepared by the then Majors

John Gowans and John Larsson, "The Blood of the Lamb," which was to be one of the major events of the international congress twelve months hence. Even though months of refining rehearsal lay ahead, the portrayal electrified the audience, none more so than myself as the newest successor to William Booth whose crowning moment when he meets his Saviour, touchingly imagined by Vachel Lindsay in the poem, "General Booth Enters Heaven," was movingly acted out.

In the darkened theatre the idea of a Salvation Army repertory company was born. I envisaged the most accomplished Salvationist actors and singers being brought together and sent on an around-the-world tour arranged by a leading impresario who, on a professional basis, would book the group into theatres where non-churchgoers could be reached with this and other message-musicals such as "Spirit," "Jesus Folk" and "Hosea." In addition, the company would present twenty-minute "condensations" to luncheon meetings of service and fraternal clubs. I was convinced of the power of the medium to communicate Divine truth, and saw the plan as a new form of evangelical outreach. For long enough I will feel the sting of self-reproach that I did not override all objections and insist on the idea becoming a reality. Perhaps there is yet the possibility.

Certain serious concerns arose during my term as General, and to a review of these I have devoted some of the succeeding chapters. I have also found it more convenient to write separately about our visits to the various continents. Concerns and campaigns there certainly were, but arching above them was a series of exciting centenary celebrations that forcefully reminded me that I had come to office at a singularly historic moment. The calendar put before me noted massive gatherings in London in July, 1978 to which delegates would come from all parts of the globe; in Scotland in 1979; in the United States and Australia in 1980, and in France in 1981. The several centenary observances were ushered in with a stirring and fruitful visit early in 1978 to historic Plymouth where James Dowdle, with his violin, had pioneered the work. The following weekend my wife and I visited Coventry for the purpose of presenting new colours to the corps. Enroute, on the famed M-1 motorway, a car swerved out from the next lane at high speed and virtually lifted our vehicle on to the median. Skilful driving by Brigadier Syd. Woodall saved us from crashing into the rails and somersaulting. Our four occupants walked away from a wrecked car with only a shaking up and some bruises. A passing Salvationist motorist seeing our plight ferried us into Coventry where an anxious lord mayor, already aware of the accident, awaited our arrival at the entrance to the city hall. We were just in time for the luncheon being tendered by the city in the fourteenth-century armoury of the council house.

One hundred years before, the first Salvation Army flag had been presented to the Coventry Salvationists by Catherine Booth herself, she being responsible for the design and fabricating of it. Through the century, the design, with only one change, had remained the same. The original banner had at its centre a yellow sun which, it was soon discovered, caused confusion in countries where sun-worship was practised. The flag's symbolism is simple and comprehensive: the blue border speaks of holiness of heart and life; the red field signifies the shed Blood of Christ as the cost of man's salvation; and the eight-pointed star which replaced the sun represents the light and fire of the regenerating and animating Holy Spirit. When my wife ceremonially presented the "Centenary Flag" it was to none other than a great-grandson of the man who had received the original flag from the hand of Catherine Booth. On the platform, supporting us, were the then Colonel (now Commissioner) and Mrs. Francy Cachelin, she being a great-granddaughter of Catherine Booth. It was as if the flag had its own preserved lineage.

The international congress encompassed not only the centenary of the flag, but also of Salvation Army bands, the formulation and registration by deed poll of the Army's eleven articles of doctrine, and of the name, "The Salvation Army." For this most spectacular of all assemblies in the movement's history, the Wembley Conference Centre, the Royal Albert Hall and other large London buildings had been reserved, and plans, master-minded by Colonel Brindley Boon, were well advanced. To these I added events in Westminster Abbey, where the flag was to lie across the high altar, and the singing of the Soweto Singers from South Africa would precede the chiming of the carillon. In St. Paul's Cathedral advisory board members would join with the International Staff Band and the Agincourt Songsters from Toronto, Canada. I also felt that there should be a grand march, ending in Trafalgar Square, as an acknowledgement of the Army's *al fresco* beginnings and its sustained outdoor ministry.

A note from General Coutts suggested a service in one of the Free Churches as a "balance" to those in state churches. The idea appealed to me, and I found Dr. Brian Johanson, minister of the historic City Temple, more than willing to cooperate. It was from the pulpit of this church, destroyed in World War II and afterwards rebuilt, that Catherine Booth, though ill, preached her last sermon in public. Speaking passionately for an hour and a quarter she collapsed at the end and could not be moved for almost an hour. It seemed especially appropriate that my wife should be the speaker on this occasion. In doing so, she not only historically bridged the years but reaffirmed the principle of equal opportunity for women to preach which, from the start, had been a vital aspect of the Army's evangelism. To further strengthen the link with Catherine Booth my wife took for her text the one used by Mrs. Booth in her first public sermon, "Be filled with the Spirit" (Eph. 5: 18).

I had designated this greatest-ever convocation of Salvationists as "The Gathering and the Glory," based on the words of the prophet Isaiah, chapter 66 and verse 18: "I will gather all nations and tongues, and they shall come and see My glory." In the context there is judgement as well as joy and a looking forward to that "one far-off divine event, to which the whole creation moves." In some senses, I felt, the international congress would foreshadow that eternal event. With more than thirty thousand attending, the Army uniform was everywhere. On the final Saturday, when busloads of British Salvationists joined the overseas delegations, Wembley Stadium, with more than fifty thousand participating, was a vast sea of colour and movement. Future historians, happily, will have access to microfilmed reports, to sound-films and recordings that will have preserved all the congress features, thus rendering any lengthy, detailed record here unnecessary.

The congress was launched in the presence of H.R.H. Prince Charles, the Prince of Wales who, travelling by helicopter from another appointment, landed near the Wembley complex. He was given a tumultuous reception, repeated when I asked him to bring greetings. The media people were present in force seeing His Royal Highness was with The Salvation Army and not at the marriage ceremony of a cousin, certain aspects of the wedding having been the subject of wide press coverage. Some of the Prince's remarks were taken as being an oblique rebuke to obstructive church authority, but the Salvationists, myself among them, did not put any such construction on his words. For us, they were exceptionally pertinent and wholly encouraging. "In an age when we are assailed by a host of outlandish philosophies and inhuman beliefs, when people are uncertain about what is right and what is wrong and anxious about being considered old-fashioned and out of date, it seems worse than folly that Christians should still argue and bicker," said His Royal Highness. "What we should be worried about now is whether people are going to become atheists, whether they are going to be given any idea of what is right and wrong, whether they are going to be given an awareness of the things of the spirit ..." The upshot was worldwide coverage of the first congress event in which the Heir-apparent and the Army were newsworthily linked.

There was a royal sequel. Invited to a reception at Canada House marking the centenary of a Canadian diplomatic presence at the Court of St. James, my wife and I were presented to Her Majesty The Queen who graciously enquired about the international congress. I seized the opportunity to say that Prince Charles, whose participation had been so tremendously appreciated, had got us off to "a roaring start." The Queen, obviously informed as to the extensive media coverage and the delicate circumstances that provoked it, smiled knowingly and said, "Almost too much, perhaps."

During the congress, emphasis in a unique way was given to the Army's century-old eleven articles of faith. Two of the four congress choruses, each of a thousand voices, sang a setting of the doctrines which I had requested Lieut-Colonel Ray Steadman Allen to compose. It was a *magnum opus* perfectly suited to the occasion but, one felt, beyond those average capabilities that would ensure its general use. But, shortly after, to my surprise, I was to hear it admirably sung in their pagoda-like hall by vocalists of the Singapore central corps. The taxing accompaniment was brilliantly managed by the two teen-age children of the then general secretary and Mrs. Major Lim Ah Ang, one at the organ, the other at the pianoforte.

The preparation of the addresses I was expected to give during the congress exercised me greatly. With such multicultural congregations the messages had to span a wide spectrum of comprehension, and the language problem could not be dismissed. Particularly challenging was the addressing of the largest gathering of officers, about eight thousand of them, ever to come together in the entire history of the Army. As I stood at the speaking desk, the unrepeatability of such an event, not only in my lifetime but in the lifetime of most present, swept over me. I spoke of the binding covenants which officers make, and in a succeeding chapter dwell at some length on one which was particularly emphasized. The spirit and quality of the officers' singing was at times more than one could emotionally bear. Only one adjective, "heavenly," could adequately describe it. The all-pervasive atmosphere of unity bespoke the universality of the Gospel and the truly international nature of our movement.

There were some unrecorded moments of immense significance. Ten former Salvation Army officers from Czechoslovakia and Hungary, where the work had been proscribed after World War II, were among the delegates. For the first time since totalitarianism had denied them their ministry they wore Salvation Army uniform. The insignia provided was English so that these "phantoms" from another era could move freely without incurring any unfortunate aftermath. Their presence in meetings was more hinted at than revealed, but the mere mention of their attendance electrified the congregations. It was to be expected that the group would wish to visit the General, and I asked for this to be arranged. For them, the General's office was the heart and nerve centre of a movement they had never ceased to love. One of the number, reasonably fluent in English, was kept busy passing on the exclamations of fidelity to God and the Army that all wanted to express. There was an exchange of promises to pray for each other, and we knelt in a circle on the carpet, arms around each other tightening the sphere of commitment, and thanked God for a moment, bathed in tears, that had eternal import. Minutes passed before I could control my feelings sufficiently to speak.

It was on the eve of the international congress that I was made a Freeman of the City of London, a recognition which I cherish for three reasons. Firstly, because London was my birthplace; secondly, because in this distinction I was, as *The War Cry* reported, "following in the footsteps of the Army's Founder"; and, thirdly, as I made plain to our hosts, Sir Edward Howard, a former Lord Mayor, and Lady Howard, the honour, as I saw it, was actually a tribute to all Salvationists, and on their behalf I was proud to accept it. At the luncheon in the Irish Chamber, Guildhall Yard, which followed the ceremony conducted by the city's chamberlain, I repeated the story told by William Booth to the City Fathers when he was made a Freeman in 1905. In a town under siege during the Boer War supplies were dwindling dangerously and the citizens were beginning to suffer. Help was organized and the rations were to be denominationally distributed. The clergy were instructed to march off their own flock and dispense the badly-needed food. One after another, like Eastern shepherds, the ministers called their sheep to follow. Last of all was the Salvation Army captain who shouted, "All of you who don't belong to anybody, follow me."

If frequently the chronicler is overshadowed by the happenings he chronicles, it was not to be so for the Army's "official organ," *The War Cry* which, in 1979, also reached its century. Only once had an issue been missed when in 1947, during an electricity power-cut, two issues were telescoped into one. The Army's founders well knew the power of the press. What they could not know was that one hundred years on *The War Cry* would be familiar to millions of readers in scores of countries, a continuing enigma to the publishing world seeing its circulation does not depend upon paid advertising. I commissioned Lieut-Colonel Cyril Barnes to produce a monograph so that the remarkable history of the Army's newspaper would be preserved as well as commemorated. The brochure, *Ever Is The War Cry,* tells the captivating story in word and picture.

To mark the anniversary publicly, the editor-in-chief, Lieut-Colonel Wm. Clark, arranged a celebratory occasion in the Regent Hall over which, as a former editor, I was happy to preside. The distribution of *The War Cry* depends upon volunteers, often referred to as "heralds." The Colonel hit on the novel idea of asking the owners and patrons of public houses, where many copies are sold each week, to nominate their favourite Salvationist for a "Herald of the Year" award. To his surprise, hundreds of nominations flowed in and, finally, five awards were required. The idea caught the interest of press and radio, and as soon as the recipients were announced the news was broadcast to the nation. With great difficulty the winner was persuaded to leave her native Kilmarnock and make her very first visit out of Scotland and to London. Margaret ("Maggie") Rubie, 74-years of age and a retired bus despatcher, after fifty-six years as a spare-time herald, was still distributing more than a thousand papers each week.

Scottish Salvationists, unlike their English counterparts, meet annually for congress gatherings. Even so, the centenary congress in the late summer of 1979 was far from usual. In few corners of the Army world can be found greater enthusiasm for a similar series of meetings. From the Western Isles, from towns on both sides of the Grampians, from beyond the Moray Forth as well as from the more populous areas of the south, Scottish Salvationists of all ages flood to Glasgow where, on March 23, 1879 two girl officers pioneered the work. Seldom, it seems, does the weather cooperate. "And ghastly thro' the drizzling rain," to borrow Tennyson's lines, "On the bald streets breaks the bland day." But inclemency is a small hindrance. On one occasion I was notified by the then territorial commander, Colonel Ernest Anderson, to remain in our quarters as the early Sunday morning march was to be cancelled because of the unremitting downpour of rain. Minutes later a telephone call requested our earliest presence at the reviewing stand. The sublimated spirit of Bannockburn is not easily dampened. The march, so a frantic voice said, was already nearing the saluting base and the genial lord provost, the Rt. Hon. David Hodge, O.St.J., JP. had already arrived. We raced to join him, and gratefully shared the big umbrella dutifully held by an attendant. I rejoiced that we were there in time to return the salute of diminutive Sister Mrs. Jeannie Fraser, OF., of Arbroath, striding by quite unperturbed by the saturating rain and showing no decline of vigour in her 92nd year. Standing at the salute, the rain poured from the lord provost's umbrella down my right sleeve until I was as uncomfortable as I assumed most of the marchers to be, yet too respectful to ask a generous lord provost to "move over." One felt that Baring-Gould's famous hymn, "Onward, Christian soldiers," could have been revised to read, "*sodden* soldiers," except that, soaked or not, these Scots in Salvation Army uniform were above all "*Christian* soldiers." They had in their hearts, as I reminded them, something the rain could not wash away.

No congress in Scotland is complete without at some juncture "the skirl o' the pipes," and no congress meeting could be more "Scottish" than when a kilted peer, the Viscount Thurso, rises, as he occasionally did, to lead the immense congregation in singing the refrain: "Wide, wide as the ocean, high as the heavens above,/ Deep, deep as the deepest sea is my Saviour's love ..."

To launch Scotland's centenary year my wife and I had visited both

Glasgow and Edinburgh in February. Visits to Glasgow had special appeal for my wife. Her father, as a lad, had left the family business in Glasgow to make a career for himself in Winnipeg, Canada. There, for the first time, he met The Salvation Army, became converted, and gave the whole of his life to Salvation Army officership. In Glasgow, following a recognition luncheon in the city chambers, I admitted Lord Wallace of Campsie, KSt.J., JP., DL., SSC., chairman of the Strathclyde advisory board and an unrelenting contestant for Salvation Army progress, to the Order of Distinguished Auxiliary Service.

The winter snow was disappearing and the fog of the morning had lifted as we drove with the territorial commander, Colonel (now Commissioner) Denis Hunter and his wife from Glasgow to Edinburgh where a crowd of officers had been awaiting our arrival. We had been greatly delayed and I was hurriedly ushered into the pulpit of the church in which the assembly was being held, minus Bible and notes, but somehow managed. Later, in the presence of the lord provost, the Rt. Hon. Kenneth Borthwick and the lady provost, Salvationists attended a reception prior to the centenary rally. With the exception of events in India, I cannot recall so many people being accommodated in so limited a space, and so happily. In the main event, the Very Rev. Leonard Small, DD., (whose height seriously belied his name), moderator of the Church of Scotland, brought greetings, and a friend to whom I, and the Army, owe an immeasurable debt, the always-kilted Lord Birsay, whose speech-making gifts were of unparalleled quality, offered the final prayer.

The fervour of the Welsh, expressed in matchless singing, eloquent speech and affectionate comradeship, lifted the centenary rally in Cardiff to the highest heights of inspiration. Masefield has it that "One road leads to London. One road runs to Wales." But all roads that days seemed to run to the Welsh capital, and accommodation in the spacious city hall assembly rooms was stretched to the limit, with hundreds throughout the Principality unable to secure tickets of admission. The British Commissioner and Mrs. Commissioner Dalziel who accompanied us were paying their final visit to Wales as leaders. The Commissioner had been born in Monmouthshire, and he and his wife had spent some years in the country as corps officers. With us, they shared the civic luncheon presided over by the lady lord mayor, Councillor Bella Brown, who tried without success to match our respective genealo-

An infant Arnold Brown sits on his mother's knee (front row, right). His father stands at the right of the group. Grandmother Brown (seated, centre) presides over a gathering of her Salvation Army officer-children (circa 1914)

General and Mrs. Arnold Brown take office at The Salvation Army's International Headquarters, Queen Victoria Street, London, Eng., July, 1977

An international Centenary Congress drew 32,000 Salvationists to London in 1978. H.R.H. Prince Charles welcomed the delegates during the opening ceremonies

H.R.H. Prince Charles with the General and his Chief of the Staff, Commissioner W. Stan. Cottrill

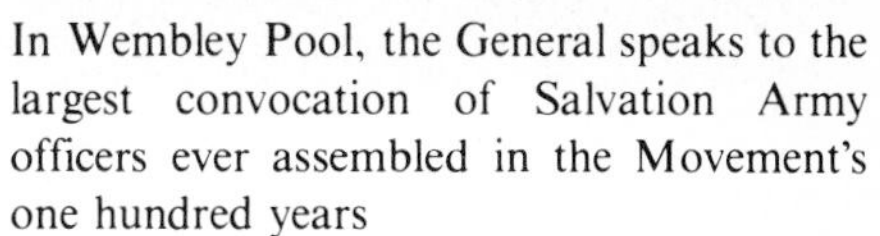

In Wembley Pool, the General speaks to the largest convocation of Salvation Army officers ever assembled in the Movement's one hundred years

During the congress, Mrs. General Brown addresses a congregation that overflowed the historic City Temple

A Doctor of Humanities (L.H.D.) degree is conferred by Dr. Denis Kinlaw, president of Asbury College, U.S.A. Commissioner Andrew Miller, a member of the college's Board of Governors, is at the reading desk

Turbanned Salvation Army officers in Northern India give a welcoming salute to their visiting General

As a newly-created Freeman of the City of London, the General poses with the City Chamberlain outside the fifteenth century Guildhall

Children in the care of The Salvation Army in Rangoon, Burma, give a wide-eyed welcome to the General

During a visit to Japan, General and Mrs. Brown are received by Crown Prince Akihito and Crown Princess Michiko

Her Majesty Queen Elizabeth II opens "Hope Town," a new home for women in the east end of London. With the General is Lord Cadogan, chairman of The Salvation Army's London Advisory Board

The General served a five-year apprenticeship with one of his predecessors in office, General Erik Wickberg, seen here (centre) with Professor Jürgen Winterhager, of West Berlin

Discussing relief possibilities with a leader of thousands of war-harassed Cambodians near the border of Thailand. With the General is Major Eva den Hartog, in charge of The Salvation Army's medical aid programme

A Nigerian chief beamingly welcomes the General to the Eastern States of Nigeria

Commissioner Wycliffe Booth, grandson of The Salvation Army's founder, with Mrs. Booth and (left) *le petit copain*

A retiring General Brown wishes his successor, General-elect Jarl Wahlström, well following his election to international leadership

gies. The South Glamorgan County Council received us with warm dignity, and an advisory board reception was presided over by its chairman, Mr. Percy Jones, JP., whose musical gifts were "eternally satisfied" when, on one occasion, he was invited to conduct the Army's International Staff Band. The Lord Lieutenant of Glamorgan, Colonel Sir Cennyydd Trahern, spoke glowingly of the Army's relief work among the Kampucheans.

A centenary observance of another kind occurred in June, 1980, marking a century of officer-training. The panelled assembly hall of the International Training College at Denmark Hill, London, was filled to capacity with officers, the oldest being Lieut-Commissioner Herbert Hodgson who completed his training in 1902. While presiding, I sought the financial aid of those present to help meet the cost of placing a floodlit cross on the north face of the central tower, one of the highest landmarks in South London, a project I had launched a year before. The college, conceived by Bramwell Booth as a memorial to his father, to be opened on the 100th anniversary of his birth, was described in the Year Book for 1929 as having "a lofty central tower ... visible from afar. Continually lit up it would perpetually remind all that all may call upon God for Salvation, and that those living in the precincts below are dedicated to the service of God and man." Fifty-two years were to pass before the tower could be illuminated. The securing of permission from the local authorities turned out to be a complicated, drawn-out business, but on the evening of January 27, 1981, as a large crowd spilled over the college lawns, I pressed the button which illuminated the 23-foot stainless steel cross, 188-feet from the ground, with its white enamelled background. No longer would passers-by be in doubt as to the spiritual purposes of the buildings. Nurses at nearby Kings College and Maudesley hospitals reported their own and their patients' excitement when the cross suddenly flashed into view. One supervisor wrote to say that when the cross broke the darkness she could not help shouting, "Christ is alive! Jesus lives!"

Despite the differences in tradition and location, the centenary congress in the United States, held in June, 1980, bore many similarities to those held earlier in London and Glasgow. Kansas City, because of its geographically central position, was chosen as the venue. The city, noted as a convention centre, nevertheless found the invasion of some fourteen thousand Salvationists to be quite out of the ordinary. American hospitality overflowed. The interest of all levels of government was obvious, with a message of greeting from the president and the personal participation of state and community leaders. American technology added its dimension in vivid, multi-media presentations. In the enormous Heritage Hall, where more than two hundred booths portrayed every aspect of Salvation Army life, achievement and interest, a startlingly lifelike figure of William Booth, electronically animated, called the spectators to enter the second century with the passion of the pioneers. American originality effervesced when, during a civic dinner attended by almost fifteen hundred persons, I was presented with a live steer which, despite its youth, already weighed eighteen hundred pounds. The animal had been beautifully groomed, even its hooves being immaculately polished. I was warned to make the acceptance verbal only and leave any handling to the posse of cowboys who had brought the reluctant beast to the stage. I was more than ready to oblige! Donated by the city's cattle market it was eventually "to feed the hungry" at one of the Army's camps. All this in the same city where early-day Salvationists had been imprisoned, among them a young, pregnant officer who was to be the grandmother of a future national commander of the work throughout the United States. Thoughts of the city's changed attitudes occupied my mind as I dedicated a plaque marking the spot where the Army's ministry had begun in 1883.

The long air journeys undertaken by the delegates in order to attend can hardly be understood by Europeans, the compactness of whose countries contrasts markedly with the vastness of America, including as it does Alaska in the north, the Hawaiian Islands beyond the western coast, and the Commonwealth of Puerto Rico off its south-eastern shores. The convention auditorium, splendidly appointed in contrast to the rather rough appearance of Wembley Pool where so many of the London gatherings took place, was "made to order" for the size of the congregations attending the major events. Filled, it became a massive sanctuary so that the spirit of worship fell easily upon the congregations. Cadets from the New York, Chicago, Atlanta and Los Angeles schools for officer training, one hundred and eighty-three in all, united for their commissioning and ordination. The length of the ceremony in no way militated against its solemnity and significance. I stood for the longest period of time in my career to receive individually the missionary gifts of all divisions in the United States, while projected on an extended screen, in magnificent colour, contributors and beneficiaries were visually united. American Salvationists on this occasion had donated almost five and a half million dollars.

The congress Sunday morning meeting was alive with fervour, so much so that during the Bible message my emphasized statements were given prolonged rounds of applause. Was this an American substitution for loud "Amens" and other ejaculations of concurrence? I did not find the applause interruptive or undesirable, surprised as I was by it. Actually, I was as encouraged by it as the Pontiff at a St. Peter's rally must be, or as certain television evangelists who gather force from such congregational punctuations. My recollections of the Kansas City meetings are most luminous with the memory of the many hundreds who sought Divine grace in greater measure, and who knelt not only at the long altar but in aisles, hallways and even doorways.

Others led Ireland's various celebrations during its centennial year, but in September, 1980, I shared appreciatively in a service of thanksgiving in the Belfast cathedral. For one short evening Ulster appeared to forget its troubles. The security screen was thrown open for five hundred representative Salvationists to pass through Royal Avenue without being searched. The presence of armed soldiers, police and military vehicles was a grim reminder of the underlying and continuing tensions. I took the salute as five bands, two-score Army flags and ranks of courageous Salvationists marched into the sanctuary where unity, rather than division, reigned. In the pulpit I faced the Lord Lieutenant of Belfast and Lady Glentoran; the Rt. Worshipful the Lord Mayor of Belfast and Mrs. Carson; Lieut-General Sir Richard Lawson, in supreme command of the military forces; the Lord Bishop of Armagh, the Most Reverend John Armstrong; leaders of all the denominations and a congregation which overflowed the ancient house of worship.

If the inspiring service lifted the spirit out of the fear with which the citizens of Northern Ireland cannot help but be enveloped, the post-Benediction minutes plunged me, at least, into reality. To enter the hotel where we were to spend the night, we had to pass through a barbed-wire enclosure, be subject to a thorough identity check and once inside, be searched. The precautions were intensive. I was asked what I had in a small leather case, and said it was a miniature transistor radio. I was instructed to take it to the far end of the hall and then turn it on so that it could be heard. Obviously, destructive devices can assume many shapes and sizes. Despite the fact that the hotel had been bombed twenty-eight times, I fell asleep to inner echoes of the praiseful music that had filled the cathedral. When I awoke in safety the next morning the music was still reverberating within.

Only those who have seen the scars of Belfast know the bitterness of the struggle and the sadness of its consequences. Not buildings only, but human lives have been irremediably marked. Yet amid the mayhem and murder compassion and brotherly kindness may still be seen. I arrived in Belfast one evening by air just as a large departmental store had been bombed. The divisional comander drove me swiftly to the scene. The once proud building had been cordoned off, and only firemen, soldiers, police and Salvationists were allowed near. Flames leapt into the night sky and windows on every floor spewed out clouds of black smoke. The streets were awash with water from a dozen hydrants. A burly fire chief, holding coffee and biscuits he had just been given by a girl Salvationist spoke with a brogue as rolling as the mountains of Mourne. "It may not be wine and wafer," he said to me, "but it's sacramental. Your people bring the presence of Christ with them." Later, I was to see standing in the shadows the manager of the store, weeping, his head on the shoulder of a man captain who was trying to comfort him. What a subject for a sensitive artist.

The buoyant, thrusting temperament of Australians is characteristic of the Army itself in this largest and flattest of all island continents. Here, in 1880, two young Salvationist immigrants from England began the unabashed witness for Christ which their successors have vigorously maintained. The organizers might have found it easier to mount the centenary congress in either Melbourne or Sydney where the Army's two chief centres of administration are located. But it was a wise decision to go back to the place of beginnings, and no city could have outshone Adelaide in its hosting of the eight thousand Salvationists who, by their obvious presence, seemed to outnumber the one-million population of this gracious state capital of South Australia, named after the wife of William IV, the first city in Australia to be designated as a city.

What the city lacked in convention facilities it made up for in enthusiastic participation. King William Street, a principal thoroughfare, was ablaze with yellow, red and blue bunting and with Army flags flying from one hundred flagpoles. His Excellency, the Governor-General, Sir Zelman Cowen, officially opened the congress at an afternoon ceremony in the Royal Botanic Gardens beside the gum tree where the two pioneers stood for their first open-air meeting. On this occasion the two had become nine thousand, and, linking the present with the past, at the centre of the crowd was a replica of the greengrocer's cart from which the first meeting had been addressed. John Gore would hardly have imagined that one hundred years later, at the precise spot, his great-granddaughter, Mrs. Captain Margaret Watters, would offer prayer, nor Edward Saunders that his grandson, Lieut-Commissioner Frank Saunders (R), would read the Scriptures.

I read to the crowd a postcard I had received that day. It was written in shaky handwriting. "Dear General," it said, "love from Archie Gale." Now 104-years old, Gale was an infant in the original meetings held a century before. Nearby, splashed with the sunshine of an Antipodean Spring, Heritage Village, a spreading canvas community, housed the memorabilia of the years and displayed in demonstration, photograph and model the manifold aspects of the Army's active witness from Perth to Brisbane and from Hobart to Alice Springs. Earlier, I had planted the first of one hundred trees which would eventually form a commemorative avenue in the Gardens. The novel idea appealed to me—a corridor of trees marking the corridor of the years.

Three other events that remain vividly in the memory were held outdoors. The first was the Saturday morning procession when an estimated eight thousand marchers filled the heart of the city with music and movement. A phalanx of vintage automobiles carrying retired officers contrasted dramatically with the flypast of planes which roared over the route of march. Piloted by Salvation Army officers the aerial display was a reminder of the Army's unique outback ministry. Remote as Australia may seem to many parts of the world it was not beyond the interest of Salvationists in Sweden from whence came a competent, composite stringband in their brilliant red and white blouses, or neighbouring New Zealand—next door but still miles away—where work had been pioneered by Australian Salvationists, which sent a youth band, the mature capabilities of which denied the average age of the players.

Representatives from Hong Kong, Indonesia, India, Papua New Guinea, the Bahamas, Uganda and Fiji were cheered by the sidewalk crowds. Such processions obviously did not happen often in Adelaide. Traffic was thrown into chaos. Unfortunate motorists who could not move their vehicles because of the march became unhappy parking offenders, but as soon as news reached the city council amnesty was granted.

When one has seen the Edinburgh Tattoo the conclusion is that nowhere in the world could such a spectacle be duplicated. Perhaps not, but the impression could have been seriously challenged by the centenary congress tattoo, a masterpiece of organization and presentation. True, the tessellated towers of Edinburgh castle were missing, and in place of the Castle Rock parade ground were the Memorial Drive tennis courts. But the thousands of spectators in the tiered seats were treated to as fine a display of marching, and certainly to equal quality in the music of the bands (Enfield Citadel Band having travelled all the way from London), as their rug-wrapped counterparts in distant Scotland. The magnificent production concluded just as a fine mist of rain began to fall and a fireworks display filled the night sky with cascades of colour. Appropriately, the massed bands were playing Handel's "Music for the Royal Fireworks."

One other outdoor gathering imprinted itself on my mind. Due to limited facilities meetings were often going on simultaneously in various buildings, but for the Sunday afternoon delegates and general public came together, some thirteen thousand in the crowd, at the Adelaide Football Oval. The creating of a worshipping atmosphere and the establishing of rapport when the lectern is far removed from the listeners might seem impossible. But the attention given to every participation corroborated William Cowper's words: "Where'er they seek Thee Thou art found,/ And every place is hallowed ground." I called for a more positive Christian witness and asked those who would genuinely pledge themselves to seek to win someone for Christ to raise their hands. It was a mighty response. Thousands of hands were lifted high in commitment. There could be no doubt as to the evangelistic zeal with which Australian Salvationists were determined to enter their second century.

The many, varied events and meetings ended with a service of thanksgiving which the organizers feared might be anticlimactic. Not in the slightest! It was a powerful meeting concluding with queues of seekers standing in the aisles awaiting their turn to kneel at the congress altar in rededication.

It was revealing to me that Australian officers, after a lifetime of service, were meeting counterparts from "the other territory" for the first time. All were Australians and all were serving in the same Salvation Army. Territorial boundaries, however, all the more entrenched because of the vastness of the country and the passage of years since their establishment in 1921, had imposed an insularity that for the first time since had been dissolved by a united congress. During the final meeting Commissioners Arthur Linnett and Leo. Ward had represented their territories in expressing thanks, each to the other, for faultless cooperation and outpoured comradeship. The congregation enjoyed my slightly ironic comment that this brotherly love, expressed in such gushing words, seemed to evaporate whenever I brought up the subject of one training college for both territories. On certain issues, evidently, "Never the twain shall meet."

Of all the centenary congresses, the one in Paris in April, 1981, held the most surprises. Paris in the Spring has its own magical attraction, and Salvationists from more than a score of countries joined in the celebrations: Norway sent its accomplished Oslo III Band, Denmark an attractive stringband, Scotland a singing company comprised of boys and girls from Springburn, England a dramatic group, Canada a delegation of officers and the United States a company of singing and timbrel-playing young people. From distant Zaire and the Congo came French-speaking groups, while from neighbouring countries came large supporting delegations.

If any doubted the joyousness of the congress a glimpse, on the Saturday afternoon, of the crowded *bateaux-mouches,* the modern pleasure craft which ply the Seine, crowded with Salvationists, would have confirmed it. The boats passed and re-passed each other with Army flags flying, bands playing and passengers singing. Loud hallelujahs echoed as the vessels glided by the Army's barge, *La Peniche,* moored near the Austerlitz Bridge, which accommodates 150 homeless men of Paris each night. I had the privilege of conducting the Oslo III Band as our *bateau-mouche* slid by the Ile de la Cité, the strains of the march, "Montreal Citadel," (a link with French Canada) rising up against the walls of the Cathedral of Notre Dame and the Palace of Justice.

Also surprising was the extent of the public interest. A splendid reception at the Hôtel de Ville, the city hall of Paris, a magnificent structure in the style of the French Renaissance, indicated the appreciation of the authorities for the Army's century of service. The dramatic story of Devil's Island and the Army's part in its dissolution was certainly not forgotten. I had previously been made aware of the city's appreciation on an earlier visit when I had been presented with the Medaille d'Argent of the City of Paris by M. le Maire, Jacques Chirac. On another occasion I had shared in the opening of an addition to the impressive Cité de Refuge with the elegant and brilliant Mme. Simone Veil, then minister of health in the French government and soon afterwards to be the first woman president of the expanded European parliament. In conversation she left me in no doubt as to the value placed on the Army's services by France, its government and its people.

In the congress soldiers' rally I ventured, with considerable nervousness, to give the address in French. I had been counselled not to do so by a solicitous wife who thought that leadership of the gatherings was sufficiently burdensome without adding what she knew would leave me limp as a dishrag, even if the undertaking were successful. To this day I do not know with what degree of acceptability I spoke, nor does it matter, since the gathering ended in a tender spirit of consecration and an altar lined with seekers, as did so many other of the commemorative gatherings.

After Paris it was Halifax, Nova Scotia, for a centenary congress marking the landing on Canadian shores of the first uniformed Salvationist, George Scott Railton, William Booth's first lieutenant and, incidentally, also his first commissioner. This multilingual nomad, in the best apostolic tradition, wanted nothing more than to take the Gospel to as many lands as his wanderings could lead him. Having pioneered the work in the United States he was being recalled, against his own judgement, to London. The ship in which he was sailing docked at Halifax and he disembarked to hold an open-air meeting in the downtown area. So engrossed did he become in his preaching that the boat sailed without him. An enforced ten-day stay allowed him to hold a series of evangelistic gatherings which served also to introduce The Salvation Army to the city. No permanent work resulted from Railton's sojourn, but Canadian Salvationists felt that the episode was worthy of recall and commemoration.

A dramatic re-enactment of the commissioner's arrival captivated the attention of hundreds of onlookers at the Halifax harbour-front as the congress began. To the dull sound of fog horns a ship emerged out of the early morning mist and steamed to the quayside. In the prow, Bible uplifted, was a life-like impersonation of Railton. Stepping ashore, the impersonator gave a powerful, memorized recital of one of Railton's stirring sermons. With the blessing of the city, the mayor being present, and the cooperation of the harbour control authorities, a large bronze plaque telling the story of the original landing was unveiled.

The series of meetings which followed brought together Salvationists from the maritime provinces, from Newfoundland and from Bermuda. To the lieutenant-governor of the province and the congress crowd I read the greetings I had brought from Dame Ruth Railton, founder of Britain's prestigious national youth orchestra, and a granddaughter of the pioneer Salvationist. The congress was reminded that the Railton family had made another significant contribution to British tradition. One of Railton's sons, a clergyman who served as a padre in the First World War, conceived the idea of honouring "The Unknown Soldier." Few of the millions who have stood by the tomb of the unknown warrior in the centre of the nave of Westminster Abbey have known that its instigator's father was a Salvation Army officer who, in his war against sin, cared most about being a *faithful* soldier, and cared not at all if he were totally *unknown.*

During my final year in office the centenary of the Army's occupancy of its premises at 101 Queen Victoria Street, in London, was noted. On Tuesday morning, September 8, 1981, a special gathering was convened in the Bramwell Booth memorial hall. The Army's archivist, Lieut-Colonel Cyril Barnes, told the congregation how the property—a vacant billiards hall—had been acquired and how unimpressively all the paraphernalia of this incipiently worldwide movement was moved from the previous headquarters—on a tarpaulin-covered greengrocer's handcart. For sixty years the original buildings served the Army's purposes until, during the fiery night of May 10/11, 1941, they were destroyed in the blitz. The sentiments of Salvationists around the world insisted that rebuilding take place on the same site, and their gifts, together with war compensation monies, eventually made it possible. More than twenty years were to elapse before the present headquarters building would be opened by Her Majesty The Queen Mother on October 1, 1963. At the close of our 1981 commemorative service the crowd stood, quietly reflecting on all the good that had flowed out from this centre during the past century while I, with similar thoughts, unveiled a plaque noting the one hundred years of occupancy. The property, acquired within the meagre means of the Army a century ago, is now among the most valuable pieces of real estate in the world. Sentiment and goodwill of the Common Council of the City of London encourage its retention, but with the urgent need for a new international training college for officers, one wonders how long it will be before headquarters takes over the present college at Denmark Hill and, with the realization of its Queen Victoria Street asset, provides proper facilities for the training of those who will lead the movement into the future.

Centenary celebrations of many kinds marking the Army's beginnings will now go on for many years. That I should have had the honour of leading the first of them all, and of taking Salvation Army history across the threshold of its second century leaves me humbly marvelling. What a rare and prized privilege!

CHAPTER 17

"No Time To Be Weary"

Centenary occasions, as sketched in the preceding chapter, while spanning my term as international leader, by no means dominated all else. Business was unceasing, and, when in London, the working day was a long one. Rising time was 5.30 a.m., but I was often awakened still earlier in the English summer by "the dawn chorus" of the birds, marvellous to hear, signalling that "the day had arrived but had not yet appeared." An early departure, before the road traffic multiplied into sluggishness, considerably shortened the time it took to drive the 9.1 miles from home desk to office desk. Leaving at 7 o'clock it was an half-hour drive, give or take a minute or two either way. Leaving at 8 o'clock the journey could last an hour and a half.

The evening meal at home was inevitably followed by hours in the study, preparing matters for the next day's business, addresses for imminent public engagements, or articles for publication. I could not bring myself to use ghost writers, and painstakingly answered letters which others might easily have written for me, and perhaps with better effect. Those who received letters signed by me can know that the words were my own. The shaping up of addresses was an unceasing occupation. Any who thought that whenever the faucet was turned liquid speech flowed out effortlessly were unaware of how often the crowded mind was forced into concentration and the tired body into the discipline of preparation.

Salvationists who see and hear their international leader once or twice in a lifetime base their impressions on his platform presence and his public utterances. They know little, if anything, of his ability at the desk or in conference. They do not know with what ease, or otherwise, he meets the world's influence-makers. They cannot be aware of the newest anxiety that is thrust on him a moment before he steps into public view. They know only what fleetingly they hear and what briefly they see. It may be the reader's opinion that this applies to all public persons, and I would agree except for one dimension. The General is not a politician whose interests stop with the material wellbeing of his voters. He is preaching a Gospel that can affect the eternal destiny of his hearers, and it is a saving element, as I repeatedly proved, that he can have the Holy Spirit's divine empowering to compensate for his human inadequacies.

Despite pressures, the international leader is expected to remain physically well. Twice on long tours I lost my voice "with much speaking." Twice I realized that interest in one's face and form is short-lived. Unless one can *say* something, the contact might just as well be aborted. In Johannesburg, on one occasion, I whispered into a microphone for three-quarters of an hour. It was perhaps a little better than silence and smiles, but only the patience of the listeners made it in any degree tolerable. Days lost to illness during all the years of officership could be counted on the fingers of one's hand, and for the period as Chief of the Staff and General only a thumb and finger would be needed. For that I am inexpressibly grateful.

One episode was a rather humourous reminder of how much one is within the sphere of general comment. I had, in one fortnight, spoken in Lausanne, Switzerland, New York City, Glasgow, Scotland, at the Swanwick conference centre in Derbyshire, England, and in Stockholm, Sweden. All were important events making their claim on mind and body. Returning from Stockholm to London I felt dizzy and nauseous. When the doctor learned about the schedule he prescribed a day or two of total rest—"simply to allow your body to catch up with your spirit." On the Saturday evening I was expected to preside over a musical festival in the Royal Albert Hall, and had to ask Commissioner Kaare Westergaard to deputize for me. News of my absence flashed around the world, and each retelling added to the gravity of my illness. Within hours I was on my deathbed and my successor had been nominated! How this was reconciled with my return to the office on the Monday morning I have no idea. The words of a former Chief of the Staff, Commissioner John J. Allan, with whom I had travelled as a young officer, were now more clearly understood. "Remember this, Brown," he counselled, "the higher up you go the more people talk about you—and the less you hear it."

If the maintaining of bodily health is important, the health of mind and spirit is equally so. One has to be careful not to let one's limitations in the face of enormous demands become a debilitating nemesis. I drew strength from the confession of Archbishop Cosmo Gordon Lang: "... the work which has been set me to do ... seems utterly beyond my power. It goes wrong; there is no response, there is a dreary succession of difficulties and disappointments. The doors of entry into the hearts of the people seem closed; the walls of prejudice, of ignorance, of callousness stand thick and grim before me. But if I have not light, I can have faith; if I have no success, I can pray; I can bring my work to Him who called me to do it."

There were days when the morning post brought a bagful of disappointments or annoyances, each capable of dealing a body-blow to self control. In such moments, gratefully, I could "bring my work to Him who called me to do it." If trouble had arisen with one officer, it restored the balance to remember that the other twenty-five thousand were alive and well and living up to their possibilities. Occasionally, there would be the uneducated and perhaps unfair criticism, and human ire would momentarily erupt. At such a moment inner voices would shout that smallness in the generalship, no matter who or what the target, insulted all. The General must be "restrained when accused, dignified when belittled and generous when challenged."

The work was satisfyingly obsessive, and I delighted in it. As the Founder quoted in the preface to his "Darkest England and the Way Out," "there was no time to be weary." That famous document, and General Coutts's "Bread for my Neighbour" (which was "an appreciation of the social action and influence of William Booth"), pushed my thinking towards the needs of the "darkest Third World." The illuminated globe revolving at the side of my desk signalled my sphere of responsibility—not only those lands coloured pink, where affluence and near-affluence existed, but the drab-grey areas where even existence itself was not a guaranteed commodity. The "Third World" was by now a familiar term.

Nations coming to independence had aspirations that could best be aided, for a start, by providing the basic necessities of life for their people. The "have needs" people were looking to the "have resources" people, and increasingly governments were making ever larger grants for Third World assistance through their overseas aid and international development agencies. Leaders of the self-sufficient countries were pledging fixed percentages of the gross national product to better the lot of the emerging peoples. There were also large church-related and other specialist fund-raising enterprises interested in the betterment of those who had for too long been denied minimum sustenance. All were looking for reliable almoners to act on their behalf.

What was required was a conduit that could link benefactor and beneficiary, that could actually discover vitally needed projects knowing how, and from what sources, they could be funded. All this led me to bring into being in 1978 a Planning and Development department at International Headquarters with Commissioner (Dr.) Harry Williams, OBE., FRCS (Edin.), FICS., as its first director. The department was immediately linked with the Salvation Army World Services Office (SAWSO) in Washington, DC., an arm of national headquarters directed by Lieut-Colonel Ernest Miller, through which the U.S. government was channelling financial aid. In this innovation I saw the spirit of William Booth striding again through those areas of misery where men and women were powerless to help themselves. His ambition would be ours: "to bring not only heavenly hopes and earthly gladness to the hearts of multitudes of these wretched crowds, but also many material blessings, including such commonplace things as food, raiment, home and work, the parent of so many other temporal benefits."

Merely to record that within three years, in fifty-three countries, nearly one thousand projects were undertaken in the amount of US$30-million is to miss the practical impact of the assistance. The dollars became coconut trees, fresh water from new, deep wells, goats for milk and meat, and bicycles and rickshaws to encourage self-support. Housing, agriculture, education and feeding programmes were all aspects of the aid rendered in everything from instruction in bee-keeping to the erection of sturdy houses for suffering earthquake victims. Never before in the Army's history had the world refugee problem been so vast or the Army's involvement so extensive. I was shaken by my visit to the

Thai camps for Kampuchean refugees. The result was The Salvation Army's Relief and Refugee Operation (SARRO), which embraced emergency and rehabilitative effort in Zimbabwe and Uganda, with the Vietnamese "boat people" in the Philippines, and Hong Kong where illegal immigrants from the Chinese mainland were also given supportive care, as well as in Somalia and among Afghan refugees flooding into northern Pakistan. Aid for this enormous programme was stimulated greatly by the powerful, award-winning film, "The Uprooted."

To stroll across the border from Thailand into Cambodia was to walk into a wilderness of tragedy. Two kilometres away, that Sunday afternoon, there was gunfire. Around us—Major Eva den Hartog, Major John Bate, the private secretary, and myself—were scores of thousands of hapless victims caught between the political pressures forcing them eastwards and military action surging westwards. At one period it was estimated that there were half-a-million of these dislodged unfortunates without any of the accommodation, medicine and sanitation that world relief organizations had provided in the nearby camp-cities such as Sa-Kaeo. I watched as tons of rice were unloaded from a convoy of lorries at the border. From rough tents and dugouts the Kampucheans rushed to carry the sacks of life-saving cereal into their own areas—a pathetic scene, devoid of dignity, like a farmyard scramble when the feeding troughs are filled.

The vastness of the privation and the primitiveness of the existence to which these wandering hordes were reduced staggered me. Families had handcarts loaded with their life's possessions. Underneath, the earth had been scraped away so that the floor of the handcart served as the roof of a makeshift home. In these "cellars" there were sick adults and sicker children. The extent of the tragedy echoed in the piteous cries of mothers offering up their new-born infants: "Please, take my baby, please!" Their own hope of survival had utterly evaporated, but with the strangers in the strange uniform perhaps the innocents at least might have a chance.

Appreciation of the Army's relief work sometimes seemed to be generously out of proportion to the contribution that limited resources permitted. Nonetheless, to receive on the Army's behalf the World Humanity Award from the Earl Mountbatten, FG., PC., GCB., OM., OC., SI., in the presence of a crowd filling the Westminster Central Hall was recognition indeed. Earlier, at a luncheon in my honour in the House of Lords, I was seated next to Lord Mountbatten. He had met Salvationists all over the world, particularly during active service as a sailor, and he fairly brimmed with sparkling stories of his contacts, one or two of them, I suspected, being wardroom inventions. Apocryphal or not, the stories continued as we walked together across Parliament Square to the presentation event.

After receiving the award I gave the third Edwina Mountbatten memorial lecture, following in the footsteps of Sir Harold Wilson, the former prime minister of the United Kingdom, and the dedicated champion of Latin-America's poor, Dom Helda Camara. It was an opportunity for chronicling landmarks in the caring history of the Army, and for recalling the immense humanitarian work of Lady Mountbatten whose last public engagement was to open an exhibition depicting world poverty in the very same hall. Also present were the Earl's daughter, Lady Pamela Hicks, whose warm sincerity and informed concern for the less-fortunate greatly impressed me; Dame Anne Bryant, DBE., with whom my wife and I had had previous happy association and who introduced Lord Mountbatten; and Livia, daughter of the noted publisher and author, Victor Gallancz, a set of whose books was presented to me. Mr. Harcourt-Munning, recorder of the Award, received a prolonged ovation when he announced that he had set up a trust fund to aid the Army in Portugal where foundation work was in progress.

It is not often that one receives a letter signed individually by both a prime minister and his wife, but the message of greeting from No. 10 Downing Street which was read to the congregation came from the Rt. Hon. James Callaghan and Mrs. Callaghan and bore the signatures, "Audrey and Jim Callaghan." It read in part: "It is marvellously right and fitting that The Salvation Army should be the recipient of the World Humanity Award. They proclaim with selfless conviction and sincerity that people matter, and that there is no greater calling than the service of others, especially those in any kind of need. Our world would have fewer problems if their dedication and compassion were more widespread."

Afterwards, Lord Mountbatten asked if he might have a copy of the memorial lecture. He was anxious, he said, that it not be omitted from the family archives. Having had such a pleasant, if passing, association with "the last viceroy," his assassination not long after seemed all the more dastardly and the loss all the more personal.

"Those in any kind of need," to whom the prime minister had made reference, would have included the first offenders appearing in the courts. My attention was focussed on them because of the burning concern of a philanthropist-friend, Mrs. Xenia Field, whose name now adorns a wing of Booth House in Whitechapel. A no-nonsense helper of good causes she combined the unlikely lives of a gardening columnist for one of the prominent national newspapers and a tireless crusader for the proper treatment of prisoners. We met soon after my appointment as Chief of the Staff to discuss the subject of first offenders who, unable to raise bail, were being sent while awaiting trial to already overcrowded prisons, an experience which would have detrimentally lasting effects. More than fifty percent of all first offenders were being released by the courts, either conditionally discharged, fined, or under probation or suspended sentence. These, Xenia Field maintained, should be spared the stigma of imprisonment. What was needed was a facility with proper supervision to which magistrates, having no alternative but prison, could send first offenders of seventeen years of age and over who were "neither addicted to drugs or drink, were not disturbingly mentally sick, and who had no record of sexual offences against children." I brought the late Commissioner Ernest Fewster, then responsible for the men's social services, into the discussions and, as a three-year experiment, a wing of Booth House was set aside for the purpose and became known as the Field Hostel in November, 1971.

Ten years later, a large gathering of magistrates and probation officers met at Reed House, Piccadilly, at the kind invitation of Mr. Alex Jarrett, chairman and chief executive of Reed International Ltd., to review a decade's work. The "experiment" had been a shining success. Sir Edward Howard presided, and Sir Robert Armstrong, permanent under-secretary of state at the Home Office, and shortly afterwards to become secretary to the cabinet, supported. So abundantly had the bail hostel proven its worth that the government was to institute similar arrangements in some twenty-one cities. With particular satisfaction I related how a number of those referred to the Field Bail Wing had not only benefited from its amenities, but had responded to the spiritual influences of the place, and had gone on to worthy achievement as Christian citizens.

It was to be expected that a number of harassed magistrates would want the terms of admission to the bail hostel broadened so that other than first offenders could be referred. Xenia Field, however, was convinced that there were special considerations surrounding the first offender, and I stood completely with her in this. William Booth would have cheered the innovation, I thought, as, a few days later, on April 10, 1979, the 150th anniversary of his birth, I unveiled a larger-than-life statue of him within a stone's throw of Booth House and the bail hostel. The intention was both to commemorate Booth's life and work and to memorialize the centenary congress held the year before. Unfortunately, during the first night after the ceremony, the outstretched hand on the statue was removed. Vandalism, evidently, was not confined to the Booth era.

Though the needs of the world which the Army was seeking to meet were unceasing, I was not disposed to treat the wellbeing of the movement itself as a side-issue. The setting and maintaining of high standards within the ranks was never far from mind. This led to the formation of the International Staff Songsters, a group I had long hoped to see instituted. From 1891 on, the International Staff Band had demonstrated universally to the Army's nearly eighty thousand senior and junior bandsmen those standards of musical excellence, deportment and Christian life and witness that were to be emulated. By its virtuosity it had impressed that wider world of music-makers far beyond the Army's borders. I recall a tribute paid by an unknown but perceptive commentator talking to a radio audience about Salvation Army bands: "What is most impressive," he said, "is that they play with the skill of professionals but with the love of amateurs." I wanted exactly the same achievement in the vocal realm. With nearly 125,000 senior and junior vocalists singing "to the glory of God and the blessing of the people," similar standards were equally required. There was no thought that all our vocal groups, some of them small and struggling, would, as a result, demonstrate professional ability. John James Audobon, the noted ornithologist and artist, believed that "the woods would be very silent if no birds sang except those who sang best." Song, not silence, was what was wanted, and if it could not be the best, it could be better.

There was much discussion during many months, and all aspects of the proposal to bring into being a standard-setting vocal group, matching the International Staff Band in quality, were carefully weighed by Army leaders before the decision was taken. The then Major Norman Bearcroft was selected to organize the group and be its conductor. Colonel Ken. Bridge, a New Zealand officer serving at International Headquarters, was appointed as executive leader. I laid down some strict rules. Not only should the group have the competence to present the most difficult of festival items and to introduce new music, but it should, with new arrangements, revive many of the "heart songs" of the Army, and essay the best of those gospel songs which suit the Army spirit. The group's music should be functional rather than esoteric, since the vocalist has the priceless opportunity of investing his music with a verbal message. To beauty of sound can be added a direct call to salvation or sanctification, not only by the stirring of mood or emotion only, but also by words whose meaning and challenge cannot be mistaken or evaded.

The inauguration festival in the Fairfield Halls, Croydon, on March 8th, 1980, was a triumph. That such a degree of excellence had been reached in so few months of rehearsal was astonishing. In the utter silence, with a whole audience holding its breath during the singing of a simple song, unaccompanied and with unadorned harmonies, I knew that the venture was justified. The group's many appointments in the United Kingdom and overseas so soon after its formation validated my conclusion.

Since its formation the Army has seen great changes in the social, economic and constitutional life of the world around it. Very early, Salvationists established in the courts and in the British Parliament their rights to proclaim the Gospel in the ways they felt called to do. Other bodies with different motives had long envied us our freedom to hold open-air rallies, to make music and to march the streets. In some instances the freedom we enjoyed, and for which our forbears suffered to achieve, was being abused by those whose aim was not the improvement of the human lot, but the subjugation of all who disagreed with their political or sectarian views. Because of this, and the riots which resulted, some concerned authorities were seeking restrictions on all freedom of expression.

Four Bills were being promoted in parliament. It was realized that if passed as drafted they would hinder, and perhaps prevent, the Army's open-air ministry. The Bills required the organizers of all marches to notify their intention seven days in advance, giving the exact time and route to be followed. Failure to do so would be a criminal offence. Other provisions could make it necessary to obtain a license for the holding of meetings in Army halls; another clause could prevent the sale of Army literature in public places; and another inclusion could prevent the holding of religious meetings in public places.

It was known that the majority of those seeking to impose restrictions had no wish to prevent the Army doing its work. They were aiming only at those using violence either in word or action, or who wished to silence the voice of reason altogether. I decided that at whatever cost the Army must petition against these Bills. What had been won at such a costly price—imprisonment, injury, and even the death of early-day Salvationists—must not be lost because of any disinterest or lethargy on our part. Our legal secretary and solicitors carefully prepared our briefs. In one instance only did I personally have to appear at a formal hearing in the House of Lords. I was not called upon to give evidence, it being clear early in the cross-examination of the proposers' representatives that they, too, would regret any statute that might impinge in a limiting way upon the Army's ministry. When the amended Bills were passed, one exempted The Salvation Army specifically by name. The others had a "model" form of wording that fully protected the Army's long-held rights and those of other religious bodies.

Many Salvationists would, I knew, be unaware of the care and cost expended to preserve legally their right to bear a Christian witness at the street-corner or while marching along the high street; but I felt they would have expected nothing less from those to whom they had entrusted the Army's leadership. Queueing up in the reception line at a Guildhall function, my wife and I were immediately preceding the Bishop of London and his lady. Referring to the debates on the Bills the bishop said, "The church owes the Army a vote of thanks. The Army led the way. We hung on to your coat-tails."

Not infrequently I hear the comment that our forces are not seen so often in public places as in earlier times. One hopes that the absence is only in the eye of the beholder. But if there is an actual decline in this vital form of witness and ministry it would be salutary to remember that a privilege unused, like a privilege abused, can all too easily be taken away. If the privilege means the possibility of influencing someone towards a new and better life, the price of loss is infinitely too high to pay.

Certain days were less desk-bound than others and more deeply etched into the memory. One such had to do with the opening of "Hopetown," a haven for the homeless and dolorous women of London's east end, by Her Majesty Queen Elizabeth II who, following the service of dedication, went from room to room to greet the residents. The strict protocol rigidly observed during the ceremonial exercises by "my Lords, ladies and gentlemen," meant little to the odd assortment of women who chatted with The Queen in over-the-fence intimacy, passing along all sorts of backyard gossip. "To walk with kings nor lose the common touch," is both a virtue and an art. Nowhere could it have been more graciously demonstrated, and with greater sincerity, than during The Queen's inspection tour that afternoon.

The new facility happily banished recollection of its forbidding predecessor opened in 1931 by The Queen's grandmother, Queen Mary, and reopened by the Duchess of Gloucester in 1948 following repairs necessitated by the severe bombing. In its first life the building had been a public baths, the glazed-brick walls being the only remaining witness to the belief of an earlier, splashing generation of East-enders that "cleanliness is next to godliness." Despite the herculean efforts of successive staffs, the wear and the weather had taken its dilapidating toll until, as one resident blithely informed The Queen, "The thing I'll miss most of all in this luverly spot will be the rats."

Sir Maurice Dean, while chairman of the Army's London advisory board, had taken time off from writing his book, *The Royal Air Force and Two World Wars* (he having been for some years head of the Air Staff Secretariat), to show the old "Hopetown" to his wife who was most distressed by what she saw. Lady Dean determined to prod her husband and the advisory board to action, and it must have given her some satisfaction to watch me, following the unveiling of a commemorative plaque by The Queen, unveil a second plaque in memory of Sir Maurice who, having worked so tirelessly for the project, had not lived to see its completion. In his place, the Earl Cadogan, the board's incumbent chairman, had just as indefatigably pushed the project to realization.

In one respect the event contrasted markedly with The Queen's opening of Booth House a decade earlier, an occasion I have already described.

For that earlier event I gave no thought whatever to the personal safety of Her Majesty. Undoubtedly there were those who did, but I was not among them. But with the escalation of terrorist activity, I was this time greatly concerned that there should be no unfortunate occurrence. That the slightest harm should befall Her Majesty while granting us her prestigious presence and her royal blessing was too awful to contemplate. As the mayor of Tower Hamlets and myself saw Her Majesty draw away in her limousine, smiling and waving, a surge of relief lifted my gaze to the building site opposite. Several of the workmen who had been interested spectators appeared to have finished for the day and were clambering down from their vantage points along the partially-constructed walls. Inside the workmen's overalls, I was told, were some of "London's finest," disastrously inept with hod and trowel, but expert in the art of preserving royal safety.

When I arrived at the desk the next morning a letter, obviously delivered by hand, topped the pile of correspondence. It began: "As we returned to the Palace this afternoon The Queen told me to write straight away to say how very much she appreciated the opportunity of opening the new 'Hopetown' Hostel and how much she had enjoyed her afternoon with the Army." Nor did this seem to end the matter. Not long after, Sir Peter Ashmore, KCB., MVO., Master of the Queen's Household, telephoned on Her Majesty's behalf inviting my wife and myself to dinner at Windsor Castle and to stay overnight. It is with pardonable (I hope!) melancholy that I add the sad fact that we were unable to accept "the invitation of a lifetime." On the date proposed we were to be in Africa. Sir Peter suggested another, later date. We would, alas, still be in Africa. I hope our African comrades did not catch the wistful, and wish-ful gleam in our eyes on the two days when Windsor Castle called and we could not answer. I tried to convey to the Sovereign how honoured we were by the invitation, and sought to console ourselves with the thought that "to be invited and unable to attend is better than never to be invited at all." A daughter humourously added her own brand of solace. We were, she felt, fortunate to be spared the cost of gold-plated tooth-brushes and nightwear that would merit a valet's approbation.

An invitation of another kind which a diary of international commitments did permit acceptance was the enthronement on March 25th, 1980, of the Rt. Rev. the Lord Bishop of St. Albans, Dr. Robert Runcie, as the 102nd Archbishop of Canterbury. A few months before, the Lord Bishop had introduced himself to me prior to a dinner at No. 10 Downing Street given by the prime minister, the Rt. Hon. Mrs. Margaret Thatcher, at which farewells were said to His Grace the Lord Archbishop of Canterbury, Dr. Donald Coggan, who was retiring. Dr. Runcie mentioned some recent and joyful contacts with the Army, and I assured him of the prayers of all Salvationists as he began his influential ministry as "the Most Reverend Father in God, Robert, Archbishop of Canterbury and Primate of all England."

The dinner was memorable for several reasons. It was not a large company, about sixty occupying the U-shaped table. My wife was seated across from the Rt. Hon. Sir Philip Moore, principal private secretary to The Queen, who had been most helpful in respect of royal participation in Salvation Army events, and whom she knew. According to the printed seating plan, I was to have been placed between Lady Armstrong, the wife of Sir Robert, and the wife of the Chief Rabbi, Mrs. Immanuel Jakobovits, but a change put me next to Sir Norman Anderson with whom I had had correspondence and who had contributed an inspiring essay, "The Finality of Christ," to the Erik Wickberg symposium. I was excited at being able to converse with this Professor of Advanced Legal Studies at the University of London whose Christian outlook, evangelical fervour, eminent scholarship and vast experience of men and affairs enriched everything he said.

Prior to the dinner, my wife had conversed with the Rt. Hon. Lord Hailsham of St. Marylebone, Lord High Chancellor, and had sympathized with him in the recent loss of his wife in a riding accident in Australia. She told him that Salvationists remembered him prayerfully, and he confessed that only his faith in the everlasting wisdom of God had sustained him. "Pain," he had concluded, "is the price of love."

The prime minister was in excellent form and spoke brilliantly, setting a standard to which Dr. Coggan himself seemed to rise with ease as he reflected on his long ecclesiastical experience and looked into a quieter future. Because of his seven years in Toronto as Professor of New Testament at Wycliffe College the two Canadians present felt a special affinity with the retiring archbishop and his wife.

The enthronement of his successor was the most colourful spectacle I had ever witnessed within sacred precincts, with, perhaps, the one exception of the jubilant service of thanksgiving in St. Paul's Cathedral marking the 80th birthday of Her Majesty The Queen Mother, for which my wife and I had privileged seating near to the Royal family. There was a notable difference between the two occasions. In St. Paul's, the colour was provided by military dress uniforms with all decorations and honours being worn—a magnificent display. At the enthronement, the colour was provided by the vestments of richest hues embroidered with the most exquisite symbolic designs. If one were left breathless at the latter's lavish pageantry, one could not forget that "All things bright and beautiful, the Lord God made them all."

The ancient Marble Chair of the Primate and the High Altar in the cathedral had recently been restored to the positions they had occupied from about 1180 AD, and it was the first enthronement for at least two and a half centuries to take place in this historic setting. I was seated with leaders of the Free Churches only a few feet away from the Nave Altar.

For the long processional from the crypt, where robing had taken place, I was accompanied by the Rev. Elsie Chamberlain who said she knew where she stood with The Salvation Army as a female minister, but with the archbishop soon to be installed she was not so sure. I, of course, needed no time at all for robing. Salvation Army uniform is *de rigueur* for all occasions. But the sojourn in the crypt allowed time for conversation with church leaders from many parts of the world, including the Most Reverend Olof Sundby, the Swedish archbishop from Uppsala, who said he was glad that he and General Wickberg could now meet as equals (both had been similarly honoured by the King of Sweden); the Rev. Dr. Billy Graham, who told me he was present because of a handwritten invitation from Dr. Runcie, a result of the great crusade which had shaken London some years before; the Rev. Dr. Andre Appel, of France, who revealed early Salvation Army connections; the Most Reverend Dr. Alexander Mar Thomas, of Kerala, India, an amazingly fluent speaker whom we had met twice previously, and many others.

The new archbishop's sermon, dealing with his enthronement, made the point that God's throne is a mercy-seat, and that while the emperor's throne reflects the love of power, the throne of Christ bespeaks the power of love. There were subdued "Amens" from our part of the vast congregation.

The day ended with a dinner given by the Nikean Club in Eliot College, University of Kent. In the queue, moving towards the receiving line, I was joined by a young man on the archbishop's staff. He wanted me to know that in his home in Broken Hill, Australia, he had been "dedicated to God" by two girl officers of the local corps who had made a profound impression on his parents. He described himself as "an Anglican Salvationist." At the table I sat by a deputy-moderator from one of the world's less-affluent areas. Pulling up his white gown, he showed me his shoes. "I got them at one your thrift stores," he said gratefully. "They're a little tight, but what can you expect for $1.50?" From the afternoon heights of splendour I had descended to the practicalities of life. My feet, like the deputy-moderator's, were once again on solid ground.

Appointments in the United Kingdom often included church gatherings where John Betjeman's lines occasionally sprang to actuality: "The organ set them singing and the sermon let them nod,/ And up this coloured brickwork the same long shadows grew / As these in the stencilled chancel where I kneel in the presence of God." Of the many "stencilled chancels" where I myself knelt in the presence of the Almighty, St. Martin-in-the Fields, watching over Trafalgar Square with its unceasing vehicular and human traffic, holds a special place. By shortwave radio on our travels I frequently heard in the night watches the voice of the Rev. Austin Williams and the sounds of the worship services he led. Venerable St. Martin's, with down-and-outers sheltered in its crypt, and the finest of orchestral music emanating from its sanctuary, belies the all-too-general view that the church is grinding into extinction. Its pulpit was one from which I felt privileged to preach, and in the sermon I pleaded the cause of the multiplied thousands in the world who are totally forsaken and whose lament echoes Christ's cry of dereliction from the Cross. The celebrated actress, Dame Flora Robson, and Mr. Richard Baker, the BBC newscaster and music commentator, read the Scripture lessons, adding the beauty of perfect enunciation to the majesty of the passages.

From the ornate pulpit of St. Michael's, Cornhill, the work of a 19th century wood carver, William Gibbs Rogers, I preached the sermon during a Divine service for employees of Lloyds Bank Limited. The church, believed to have been in existence before the Norman conquest, echoed to the singing of a choir comprised of the bank's staff, with the manager of the tax department serving as choirmaster. I tried to prepare an address on the text, "You should at least have put my money into the bank so I could have some interest" (Matthew 25: 27.LB), but lacked inspiration and moved to a less fiscal theme.

History was evoked by a visit to the Lambeth Methodist Mission, London, where William Booth had been the minister in the late 1850's. The Rev. Walter Newby apologized on behalf of an earlier congregation which, he regretted, had lacked sympathy for William and Catherine Booth and had resented their bringing "people of lower class" to the services. Booth, not to be deflected in his passion to reach the neediest, had moved on to the east end of London. But all had been in the purposes of God, the minister felt; the Army had arisen and the Lambeth Mission, in its 241st year, was now a place where William Booth would feel at home since it was doing well the work he had wanted done so long before.

Preaching in a variety of denominational churches around the world I could not help comparing Salvation Army-church relationships at the beginning and end of my active career. An Anglican friend who had become a vicar invited me (who had become a Salvation Army lieutenant) to preach in his church. He was so nervous about having done so that I offered to withdraw. To this he would not agree, but insisted that I wear a Geneva gown over my uniform and did not preach from the pulpit. He fervently hoped that his bishop would take an enlightened view of his daring. Now, the interchange of pulpit and platform is commonplace. No longer do clergy pass each other, or Salvation Army officers, with denominationally stony faces. What of faith is held in common is now more commonly valued. I had always believed that Christians of whatever genre should be able to shake hands or, at the least, to smile at each other, and there is no doubt that generally speaking this is now customary. I have discovered that the most able of the clergy are not lacking in sincerity or dedication. The misconceived equation that class, plus scholarship, equals minus devotion, has long since been corrected. For the goodwill and encouragement I have received from so many brothers in the faith I privately raise my own *Te Deum Laudamus,* though more in the idiom of the pioneer Salvationist, William Pearson, than Giovanni Palestrina. One small vexation should be confessed and dismissed for ever. Why do so many parsons who accept an invitation to a special gathering put in such a brief appearance and with such overt ceremony take their early departure? The prime minister, with a thousand burdens of state on his mind, stays to the end. One can only assume that there are funerals to rival every function.

In this chapter I have mentioned some of the events of either interest or importance that occurred in the United Kingdom during my term of office as General. To the reader who notes omissions let me explain that a day-to-day record would have required several folios of unavailable pages. Visits to various cities could each have occupied an entire chapter, but must be telegraphically condensed. At Nottingham, birthplace of William Booth, my wife and I were always accorded full civic honours. The position was reversed when, at International Headquarters, we were able reciprocally to receive the lord mayor and lady mayoress, the sheriff and his lady and a delegation from the advisory board.

At Leicester, a Roman city in AD 120 and, since the 13th century noted for its manufacture of woollen goods, I had seven full engagements during a one-day visit. At one of them Royal Air Force officers persented me with a magnificent cake weighing sixty pounds and artistically iced in acknowledgement of the RAF's 60th anniversary and The Salvation Army's centenary. Delegates to the international congress at Wembley saw the cake on display. A civic reception tendered by the lord mayor was followed by a ceremony in the town hall square where I accepted a new marching drum for use by the International Staff Band. I regretted that I was incompetent to accede to the men of the massed bands' repeated request for "a dedicatory solo."

At Portsmouth, where the Army flag flew from the city hall masthead, the centenary of the citadel's excellent band was observed and tribute paid to Bandmaster Harold Nobes's 42-years of leadership.

At Manchester, in opening a new men's hostel housing 210 men, described by the lord mayor, Councillor Robert Crawford, as "truly magnificent," I saw a fourteen-year dream come true. The project had been initiated when the Manchester advisory board was formed. The first chairman, Mr. Joseph Cox, an affectionately honoured supporter of all good causes, had kept the project alive through alternating periods of expectation and frustration. I remembered his many kindnesses to the Army and to me personally as I unveiled a plaque in his memory. He had died not long before.

At Wood Green, in North London, I spent a unique weekend "in the heart of," rather than "in the arms of" the law, with members of the Blue Shield Fellowship composed of Salvationists who serve as policemen and policewomen. Sixty of the fellowship's members, from constables to inspectors, with visiting law-enforcement officers from Canada and West Germany, participated. From among the delegates a first-class band was formed, and vocal talent of rich quality was also available.

Skegness, England's north-east coastal resort, favoured by the hardy who like the bite of North Sea breezes, was the venue for a national conference of YMCA secretaries to which I had been invited as speaker by the national director, Mr. Ray Collins, LRAM., an appreciated friend whose Christian character was as evident as his brilliance at the keyboard of the piano. To the assembly I recalled the fact that Sir George Williams, founder of the YMCA, was a contemporary of William Booth. Williams, as the result of a conversation with a friend on Blackfriars bridge, dedicated his life to evangelizing fellow-workers on Ludgate Hill. Booth found his destiny in the more depressed regions a mile or so to the east. Both became notable social reformers, but neither lost their primary spiritual aim. The conference did me good. In the early morning prayer sessions and in Bible study periods I was jolted out of any misconception that the "Christian" in the movement's name was meaningless. I was teamed with the Rev. Dr. Johanson, of the City Temple, and the Rev. Eric S. Allen, of Leeds (whose father had been a longtime employee of the Army's Campfield Press at St. Albans), to form a panel giving answers to delegates' questions. There are times when "unity is strength," and I was thankful not to be alone in such a lively open forum.

In 1979 the golden jubilee of the William Booth Memorial Training College (commonly referred to as the International Training College, though inaccurately according to the trust which governs it) at Denmark Hill, London, was observed on the precise date of its opening, July 8. Through its corridors in its fifty years had marched nine thousand men and women into Salvation Army officership. In the commemorative gathering arranged by the training principal, Colonel (now Commissioner) Harry Read, flags of the first and current sessions of cadets were marched in and received as "battle honours." I expressed what was not only a personal hope but an imperative for the movement's future that "all who arrive at this place, and all similar places around the world, should desire nothing of self-comfort, but only the glory of God."

Though life lunged ahead, thrusting through a taxing agenda, every now and again "death's pale flag," as Shakespeare called it, was raised and pause made to honour a colleague's selfless leadership. In December, 1977, General Wilfred Kitching's earthly remains were laid to rest in Camberwell cemetery, London, alongside those of other leaders. There is a strange prefiguring in conducting the funeral of one's predecessor in office; the mortality of leadership is realized, as is the challenge to final accountability. I felt that General Kitching, international leader from 1954 to 1963, had, by his influence left a beneficial mark on the movement he loved. His autobiography's title, *A Goodly Heritage,* summed up his sense of indebtedness to the Army in which he found a lifetime of personal happiness and sanctified service. Ordinarily meticulous, he left no suggested order of service for his funeral and commital. In conversation with his wife he had repeatedly said, "I simply want the occasion to be *real* Army." It was. The songs were bright with eternal hope and, instead of the depressing sound of gravel falling on the lowered coffin, I matched the ritual words, "... earth to earth, dust to dust, ashes to ashes ..." with the dropping of a yellow, red and blue flower, the colours of the movement he championed, served and led.

I had promised the High Council which had elected me that I would call Salvationists to a renewed emphasis upon our doctrine (cf. Appendix). In India I had seen large congregations stand and recite in unison the eleven articles of faith to which all Salvationists subscribe, but I suspected that this kind of memorization was not universal. As well as being committed to memory, the beliefs also required intellectual acceptance. Neither were they to be regarded as time-worn engravings on moss-covered foundation stones, historic but functionless; but rather as magnificent branches of a firmly-rooted, healthy tree providing fruit for the soul and shade from "man-made myths." *The Expository Times* (April, 1980) claimed that "the church has a continuing mandate to do theology. Trying faithfully to discharge it, the church keeps mobile and alert. Neglecting it, the church slithers into stagnation and indolence."

Periodically, questions concerning the doctrine reached the General's desk. Most came from respectful seekers after elucidation. A frequently-raised query had to do with Christ's resurrection which was the basis of the early church's conquering message but which was not specifically included in our statement of faith, though unquestionably implied. No branch of the church of Christ in the world sings more believingly, or joyously, to the fanfaric accompaniment of its numerous bands, "He arose! He arose! Hallelujah! Christ arose!" But honest questions deserve careful answers, and taking what I considered to be a vitally necessary step, I reinstituted a doctrine council. Beyond dealing with enquiries, the council has occupied itself with reviewing the Handbook of Doctrine, the last edition of which was published in 1969. This is a long task. As a more immediate achievement, a simplification of the manual, under the title, *The Doctrine We Adorn,* has already been published. It will meet the needs of those areas where the "things of the spirit" require to be expressed in the simplest of terms.

For the first time in thirty years the face of China was turning outwards. The People's Republic established by Mao-Zedong on October 1, 1949, was now looking to that world of high technology which lay beyond the hitherto impenetrable bamboo curtain behind which it had sought to organize its more than one-billion "people mouths"—which is the literal meaning of the Chinese word for population. Trade missions were moving out and coming in. Great symphony orchestras from abroad were eagerly greeted by throngs suffering from cultural starvation. The overthrow of the so-called "Gang of Four" was opening many doors, including those of the churches. Nearly seventy years earlier, in a deathbed conversation with his son, William Booth had said: "Bramwell, I have been thinking very much during the last few nights about China," and he extracted a promise that "you will unfurl our flag in that wonderful land." The promise was sealed with a handshake and a prayer, and had been kept.

But now, the once-flourishing Salvation Army, as an organized body, had disappeared. Its buildings had been confiscated and turned into storehouses or cultural centres leaving thousands without a place of worship. Its officers, almost 150 of them, had been forced to seek other occupations. A number had been drafted into labour camps. From the scanty information available many, it was understood, remained Salvationists in spirit, but in respect of any visibility it was as though the movement had never existed. For The Salvation Army, national "liberation" in 1949 meant total disqualification.

I asked the Canadian High Commissioner in London, the Hon. Paul Martin, PC., QC., then dean of the diplomatic corps at the Court of St. James, if he would introduce me to the Chinese ambassador. He said he would do more. He would accompany me to the Chinese embassy. We rode in his limousine past All Souls Church in Langham Place and the BBC, and on to the embassy in Portland Place. Of all the embassies seen in our travels, this was the most austerely furnished. It mirrored so much of what I would see when, in early retirement, I would actually visit China. Once inside, we were no longer in London. We were in China. We were received with the same smiling delicacy with which, months later, I would be greeted by a commune family in a village beyond Beijing's vast duck farms with their fluttering colonies of white birds fattening for the table. Where else in London for "elevenses" would we have been served tea with large, viridescent leaves floating like lotus plants on a miniature pond, and dates, pitted, and prettily, individually wrapped?

The Canadian High Commissioner told the Chinese ambassador that he had come with me because he knew I had something of the utmost importance to say. I reminded His Excellency that the Army's history in China began as far back as 1887, though it was not until 1916 when pioneer officers entered Peking, as the city was then called, that permanent work was established. In 1930 it spread to Manchuria and Hong Kong. More than two hundred officers drawn from twelve countries had served in North China. Large-scale relief operations had been characteristic of the work from its inception, as had also the homes where derelict men and women and abandoned children had been sheltered. In the days of battle, officer-nurses had rendered efficient aid to the wounded, bravely remaining at their posts.

Reports reaching International Headquarters during that turbulent period stated that "in face of the grave uncertainties of war, officers with their wives and families have stood firm at their posts in unassuming, heroic determination"—with only one consuming intention, that of bringing succour and encouragement to a bewildered people. Another message stated that "though faced by greater odds than ever before, in conditions not conducive to anything spectacular, persistent, and in some places, aggressive, efforts continue." Later still: "The Army in China is passing through momentous days. Far-reaching changes are taking place and full responsibility for the continuance of the Army's work will soon be placed entirely on national officers. The work may be drastically reorganized, probably reduced and restricted, but our Chinese officers deeply desire to continue the Army's great soul-saving work long after the last overseas missionary has left the land."

It was impossible to tell whether my review was making any impression on the ambassador. He listened intently but impassively. I recalled with what universal sadness Salvationists had learned of the general exodus of missionaries at the end of 1951 when communication was no longer permitted between International Headquarters and the indigenous administration which, alas, was all too soon to collapse under unbearable pressures. I respectfully submitted to His Excellency a list of the properties we had lost in the upheaval in the vague hope of eventual reparation. Mr. Martin, with gladiatorial energy, pleaded that the Chinese government should allow the Army to resume its work at once. "Canada, the United Kingdom and more than eighty countries," he said, "would join in testifying that they could not do without this movement, and neither can China. Every country needs the example set by the high standards of compassionate service it displays." He urged the ambassador to arrange for me to make an early visit to Beijing and confer with the appropriate ministries.

As we prepared to leave, I addressed myself directly to the ambassador. "Sir," I said, "I think you and I are about the same age. That means you would have been old enough to have seen or heard something of The Salvation Army before it was proscribed and sank into the shadows of the unknown. Did you ever come across The Salvation Army in your youth?"

To our surprise, he answered in perfect English. "Yes," he said reflectively, "I remember *Chiu Shih Chun*—God's soldiers without guns." I thanked him for the recollection and the definition, and the interview was over. A gracious but non-committal letter came afterwards from the ambassador. "At the moment our government is engrossed with many matters ..."

When I reached China in 1982 I had cause to think that the visit to Portland Place had not been entirely fruitless. I felt sure it had opened the way for my discussion with Mr. Shen De-rong, secretary-general of the National Committee of the Three-self Movement of the Protestant Churches in China, the agency through which the government intends to direct ecclesiastical affairs. What I had said to the Chinese ambassador in London I repeated to the secretary-general and his assistant while the sounds of Shanghai floated through the open windows of the office on Yuan Ming Yuan Road in which we talked. The conference made many things clear. No "overseas" oversight or support would be permitted. Bible-smuggling was an absurd measure; the government had assigned stocks of the best paper and had commissioned one of China's leading printing houses to produce one-million copies. The church would not engage in such activities as education and health-care, these being the well-discharged responsibilities of the state. The church would be a "worshipping community" only. There would be no denominational "labels." The government had recognized Christianity as an "indigenous" religion, and had approved the formation of "The Christian Church of China." The abolition of denominationalism might mean little to some, but, I intimated, a Salvation Army uniform is a "label" that conspicuously proclaims its wearer's affiliation. How strange that a secular government could bring into existence a "realized ecumenism" which, in the churches' best days in China, would have been regarded as impossible. One fervently hopes that the officially-blessed church will survive without that transfusion of spiritual vitality which flows from universal fellowship, that it will not languish in its detachment from those works of mercy which, springing benignly from the early Christian church, have been part of its ministry ever since, and that it will not shrivel into itself if denied evangelistic adventure.

In Beijing I was to meet a tattered remnant of our Salvation Army. For the twenty-one who met in an "upper room" of the once proud headquarters building on Wangfujing Street it was like the reunion of long-lost relatives—eyes filled with tears, words quivering in the throat, hands reaching for hands, with floods of questions, unasked through the years, hoping for reassuring answers. At the centre of the group was the former Major Yin Hung-shun, erect in his 78th year and with a face wreathed in serenity. He was the last of the four Chinese officers into whose care the Army had been committed when all expatriate officers were repatriated. His story deserves a book of its own by an inspired pen. It is a remarkable saga of faith under fire.

No General had been able to visit China. (William Booth, during a tour of the Far East, had been expected, but having reached Tokyo he turned back to London. The records do not say why.) Even now it was a General who had already entered retirement. But that mattered not at all. To this group it was a miraculous moment. In the presence of an international leader, and to the accompaniment of a single cornet, the song was raised in Chinese and English, "O boundless Salvation! deep ocean of love." I was asked to speak. I opened the New Testament and saw the words, "Let not your heart be troubled ..." The group, once scattered like sand-crystals in a violent storm and marvellously gathered together again, had had to rely solely on the comforting presence of the Holy Spirit for their spiritual preservation. I did my best to remind them that they were never forgotten by their fellow-Salvationists around the world, and certainly not by a Heavenly Father whose Son had already gone "to prepare a place ..."

When the Hon. Paul Martin and myself said goodbye to the Chinese ambassador in London, all the foregoing was in the future and beyond expectation. It is not slighting to speak of Chinese inscrutability; it is a national characteristic. But its effect on me, as I stepped again into the High Commissioner's automobile, was to make me wonder whether I had actually had an interview about a painful past and an uncertain future, or whether I had just imagined it.

CHAPTER 18

"One In Charity"

My wife and I were again in charming Leysin, resting for a few days amid the beauty of the Swiss Alps, when a telephone call from London, England, disturbed more than our furlough. The outcome of this conversation with the Chief of the Staff—"suspension from the World Council of Churches pending dialogue"—was to stir the minds and feelings of Salvationists around the world. It was also to engender enormous media coverage and to be the subject of impassioned debates in the church councils of the world. The Chief conveyed the news that the fires of uneasiness, smouldering since 1970 concerning the direction of the World Council of Churches' policies, had been fuelled by a grant of $85,000 to the Rhodesian Patriotic Front led by Joshua Nkomo.

It was a particularly bitter period in the Rhodesian debacle, and, immediately following the announcement, perplexed Salvationists and others were demanding to know if the grant meant the espousal of violence by the World Council and whether the Army, by the law of association, was party to it. Donors flooded the various headquarters with letters and telephone calls asking if monies given to the Army had found their way, via the WCC, to this allocation. I knew that no contribution had been made by the Army to the Programme to Combat Racism. I also knew that no movement could more visibly have demonstrated its total commitment in a practical way to all in need, of whatever colour or culture.

It would be unfair to make a sweeping denunciation of the council's grant aid programme. Many allocations were to worthy causes and deserved commendation. But there were aspects of this latest, and similarly placed grants since 1971, that created criticism. The grant was ostensibly for relief in food, clothing and medicine, but there was no guarantee that the funds would be so applied. Even if they were, it meant that such aid would be releasing other monies with which the war effort could be pursued. Simple logic suggested that one way or the other the grant could subsidize the escalating violence. I wanted it made clear that the Army was not protesting against the aims of the Patriotic Front. Our reaction was certainly not anti-liberation nor pro-white. That the WCC should be pleading for disarmament and peace and, at the same time, be supporting users of armed terrorism was, to our way of thinking, inconsistent. The grant appeared to be so specifically placed as to indicate a political inclination on the part of the council, in contrast to The Salvation Army's traditional non-political basis.

For ninety years the Army had been part of Rhodesia's national life, with strong participation in the fields of education and health care. Its officers knew that not only Nkomo's followers, but numbers of black Rhodesians holding quite different political aspirations, were in dire need due to the internecine struggle that had disastrously interfered with the production and availability of life's necessities. Grants made equally to all factions at this particularly tense moment would, it was felt, have reflected the concern of the churches for the total problem, and would have eliminated any undesirable element of partiality from which political conclusions could rightly or wrongly be drawn. The grant was also given without any requirement of accountability. To my mind this was unwise. The giving of funds "on trust as an evidence of total commitment" seemed exceedingly naive. Our own indigenous leaders were aware of widespread indiscipline in the handling of monies and were doing their best to develop a high degree of fiscal responsibility. Generosity of this kind, however highly motivated, splintered respect for those standards of accountability which were being established with much difficulty.

A further point was the disregard of the presence in Rhodesia of the council's member churches and their ability to be the purveyors of relief. Their long and intimate knowledge of both the people and their needs, and, for certain of them, proven experience in meeting calamitous situations, apparently counted for little. To have used them, and among them The Salvation Army, would have enhanced the churches' relationships with the people. By-passing them created the impression that the council was uncertain about the expertise of their own member churches, but were confident of the Patriotic Front's management capabilities.

It is now history that the Patriotic Front did not come to power. If the grant had been made on the basis of the rightness of this particular faction's cause above all others, then politically it failed. One can only hope that the grant eased the severe lot of some whose husbands and fathers were caught up, many of them unwittingly and unwillingly, in a conflict for power about which they knew little or nothing.

It is necessary in the interests of accuracy, and for the record, to state that the grants by the Programme to Combat Racism were not the sole or chief cause for the rift between the Army and the council, a rift that had widened with the passing years, and particularly during the Seventies. The growing gap was regrettable since the Army was involved with the World Council of Churches from its inception. In 1910 a World Missionary Conference held in Edinburgh discussed European and American responsibility for spreading the Gospel and this led, in 1921, to the formation of the International Missionary Council. Four years later, delegates from various Christian denominations met in Stockholm and discussed the application of Christian principles to world problems. The result was the creation of the Universal Christian Council on Life and Work. In 1927 a World Conference on Faith and Order was held to deal with doctrinal divisions between denominations. The two last-mentioned conferences met respectively in Oxford and Edinburgh in the same year, 1937, to agree on a plan for union. Only a year later a group of representatives met in Utrecht and laid plans for an envisaged World Council of Churches. It existed in embryo for the next decade sponsoring inter-church relationships and rendering worthy service during the years of the Second World War. The World Council of Churches' inaugural Assembly was held in Amsterdam in August, 1948, with 146 member churches representing forty-six countries, of which forty-two churches were from the Third World. Included in the church representation were ten "black" churches. All member churches were to be autonomous, and a minimum membership of 25,000 was required for admission to the council. Twenty years later, at the Uppsala

Assembly, one hundred and three Third World churches, including forty-one African, were registered, reflecting the upsurge of indigenous denominations. Today there are some three hundred member churches representing one hundred countries.

Prior to the first Assembly in 1948, the advisory council to the General, brought into being as the result of a pledge given by General Albert Orsborn to his electors in 1946, had, as one of its first matters for consideration, "The Salvation Army's relation with national and world councils of churches." The General, in his request for a recommendation, said, "I have my own views, but I do not wish to impose them on others," and then went on to express them in a six-page memorandum. The document concluded with: "I do not wish my period of leadership to be associated with the gravitation of The Salvation Army nearer to church life in faith and order," a view evidently not generally held seeing the advisory council responded with an eight-page statement summarized in one sentence: "The advisory council has no hesitation in recommending that The Salvation Army continues its membership of the World Council of Churches." The General then gave his decision concerning Salvation Army representation at the first Assembly in grudging terms: "It occurs to me to wonder why we should participate in the Assembly ... but the majority of our leaders think that we should be represented and therefore I have told the chief to arrange it."

As defined by its constitution the World Council "is a fellowship of churches which confess the Lord Jesus Christ as God and Saviour according to the Scriptures and therefore seek to fulfil together their common calling to the glory of the one God, Father, Son and Holy Spirit." To this theological basis for admission The Salvation Army could commit itself unreservedly, and sent representatives to all meetings of the highest authoritative body of the council—the Assembly; in 1948 at Amsterdam, Netherlands; in 1954 at Evanston, USA.; in 1961 at New Delhi, India; in 1968 at Uppsala, Sweden and in 1975 at Nairobi, Kenya. A Salvation Army leader, Commissioner A. G. Cunningham, was elected to the first central committee of the World Council thus confirming the Army's membership as a constituent "church" from the beginning. He was succeeded by a number of outstanding leaders including Commissioners Frank Evans, Clarence D. Wiseman, Herbert Westcott, Harry Williams and Victor Keanie, and Colonel Ernest N. Denham.

Only weeks before the controversial grant was made to the Patriotic Front two Salvation Army girls, one a Lieutenant, Diane Thompson, of London, England, and the other a lay worker from Northern Ireland, Sharon Swindells, had been murdered by freedom fighters at the Usher Secondary School where they were serving. The killing appalled Salvationists. Some were angered. They, like many non-Salvationists, felt that the death of the two young women was a clear signal that violence had gone mad and that any control of men under arms was mythical. Not once, however, was this happening mentioned officially in our dealings with the World Council of Churches. We did not want our protest over the grant to be in any way regarded as an emotional reaction to the death of the girl Salvationists. Other missions suffered more severely than the Army in the loss of expatriate workers' lives and, as grievous as was the loss of the two splendid women, it was well-known to me and my associates that the lives of many other Salvationists had been taken. That they were black did not make their death any less a loss to the Army. At war's end, when the rolls were cursorily checked, our leaders in the renamed Zimbabwe informed me that, sadly, somewhere between four and six thousand of our people had lost their lives in the struggle.

The 1978 grant, however, seemed to be "the last straw." Protests concerning earlier grants registered by the Army's representatives serving as members of the central committee had merited little response. What little acknowledgement there had been was patronizing. More importantly, through the decade the council's tendency to politically-inclined action appeared increasingly to override that evangelical thrust which the Army and other church bodies had longed for as a result of the closer inter-involvement of the denominations. A spreading acceptance of "liberation theology" as being primarily a Scriptural mandate to social action in the temporal sphere, and in certain circumstances justifying violence, was viewed with profound misgiving. Christ's testimony, "The Spirit of the Lord is upon me, because He hath anointed me ... to preach deliverance to the captives ... to set at liberty them that are bruised" (Luke 4: 18), for us meant the possibility of spiritual liberation for the sin-bound individual through Christ's sacrifice on the Cross. It appeared as if the word of Dr. Headlam, Bishop of Gloucester, at the Malvern Conference in 1924, was prophetic. He foresaw that a World Council would be "continually involved in political matters and controversy, and largely influenced by the passion for identifying Christianity with socialism."

In proposing to the Chief "suspension pending dialogue," I asked for the opinion not only of Commissioner Williams, our current member of the central committee, but also of the advisory council to the general, before such a step were taken. All felt that "dialogue" was important, and that the step of "suspension" was the only way by which this could be hastened. Commissioner Williams's views were particularly important. He had been nominated by General Wiseman during a commissioners' conference at Sunbury Court in 1975 to fill the vacancy on the central committee (left open since the retirement of Commissioner Westcott) in view of the imminent Assembly at Nairobi. Some felt that this particular Assembly could be a "watershed," and that the direction of its flow, theologically and practically, would determine whether or not the Army should remain in membership.

Before leaving Leysin I authorized the Chief to give the decision to the World Council and to Army leaders. By the time my wife and I reached London the following weekend the whole world, it seemed, also knew of the decision. The "dialogue" aspect, generally speaking, was ignored by the media. The "suspension" element was headlined as "Salvation Army quits World Council of Churches." Perhaps I had been ingenuous in thinking that the matter was a private one between a member and the body with which the member was affiliated. Seated at lunch almost two years later beside the venerable ecumenist, Dr. Visser't Hooft, he likened our suspension to a family disagreement. "All families have them," he said, "but the family doesn't break up because of them." I admit to having thought of our suspension, and the need for conversation, as purely a family affair, but privacy within the house of *Oikumene* was not to be. The world took sides, and I found myself to be a tennis net above which balls flew with speed and force and, into which, not infrequently, volleys landed rather painfully.

Dr. Philip Potter, general secretary of the council, responded quickly by coming from Geneva to see me at International Headquarters. It was our first meeting and it confirmed all I had heard of his many gifts. Personable and articulate, he had my immediate respect. The reason for any misunderstanding was defined by him as due to lack of communication. We, perhaps, had not fully understood the council's motives and philosophy, while he and his colleagues, he admitted somewhat ruefully, had taken the Army very much for granted, though tremendously appreciating its work and witness. In this discussion I expressed the deep concern of many Salvationists at what appeared to be the politicization of the council. I asked if the council, by involving itself in certain sensitive national issues was not subscribing to a lesser function rather than honouring its greater mission, the evangelization of the world by the power of the Gospel? The views of Dr. Potter and myself on the "revolutionary" character of Jesus hardly coincided.

Dr. Potter proposed a meeting of members of his secretariat with Army leaders, and this was set for the 12th of December at International Headquarters in London. The date was easy to remember; it would be the eve of my 65th birthday. The group met in the board room of the Advisory Council to the General, a room dominated by a large and excellent portrait of General Bramwell Booth, cloak about his shoulders and pince-nez in hand. Supporting me were the Chief of the Staff and several commissioners. The Geneva delegation was led by the moderator, Archbishop Ted. Scott, of Canada, who suggested that he and I should jointly preside. If differing views were to be expressed the accent would be the same! The day and the discussions left me with a mosaic of impressions—the compelling quality of Christian fraternity; the almost fanatical commitment to the cause of ecumenism of certain of our visitors; the solidarity of Salvationists in their less-articulated but unequivocal allegiance to evangelism; my own nervousness when frequently required to advance a proposition or sum up for our side; and not least the inspiration I received from the choicely-phrased prayers offered by the archbishop. He, I felt, was uncomfortable in confrontation; he is more pastor than prefect.

To the theological basis of membership in the council, adopted in 1948 at the Amsterdam Assembly, a later, additional statement implied that the World Council of Churches was to be a "Eucharistic fellowship." For the Army, as a non-sacramental body, this could mean exclusion, certainly so if organic union became a reality. The archbishop took pains to explain that the phrase should be interpreted in its widest sense as "a fellowship of thanksgiving," which, he insisted, could not debar the Army and its joyous witness. The elucidation was offered helpfully, but it remained clear that for a vast number of leading churchmen the

Eucharist meant the celebration of a rite not practised by Salvationists, a fact which, in their thinking, determined the "church-ness," or otherwise, of a religious group.

The fact that printed references to the Army's membership in the Council's publications had relegated us as an international movement to a London, England, group, was something that could immediately be corrected. This point was quickly and good-naturedly despatched. Discussion concerning the Programme to Combat Racism was less easily dealt with, and there was an animated exchange when certain commissioners wanted to know what was, in the mind of the Council, its true magnetic North in respect of global evangelism and world ministry. Regrettably, the day did not finish as it began. In the final half-hour restraint somehow evaporated. In astringent and, at one point, emotional terms, the general secretary, and the one woman member of the council's delegation, gave the Army a "woodshed lecture." The mature adult sought to instruct the wilful child. Perhaps the dispensers felt they could not be true to themselves without doing so, but it was an exercise that put a sting into the tail of the conference. I went home with my own emotions in turmoil.

I had informed the conference that no final decision concerning the Army's future relationship with the Council could be given until after the international conference of leaders scheduled to be held in Toronto in September, 1979, and, apart from providing Army leaders with details of the meeting and gaining their reaction, the matter was dormant through the intervening months. In Toronto, the debate was serious and frequently intense. All knew that a decision would have to be reached; we could not stay "in suspension" indefinitely, and I had indicated that I did not want to enter retirement with this piece of business unfinished. There were various views and an early consensus was obviously impossible. Delegates were asked on returning to their appointments to review the whole subject in the light of the latest information given them. The conference then asked that a letter be sent to Dr. Potter, and on behalf of the delegates I signed the following prepared message:

1st October, 1979

Dear Dr. Potter,

I promised that after free consultation with the commissioners of The Salvation Army in September, 1979, I would give you an answer on the matter of The Salvation Army's membership of the World Council of Churches.

When the subject was reviewed during an international conference of leaders it became evident that there were several deeper aspects of the relationship which required that further kind of examination which the duration of our conference did not allow. Our leaders did feel it would be helpful if I restated the priorities for which our world-wide movement is known:

(1) Evangelism.

(2) Concern for the poor and oppressed without distinction of race or creed and which is not partisan in terms of support for any specific party.

(3) A history of support for socio-political changes which eschew violence.

(4) A branch of the church which does not practice the rites of Baptism and the Eucharist, and commissions women equally with men, admitting them to all offices.

Committed as we are to these priorities it is felt that there has been a gradual shift in the World Council of Churches' own emphasis which often makes us appear out of step.

In view of the recommendation made at the central committee of the World Council of Churches at Kingston in January, 1979, to institute consultations with the churches on the administration of the Special Fund to Combat Racism, deferring decision until the next meeting of the central committee, I would express the hope that the executive committee will permit the *status quo* to continue until that date. During this period we will be able to conduct the further examination of our relationship referred to above.

It will be for you to state whether our representative would be welcome at the next central committee meeting and at any appropriate consultations before that.

In the Name of Christ the conference sends, through you, its greetings to all the churches, with the prayer that the Holy Spirit will continue to enlarge and prosper their mission and ministry.

Yours sincerely,
(Sgd.) Arnold Brown, General

As the months went by the returns came in, but many were inconclusively couched. Finally, a simple questionnaire offered three courses of action for which "yes" or "no" answers were required. Few wanted total severance. The majority wanted a form of relationship which preserved a spiritual unity with all member churches of the council but which unshackled the Army from the policy decisions of the executive and central committees.

By the time we were ready to submit our request for a change to fraternal status, Dr. Potter had gone on a sabbatical. His deputy, however, invited us to come to Geneva immediately following the general secretary's return, and on June 3, 1981, we were warmly received in conference, Archbishop Scott acting as chairman. One could only admire the persistence of the chairman, the general secretary and others who represented the World Council in seeking to retain the Army's full membership. I explained that the best possible consensus of Salvation Army views had been secured, and that our delegation, with the recommendation of the Advisory Council to the General, had come not to debate the issue but to conclude it. I can only describe the atmosphere as one of affable emptiness in which all arguments had been neutralized. Only one outburst momentarily altered the ambience. A recent appointee of the Council charged us with "deliberately amputating the Body of Christ." The statement was extravagant, and I assured our friend that we had no desire to "amputate" ourselves from any unity of the spirit or in any way to dismember the body of Christian kinship.

Under the council's constitution the change of status we sought could not be effected without first withdrawing from full membership and afterwards applying for fraternal relationship. The technical procedure was recognized but, sensing what the media treatment would be, I had hoped that "withdrawal" would be less emphasized than a "change of relationship." This was not to be. The chairman then proposed that each delegation should separately have a period of reflection and prayer. When we regrouped the Council's delegation appeared to have given up any attempt to retain our membership and manifested only a desire to work out the mechanics of the change as efficiently and cooperatively as possible. It was agreed that our letter requesting a change of status should be presented at the next meeting of the central committee due to be held in Dresden, East Germany and, on the basis of the committee's decision, an agreed news release would be issued jointly.

I sent the following letter from London:

31st July, 1981

Dear Dr. Potter,

Members of the Salvation Army delegation which you and your colleagues received so cordially in Geneva on June 3rd have given further prayerful reflection to those helpful deliberations, and the subject of The Salvation Army's relationship with the World Council of Churches has also had the renewed attention of the Advisory Council to the General.

The feeling is that those who carry the chief responsibility for the World Council of Churches have been exceedingly patient not only in correspondence but also in allowing us ample time to study those aspects of the relationship that have troubled many Salvationists. We are aware that to be "in suspension pending dialogue" was, under the World Council of Churches' constitution, an unrecognized status and, because of this, your tolerance has been all the more appreciated.

The time has come, however, to resolve the situation, and we therefore ask for an adjustment in the relationship that presently exists. The Salvation Army wishes to move from full membership to fraternal status under the provision in the Constitution (Section VI, 1, and Section XII of the Rules).

In making this request we are acting on the best consensus we can gain, based on the most careful polling of our world-wide leadership, and via the processes explained in detail during our deliberations in Geneva on June 3rd.

The reasons for this submission have been shared with you, and at length. In summary, they revolve around the fact of The Salvation Army's internationality which itself implies diversity of views concerning our relationship. The preservation of that internationality, by the very nature of our movement, is vital to us, and, we feel, to those whom we serve.

To lose any spiritual fellowship with the World Council of Churches would be for us as undesirable and painful as it would be if we were to sever the happy relationship we enjoy with local, regional and national councils of churches around the world, as well as with the various communions and denominations whose witness and work for Christ we prayerfully uphold and in which, in our unique way, we share.

There are unquestionably aspects of the World Council of Churches' activity which demand our full support, e.g., the Commission on Evangelism, the Commission on Faith and Order, CICARWS, and CMC. We would certainly wish to demonstrate such support in more positive and practical ways. Our gravamen has to do with the issuance by the World Council of Churches of statements, the developing of policies and the carrying out of actions which we regard as political, and which, as such endanger the non-political nature of the Army, the preservation of which is basic to the movement's effectiveness in a number of countries. Refusal to identify with political factions, as distinct from deep social concern for the needy people of all lands regardless of creed, colour or political persuasion, has been the essence of the Army's life and endeavour from its very begining. Indeed, we see clearly that any such political identification would inevitably cut us off from large numbers of those very people we seek to succour. The Salvation Army's foundation belief is that the only real hope for the transformation of society lies in personal salvation through faith in the redemptive grace of Christ.

This submission comes to you in the prayerful hope that all who will be related to its consideration can accept that it is motivated only by a desire, on the one hand, to remain in the most harmonious relationship with the World Council of Churches that our position will allow, and, on the other hand, to follow a course which appears to us, after relentless heartsearching and long and prayerful study, the proper one at this particular time.

No-one knows what the future may bring. Should the day come when circumstances encourage The Salvation Army to leave fraternal status and seek full membership, I hope that our readiness to apply would be matched by the World Council of Churches' understanding.

Our constant prayer is that for you and all who share your immense responsibilities there may continue to be granted "the wisdom that cometh from above."

With warmest personal greetings and every good wish. May Divine grace be yours in overflowing measure.

Yours sincerely,
(Sgd.) Arnold Brown
General

In acknowledgement, the central committee wrote as follows:

Dear General Brown,

The central committee of the WCC received with deep regret the news of The Salvation Army's decision to resign its membership of the World Council of Churches. In your letter of 31 July, 1981, you express the desire to remain in the most harmonious possible relationship with the WCC. The committee accepts your resignation and accedes to your request for fraternal status as a world confessional body. Formally, in terms of our constitution, this means that you may be invited to send non-voting representatives to our meetings in such numbers as the central committee shall determine.

As a founding member of the WCC, The Salvation Army has belonged since 1948 to the worldwide fellowship of churches which "confess the Lord Jesus Christ as God and Saviour according to the Scriptures and therefore seek to fulfil their common calling to the glory of the one God, Father, Son and Holy Spirit." This basis of membership is open to the variety of emphases and gifts that different members bring to the total fellowship. Expression of this variety is ensured by the WCC's constitution. The central committee regrets that The Salvation Army feels that, as a member of our fellowship, it compromises its special emphasis on personal salvation through Christ as "the only real hope for the transformation of society."

In explaining the reason for your resignation of membership, you refer to statements, policies and actions of the WCC with which you take issue. Yet it has been clear from the earliest years of the council's life that no member is bound by any action of the whole council. To quote from the WCC central committee statement in 1950: "Membership in the council does not in any sense mean that the churches belong to a body which can take decisions for them. Each church retains the constitutional right to ratify or to reject utterances or actions of the council."

You describe in your letter that you have agonized over this decision since 1978 when you first suspended membership. The central committee appreciates the difficulties you found, but wishes it had been possible for you to continue the dialogue on the issues you had raised.

We feel compelled to disagree with the contrast you draw between the so-called political nature of the action of the World Council of Churches and your own claim to have a non-political stance. From its inception the World Council of Churches has always acted from the deep conviction that the imperatives of the Christian gospel affect all realms of life. Indeed, one of the constitutional functions of the council is to promote "one human family in justice and peace."

We welcome the continuing support you express in your letter for large areas of the council's work, especially world mission and evangelism, faith and order, inter-church aid and the Christian medical commission. But these programmes are inextricably bound up with all the policies of the council in all areas of its work, including the programme to combat racism, over which you have had particular difficulty.

We are aware from our conversations with you, that the World Council's search for "full eucharistic fellowship" poses problems for you as a non-sacramental movement. We can only reiterate the assurances we have given you that this phrase is not a part of the basis for membership and therefore does not exclude you from our fellowship.

You express the hope that should the day come when The Salvation Army re-applies for membership the World Council would meet you with understanding. We can assure you of our willingness to do so.

Meanwhile, we shall maintain cooperative working relationship at the international level, and we share your hope that at local, national and regional levels the ecumenical relationship which The Salvation Army enjoys will continue to grow.

We greet you in the Name of our Lord and Saviour Jesus Christ.

On behalf of the central committee,

Edward W. Scott, Moderator
Philip A. Potter, General Secretary

Our submission was presented during the Dresden meeting and the change was agreed with accompanying expressions of regret. Something, however, went awry with the plan for a bilaterally-agreed news release. The World Council prepared its own release, embargoed until noon the following Monday; but, on the previous Sunday evening, newspapers in the Netherlands were already informing our leaders of the Army's "withdrawal" and asking for comment. When the telexed text of the release reached International Headquarters we cabled immediately asking for a revision of the heading which was worded negatively, emphasizing "withdrawal." But it was too late for change. The damage was done. Media comment, in avalanche volume, generally stressed "withdrawal," and all too many reports invested the events leading to the decision with a bitterness that existed only in the journalist's imagination.

I did not want the Army's offer of help in those areas of work on which the council and the Army saw eye to eye to be thought of as a polite, empty gesture. The offer had been made in good faith, and I was prepared to second suitable officers to the Council's staff and meet their subsistence. I felt that I should emphasize this, and accordingly wrote to the archbishop and general secretary the following letter which concluded the exchange of correspondence:

> Dear friends:
>
> Though you were kind enough to telex the contents of the central committee's letter of decision, the letter itself has now come safely to hand and, in order that the file may be left in a tidy condition for my successor and the future, I acknowledge with thanks its receipt.
>
> It was our hope that our request for fraternal status would engender minimum media comment. Unfortunately, we felt that media stress fell more on the aspect of "withdrawal" and less on the desire of the Army to maintain a helpful relationship.
>
> We would wish, however, to emphasize that the offers of support made during our Geneva discussions reflected our desire to be involved in those areas of Christian work and witness to which we are equally committed. I am hopeful that Commissioner Keanie will have opportunity to discuss possible ways and means with those of your officers with whom you might wish him to confer.
>
> We are grateful for every expression and gesture of Christian fellowship you have extended to us. We have the feeling that wearers of Salvation Army uniform will always be welcome at your headquarters in Geneva, and we appreciate this. Equally, the doors of our International Headquarters will be wide open to any associated with the World Council of Churches who can visit us.
>
> With both official and warmest personal greetings. May God continue abundantly to bless and be with you.
>
> Yours sincerely,
> (Sgd.) Arnold Brown
> General

The Army's decision, when understood, was widely supported. Only in Zimbabwe was there any kind of unhappy reaction. That, I felt, came about because the explanatory material provided to each command had not yet reached the small group of well-meaning but uninformed Salvationists who made a public protest outside our headquarters in Salisbury (now Harare). Fear that the Army's decision would forestall any further, badly-needed grants appeared to be the basis of the protest, a fear that was soon allayed by the receipt of a grant of $100,000 from the World Council for relief purposes, the money being drawn from sources other than the Programme to Combat Racism Fund. The demonstration was brief, but long enough for the news cameras to film the "Down with Brown" placards. The chief participants were invited to join in discussion and a climate of understanding was soon created. Shortly afterwards the territorial commander reported that "the Army in Zimbabwe is in good health."

On reflection I see the episode of the Army's relationship to the World Council of Churches as a two-dimensional experience. One had to do with my official involvement, beginning in 1970 while Chief of the Staff, and coming to a climax in my final months as international leader. It was an organization-to-organization dimension—two international, multi-national bodies seeking to learn each other's place and function; the one, eucharistic, influential, status-conscious and somewhat monolithic. The other, non-sacramental and attempting to unite in one discipline a variety of races and views; perhaps the only truly international member of the World Council's growing family.

The other dimension was personal. I found myself dealing with individuals rather than an organization; persons for whom I developed high respect and warm regard. Through the long months of negotiation and mounting strain I came to see them as "apostles of unity" who, like myself, were not without an occasional "thorn in the flesh." What is here recorded will, I am certain, convince the most sceptical that we were, at the least, "... one in charity."

CHAPTER 19

Unfinished Debate

Both my parents came from large families the members of which, despite all sorts of tensions and trials, had lasting marriages. Always I saw perfect love demonstrated in their relationships by my father and mother. With such a background it is understandable that I was led to alert Salvationists, and to make public statements, concerning what I regarded as a major threat to the Divinely-intended order of society. The demolition of family life, the torn lives of children because of broken homes, and the growing acceptance of infidelity in marriage leading to divorce, were increasingly observable in sorry human terms and blatantly apparent in divorce statistics. Lord Shawcross in *The Observer* had put into words what I felt in my bones. "The so-called new morality is too often the old immorality condoned."

The Salvation Army's view is that the Christian marriage should be permanent and monogamous. It is not to be an ephemeral relationship, but one that is exclusive and enduring. That is why both partners are required to make vows of fidelity to one another in the presence of God. The fact that The Salvation Army's marriage ceremony contains much more than the actual words required by law is further proof that ours is not just a civil ceremony. It could be argued that the knot which the civil law ties can be untied by the same civil law, but not promises made "in the name of the Father, and of the Son, and of the Holy Ghost."

The crisis of marriage in our time is largely due to the fact that many have come to doubt whether this ideal, as well as the conception of sex with which it has always been associated, is still relevant and practical in contemporary life. If they marry, some ask, why should it be necessary for them to commit themselves to a permanent and exclusive relationship? Would it not be more sensible to acknowledge that love may not last, and that a door should be left open for escape? Why not look upon marriage as an experiment? If one fails the first time, let him/her try again. Perhaps he /she will be more successful the second time.

It is a strong tradition, generally borne out in practice, that Salvationists must be living examples of the joy and satisfaction that flows from a Christian marriage. The standards of a society that seeks only the satisfaction of self are not the standards of the Army. From the Sixties on an increasing number of young people were applying for officership who had already been divorced and remarried. There were among my advisors those who said that this should simply be charged up to immaturity; that these young people were "the children of their time." Others counselled a "positive" attitude. Would not these young men and women, because of their experience, be better able, as officers, to shepherd any wilful members of their flock? My own feeling was that it was just as likely that some of the flock would doubt the shepherd's credibility.

Here, I felt a kind of line could be drawn. If the candidate's divorce had occurred prior to conversion and Salvation Army soldiership, that was one thing. If it had happened after a commitment to Christian discipleship and to the standards of the Army, that was definitely another situation. In any event, the most exacting care should be exercised by those charged with deciding a candidate's acceptance or rejection in instances where the Christian standard of marriage had not been maintained.

For Salvationists contemplating divorce I had grave concern. Often their living was earned while working among non-religious people whose views were secularist and sometimes regrettably amoral. Not to succumb to such views required a moment-by-moment claiming of Divine grace. My concern was certainly no less for the very few officer-couples who felt they had come to a parting of the way; but here the problem was more difficult. I subscribed to Helmut Thielicke's view. This eminent German theologian, preacher and writer, had said: "Even in the case where from the legal point of view the minister is the innocent party, the continuation of his office presents him and the church which has commissioned him with problems whose gravity dare not be underestimated. The bearer of a public office is not in a position to make his motives plausible and, what is more, to reveal the background of his intimate personal life. He has no possibility of controlling the judgements people make before or after the fact and preventing them from casting doubt upon the credibility of his office and his message. To hear the word, 'till death us do part,' spoken as a vow by one who himself could not, or did not, satisfy that obligation, can provoke offence and seriously increase the already threatening danger that the church's blessing will be misunderstood as a mere conventional ceremony."

Of the complications that could arise with the reacceptance of divorced officers, particularly if both parties involved in the divorce proceedings claimed "no fault," and equally claimed reinstatement and the right to remarry, I hardly dare to speak. Whatever difficulties the historic churches might have in the reinstatement of a divorced clergyman, the difficulties are doubled for the Army inasmuch as both husband and wife are equally commissioned and, in several countries, equally licensed to conduct weddings. Both are equally responsible for the demonstration of Christian standards in everything they say or do. As well as "the man of God," there is "the woman of God."

Included in the schedule of events of the international congress in the midsummer of 1978 were two sessions for officers. These were the largest convocations of officers in the Army's history. For months prior to the congress I prayed and agonized over what I should say to this splendid company of dedicated men and women, many of whom had experienced hardship in difficult places for the Gospel's sake, and "the latchets of whose shoes I was unworthy to unloose." In the first session I chose for my text, "He will ever be mindful of His covenant" (Psalm 111: 5), and pointed out that a covenant is not the forcible exerting of authority by one over another. A covenant is an agreement entered into voluntarily as binding on both sides. That an infinite God, possessing the power of creation and government, to Whom all law is answerable, beyond Whom is no other, should pledge Himself to those who have inherited all the frailties of human nature is, in itself, a remarkable indication not only of God's justice and holiness, but also of His kindness. Under that all-important and all-embracing covenant into which Salvationists have entered with the Lord of life Himself in respect of their salvation and sanctification, I dealt with some of the covenants which must be kept sacred. One was the covenant of marriage. The couples comprising this unique congregation were themselves an impressive validation of the radiant way in which the covenant of marriage is generally honoured in the movement.

I felt I was given close attention, but with several thousand officers seated in the vast Wembley Pool (as the arena is curiously named), it was difficult to guage precise reaction. Many present had carefully studied the matter for themselves and had reached certain conclusions. Among them were officers who steadfastly refused to conduct the marriage of divorced persons. There were others who felt it was a Christly act to be performed when all others of the clergy had said No. As subsequent correspondence revealed, the congregation included at least two who had passed through the trauma of being deserted and, finally and against their will, but within the provisions of the law, had been divorced by their spouses. For them, my address must have been an admixture of bitterness and balm.

I emphasized that our Christian faith insists upon a *responsible* freedom. It is not a freedom to pursue one's happiness in one's own way. It is a freedom to fulfill *the demands of love* which are not less, but actually more rigorous than any code of laws. If so, the desire for greater satisfaction for the self, or the unwillingness to face ordinary difficulties and, at times, extraordinary problems, can never be an adequate ground for divorce. The Christian will be prepared to endure unhappiness so long as there is any chance of overcoming the obstacles that endanger the marriage, especially when the happiness and security of the other partner and children are at stake.

I called upon the officers to give emphasis to the positive blessings of a Christian marriage, and stressed that it contributed to the moral development of men and women, that it stabilized the sexual impulse and transforms it into creative energy, and that it is superior to all other forms of relationship because of the attitude it fosters towards children. The fidelity of husband and wife to one another entails the faithful concern of both for the happiness of the children. I pleaded that Salvationists, when tempted to think of divorce as an easy way out, should be reminded of their solemn vow to take the partner "for better *for worse,* for richer *for poorer, in sickness* and in health, to love and to cherish till death us do part, according to God's holy ordinance."

Flowing out of this congress challenge two commissions were set up. One was to survey the whole subject of marriage within the Army and to find ways of improving pre-marriage counselling and of lessening the stresses that fall upon busy Salvationists and which could threaten a marriage. The terms of reference allowed the members of the commission to range far and wide over this admittedly vast subject. When my term as General ended, their work, like my own, was unfinished. When concluded, I predict that it will be enormously valuable.

Another commission was set up to determine what discipline was appropriate in respect of officers and soldiers who, having passed through the divorce court, sought to maintain their affiliation and, in the case of officers, their officership. This commission was as thorough and searching as any with which I had experience. I was surprised at the strength of feeling, in the findings, against officers who had been party to a divorce ever resuming active officership. Sanctions were wanted that would convey to the Salvationist community, and especially to young people so susceptible to example and particularly critical of double standards, the fact that The Salvation Army believes Christian marriage to be inviolate. I spent several weeks reflecting on the submissions and in discussing them with other leaders. Without, I hoped, any eroding of Biblical standards, as far as these could be interpreted and applied in a modern society, I modified the proposed regulations. The Bible does not prescribe a detailed canon of discipline for The Salvation Army. Ways had to be found so that certain conditions could be established and certain ends achieved, not by any totalitarian, cultic or fanatical imposition, but simply to make it plain that there were standards which Salvationists intended to keep whatever "the ways of the world."

The work of the latter commission was studied during the international conference of leaders held in glorious autumn weather in Toronto in 1979. Some of the delegates described the draft as "legalistic," and were concerned that the proposed sanctions reflected little compassion. Asking an "innocent" party to accept a period of suspension at a time when the individual needed all the support and Christian fellowship available was felt to be unjustifiably harsh. In rebuttal it had to be pointed out that compassion can sometimes, unfortunately, lead to a picking and choosing of the rules to be kept, while disregarding others. Perplexity issued in incisive questions. Was there ever a totally "innocent" party, even where a "no fault" divorce was granted? Who would ever really know what went on behind the closed curtains of the home? Should our youth see the administration turn "a blind eye" to what, in admittedly isolated instances, might distastefully be described as "a swapping of partners" when divorced parties remarried within the same congregation?

The leaders were more united in their views about officers who were the unfortunate victims of an irretrievable breakdown of their marriage. Consolation should be generous. There should be "caring without condoning." Fellowship in the congregation should be flooded with sincerity. But a return to the platform as spiritual head of a worshipping and witnessing community had grave implications.

As conference time dwindled, it was decided that the drafts should be taken back to the various countries and that study groups should be set up to re-examine the proposed sanctions. Not all the territories and commands did this. Those who did, and submitted comments, had the satisfaction of knowing that their submissions were carefully regarded by the commission at International Headquarters and, as a result, further modifications were made.

Early in 1981 the *Orders and Regulations Governing Separation, Divorce, Reinstatement and Remarriage* were printed and distributed. Aware that there were pending cases, and that time would be needed for leaders at various levels to make themselves familiar with the new rulings, the *Orders* were promulgated six months before the date of implementation. This new procedure, hailed by some, gave time, I was dissappointedly to realize, for further reflection by those leaders who had not given earlier thought to the subject but who were now faced with the responsibility of imposing the new regulations. In my last year of office as General I had decided that the coming together of leaders to elect my successor was too valuable an opportunity to miss for conference. The pre-High Council conference began at Sunbury Court twelve days after the new regulation was supposed to have come into force. With other important subjects, this item was again on the agenda. The promulgation had stimulated still further reaction. Some delegates pleaded for further study; others to be granted unilateral decision-making powers.

Discussion concentrated on the treatment of the "obviously innocent" party (though, as earlier remarked, cold logic asked who would be able infallibly to classify a person as such). Another aspect that concerned certain delegates was the length and timing of any period of suspension. Other delegates were troubled because a Salvationist wishing to resume soldiership after a divorce was required to complete an application as searching as one for a convert from a dubious, but forgiven, past who wanted to become a recruit.

The conference ended with my outlining possible courses of action. The regulations could be withdrawn, except that this could be taken by Salvationists as a sign of hasty drafting or, worse, the lack of will to maintain a standard and administer required discipline. I was concerned lest a withdrawal might make all other regulation suspect. Strong regulations had contributed to the fibre of the movement's life and work. I recalled that a solicitor, after studying all our orders and regulations before he could make a finding in a particular case, said he wished all the bodies he had represented in his lifetime had, in such clear, strong and yet compassionate terms, a comparable corpus of guidance for their members, protecting their rights and privileges and spelling out the terms of their commitment.

Another option would be to modify the regulations in the three aspects that were proving troublesome, and I saw little difficulty in this. Still another possibility would to insist on the application of what was now technically effective regulation, but to notify all leaders that it would be considered experimental for two years. Thereafter, in the light of hard, practical experience, the regulation could be reviewed at the next international conference of leaders, by which time my successor, at that moment unknown, would himself have gained his own insights and be able knowledgeably to plot the best course.

A combination of two options was my own preference; to modify the three vexed points and to consider the whole regulation as experimental for two years. If what is decided, whatever it is, succeeds in upholding the sanctity of the Christian marriage within the Army's ranks, then the challenge I initiated will have evoked a right response. That high aim will not be accomplished by expecting the goblins of infidelity, divorce and fragmented families quietly to disappear. Like others before it, this is "a sinful and adulterous generation."

One comment cannot be omitted. The whole issue was debated in conference and by correspondence in an atmosphere of impervious goodwill and mutual trust. Not all men and women think alike, and for that we can be grateful. But when it comes to guiding God's people in such a delicate but vital matter, all Army leaders in my experience were one on their knees before the Throne of Grace.

For the Army's administration the debate is unfinished. For me, as both prosecutor and defendant, the case rests.

CHAPTER 20

A Necessary Act

Possibly the single most important and far-reaching administrative action with which I was associated during the period spent as Chief of the Staff and the General was the bringing in of a new constitution. Through the years of negotiation I was inclined to agree with Niccolo Machiavelli that "it should be borne in mind that there is nothing more difficult to arrange, more doubtful of success, and more dangerous to carry through than initiating changes in a state's constitution."

What was referred to as "The Constitution" was in reality a brace of five documents, three being Deeds Poll, executed by one person only, and two being Acts of the British Parliament. The first of the Deeds Poll, "A Deed of Constitution," had been executed by William Booth himself in 1878 in the days of the East London Christian Mission. The most substantial document was The Salvation Army Act 1931, The Salvation Army Act 1968 only amending certain aspects of it by making provision for the management of trusts connected with or related to the interests, aims or purposes of The Salvation Army.

The 1931 Act was born of necessity. A large majority of the commissioners attending the first High Council which had adjudicated on the unfitness of General Bramwell Booth to continue in office on the grounds of ill-health, had voted for a Bill which would ratify the decisions made in conference. They were (1) the abolition of the General's right to nominate his successor and the subsitution of the method of election by the High Council; (2) the fixing of an age limit for the retirement of the

General in harmony with the existing regulations for the retirement of all other officers; (3) the substitution of a trustee company to hold the properties and capital assets of the Army in place of the sole trusteeship of the General.

Resorting to Parliament was regarded as a serious and somewhat hazardous undertaking. Public comment on the events of 1929 had been widespread, and members of parliament, like other citizens, had formed their own, and in some instances strong, views concerning the deposition of Bramwell Booth and the actions of the High Council. Commissioner Samuel Logan Brengle, highly regarded by all his colleagues, writing in *The Staff Review* of October, 1930, advocated caution. "Reform is in the air," he wrote. "To meet the age, the new spirit, and the new needs of this huge, worldwide organization and organism—called The Salvation Army—changes, developments, reforms—call them what you please—will come, must come, should come. But I question the wisdom of too many, too radical, too far-reaching reforms. Therefore I would earnestly suggest to those upon whom the task of making changes falls, not to look too far ahead and imagine that they can foresee and legislate for all the needs of those who come after us. The Army may be bound and crippled in its efficiency as surely by too drastic and far-reaching reforms as it came to be by the rigid, cast-iron Deed of 1878 ..."

One of the members of an advisory commission set up to recommend a course of action, Commissioner Charles H. Jeffries, expressed himself in a letter dated 24th February, 1931, to General Edward Higgins who had been elected by the High Council to succeed General Bramwell Booth: "If, later on, further reforms are demanded and there is sufficient body of opinion in the Army to back up such a demand, there is no reason why a further appeal to Parliament should not be made, but, in my opinion, it is not likely that any such demand will be made within ten years, and by that time the Army will have had experience of the working of our system under the modifications secured, and will be able to formulate calmly and wisely any further reforms thought to be necessary."

The passage of the Bill which became the Salvation Army Act 1931 is described in a full and fascinating way by General Frederick Coutts in Volume VI *(The Better Fight)* of *The History of The Salvation Army.* The Bill was discussed in ten sittings of the House of Commons Select Committee presided over by Mr. Frank Lee, six petitions being presented against the Bill. The Bill was then debated in the House of Commons and against some notable opposition was approved by 221 votes to 31. When the measure went to the House of Lords Select Committee on Private Bills, chaired by Viscount Chelmsford, GCSI., GCMG., five petitions against it were heard, occupying five sittings. The eventual decision was that "the preamble of the Bill is approved," and on July 31, 1931, the Bill, given Royal Assent, became the Salvation Army Act 1931. Two fundamental changes in the Army's constitution had been secured: it became the responsibility of the High Council to elect a new General whenever the office fell vacant and, in second place, a Salvation Army Trustee Company would be formed whose duty it would be to hold, as custodian trustee, all property hitherto vested, or which might subsequently be vested, in the General. The retiring age of the General, parliament decreed, was a matter for the Army itself to decide.

Thirty-seven years were to pass before a further resort to Parliament was made, though soon after the passing of the 1931 Act it began to appear that the terms of it had not achieved in full the purposes for which it had been prepared. When Counsel's opinion was sought it became clear that there were internal inconsistencies in the statute itself, and steps were taken to remedy the situation by a Deed of Variation under the hand and seal of General Coutts dated 14th July, 1965, and by the Salvation Army Act 1968 which became law on 30th May of that year.

In 1969 the Charity Commissioners for England and Wales notified the Army's solicitor that in their view what was required was "an entirely new constitution to be embodied in a deed, and that the deed should then be submitted to parliament with a view to its being confirmed by Act of Parliament." I took this suggestion as being timely seeing alterations in the wording of the constitution would be required by the changes in the ranks system for officers which were soon to be introduced. If for no other reason than this, a revision would be necessary. Discussions were initiated with a view to implementing the Charity Commissioners' proposal, but I found little encouragement, apart from my superior, General Wickberg, to proceed. Extreme arguments were used to reinforce resistance. One was that the constitution could not possibly be changed unless all Salvationists agreed in writing. One had visions of signatures being sought in remote and wild areas where the intricacies of the constitution would mean absolutely nothing. Why, when we were dealing with a British Act of Parliament the agreement of Salvationists outside of the United Kingdom should be required was as illogical as the idea was preposterous. Equally ill-balanced was the proposition that the signatures of British Salvationists should determine the constitutional requirements for the rest of the Army world.

It puzzled some leaders why such importance should be laid upon an Act of the British Parliament seeing no national parliament can legislate for another country. The explanation is simple. The Act outlines, *inter alia,* the duties, powers and responsibilities of the General whose leadership embraces Salvation Army activity in whatever country it exists, and also lays out the function of, and certain procedures to be followed by, the High Council. Both of these aspects have vital effect on the Army wherever it manifests itself.

As the Army expanded overseas, indigenous constitutions had to be established. At first these were mainly in Europe and the English-speaking countries of the British Commonwealth, but with the establishment of the Army in lands of other languages, other cultures and other legal systems, the form of our constitutional framework underwent considerable change. It has been a continuing responsibility to monitor these different systems and to secure the highest measure of consistency in the world pattern of Salvation Army legal arrangements. The Army in the United Kingdom is the "original" Salvation Army. It is the parent body to which the legal system of an overseas country looks for a model form of constitution.

With only minor amendments the Salvation Army Act 1931 lasted through almost fifty years of rapid social and economic change, but its language had become archaic, it was silent on some matters of great importance to the movement and, regrettably, it consisted of a number of separate documents. The Charity Commissioners were right. A shorter and simpler document was needed. Inexplicably missing from the 1931 Act and the previous documents, but now vitally necessary, was a brief but comprehensive statement of objects. What was required was a statement that granted to the Army the right to engage in any activity which might further, or be motivated by, its religious nature. There had been cases where the Army's legitimacy in establishing certain forms of social service had been questioned by lawyers acting for various levels of government. Accordingly, our ability, as a legal entity, to receive grant aid for certain forms of endeavour had been challenged.

A more effective procedure for the High Council was also desirable. I had strong feelings about the appropriateness of only seven commissioners being able to requisition a meeting of the High Council for the purpose of adjudicating on the fitness, or otherwise, of a general to continue in office. Was this a sufficient number for so serious a purpose? I also felt that a vote of three-fourths of the membership of the High Council should be required to pass a resolution of deposition. In other words, so grave a step should not be taken without the decision being virtually unanimous. Also, provision should be made for any General under adjudication to present his defence either in person or through counsel. Mr. Justice Eve, presiding over the action against the High Council in the Chancery Division of the High Court of Justice on 31st January, 1929, said, according to *The Times,* "he could not help thinking that a mistake had been made in not giving the General an opportunity of attending by his agents. It was for the council to decide what agents, whether lay persons or persons in the position of solicitors or counsel. That was a matter which rested with them, but, subject to that, it was in his opinion a mistake—a perfectly innocent mistake he doubted not—that they did not give General Booth an opportunity of stating the grounds on which he was seeking to continue in office for the present."

I had not long been in the Chief of the Staff's office without realizing that the provision which allowed a General to retire whenever he wished, simply by giving six months' notice in writing to the Chief of the Staff, was a weak arrangement. Suppose that within weeks of taking office a General gave six months' notice and retired. What effect would another early convening of the High Council have on the Army and, indeed, on the general public?

Any revision of the constitution should, I was convinced, provide for a more realistic distinction between the international Salvation Army, as represented by the General, and the purely domestic arrangements of the Army in the United Kingdom. The General should be relieved of some of the routine work which devolved on him, without in any way limiting the authority or discretion which Salvationists by common consent have accorded to his high office. It was not generally known that no property transaction in the United Kingdom, however trivial, could not be accomplished without the General's attention, and unhappy reflection on the competence of the individuals and boards charged with the proper administration of such business.

A number of other matters needed adjustment. By the 1931 Act the High Council could elect any person outside of High Council membership, or even Salvation Army soldiership, as General. This, most conceded, was too expansive a clause and went far beyond the original intention. Also by the Act the voting, when seeking to elect a General, could go on *ad infinitum,* there being no procedure to limit the number of ballots. Aware of the tensions that build during this solemn exercise, I asked our constitutional lawyers to provide a system which, while allowing for an adequate expression of preference in order to reach the necessary plurality, would also include a reasonable form of closure.

Most wanted of all was the right to make future changes to the constitution without recourse to parliament. According to our advisors, by appending to the body of the Act a number of schedules this would be possible.

Discussions with the Army's solicitors, Messrs. Slaughter and May, stretched over a period of two years and, in the summer of 1979, it was decided to initiate a Bill in parliament. This set off a new series of consultations with our own solicitors, our parliamentary agents, Messrs. Dyson, Bell and Co., and, in particular, with Mr. Jeremy Francis, a partner in that firm, together with the Army's own legal advisor, the then Major Bramwell Baird, as well as with our auditors, Messrs. Knox Cropper and our stock-brokers, Scrimegour & Co. Not only did Salvation Army and legal views have to be satisfied, but also those of the Charity Commission and the Treasury Solicitor. Eventually, all matters were cleared and the report of the Attorney-General on the Bill was wholly favourable.

To achieve this approval the Army was asked to make two concessions: (1) to limit the wide powers of investment for Army funds which the Bill had originally sought; and (2) to substitute for the General, the Central Finance Council of the Army which would have scheme-making powers in respect of common investment schemes. We acquiesced on both counts, since not to have done so would have added considerable difficulty to the passage of the Bill.

An early draft was referred to the Advisory Council to the General and the recommendations made by that council were incorporated so far as possible in later drafts. In September, 1979, the latest draft was submitted to the international conference of leaders meeting in Toronto, the largest and most representative conference of its kind ever held. It was considered by the delegates in two full sessions, and again studied at a private meeting of the commissioners seeing the assent of two-thirds of their number would be necessary if the submission to parliament were to proceed. At each meeting Mr. Keith E. Wright, MA., senior partner in the firm of Slaughter and May, was present to explain the purpose of the Bill and to answer questions. Once more, shortly before the printed Bill was laid before parliament, it was carefully scrutinized by the General's advisory council.

The Bill was deposited on 27th November, 1979, and was allocated to the House of Lords. By the closing date, 6th February, 1980, no petitions against it had been filed. We were far more fortunate than our predecessors in 1931! I invited the Rev. Dr. Lord Soper, well-known Methodist minister and life peer, to come to International Headquarters and take lunch with my wife and me. He was in great form and regaled us with amusing and moving stories from his half-century of open-air ministry on Tower Hill. Only a few days before, while preaching, a young constable had threatened to arrest him for causing an obstruction. Lord Soper suggested that the constable should do his duty as he saw it, though he maintained his own right to continue what he had been doing for fifty years. The officer persisted and called for a patrol car to take the arrested preacher away. As excitement grew, the crowd being very much on the side of Lord Soper, an official of the Metropolitan Police Force arrived and took charge. He was full of apologies for the policeman's excessive display of authority, and promised that "a suitable word or two" would be whispered in his ear. The mix-up ended with Lord Soper pleading the young constable's case and asking the superior to forget "the whispered words." Between stories I asked Lord Soper if he would agree to introduce our Bill on Second Reading if that should prove necessary, and he immediately and enthusiastically acceded. In the event, the Bill was read a second time on the 19th February without a Division, and Lord Soper's services were not required.

The Bill was considered in committee by Lord Aberdare, Lord Chairman of Committees, sitting with Counsel to the Lord Chairman, in the Moses Room of the House of Lords, at a few minutes past eleven on

Tuesday morning, 13th May, 1980. Members of the committee were assured that the Bill had been fully discussed with the government departments concerned and that they had expressed themselves as satisfied with it, subject to certain agreed amendments. The chief accountant from International Headquarters, the then Lieut-Colonel Roy Lovatt, gave formal evidence to prove the Preamble. He and members of the Army's legal team were prepared for extensive questioning, but only formal evidence was given, and the Lord Chairman announced that he would report the Bill as amended to the House. There was no further action until 11th June 1980, when the Bill was read for a third time in the Lords, and, on the same day, was read for the first time in the House of Commons.

In the unlikely event that objection was made to a Second Reading, preparations were made to provide support, and a number of members of parliament known to be favourable to the Army were briefed to speak on its behalf. Among them were Mr. Derek Foster, the Salvationist member for Bishop Auckland, the Rt. Hon. Roy Hattersley, a former cabinet minister, Mr. John Blackburn and Sir Bernard Braine, the member for Essex South-East who had cooperated with the Army on a number of issues and whose wide parliamentary experience generated respect. The precautions were unnecessary and the Bill had a Second Reading without a Division on the 24th June. It was committed to the Select Committee on Unopposed Bills for consideration at four o'clock on Wednesday afternoon, 9th July, in Committee Room 9, and I was instructed to attend.

There was no way of knowing the outcome of the meeting. The whole scene was one of mingled dignity and efficiency. The cheerful conversation that dominated the pre-meeting briefing session had subsided. The hush that now prevailed was funereal. I found myself tensing as members of the committee filed in and took their places. As they sat, a two-way evaluation began. We surveyed them; they silently contemplated us. With the chairman, Mr. Richard Crawshaw, were Messrs. John Forester, Archie Hamilton and Robert Rhodes James. Mr. Michael O'Halloran was appointed a member but did not attend. Sir Robert Speed, counsel to Mr. Speaker, and counsel-designate, Mr. T.R.F. Skemp, CB., were also present.

The chairman began by stating that the Attorney-General had reported on the Bill and asked whether the amendments already made, and those proposed, were acceptable to him and to the Charity Commissioners. Mr. Francis, speaking for our parliamentary agents, assured the committee that they were acceptable and went on to outline the amendments. He then read a statement of the objects and gave a précis of the Bill, similar to the statement made to the committee in "Another Place" (the House of Lords). Detail relating to the Army trusts was provided by the Army's legal secretary. The chairman then wanted to know whether, in exercising his power to appoint members to the Central Finance Council, the General would be following an established procedure or if he would have discretion to appoint whoever he chose. Mr. Francis indicated the discretion was unfettered in terms, but that in practice there was a consultative procedure which would always be followed, and that appointments would only be made of officers with specialized knowledge or experience. I confirmed that this was so and would be so.

Mr. Robert Rhodes James then asked me, rather pointedly, why it had taken ten years to implement the advice of the Charity Commissioners. I was unsure whether the inflection in his voice conveyed cynicism or humour. I hoped the latter, and told the committee that while I had begun as Chief of the Staff, with General Wickberg's approval, to implement the Charity Commissioners' suggestion, I was able to take it up again only after being elected as General in 1977. Mr. James then asked if the intention behind the financial provisions of the Bill was to separate the General from day-to-day administration of the Army's finance and property. I explained that part of the purpose of the Bill was to distance the General from the daily routine of the Army's business affairs in the United Kingdom, and legally to put him in relation to the British Territory in much the same position as he stood in respect of other territories. I pointed out that I relied on my advisors in great measure for decision-making in business, and suggested that the Bill would give formal recognition to what was already a fact.

Invited to make any further comment I wished, I added that I was anxious to secure passage of the Bill because the constitution in Britain served as a model for many other countries throughout the world. It would be translated so that it could be presented to the appropriate authorities in their own language to form the basis of the Army's constitution in such countries. There were no more questions and I was invited formally to prove the Preamble as amended by evidence. This done, the chairman announced that the committee accepted the case for the Bill and would so report to the House. The proceedings ended at 4.35 p.m., and we walked out of the venerable parliament buildings into a bright summer evening, relieved that the last challenge had been hurdled. Mr. Francis had been accompanied by three of his assistants. Mr. Keith Wright had been supported by another partner and two assistants. The Salvation Army oficers accompanying me were the chief accountant, Lieut-Colonel Peter Hawkins; the legal secretary, Major W. Bramwell Baird; and my personal assistant, Major John Bate. We parted with much hand-shaking and a high degree of satisfaction.

In accordance with procedure for Private Bills in the House of Commons, the Bill was considered again by the Examiners on 21st of July to ensure compliance with the decisions of the Select Committee. It was read a third time on 24th July and the Commons Amendments were then considered and approved by the House of Lords. Finally, on 1st August, 1980, the Bill received Royal Assent and became an Act of Parliament (Chapter XXX), coming into force immediately.

The new Act embodies almost all of the hoped-for revisions. Schedule 1 comprises the Doctrines of the Army, parliament having decided that it was not their desire or within their ability to tell Salvationists what they should believe. Other Schedules cover matters related to the vacating of office by the General and the convening and function of the High Council. These subjects need not again be referred to parliament should the necessity for change arise. Revisions can be effected by the General, provided there is the written agreement of a full two-thirds of the active commissioners. The Act also moved the Army's Trustee Company from being a custodial trustee to being an ordinary trustee, the general ceasing to be the managing trustee. This broader base of management more closely meets the spirit and expectation of current company law and heightens the degree of accountability. Flowing from this change has been the regularizing, rather overdue, of the structure and operation of the subsidiary companies such as Salvationist Publishing and Supplies, Ltd., Reliance World Travel Ltd., and the Salvation Army General Insurance Corporation Ltd. The Reliance Trust Limited (formerly the Reliance Bank Ltd.) conforms in its operation to the Banking Act 1979.

Copies of The Salvation Army Act 1980 were printed quickly and distributed to all English-speaking officers. Translation in a number of languages was to follow. My foreword concluded in the following terms: "A constitution, however, is no more than a legal framework within which a movement like ours can grow and develop. The heart of the Army beats within the lives of its soldiers and officers as they carry the imperishable message of the Gospel to the needy world around them. I commend this new constitution to you, but most of all I commend to you the grace of the Lord and the power of the Holy Spirit to motivate and inspire you as we move towards the twenty-first century."

CHAPTER 21

"This Is My Father's World"

Our global travels convinced us that the five continents affect the five senses differently. Europe does not look like South America, and Asia has a different taste to Australia. Touch varies from continent to continent. In North America hands operate a vending machine. In Africa they encircle a freshly-fallen coconut. The sounds differ. The bells of Switzerland are in auditory contrast to the call of the muezzin in Indonesia. No two continents smell alike. One can sniff Calcutta miles away. Likewise Christchurch in New Zealand's southern island; but the redolence of the one differs from the fragrance of the other. Five senses are ample for the average tourist, but I was not a tourist. I needed a sixth sense—the ability to sense the "real" under the programmed; the discernment to glimpse the "actual" when overlaid with the trappings of welcome and celebration. Not being a tourist I perhaps missed many of the sights that reward the ordinary traveller. But my wife and I saw sights the ordinary tourist never sees, and heard sounds he would never hear. We possibly smelled what he would never smell. Fortunately, since I carried no camera, certain scenes and situations, certain people and their characteristics were photographed by the mind and memory as permanently as on film.

Our first visit to Africa was to Nigeria in 1970 for golden jubilee celebrations. The country was still reeling from the Biafran war. The territorial commander had announced congress gatherings in Etinan in the Eastern States but had no idea how many would, or could, attend.

Judging by the number of armed soldiers at the Port Harcourt airport where we landed, and the microscopic search of our belongings, the people hardly realized that the war was over. On a particularly brilliant Sunday morning we stood at a reviewing stand beside a tall flagpole from which fluttered the Salvation Army flag. My wife and I, with Colonel and Mrs. Len. Kirby and the then Major Frank Fullarton, the private secretary, were the only people in sight, apart from a group of seven or eight bandsmen from Calabar who shattered the silence with alternate renderings of two tunes, one of which caused me to go over to the bandmaster and shake hands with him.

"Thank you, bandmaster," I said, "for playing one of our national songs. It was thoughtful of you to honour us in this way."

He looked at me blankly and asked, "What song did you say?"

"The Maple Leaf for Ever," I replied. "It's one of Canada's national songs."

He shook his head negatively and his large eyes pleaded for forgiveness at having to correct me. "Oh, no, sir," he said firmly, "that's not 'The Maple Leaf,' that's 'God bless our Army round the world, and keep us true for ever.'" For him, the tune's nationality meant nothing. It was simply a melody that allowed him, as a Salvationist, to express his own internationality.

Through a mile of palm-leaf arches, a green corridor of greeting, several thousands of white-uniformed Salvationists (according to the report, "The largest concourse of uniformed Salvationists in living memory in the south-eastern state") marched—or danced!—past us, singing the two songs in the band's repertoire. The second appeared more popular than "The Maple Leaf." With two years of fierce horror behind them, the marchers, many of whom had barely escaped with their lives while hiding in the bush, had good reason to sing, "When the saints come marching in, I want to be among that number ..." In the afternoon, to roars of approval, local chieftains clothed me in traditional Nigerian dress —several sizes too large!

There was a dramatic episode as we drove, still talking about the day which had marked the rebirth of our movement in that part of Nigeria, towards Aba and a government rest centre. A bridge we had crossed with considerable caution early in the day was now closed by the military. The detour meant an extra ninety miles by an unfamiliar route, and our driver was weary. Out of the darkness, as we tried to control our disappointment, a soldier appeared. Waving his bayoneted gun he told me to get out of the van. Quietly, the Colonel beside me said, "Sit still." The point of the bayonet came closer and the soldier repeated his command much more roughly. Again the Colonel said, "Sit still." A bayonet, I now know, can be an intimidating persuader, but then I heard the Colonel saying, "These are for you. I know you can read," as he handed the sentry a Gospel and other religious literature. In an instant the soldier was all deference and gratitude. He waved us on, obviously impatient to be alone with his precious gift. After that frightening incident, the escape of one of two live chickens with which my wife had been presented caused minimal panic, even though it fluttered dementedly around our heads in the van, evading capture as we plunged through the night avoiding the huge bomb craters in the roads.

It is a custom in Nigeria for all forms of transportation to carry brightly painted mottoes, many of them Scriptural phrases imploring the Almighty's providential oversight. Speeding towards us we saw an open truck, dangerously overloaded with its human freight, and commandeering most of the road. It was obvious we would pass, if we passed at all, just where an unusually large crater had destroyed our side of the highway. With strong hands on the steering wheel our van clung precariously to the crater's edge as the lorry flashed by. On its side was painted: "Thank God. No condition is permanent!"

In Lagos I met General Yakubu Gowon, the 36-year-old head of state responsible for sixty million people. He received me in the military barracks where he lived, refusing to occupy the presidential premises. He told me that he was a soldier, not a politician. To Britain, he said, he owed an enormous debt. From the dusty streets of a small Nigerian village he had gone to a government college at Zaria and thereafter had been given an excellent education in England. At Sandhurst, he said, he had been taught the value of discipline. "These two, education and discipline," he told me earnestly, "are what my people need." Knowing that I was a Canadian, he took the opportunity to express his annoyance concerning the stand taken by certain Canadian church leaders whose sympathies during the war had been with those in revolt and to whom they had provided generous relief assistance. With some bitterness he observed that they had been totally misguided and, he hoped, when I had opportunity, I would tell them so. He then asked me to pray with him and for Nigeria. Not long after he was exiled in the United Kingdom to which he owed so much.

Another imposing figure who received us with ready cordiality was the Oba (King) of Lagos. Tall and commanding in appearance he obviously dominated life in the palace where we met. Women bowed almost to the ground as they passed, and children scurried by on all fours. Cast in a traditional rôle, he had all of natural refinement plus western education and experience. His address to the golden jubilee congress was masterly by any standard, as flashing with wit as the enormous gem he wore on his finger, and which refracted brilliantly whenever it caught the light.

Ten years later, accompanied by the international secretary for Africa, Commissioner Richard Atwell, I visited Calabar in Nigeria's Cross River State. Fifty years before, the late Colonel and Mrs. Walter Sully, then young officers, had followed in the footsteps of the heroic Scottish missionary, Mary Mitchell Slessor, to begin the work of the Army. They knew no-one in Calabar and spent their first night sleeping on the mud floor of a hut. How incomparably different was my visit! As I deplaned, fifty motorcycles (apropos the Army's golden jubilee in the area) each bearing two fully-uniformed Salvationists and a large flag, formed up as an escort, and, with a roar like thunder, opened a way through the traffic for the car in which I rode. I laid a wreath on Mary Slessor's monument, a huge grey stone cross on a hill overlooking the harbour. On the base are chiselled the words: "The people that sat in darkness saw great light" (Matthew 4: 16), and "They that turn many to righteousness shall shine as the stars for ever and ever" (Daniel 12: 3).

In the harbour below oil-tankers were moving Nigeria's new wealth while we stood and sang a verse of William Booth's anthem, "And now, Hallelujah! the rest of my days/Shall gladly be spent in promoting His praise ..." That afternoon in the stadium I faced more than five thousand Salvationists in white uniforms who sang, with rhythmic movement, the African folk-tune we now call, "Calabar." In English they used the words, "Guide me, O Thou great Jehovah," by William Williams (the "Sweet Singer of Wales"). The spirits of Slessor and Sully seemed inspiringly close. An exuberant march around the stadium track concluded the jubilee. A platoon of cripples from the Army's Oji River centre brought up the rear. Calipers and crutches slowed their pace, but determination was evident in every awkward step. They made a pathetically proud sight.

Africa is one continent but many countries of many contrasts. The African, generally speaking, is one of the most likeable members of the human family. He has inherited a largesse of ancient wisdom. He is imitative and learns quickly, which can mean progress. He is a "natural" Salvationist. Once he claims the faith, the faith claims him; he will die for it. Music stirs him to the depths of his being. The beating of the drums quickens his heart-beat. Uniforms, marching, singing, flags and banners all warm his blood. William Booth, interviewed by *The British Weekly* after a visit to South Africa in 1909 said, "The natives ... are ingenious in trade and industrious in work, and are growing both in numbers and power. You must do something with the black man and you must do it quickly. You must ... make him a self-respecting individual. You must Christianize him. You must befriend him ... otherwise there will be terrible and appalling trouble."

* * *

In few countries can the phenomenal growth of The Salvation Army match that of Kenya, a land of vivid natural beauty where multiracial harmony has meant prosperity and progress. In Kenya I was dubbed "the rain maker," no small honour since, prior to my arrival, the drought had been severe and in the north crops had failed and elephants were dying. In the mind of the territorial commander of the day, Commissioner Geoffrey Dalziel, however, timing was faulty. Months of hard preparation for the congress threatened to be washed away in successive downpours. So great was the rejoicing of the crowds, however, that the rains were ultimately accepted as an answer to prayer, and he and his organizers allowed their mourning to be turned into joy. Many Salvationists had walked scores of miles to Nairobi spurred by the hope that congress petitions would cause the reluctant heavens to open.

Thika, not far from Kenya's modern capital, is not only a place-name but is a synonym for Salvation Army compassion in action. At the high school for the blind (one of 285 schools sponsored by the Army in Kenya) the eyes of the mind are opened and high standards of intelligence are discovered. I could not believe my ears when the school chorus sang. Intricate harmonies were beautifully negotiated and full-throated *tuttis* billowed across the sandy schoolyard. Nearby, young cripples sheltered in the Army's "Joytown" hobbled purposefully to classes where school lessons and self-supporting trades were being mastered. Lads with limbs splayed at obtuse angles performed an acrobatic display for me, much of it on hands rather than feet, the performers being upside-down in all but the faultlessness of their dexterity. I recalled pyramid-building challenges as a boy scout when possessed of all of one's faculties; but "Joytown's" pyramids were far more complicated and impressive, despite hindering handicaps.

A second visit was paid to Nairobi in 1980. The city now had one of the most impressive air terminals in the world. The Kenyatta Conference Centre, housing massive international conventions, was the scene of the commissioning of fifty new Salvation Army officers. In many lands such a function is internal, but not in Kenya. With Commissioner Ngugi on the platform were government leaders and the influentially-great from among the citizenry. To them this was an important event in the development of their country where progress for the future must rest upon Christian foundations. Three times on the Sunday the auditorium's six-thousand seats were occupied.

After a series of massive weekend events any happening on a Monday morning has every possibility of withering in the torpor of anticlimax. Many preachers regard Monday morning as a God-given period of convalescence during which reflection and recuperation reknit the ministry's "ravelled sleeve." Not so for us in Kenya. The schedule read, "Monday, 10 a.m., Tala Market," and, with only a brief stop in order to observe a distant herd of wild giraffe, their long necks and outsize heads poking out of the horizon, we arrived at Tala Market. An empty platform standing at the centre of a large waste space, with black gamins hopping on and off it, was the sole indication of future activity. But Africa has its signals, and our solitude was brief. Distant drums, metronomic in their beat, were urging unseen marchers to the meeting.

With astonishing speed the scene changed. Thousands of Salvationists in white tropical uniforms surrounded the stage, each contingent clustering about its own flag and proudly placarding the village of its origin. If distance had prevented their attending the Sunday gatherings, then Monday must be their Sunday, and the Divine purposes of worship in the presence of their international leaders must be served. If the word, "unforgettable," is often used, there are times when no other will do. Now, on ordinary Monday mornings, I lift my cup of recollection and drink to the last drop the "unforgettable" elixir of Tala, thanking God that on the second day of the week, as well as on the first, men and women can meet around the Throne of Grace, even if to some it seems to look like a temporary stage swarming with little black boys who find it to be a first-rate adventure playground.

Before we left Nairobi my wife and I were received by His Excellency, President Daniel Arap Moi, Kenya's head of state. Immediately after shaking hands we were the recipients of his Christian witness. Daniel means, "God is Judge," and Arap Moi carries his name with respect. Conservatively dressed in a dark suit, he presented a marked contrast to his predecessor, the great Mzee Jomo Kenyatta, Kenya's "founding father." Here was no traditional costume or fly-swatter flicking out exclamation marks. At some moments in the conversation the president seemed to be too gentlemanly to be part of the political struggle and too clement to administer any rough justice. But there was decision in his bearing and purpose in his gaze. The proper future of *Jamhuri ya Kenya* and its ten million citizens was his theme and, under God, he felt that the land was rich with promise. With a dash of the dramatic he explained the meaning of the republic's flag with its three horizontal stripes of black, red and green, the red edged in white and bearing in the centre an African shield in black and white with two crossed spears behind. I recall the animation with which he described how, out of the black darkness, and by the red blood of the people's heroes, had come the lush green country that was now the Kenyan's homeland.

A few days after our departure, Nairobi's famous Norfolk Hotel where we had been quietly and comfortably accommodated, fell victim to the terrorist's bomb with an unfortunate loss of life. Our recent stay made viewing of the television news coverage shudderingly personal.

* * *

Two visits to Rhodesia, both before the name was changed to Zimbabwe, italicized the startling changes that can affect a nation within so short a span of time as a decade. During the first visit there was more comment about the magnificent Jacaranda blooms than the country's political future. I was captivated by the country's natural beauty and the air of prosperity that haloed it, but did not realize how ominously volcanic feelings were swirling towards eruption. On the surface at least in 1972 all appeared peaceful, though the Unilateral Declaration of Independence and the negotiations that followed had certainly created harsh disagreement between Salisbury and Whitehall.

Looking from the pulpit of the Salisbury Cathedral, where our 85th anniversary service of thanksgiving was held, I had a clear view of Prime Minister Ian Smith, who had read one of the lessons, and his wife, seated in their special pew at the front of the large congregation. The prime minister appeared tense and distant, his face set in immobility. Was he, I wondered, pre-shaping his reactions to the results of the Pearce Commission which were to be announced the next day? One could foresee stormy negotiations with the United Kingdom over the "illegal" action which it felt the government of Rhodesia had taken, but could anyone have thought that so swiftly and disastrously argument would become bloodshed, and that internecine war would engulf this lovely land for the next seven years?

When next we visited Rhodesia the terrible struggle had ended. Independence was only days away. Lord and Lady Soames would soon vacate Government House, where we were received by them, in favour of the new occupants, Mr. and Mrs. Robert Gabriel Mugabe. I had read Lady Soames's new book about her mother, Lady Clementine Churchill, and congratulated her on it. She was intrigued by my references to William Booth's jousting contacts with her father, Sir Winston, all of which seemed new to her. I ventured to tell Lord Soames that in negotiating the independence arrangements he had, in my opinion, successfully grasped a stinging nettle while wearing the right gloves. He appeared gratified, but his large eyes held a questioning look. I asked him if he thought the Army were wise in pouring all possible resources into Zimbabwe's future, and he replied that it was a difficult question to answer.

"I know what I should tell my government," he said, "but the Army's motives and purposes are different."

He hoped that I would see Mr. Mugabe for myself, and this I tried to do. The incoming prime minister, however, was having a long meeting with tribal chiefs and was unavailable in the time I had at my disposal. I had to content myself with discussing matters with the new minister of state, the Hon. Emmerson Mnangagwa.

In conversation with Lady Soames my wife mentioned the helpfulness of Teresa of Avila's benediction which begins, "Let nothing disturb thee, nothing affright thee ..."

"I keep those words on my dressing table upstairs, and draw great comfort from them always," Lady Soames intimated. "How strange," she said, "that you should refer to this particular verse."

Relief over the war's end and hope for a halcyon future were everywhere in the air. For so long inured to conflict, the majority of Rhodesians welcomed the return of peace. In a Sunday morning gathering for which the National Sports Stadium was crowded, I presented to Colonel David Moyo a new territorial flag, the first to bear the changed name of the country. If I took longer than usual to untie the ribbons around the furled colours, it was because the excitement of the crowd was something to be savoured. It was an historic moment to be stretched to its limit of significance. As the folds dropped into place and the name, "Zimbabwe," was seen, patriotic feelings exploded. Colonel Moyo lifted the flag and ecstatically marched again and again across the wide stage, each proud wave of the colours being greeted with renewed acclamation. Later, I told the media that the Army was giving more than a flag to Zimbabwe. As evidence of our confidence in the nation's future I had, during the visit, laid three foundation stones: one for a new home for aged citizens, another for a new hospital wing, and a third for a new training college for officers. Faith could hardly have been more patently and practically demonstrated.

Though peace had returned, the pain of war still nagged. As we marched into the cemetery at Bulawayo where the two girl Salvationists, murdered at Usher Institute, were buried, a little band played, "Sweeping through the gates of the New Jerusalem." The twin graves had a single headstone bearing the testimonial words, "Love endureth all things." Remembering that the red blood of these devoted young women had mingled with the red sands of an Africa they loved, we recalled also the staggering number of African Salvationists whose lives had been claimed by the bitter conflict. Bulawayo—the name means "Place of killing"—once under the sway of cruel witchcraft, "smelling out" and murder, seemed tranquil enough on this Saturday morning. Sunshine and faint shower alternated as we prayed and sang. Then came a revealing moment. An African officer in his prayer referred to the death of the white girls.

"When I heard of it," he said as he wept, "my heart broke. My inborn, suppressed hatred of the whites melted. My bitterness disappeared. I was changed for ever; changed into a new servant for Christ. I realized then, O God, the true meaning of love. Like your Son, these women had died for me and my people." We wept with him.

The graves were overlaid with yellow, red and blue flowers. Major Jean Caldwell, whose life had been spared on that horrific night at Usher, read Paul's "hymn to love" (1 Cor. 13). She had returned to the institute to hand over a new flag to the reconstituted student body. I spoke with difficulty, glimpsing again for myself the high cost of that "greater love." The damp, warm mist, the occasional spatter of rain wetting the printed order of service, and the band playing "When the roll is called up yonder I'll be there!" coalesced in memoriam "For all the saints who from their labours rest."

In the crowd was a major whose Salvation Army cap had several bullet holes through it. His wife's knees were bullet scarred. Both had miraculously survived the terrorists' gunfire. I sorrowed with another officer paying his respects. Thirteen of his choice young people had been senselessly mowed down by terrorists' bullets as they left the Army hall and their Bible studies. Altogether it was a morning to remember!

Our final meeting in Salisbury concluded with many seekers, black and white kneeling together at the altar. It was a moving reminder that at the feet of Christ and under the binding fatherhood of God lies the secret of brotherhood.

* * *

All of our services in Africa were multiracial, and without disturbing incident. In South Africa, where black, white and coloured sat side by side, a local officer declared in his welcome address, "Here we have the most colourful and the most colour-less expression of The Salvation Army in the world." The speaker, a lecturer at the University of Witwatersrand, was the conductor of the large congress chorus. The first notes of the group (whose members were black), accompanied by the Johannesburg Citadel Band (whose instrumentalists were white), were like a tidal wave smashing against a rocky cliff. Never again will I hear a rendition of "Worthy is the Lamb" without reliving the surprise and exhilaration of that moment.

Traditional skills were also demonstrated. On the citadel platform we were joined by a group of youths who were announced to perform a "gumboot dance." All wore what the English call "Wellingtons," and by stamping their feet and slapping the sides of their rubber boots a variety of rhythmic, percussive effects were created. There was one notable drawback. The gumboot dance surely had originated in the open-air and was not intended for a carpeted platform. Each stamping raised a new cloud of dust until the platform resembled a Sahara sandstorm. The performers, like the platform party imprisoned behind them, disappeared slowly into a grey mist, all to the rollicking enjoyment of the crowd.

The South Africa visit concluded with Easter gatherings at Capetown. Early on the Sunday morning, crowds gathered at the Rhodes Memorial on Table Mountain, one of the world's great landmarks since the 15th century. Here, for more than thirty Easters, the Salvation Army had conducted the community sunrise service. In the darkness it was impossible to see whether the mountain's famous cloudy tablecloth was spread, though pouring rain indicated that it was. I had been instructed to finish, on a given signal, any remarks I might be making so that a flourish of trumpets could herald the first flash of the rising sun. But signals were unnecessary. We were not to see, as the worshippers generally did, the side of the mountain spectacularly splashed with brightness. Instead, the darkness thickened and the rain fell more heavily. I spoke to a large congregation of dripping umbrellas and sheltering tarpaulins, making the points that we were all under the umbrella of God's love, and that "as surely as the sun has risen, though we do not see it, so much more certainly has Christ risen from the dead."

* * *

I was welcomed to Zambia by the vice-president and secretary-general of the ruling United National Independence Party, the Hon. Mr. Mainza Chona, who said he wanted to greet me "as a cousin." "Whatever the disparity in age," he said, "cousins can meet on the same level of enjoyed fellowship. Thus a young man can converse, and even joke, with an old man who otherwise would require to be addressed on another plane. For the young man it is an exciting privilege. He feels that as a result he has grown tall in the councils and confidences of his adult superiors." We then shook hands "as cousins," I assuming myself to be "the old man" in the allegory.

Chikankata for the Army in Zambia has long been a focal point of interest and service. Education and health-care, on a large scale, go hand in hand with spiritual instruction. Here, I gained more than I could give, though I took heart from the Tonga aphorism, "Every visitor brings a piece of wood for the fire." Inspections over in the company of the officer commanding, Lieut-Colonel Lyndon Taylor, there was a public service in a woefully overcrowded building where the International Secretary's long experience in Africa had taught him how to handle situations that might in a Western setting be disconcerting.

"We want absolute quiet so that we can all hear what the General has to say, don't we?" he asked the mothers present. "There is no need for cry-rooms, is there? You know what to do, so do it!" As the meeting progressed I discovered what was meant. Immediate and unembarrassed breast-feeding brought the silence of contentment to every infant heckler.

Seated in the hall, wearing their white uniforms, were members of "the leper choir." I had visited their compound of little cottages, and had seen at close range the hideous ravages of Hansen's disease. Though medical science has discovered how to arrest the disease and, in many cases, to cure it, these men and women were no longer wanted in their villages or in the homes of their own people. Leprosy is still one of the most unreasoningly feared of all ills. During one service the "choir" sang same strangely moving words: "I'm waiting, Jesus, for You to take me home." The lump in my throat grew larger with the second verse: "I'm ready, Jesus, for You to take me home." When the obnoxiously self-righteous claim that Christian compassion is vanishing from off the earth I think of the young officers I saw after that meeting with their arms around these pitiable victims of an alienating disease, helping them up the hill to their little colony of comfort and care. Thankfully, there is yet an aristocracy of service.

* * *

To the north-west of the continent lies Ghana, formerly the Gold Coast, sandwiched between the Ivory Coast on the west and Togo on the east. To the north lies the Upper Volta and to the south the Gulf of Guinea from which vessels sail in to Tema Harbour, the largest man-made harbour in

Africa. In Accra, the capital, our party were guests of the state and royally treated, and the cooks went all out to cater for our Western tastes. At one meal a large dish of boiled potatoes was served with a touch of regal hospitality. No wonder! At the time, and in that part of the world, potatoes were costing one pound sterling each. Housed in palatial surroundings we had everything we needed, except water. Without it, I found, personal hygiene becomes a challenge of the first magnitude.

The president, Dr. Hilla Limann, received us at his country residence, an imposing structure on the crest of a hill from which, I was told, guards could see any movement in the surrounding country for miles around. Here, more than anywhere else in our travels, I sensed the precariousness of political office. A surprising number of big, alert attendants, smartly attired in morning coats, and with weapons, accompanied us through various halls and rooms until we came into the president's presence. I still know very little about the man, other than that he had been a diplomat, and before that had studied at the London School of Economics and the Sorbonne in Paris. But I liked him, and our conversation was easy, informative and enjoyable. His tenure, however, was to be a short one, abbreviated by another of the all-too-frequent *coups* which have plagued the stability of this rich and promising country.

By the president's courtesy, and in the company of the officer commanding, Lieut-Colonel Don. Seiler, we flew in a Royal Ghanaian Air Force plane to Kumasi in the north. With us was a prominent official of the World Bank who must have wondered who his travelling companions really were when he saw the dimensions of our welcome at the airport. They can only be described as "enormous." Thousands of Salvationists shouting "Akwaaba!" ("Welcome!"), were accommodated on temporary bleachers, carefully segregated according to their status as officers, local officers, soldiers or recruits. Nearest to the plane, in a reserved section, were all the community leaders in the uniforms or vestments of office, and I was escorted to them under a huge ceremonial umbrella carried by a panting giant of a man. As I greeted the dignitaries a military band struck up, "O Boundless Salvation," the woodwinds adding a pleasing colour to the scoring. The bandmaster was every inch the Kneller Hall graduate.

Prior to the service in St. Cyprian's Anglican cathedral, I went to meet the Asantehene—the King of the Ashantis—at his palace. A glass of water was offered as a sign of welcome, and as a sign of friendship I took a sip. The enthroned Asantahene was traditionally garbed, his flowing garments highlighted by the gold rings he wore on fingers and toes. Each was formed into the figure of a peacock, the emblem of the kingdom. Once the formalities had been discharged in the local language the king said, "Now we can talk in English" and this he proceeded to do with an accent reminiscent of one of the best British colleges.

"You are a man with great authority over many people," the Asantahene said, "and I have had prepared for you a special gift." He then handed me a wood carving of a man's hand holding up an egg. "Responsibility should be held firmly," the Asantahene said. "It must be grasped, and not carelessly dropped. And yet power must be held lightly, carefully. To forget its fragility can mean chaos." Many times afterwards the carving spoke its silent advice. Another meaningful gift was a carved stool of distinctive design. In the history of the Ashantis the original Golden Stool, after which the gift was patterned, was the symbol of unity, to be preserved at all costs. Legend has it that it descended from the heavens about the year 1700 in a black cloud amidst rumbles of thunder through air thick with white dust, alighting gently on the king's knees. Thus the chiefdoms were united in one state, and for the next two hundred years comprised the most powerful state, after Benin, in West Africa, its power residing in the quantities of gold traded across the Sahara to the Mediterranean. Whatever his ancestors thought, the Asantahene with whom I talked, as well as the majority of his people, are devoutly Christian, and there was a fervency of response when, at the Asantahene's invitation, I offered prayer. We both knew of another Golden Stool, beautifully referred to in Jemima Luke's Sunday school hymn: "Yet still to His footstool in prayer I may go,/ And ask for a share in His love."

In Accra more than three thousand people attended each of four meetings held under a spacious canopy erected for the occasion. According to the general secretary of the Christian Council it was "Ghana's big year." I was, he said, the fourth world religious leader to visit the country in 1980. Unknowingly, I had followed in the footsteps of His Holiness the Pope, Dr. Billy Graham and the Archbishop of Canterbury.

* * *

The two predominantly French-speaking areas of Africa—Congo and Zaire—are separated by a river that for many miles provides a natural border. To those on the Congo side, the river, with its green islands of tropical growth swirling seaward, is called the Congo. To those on the opposite shore it is just as definitely the Zaire River, so that in public utterance one must use the proper nomenclature depending, of course, on which side of the river one is speaking. Salvationists, happily and numerously, are on both sides of the river and, when the borders are open, can meet for fellowship. When, because of some political necessity the border is closed, the river itself becomes an impassable barrier.

In Brazzaville, the Congolese capital of what was once French Equatorial Africa, congress gatherings began on the Sunday morning with a "never-ending" march. It went on for so long that I suggested to the leaders, Lieut-Colonel and Mrs. Willy Huguenin, that many of the marchers must simply be going around the block in order to pass the reviewing stand a second or third time. But I was wrong, and obviously so when I mounted the covered platform to face the mammoth crowd of uniformed worshippers standing in the glistening sun. In this part of Africa I came to understand the Old Testament references to "dancing before the Lord," for when the offering was brought forward the collectors literally danced towards the front. Rhythmic, graceful, devoid of sensuality but overflowing with gladness, the dancing appeared to make the bringing of the congregation's gifts to God an exercise of sublime joy.

There was "dancing" of a livelier kind, effervescing in enthusiasm, when a vigorous song was sung, and when I and other visitors joined in the happiness of the crowd was unbounded. The front-page of an English-language newspaper the next morning reported it in up-to-the-minute slang: "The general 'digs' the Azbahda." Seldom had I been so modernly reported. My Bible address had to do with purity of thought, word and deed and, in order to make a positive emphasis, the negative aspects of life were mentioned. The newspaper reported that "The general lashes out against the evils of society ..." Communist party leaders attended and welcomed us. One seemed greatly pleased that I addressed fellow-Salvationists as *"mes chers camarades."* "We also address each other as 'comrades,' " he said, "and your flag has almost as much red in it as ours!" In this fleeting encounter I tried to summarize the vital differences.

We flew in a small plane to Loumobo with a French woman pilot at the controls, to the apprehension of certain members of our party. The next leg took us to Pointe Noire, the Congo's Atlantic seaport. As the stadium gathering was concluding there were signs of a gathering storm. We had not long been aloft on our return flight before the storm broke, or, more accurately, both storms broke, one above us and one below. Each seemed to have its separate sources of electricity, the one above streaking the heavens with long forks of lightning, the other spreading sheets of lightning across the tumbling black clouds beneath us. I was sitting in the co-pilot's seat. We were now in the hands of a male pilot who seemed much too nonchalant for the cosmic tumult which surrounded us. When a deluge of rain hammered our craft and the wind began to toss the plane wildly, I remember looking out of the window and wondering if our fragility could survive such untameable elements. The pilot asked the authorities for permission to go higher, and we rose into calmer atmosphere above the storms that had sandwiched us. Eventually, we heard the pilot's laconic comment, "We're now at 5,000-feet. The lights of the runway are ahead." At the near end of the landing strip were red lights in the form of a cross; beyond was a corridor of white lights marking the runway. For the Salvationists on board it was an illustrated Gospel lesson: the storm, man against threatening forces, a Cross ("You must go home by the way of the Cross ...") and safety. What it must have been for the black woman officer in our group who was making her very first plane journey I can hardly imagine. She was, I know, too terrified to look at the storm, nor could she. Her eyes were too tightly closed in prayer.

Seven uniformed delegates from Angola met me privately in Brazzaville. They were anxious that the Army's work might be officially recognized in their country, and a highly-intelligent young accountant, whose English was letter-perfect, presented their case. He submitted financial statements and bank records showing in detail income and expenditure from the day that the work had begun. The hopes of the unrecognized Salvationists in Angola were further expressed by a medical doctor who asked if a Portuguese-speaking leader might be sent from International Headquarters to deal with the authorities seeing the group had collected sufficient signatures to warrant registration as a religious movement. We prayed together, asking God that the seed already planted might be watered by the Spirit and that, in the country's quieter future, it might beneficially flourish.

* * *

We crossed the Congo/Zaire River in scorching heat. If the crowds of white-uniformed Salvationists at the Brazzaville docks gave us a touching farewell, the crowds of white-uniformed Salvationists at the Kinshasa docks gave us an equally moving welcome. As we journeyed through Africa, at centre after centre, I found myself near to tears because of the tides of affectionate respect which flowed over us. Conscious of our humble beginnings it was difficult for my wife and myself to accept that there could be satisfaction and a treasured memory for someone who had simply touched our uniforms. I could hardly bear it when, at one place, men and women knelt to kiss our shoes and then to look up into our faces with reverence. In such circumstances one could only feel himself to be, with the Apostle Paul, "the least of all the brethren."

Kinshasa, a modern city at the heart of Africa, is among the top few most expensive cities in the world to visit. Salvation Army work began here as recently as 1934, but the expansion has been phenomenal. The Palais du Peuple, an auditorium of magnificent design, constructed for Zaire during a period of Maoist influence, was filled for the Sunday afternoon rally. What followed was unique. There exists in Zaire an active group known as the "Former Salvation Army Students' Fellowship." The members are erstwhile students of Salvation Army schools who have now taken their places in the professional and business life of the country. During one of the nation's troubled periods the schools had reverted to the government but, eventually, were given back to the Army. While out of Army hands the buildings were badly damaged and much equipment was stolen. Extensive repairs were required, towards the cost of which the Swiss Government made a generous allocation. But despite the interruption, the educational work had produced doctors, lawyers, teachers, accountants and prosperous men of commerce who did not intend to forget their beginnings.

I was guest of honour at this unusual fellowship for which a tempting buffet had been prepared by an accomplished French chef. He could not understand my hesitation in accepting some slices from the huge roast which was the centrepiece. I apologized by explaining that I had never eaten monkey, and would delay my sampling of it. I wish now I had been more venturesome. Later, there were brilliant speeches from some of the members, all of which made one grateful that Salvationist visionaries had seen in the children of hundreds of villages the possibilities of rewarding academic development.

In the driving rain we proceeded to the Army's clinic in the centre of Kinshasa. Again we saw how much skilled and devoted officer-nurses can do with so little. In exceedingly limited facilities they were receiving fifteen hundred patients a day. In the presence of His Excellency, Karl H. Anderson, the Swedish ambassador to Zaire, I laid the first stone for a new, extensive health complex made possible by the gifts of various Swedish agencies.

The Republique du Zaire saluted the centenary of The Salvation Army in the United States by issuing a 10Z stamp bearing the likenesses of my wife and myself. As stamps go, it was large and beautifully printed in full colour. Even the gold trimmings on our tunics and headgear were faithfully reproduced. Later we learned how the celebratory stamp came to be issued. An important figure in the world of philately, whose advice has often been sought by the postal authorities of various countries, had negotiated the issue with the Zaire government. He was an active member of the board of management of the Army's general hospital in Flushing, New York, and from the day that his wife returned home from critical and successful surgery and praising the high level of care she had received, he could not do enough to show his gratitude. The term, "philately," is a Greek derivative translated freely as meaning love or affection for that which insures free or prepaid transit. For the sponsor of "our" stamp, affection ran beyond the study, collection and promotion of postage stamps; the commemorative stamp was only an indication of his unmeasured affection for the Army and its healing ministry. Not everyone can see himself on a postage stamp, but any tendency to boast about it was quelled when I read in a learned publication that "since stamps were first issued it has been customary throughout the world to pay postal tribute to famous and *obscure* personages, in recent years at the rate of several hundred annually."

Before leaving Kinshasa we were the dinner guests of the general secretary and his wife, Lieut-Colonel and Mrs. Emmanuel Miaglia. They had invited the territorial leaders, Colonel Mbakanu Diakanwa and his wife, and a number of representative Salvationists. Seated next to me in Army uniform was a doctor, a product of our own schools. Beside him was his rather young-looking wife, a nurse. I asked if they had a family, and they proudly informed me that they had fourteen children. Outside, it was still desperately wet; inside, illumination was limited. In the half-light we sang together and, it being the appropriate day, at the request of the hostess I lit the first of the four Advent candles. It was a comforting flame, throwing large shadows over the assorted company. How symbolic, I thought. At the centre of the continental colossus we call Africa a single candle burns brightly, and in the hush we know again the all-encompassing truth, "Immanuel—God with us!"

CHAPTER 22

"This Word It Reaches Nations"

Comparing Europe and America, Goldsworthy Lowes Dickinson says that the geography of the two continents foreshadows the differences in their civilization. America is simple, broad, large, grand in design. Europe is complex, lacking symmetry but possessing variety. My own descriptive adjective for Europe would be "intriguing," in the sense of arousing one's excitement or curiousity. For me, fascination increased with every visit, and over the years the contacts were so numerous that to these pages can be committed only a few of the highlights from the bulky files of memory.

A Canadian, I suspect, would always feel at home in that part of Europe called Scandinavia. If Norway has its fjords, so has British Columbia. The highways of Finland, often cut through rock and lined with coniferous trees, match those of Northern Ontario. If Sweden has its Gulf of Bothnia, Canada has its Gulf of St. Lawrence. The same latitudes that cross Denmark race across a wide-spreading Canada. Exceedingly common to Scandinavia and Canada is an abundance of snow. Both know the beauty, and sometimes the bitterness, of "the white winter." It was during a raging snowstorm on a winter's day in 1888 that Salvationist invaders arrived in Oslo, Norway. Ninety years later my wife and I stood on the site where the first meeting was held, and, as snow fell steadily from a grey, Nordic sky, we honoured the memory of the pioneers.

In the final anniversary gathering a well-dressed man strode down the aisle shouting, "Det fins ingen Gud her!" ("There is no God to be found here!"). He was as wrong as anyone could be, since many seekers sought and found God during the prayer meeting that followed. And Norwegian Salvationists are nothing if not sincere; they express their religion in a joyous way that does not lessen their unbending commitment to principle.

Among many significant memories, the opening of Norway's new territorial headquarters and the Oslo Temple is unforgotten largely because of an exquisitely-worked tapestry, in the form of a cross, which hangs on the wall behind the platform. The work was uncompleted at the time of the artist's death, and was finished by other competent hands. Incomparably, in my judgement, it depicts the centrality to the Christian faith of Christ's sacrifice on the cross and the eternal importance of the Army's mission. On one arm of the cross is portrayed a group of marching Salvationists, their hands reaching down to lift up those who are in the ditches of life, broken and hopeless. At the intersection of the cross there is the figure of Christ, around which are traced the words from the Book of the Prophet Isaiah (1: 18), "Though your sins be as scarlet, they shall be as white as snow." The marching Salvationists are seen emerging on the other arm of the cross with their "trophies" cleansed, upright and now part of the victorious march to Heaven. It is a powerful conception and, as an illustration, it has served my purpose on many occasions.

* * *

So much in Sweden is touched with *éclat*. Centuries of peace have permitted refinement in lifestyle and achievement. Could there possibly be a smarter manifestation of the Army than in Sweden? The massing of Salvationists on the final evening of a congress in Stockholm's famous Skansen Park, high above the city's harbour, is an inspiring spectacle. After a long march of witness, a colourful "Salute to the Flags" heralds the making of devotional music that lasts far into the undarkening night of midsummer. To have presided over three such occasions, and to have conducted one of the territory's excellent bands before a Skansen congregation of multiplied thousands, has invested the name, "Skansen," with the same telling import for my wife and me that it has for all Swedish Salvationists. Far below, one sees the ships sliding silently across the waters while the lights of the city blink in "festivitas" as the music of praise ascends to God.

In Sweden one is assured of a competent translator, though one can hardly envy the officer chosen for the task since so many in the congregation have fluency in English, the country's second language. If the translator hesitates for an instant, twenty voices might call out the precise word, heightening his anxiety and sometimes dismissing from the speaker's mind the next sentence he was ready to utter. General Wickberg, doyen of English-Swedish translators, gave me good advice. Sermon texts should be carefully compared in both languages before usage. On my first visit I spoke from the text in Psalm 116: 16 which, in English, reads: "I will pay my vows unto the Lord now in the presence of all His people." The sermon outline was simple. To whom do we pay our vows? Unto the Lord. When do we do it? Now! How do we do it? In the presence of all God's people. Curiously, the Swedish rendering omits the word, "now," so that for the careful Swedish Bible student it would appear that I was indulging in what theologians call "eisigesis," the reading into the text of more than is there—the opposite of "exegesis." One could, of course, in the giving of the address explain that "the English Bible reads thus and so," but if this is done with any regularity the practice implies that either the English or the Swedish Bible translators were at fault.

Perhaps this is as suitable a juncture as any in which to interpolate some further words on the subject of translation and translators. The sentence-by-sentence method used in the Army is highly effective, especially if the speaker and translator feel at home with each other. One learns to frame short sentences that embody a complete idea. Dangling participles are to be avoided, and parenthetical clauses can disastrously derail a train of thought. In West Berlin, however, we encountered translation of another, and, to me, incredible, method. Senator Dr. Dietrich Sauberzweig was our luncheon host at a civic reception and, in German, made a gracious speech of welcome. The woman translator, one used for important government events, apparently memorized the entire speech and then translated it. My reply was interpreted in the same way. Intrigued, I asked the translator how long an address she could commit to memory before beginning translation. She said about thirty minutes, though with occasional notes as reminders, considerably longer. People present who knew both German and English said that her translations were perfectly accurate. I still prefer the sentence-by-sentence system. Translators with a computer-like memory such as is owned by the Berlin lady are rare indeed.

Blessed be the translator who is competent enough also to "imitate" any emphasizing gestures without losing the sense of what he is translating. Humour can be translated provided it is not based on words with more than one meaning, or on puns that are considered by the interpreter to be untranslatable. Poetry, so effective a weapon in the preacher's armoury, cannot be translated "on the spot," though sometimes I have asked the translator to give a "free" rendition of some poetical lines if the truth they conveyed was more wanted than the rhyme in which it was enshrined.

The late Commissioner Gösta Blomberg was an acknowledged expert in Swedish-English and English-Swedish translation. He had a priceless story for those forced to use translators. It concerned an English Salvation Army leader who insisted with Blomberg that a certain story be translated as an "ice-breaker" in the early part of his meeting. Blomberg told the visitor that the story was positively untranslatable. Stubbornly, the visitor continued to insist. When the story was being related Blomberg took a verbal detour and explained to the congregation that "the old gentleman is now telling a story which in English is quite funny, but which is quite untranslatable. We will all help him if, when I take out my handkerchief and blow my nose, you will all laugh heartily." The congregation entered into the mischievousness of the moment and cooperated with unrestrained enthusiasm, so much so, that after the meeting the Englishman patted Blomberg on the shoulder and said gratefully, "I knew you could do it, Blomberg. I knew you could do it!" The obverse side of the incident, as Commissioner Blomberg told me, is that translators can have a speaker, without his knowledge, completely "in their pocket."

When being translated, what is known as "elaboration" is best forgotten. In quite another part of the world I once spoke of a rainstorm. What the translator said sounded like, "Oggidy blog." "Yes," I continued, "the heavens opened; the rain teemed down." "Oggidy blog," said the translator. I tried again, "And from the clouds there poured a veritable Niagara." "Oggidy blog," said the translator for the third time. It is well to remember that in some regions the limitations of the local language cannot be stretched.

Only once, in a part of the world where little English is spoken, did I feel myself cheated by a translator. He was completely fluent in English as well as his own language. But he was a compulsive talker in both languages, full of speech and full of himself. Before long I became aware that he was not saying what I was saying. If something I said caught his imagination, he presented it in his own way, and at no little length. Without doubt he became the main speaker; I was just a visitor who occasionally managed to slip in a comment or two.

I dare not indicate in which country another translation story was told me. The central character in the incident is still translating and, I have every reason to believe, with increasing efficiency. One of our leaders was speaking to a congregation of officers. He was encouraging them to "write it on your hearts. Engrave it on your mind. Etch it across the whole of your life—Salvation Army officership is a *vocation."* The novice interpreter did well until he came to the climactic thought. "Etch it across the whole of your life," he said, "Salvation Army officership is a *vacation,"* and then went on to say that every officer should take one regularly! Later, this same translator served me well, though having heard the story I was careful not to use the word, "vocation."

* * *

In Finland translation takes on another dimension since the congregation comprises both Finns and Swedes, though Swedish is the language of fewer than ten percent of the population. Here the same sentence is heard three times, and the order of speaking, as well as one's next thought, must be remembered. My wife had expressed some nervousness about the procedure before our first visit, and I had emphasized its simplicity. "Say what you want to say, and then wait until the person on your right has finished." The advice was accurate, but I had not foreseen that when a word, or phrase, came slowly to one translator, the other, with merely a glance or a nod, and by mutual agreement, would take over. During our last visit only a Finnish translator stood beside us. The Swedish translator was accommodated where he could hear the proceedings and then broadcast his translation to the Swedish-speaking people in the congregation who were provided with earphones. Thanks to advancing technology, for the long-suffering the length of the addresses diminished by one-third.

At one point in this particular congress five languages were being used, the usual Finnish, Swedish, and English being supplemented by French and German for the benefit of a Swiss holiday group of some eighty persons who were present. In earlier times, when public movement was much less, the peripatetic preacher was safe in repeating his sermons. Now, it is the public which is peripatetic, and the preacher repeats himself at his peril. This same tour group had been in our congregation only days before when we were in Bern. Following the Finnish meetings the group went touring in Lapland, but the next weekend joined the congress gatherings in Stockholm. For the third time the group sat before us. Lightheartedly I said that I had not realized my own speaking abilities. To have eighty people cross Europe in order to hear me speak on three successive Sundays was commendation indeed. Perspective was restored, however, when the officer tour-director told me conspiratorially that had I repeated myself he would, in French and German, have "invented" another sermon for the benefit of the party.

Finland's Salvationists struck me as strong in faith and devoted "searchers of the Scriptures." With a national population of fewer than five million, the strength of the Army is impressive. With nearly seventy corps congregations and fifty-five institutions it is a recognized part of Finland's national fabric. For the country's giant neighbour, Russia, where, since 1918 the Army, regrettably, has not functioned, it is the nearest evidence of the Army's continued existence. There is a modern touch to so many aspects of Finnish life, and the uninformed visitor is often taken by surprise. I saw modern ideas applied in the Army's institutions housing children and the aged. In the Helsinki accommodation for children the age groups are segregated, each group being cared for by its own supervising staff on a different floor of the building in order that, among his peers, the child's physical, psychological and academic development might thrive. In one of the delightfully-furnished homes for aged persons we saw the progressive attitudes of the government reflected in the mandatory provision of a physical fitness salon. As an encouragement to those of advancing years to keep themselves "in shape," every kind of exercise machine is available. For some, even the sight of the equipment could be beneficial!

* * *

And what of Denmark? Capitalizing on the popularity of Copenhagen's famous Tivoli Gardens we twice conducted congress meetings in this world-famous entertainment centre's concert hall. The sound of marching Salvation Army bands competing with the much less devotional music that flooded the night air was itself somehow exciting. To pass through the throngs of pleasure seekers crowding the walks, filling the restaurants, or interesting themselves in myriad forms of leisure activity was to remember William Pennick's lines: "We are witnesses for Jesus ... where the cares of life and fashion crowd the Saviour from the heart." I was gratified by the size of the crowds in our meetings. Bored by Tivoli's attractions, some had decided to see what a Salvation Army meeting could possibly be like.

In those two congresses I particularly remember the youth events. The young people, charmingly Scandinavian in looks, with blond hair and pink cheeks, wore their Salvation Army uniform with flair. Their impressive acting out of New Testament parables was enhanced by the most convincing of stage-settings. They were obviously done, if not by a professional, then by someone of unusual talent. When stage-lit, rocks really looked like rocks; trees appeared to wave in the wind; and hills undulated three-dimensionally into the distance, as hills actually do. Perhaps the props were borrowed from a theatrical company that sometimes used the same stage. From wherever, or however, the props came, the young performers' efforts were heightened because of them. Settings are important. A royal landau, liveried footmen and a mounted guard of honour add to a queen's dignity. A carelessly prepared, or unprepared, background can reduce an otherwise delightful Nativity play to a tawdry embarrassment.

Our last congress prior to retirement was spent, to our immense joy, with our Danish Salvationists. Tivoli was no longer the venue, and probably the new location was more suited to congress purposes. Still, I missed the bright illuminations and the throbbing sounds of the Gardens, recalling that, after passing through the crowds and once inside the concert hall, one had the feeling of having reached a sheltered sanctuary. Her Majesty the Queen Mother, Queen Ingrid, born Princess of Sweden and widow of the late King Frederick IX, came to the new location, and we were presented to her before the gathering. A stately, elegant lady, the Queen had not only absorbed the facts of our *curricula vitae* but was genuinely interested in them. We sat at a small table waiting for the fanfare that would herald Her Majesty's entrance, she nursing the flowers with which she had been presented, and clearly in no hurry to pass them over to her lady-in-waiting. They had been "presented," and her acceptance was not an idle gesture.

Entering the auditorium I was surprised to see that a gilded chair had been placed at the front of the centre aisle on the ground floor for Her Majesty. This meant that all participants on the platform were in full view of the royal visitor. When I spoke, the Queen was not looking at my back but studiously at my face, so studiously that the impression grew that I was speaking only to her. I did not come to know whether the arrangement was customary or by regal request. The Queen's own view, expressed in conversation afterwards, was that she had come to be part of the congregation; her intention was to be inspired equally with all others, and not less than any other. It is not a Canadian way of doing things, much less British, but it obviates the uncomfortable necessity of turning one's back on special guests, especially a royal one. It puts the relationship on a face-to-face basis, the mode of true friendship.

* * *

In Germany today The Salvation Army is a small and gallant band. Its stronger days could not fail to occupy the mind when standing on an observation platform near the Berlin Wall and looking across at a once-impressive territorial headquarters ignominiously serving as a storehouse. Owned by "a foreign body" it was being allowed to fall into decrepitude. Around it had been placed concrete tank traps. Immediately in front was a military guard hut. The last time I viewed the building the impressive dome had begun to collapse, though the flagstaff from which had often proudly flown the Army flag, was still in place. Through the Foreign Office in London we had instituted a claim for reparations in respect of the many properties expropriated during the war. This notwithstanding, the next time I visited the spot, the building, scene of so many great gatherings and a repository of bright memories, had been dynamited into extinction.

As guests of the American air force my wife and I viewed from a helicopter the entire weaving length of the infamous Berlin Wall. We hovered as near to it as military accords would allow, but near enough to see that it is not one wall but four, with stretches of barbed wire marking off dog runs and swivelling machine-gun emplacements, all emphasizing an intention to restrain and isolate. It is unbearably sad to think that on both sides of the wall people speak the same language and that by it even families are divided. East of the wall, in happier days, were many Salvation Army corps and institutions. To other machinations that have sought to fragment The Salvation Army must now be added, of all things, a wall! Returning to the base we flew close to the Spandau prison and caught sight of a lonely figure walking in the grounds at the rear. It was Herr Rudolph Hess.

Following the flight my wife and I were entertained at luncheon by Major-General Calvert P. Benedict, in command of American troops based in Berlin, and his gracious wife. They had invited Major-General Robert Richardson and Major-General Bernard d'Astorg of the British and French forces to dine with us. From the four-power occupation armies only the Russian general was absent. Nevertheless, as our host remarked, we still had four generals present! Later in the day we took tea with the Federal President and Head of State, Herr Walter Scheel, who revealed, in fluent English, a comprehensive and understanding knowledge of the Army, of its pre-war strength and service in his country, and of its notable and compassionate care of German soldiers returning dispiritedly from Russia at the war's end.

Salvation Army meetings in Berlin, still the largest city in the federal republic, reinforced one's faith. Perhaps the imminence of the unknown had its effect so that spiritual needs were more sensitively felt. Many meetings ended with tender expressions and tenderer feelings. Salvationists from the East, before making their reluctant way back to the checkpoint, would sing, "God be with you till we meet again." Hands would be uplifted and throughout the refrain some would wave their handkerchief—the kind of leave-taking that signified confidence in an eternal, unbroken fellowship.

Speaking to Salvation Army leaders from all parts of Europe during a conference hosted by Commissioner and Mrs. Caughey Gauntlett, the bishop of the Evangelical Church in Berlin and Brandenburg, Dr. Martin Kruse, pleaded with the delegates to wear their uniforms as often as possible, and wherever possible. "It makes Christianity visible," he said, "in a world where it is quickly becoming anonymous." How gladly, I thought, would former Salvationists on the other side of the Berlin Wall, if permitted, heed the good bishop's good advice.

* * *

A visit to Belgium, where the Army's work requires the use of both French and Flemish languages, allowed participation in the command's ninetieth anniversary gatherings arranged by the country's leaders, Lieut-Colonel and Mrs. John Ord. During the congress I was received at the Palais Royal in Brussels. Of all the courtesy calls paid to heads of state, none made a more spiritual impression on me than the audience granted by His Majesty King Baudoin of the Belgians. Monday morning, November 12, 1979, was grey and showery. We were driven to the palace by Retired Bandmaster Marcel Paulus, and courteously met, with guards standing at the present-arms, by the military ADC, Colonel Baron de Posch. From the moment of my being presented I felt there was in His Majesty's manner something considerably beyond schooled civility and practised courtesy. He greeted me most cordially and led me to a chair. No attendant remained, and we were left alone in the spacious, impressive chamber, seated in front of a large fireplace carefully laid with logs, but unlit.

The King began by thanking me for what the Army had meant to Belgium. Queen Fabiola, he said, had returned from a visit to our children's home, "Clair Matin," tremendously impressed by the consecration of the officers and workers to the children in their care. He expressed pleasure at meeting "someone who is entirely dedicated to the spiritual and physical betterment of humanity," and I confessed my hope that all Salvationists might merit his compliment. A host of them, I insisted, deserved it more than I did. I mentioned how, during an audience with the Crown Prince and Crown Princess in Tokyo a few days before, the Crown Prince had expressed great pleasure over his recent visit to Belgium. The King spoke of his own high regard for the

Japanese royal family, and we agreed concerning the graciousness of Her Royal Highness and the Crown Prince's informed mind.

From that point on the conversation moved from the temporal to the spiritual. All of His Majesty's questions seemed to be framed with care. How did the Army motivate and encourage its officers and soldiers to be evangelists? How were they instructed in the art of communicating the Gospel to people in various human situations? Was there a danger that the Army's better-known social action would defeat its primary evangelistic purpose? How did the call to a life of service for Christ come to me personally? In days when young people were less responsive to regimentation did the Army's admired discipline mean fewer reinforcements? If the King's questions were thoughtfully constructed, my answers were received with more than superficial interest. Such questions could not be disposed of telegraphically, and twice I voiced the thought that I had already trespassed on His Majesty's valuable time. Though he encouraged me to continue, I kept one eye on the buzzer at the end of the low table, anticipating any movement of his hand towards it, and ready immediately to rise and take my leave. There was a final question. What of the charismatic winds that had blown through the churches? The audience ended with serious, refreshing conversation concerning the Person, the work and the power of the Holy Spirit. I may in time forget the actual words spoken, but the reality of that audience as a *confrontation spirituelle* will remain.

The Lord Mayor, M. Pierre van Halteren, and the Lady Mayoress, welcomed my wife and me in Brussels' beautiful 15th-century city hall. The mayor spoke enthusiastically of "our Bruegel," and gravely of problems caused by a minority group of immigrants. "They have," said the mayor, "adopted a convenient form of morality. There must be no stealing from members of one's own family. That is positively forbidden. To steal from one's close neighbours is questionable, but to steal from anyone else is totally acceptable." That same evening, while the public meeting in which we shared proceeded with fervour and joy, my briefcase was stolen from the officer commanding's office. I now knew, at first hand, what the lord mayor was talking about. Passport, certificate of citizenship, travellers' cheques, calculator and radio disappeared with the briefcase. On the desk were scattered a few oddments, valueless souvenirs of the thief's visit. I spent the midnight hours at the central police station where lengthy forms were completed and a chain-smoking detective appeared to enjoy prolonged conversation with our dismayed colonel. The Canadian embassy provided authorization for my re-entry into the United Kingdom, but months passed before all the lost documents could be replaced. Weeks later, in London, I bought a replacement briefcase. Examining it, I saw by the manufacturer's identification that, ironically, it had been fabricated in none other than Belgium.

* * *

I was first introduced to Switzerland with its harmonious amalgamation of cultures and languages and its ravishing natural beauty by a remarkable Salvationist, Dr. Victor Kunz. He was as devoted to The Salvation Army as to his practice of medicine and travelled the world observing its work and encouraging its workers. During a visit to Toronto he came to our home and extracted a promise that I would someday visit him and accept hospitality in his house at Stafa, a small village on the northern shore of Lake Zurich. The opportunity came after I attended a congress in Sweden as an "observer," and I arranged to return to Canada by way of Stafa. The doctor met me at Zurich airport and, in the days at my disposal, took me in his aging car to see as many of the beauties of the country he loved as time allowed. Already the doctor was showing signs of the debility which was eventually to finish his extensive travels, but with great determination he negotiated the steep, narrow roads and hairpin turns that test the best of drivers. He knew where the loveliest and most majestic views were to be seen and repeatedly described them as "God's amazing handiwork" as though he were seeing them for the first time. The beauty of Zurich was irresistible on the perfect summer day of our visit. The city simply glistened beneath the proud towers of the Grössmunster, the Fraumünster and St. Peter's church. From that day I was a prisoner of Switzerland's enchantment.

Dr. Kunz, still honoured in the memory of his friends, had long since gone from the scene when, as chief of the staff and, later, as general, visits to Switzerland became more frequent, especially for the Ascensiontide gatherings which are a notable feature of the religious year. These traditional gatherings are unmatched elsewhere in spirit and significance. For those who speak German, Zurich is the venue of the devotional gatherings and a march for which many of the city's streets are closed to traffic and lined with interested townspeople. Those who speak French attend similar gatherings held in Lausanne, and do so with equal support and fervour. International leaders through the years have usually conducted the services in Zurich, but in deference to the French-Swiss, on one occasion, and gladly, I led the gatherings in Lausanne.

It is curious that only in this part of the Army world is such emphasis given to a remembrance of the Ascension of our Lord. Originally it was a unitive festival commemorating both the Ascension of Jesus and the descent of the Holy Spirit, but during the 4th-century it was resolved into two commemorations, the Ascension being celebrated forty days after Easter and Pentecost, as the word implies, fifty days after Easter. In both Zurich and Lausanne worshippers expect the Bible addresses to deal specifically with the Ascension theme, and rightly so. But the subject, though a thrilling one, is not capable of the same kind of extension as the theme of Pentecost and, I found, one had to work hard to produce sermon material, time after time, which presents the meaning of the Ascension in ways that add to an understanding of its glorious purpose. The challenge was to remind the congregations that the Scriptural word, "Set down at the right hand of God," must convey the entering of the exalted Jesus into a state and an activity which transcends the limitations of place and space as a participant in the sovereignty of God the Father. For Swiss Salvationists and their friends the observances are of the highest devotional order, illuminating and enriching, and serving to prepare heart and mind for the imminent Whitsuntide assemblies that recall the establishing of the Church as "a new fact marked by a new quality of life."

To be in Zurich on Ascension Day as the visiting "missioner" is to awake to the sweet sounds of a Salvation Army band playing under one's hotel window, instruments gleaming in the early morning light and the red tunics of the instrumentalists giving a rich dash of colour to the scene. While the music floats through the holiday-quiet streets the bandmaster brings a bouquet of flowers to the hotel room—not only a gesture of welcome, but also an expression of hope that the exercises of the day will cause the flowers of faith and love to blossom in the soul.

Two events convinced me of the trustful regard in which the Army is held by the public of Switzerland. The first was a most responsive assembly of Zurich's influential city leaders to whom I spoke of the Army's international outreach. I sat between two men whose names were almost alike. On my left was Commissioner Robert Chevalley, the territorial commander, amazingly fluent in three languages at least and, on my right, brimming with vitality, Dr. Georges-Andre Chevallez, finance minister in the federal council, a human cornucopia out of which tumbled impressive fact and delightful anecdote.

The second was a luncheon gathering at Villa Monchoisy, Vandeuvres, on the outskirts of Geneva, generously hosted by two gracious supporters, M. and Mme. Yves Oltramare. The guests, distinguished citizens of this patrician and cosmopolitan region, were received at the entrance of the imposing chateau and shown through to the gardens where a magnificent blue and white marquee had been erected. The setting was exquisite. Tranquil meadows unrolled towards the horizon and the purplish outline of the mountains. In the marquee, each supporting pole was entwined from the canvas top to the ground with fresh flowers, and the table settings, with their floral centrepieces, damask napery and shining cutlery betokened impeccable hospitality. *Dejeuner* was served in the finest French-Swiss manner. M. Oltramare's welcome and his tribute to the Army was a masterpiece of courtesy and compliment making it easy for the Commissioner and myself to speak of the Army's plans for the future.

Strolling among the guests I met the chairman of one of Switzerland's leading banks. With tongue in cheek I told him that we had much in common seeing I was the president of an English bank. He remarked uncomfortably that he had never heard of the Reliance Bank (now the Reliance Trust Company, Ltd.), but that he would look it up. I took the opportunity to tell the story of "our" bank, small in comparison with his own, but exceedingly useful. He shook my hand with friendly warmth, as one banker to another and, as a coda to our conversation said, "What a good idea, a very good idea, to have one's own, one's very own, bank."

Also present was the wife of Dr. Philip Potter, general secretary of the World Council of Churches. Sadly, the illness which soon afterwards caused her death was apparent. Our conversation was not about banks and money, but of spiritual treasure deposited "where neither moth nor rust doth corrupt, and where thieves do not break through nor steal."

Doreen Potter had for some years, and with marked capacity, devoted herself to the production of a revised "Cantata Domino," an ecumenical hymnary published on behalf of the World Council of Churches. Because of that conversation I particularly value the copy of the new edition which Dr. Potter kindly inscribed and sent to me.

* * *

A letter from a veteran Salvationist expressing the hope that someday an international leader would come to her island led to a visit to Iceland. The first General to reach that part of the world I was given what the press described as "an overwhelming reception." It was nothing less than that. There are six daily newspapers in Iceland, all produced in Reykjavik, the capital, and following a press conference on arrival all six carried photographs and reports the next day. Iceland is like nowhere else in the world. It is "the surprising island of the Atlantic," a heap of strata brought to the surface by the eruptions of past centuries. At once I was snared by its spell-binding ruggedness, the product of violent, clashing elements—a volcanic origin, immense fires below the earth's crust, and vast, glacial wildernesses of ice. Someone discovered that lupins could survive the winter bleakness, so that grey-black wastes were spread with softening blue, mitigating the monotony. "Lava and lupins"—that, for me, is bleak and beautiful Iceland.

Congress gatherings, in addition to a broadcast holiness meeting and other events, were held on two successive evenings in one of Reykjavik's large churches. Commissioner and Mrs. K. Solhaug had accompanied me from Norway, and the Commissioner, stationed in Iceland forty years before, found that the language had not deserted him. Appreciation for the Army in Iceland has deep roots. Seamen, grateful to escape the bitter rigours of the North Atlantic, had been cared for in warm and friendly surroundings. Aging Icelanders needing special oversight, and others for whom life was a rough passage, had found harbour in one of our convalescent or rest homes.

The republic's first woman president, Vigdis Finnbogadottir, received our party graciously. The first woman to be elected head of state anywhere in the world, she is attractive and able and an authority on the history of her own land. Her love for the past was evident in the caressing way she spoke of the huge, antique table at which we had tea, and of other items of furniture formed by pioneer hands and now in the presidential residence. The president had just returned from a state visit to Denmark where she had passionately sought the return to Iceland of some of its historic artifacts. She said she would like to share a secret with us. Heads of state around the world, she was sure, were searching for the "ideal gift" for Prince Charles and Lady Diana on the occasion of their wedding. Remembering that the Prince of Wales came annually to a remote part of Iceland for fishing, she had commissioned one of Iceland's leading artists to paint the scene of the Prince's visits. Later, we saw the public announcement concerning Iceland's appropriate wedding present. From the president we also had a proud reminder that Iceland has the world's oldest parliament, the Althing (legislature), which in 1974 at Thingvellir, to which we made a hurried visit, had celebrated 1100-years of its function.

A meal in the home of the Bishop of all Iceland, Dr. Sigurbjorn Einarsson, brought me into contact with a patriarchal personality. Tall, thin, with a shock of hair, his ascetic appearance heightened by his black garb of office, one quickly sensed the bishop's extensive scholarship seasoned with a love of pure humour. He introduced me to Hallgrimur Petursson's "Hymns of the Passion" which are read annually at the appropriate season by most of the devout Evangelical-Lutherans for whom he is responsible, and gave me a copy in English. Dressed in national costume, his diminutive wife was a motherly hostess. One could visualize the two sharing a meal-table prayer, a perfect subject for a stylistic canvas by Seurat or an eloquent cover painting by Norman Rockwell.

Reykjavik's municipal councillors provided unique hospitality at an historic village where the life and times of early settlers are recreated. I took breakfast with them out of doors in the summer sunlight, seated on a rough bench and at a handhewn table. Subjects ranged from the providing of summer employment for island-locked university students to the unbelievable unwisdom of a developer who, carried away with modern design, had built houses with flat roofs entirely unsuitable for Iceland's snowy winters and a source of unending trouble for the unfortunate tenants.

Iceland, with its abundance of geothermal springs, gave the word, "geyser," to the world. Plumes of steam and spouts of superheated water are common sights, so I was told. The one geyser we visited which, according to our hosts, performed regularly for visitors, sulked in its steamy depths, and after a tedious hour of unrewarded waiting, bubbled teasingly only an inch or two above the surface. This was our only disappointment in Iceland which, despite its chilling name, provided one of the most heart-warming experiences of our global travels.

* * *

Easter in Rome is for many of the devout a lifelong hope. For us, in our final year of international leadership, it was a felicitous realization. Not for us, of course, a packed St. Peters' Square, but crowds nevertheless that overflowed the buildings in which our meetings were held. Never, nor anywhere, did we experience spiritual ecstacy to compare with that Easter Sunday morning's service. Out of limited resources Salvationists and friends had travelled from all parts of the country, among them victims of the devastating earthquake in Southern Italy from which the villagers of Brienza, Monti, Saint Selina, Braipe, Bozzi, S'Chiaui and Atena Lucana, still suffering hardship, had come for spiritual encouragement. Fifteen thousand homeless in that area had been fed every day by Salvationist relief teams and now, months later, the rebuilding of homes by the Army was being undertaken.

I had often used the term, "Resurrection radiance," but that morning I saw it on the faces of men and women who had been forced to live in animal pens, some in cardboard huts covered with polythene and tarpaulins, and others in open fields. The terror of a home cracking open and disintegrating, or rocks falling from the mountains, was not forgotten; but neither was the eternal victory of Christ over disaster and death. It was for them, after their unnerving and horrendous experiences, a radiant celebration of new life, of everlasting life in Christ. For more than two hours the congregation exulted in the glory of Easter, including many standing in the aisles and in the vestibules, jammed together with no thought of personal discomfort in mind, but only ineffable joy in the heart. Nor did "rapture's flush" diminish; in the evening the Ponte S'Angelo Methodist church was filled for another service. Here, on the banks of the ancient Tiber, God was again praised for the triumph of the Resurrection.

Minutes before the afternoon open-air meeting concluded, the officer commanding, Lieut-Colonel Raymond Yarde, received word from the authorities that we could march back to our hall. Playing and singing, we joyously trod Rome's historic roads. Were these the very streets along which early Christians had been cruelly dragged to their death? Could it be that the Apostle Paul had walked these same lanes? If for him, also for us, a *via sacra.* It occurred to me that Paul might himself have marched with us if twenty centuries had not divided us. But, present or not, his triumphant words had echoed again to the large, attentive crowd surrounding our arc of witnesses: "But now is Christ risen from the dead ... in Christ shall all be made alive."

While in Rome, the hotel in which we were accommodated, appropriately named, "The Eden," provided another link with the Founder. Here, William Booth had been housed by the owner, a Christian woman of German nationality, who greatly admired Booth's religious zeal and his accomplishments on behalf of the poor. Ownership of the hotel had long since changed but, in the quiet, mezzanine library I saw shelves of beautifully-bound German Bibles, a reminder, I assumed, of the first owner's concern for the spiritual care of her guests. Almost every hotel room anywhere in the world in which I have stayed has had its Gideon Bible. Only "The Eden" has had a collection of Bibles so prominently displayed in one of its common rooms. Usually, a hotel's main lobby boasts of a small newsstand where, more's the pity, everything but a Bible is distastefully displayed.

* * *

For the world's music-lovers, in which company I hasten to place myself, Vienna (or Wien) is a shrine, associated as it is with the names and compositions of the musical Greats—Beethoven, Haydn, Schubert, Mozart—and remembering the proximity of the blue (?) Danube and the Vienna Woods, the Strausses. In this Austrian capital The Salvation Army's trumpet, trombone and timbrel play no master-works, but do give evidence of the movement's benign presence amid a population almost totally Roman Catholic. Like other tourists we rode in a caleche through the narrow, winding streets, noting the wall-plaques that indicate the birthplace of this or that notable composition, so many as to create the illusion of a cemetery-city with carefully placed headstones commemorating the demise of genius. Except, of course, that music is a living thing, outlasting its creators. In Vienna music still holds sway, as does the sound of the Army's trumpet, trombone and timbrel, augmented on the occasion of our visit by the officers' band from Switzerland, with their territorial leaders, Commissioner and Mrs. Gauntlett.

I had hoped to meet the Austrian chancellor, Dr. Bruno Kreisky, with whom General Wickberg had had useful association, but he was out of the country. We were received, however, at the imposing Rathaus by Vienna's Oberbürgermeister. He was greatly distressed by the murder, the day before, of a close friend and prominent citizen by a terrorist who, after firing the fatal shots, sped away while all around the dead man were lost in confusion and anger. The mayor could not understand the shooting. His friend was not a controversialist or engaged in activities that might have targeted him for elimination. Expressing his sorrow, the mayor's voice faltered, and he welcomed the suggestion that we should offer prayer for the dead man's family and his bereaved friends.

From Vienna to Linz is about one hundred miles to the west by road. Between these two major cities in which all Salvation Army work in Austria is concentrated, lies Mautthausen, a heinous concentration camp operated during the Second World War by the Gestapo. We walked through the empty, silent grounds accompanied by a professor of history who said he would give us only facts concerning what had transpired here. No sensationalizing was needed, he declared; the facts were macabre enough. The entrance is dominated by a huge sculpture memorializing the torture and death of a captured Russian general. In the block of stone one sees the imprisoned figure of a naked man, victim of the bizarre treatment that killed him. Stripped of his uniform, the general was forced to stand before all the prisoners while ice-water was poured over him until he froze solid, a human icicle.

We walked slowly and sadly down the steep, narrow, uneven steps to the bottom of the huge stone quarry we had seen in documentary films. The professor told us that the hundred or more steps would be filled with prisoners who thought they were climbing up for food. At the top, guards would push over the front row and, like tumbling dominoes, the victims would fall helplessly backwards on each other, breaking bones and sending their compatriots to death by asphyxiation. Shuddering at the horror of it all, we moved to the small chambers where hundreds of naked prisoners (the large numbers ensuring their remaining erect despite unutterable weakness) expecting only a cleansing shower breathed in the lethal gas that drifted from the water pipes. Our party did not talk to each other. Thoughts of "man's inhumanity to man" silenced conversation. We simply looked at each other, nodded our heads, and breathed little sounds which, while meaningless, expressed everything of abhorrence and unbelievability. I felt like crying, and, when no-one was looking, I did.

One was glad to reach Linz; to come from a hateful past to an hospitable present. Linz is an Army-conscious city, illustrating the ability of a small contingent of workers to make a vast, compassionate impact upon a community's life and needs, and demonstrating also a city's gratitude for such service. The mushrooming industrial estates on the city's edges have not cancelled out the beauty of the old town. Its squares and arcades are rich in charm; everywhere picture-postcard architecture is coloured by window-boxes full of flowers. In front of the red and cream town hall, rebuilt in 1513 after the great fire of 1509, the Swiss officers' band played the famous "Radetzky" march, the bandmaster adding to my enjoyment by asking me to conduct. Strauss the Elder, who wrote the piece in 1848, was no stranger to lovely Linz. He would perhaps have been fascinated by this scene and this sound. Led by the jovial bürgermeister himself, the crowd pressed around the band, clapping their hands in rhythm and adding a percussive extra that Strauss never knew. His music, however, was a happy bridge across which Salvationists could pass to their chief purpose, the preaching of the Gospel.

A reception attended by three hundred leading citizens following an evening festival left me with the conclusion that never had so much been done by so few for so many. A large men's hostel, a treatment centre for alcoholics and a tourist accommodation, all operate under the direction of one indefatigable officer-couple who know the city's hidden seaminess, and know even more intimately the empowering of the Spirit to minister in and to it.

CHAPTER 23

"Their Line Is Gone Out ..."

It is often said that no-one can visit the subcontinent of India, or indeed any part of South Asia, and be the same afterwards. It is a comment that some would dismiss as generalization, but our own visits proved that inexplicably something actually happens to the metabolism of the mind. Sensibilities are set on edge, and, for the compassionately-inclined, the floodgates of sympathy are ripped wide open.

India is The Salvation Army's oldest mission field and celebrated its centenary in 1982. The chief pioneer was Commissioner Frederick de Latour Booth-Tucker who, his biographer, Commissioner Harry Williams, states "was born in India into a wealthy English family at the height of Victorian imperialism. Abandoning a lucrative career in the Indian Civil Service he joined General William Booth in England, later returning to establish The Salvation Army in India. Braving scorn and imprisonment he adopted local garb and dialects to reach the criminal tribes and the poor." Opprobrium may have marked the beginnings, but there was no shortage of volunteers in those early days to bring the light of the Gospel to "India's coral strand." When, for example, reinforcements were called for, the territorial commander in Canada, Commissioner Thos. B. Coombs, received applications from three hundred volunteers. Among the twenty chosen was the Commissioner's own son who gave his life for India. Before the close of the century William Booth visited India twice, evidence of the importance put on the rapidly growing work and the encouragement he wished to give to it.

Mahatma Gandhi's renaming in the mid-1930's of the Untouchables as the Harijans—"children of God"—was accurate for the scores of thousands who, professing the Christian faith, had, in the intervening years become devout Salvationists.

Since India's independence the number of expatriate Salvation Army officers has steadily declined. Indigenization has always been for the Army a coveted goal, but total Indianization has not yet been thought practicable. Some overseas officers with specific skills are still needed, but the securing of entry permits has been increasingly difficult. Extraordinarily long waits have more often than not terminated unsuccessfully. The Indian High Commissioner to London, the Hon. Aba Pant, who I regarded as a highly eloquent speaker, was most sympathetic to our situation. With a corpus of nearly three thousand Indian officers I asked for a quota of one hundred expatriate officers. These would, of course, have to meet legislated requirements, but would not be subject to interminable delays or considered as blocking the appointment of Indian officers. (With some governments entry permits are transferable within a limited time and within an established quota, a system that works successfully for both the authorities and the Army.) Just when the High Commissioner's understanding seemed to be leading to an approved *modus operandi,* he was transferred to Rome. Wags had it that His Holiness the Pope would pester him less than the leaders of The Salvation Army.

I hoped that a solution to the entry problem would result from an interview in New Delhi with the home secretary whom I had met socially the previous evening at the residence of the Canadian ambassador. The minister was a mild, organized person who scuttled any discomfiture he may have personally felt about our problem in a sea of explanation about the circuitous route that every application had to follow. His brilliant diplomacy left me feeling embarrassed at having raised so "trivial" a matter with so important an officer of the government. Once outside the government building, however, the needle swung back to its compass point of utter disappointment. Even waving a note from Indira Gandhi herself, with its handwritten addition expressing her admiration for the Army's work, apparently had not sufficient magical power to cause officialdom to change its policy.

For India, not only the caste system, but a multiplicity of languages known as "mother tongues," and numbering over sixteen hundred, have made national unity difficult to achieve. Speaking in the Royal Albert Hall, London, in 1931, Winston Churchill declared that "India is a geographical term. It is no more a united nation than the equator." Fifty years later, the unification of India's polyglot population remains less than totally accomplished. How many generations will be needed before Hindi is a common language, and the Devanagari script in which it is written is generally used, would be difficult to forecast. It shocked me the first time I heard one of our commissioners speaking to fellow-Indians *through a translator.* English is the one language that bridges the gaps, and fluency in it is necessary for any leader whose appointments may take him to various parts of the country.

It is the time-worn text of every travel brochure that India is a land of contrasts. What overwhelmed me on the first visit, but which came to be more comprehensible with each succeeding visit, was the violence of the contrasts, the immense chasm between apex and nadir. Affluence and poverty, culture and coarseness, knowledge and illiteracy, epicurean satiety and raging hunger exist side by side. In a major city I was billeted in luxurious surroundings. Uniformed bearers stood waiting to fulfill my smallest wish. To walk in the gardens was sheer delight. But immediately outside was another world. A huge billboard bore the reminder: "This city is for ever. Keep it clean!" The message was evidence that the authorities wanted the best for the city and its citizens, and realized the need for improvement. Yet, beside the billboard itself were sidewalk dwellers for whom a piece of tarpaulin was for tiny children the only shelter from a relentless sun. A midden of human and animal excrement nearby more than justified the billboard's admonition, but completely ignored it. In our accommodation a printed menu for each meal of the day graced the table. On the street, gutter fires burned under old pots in which bubbled the sparse nourishment that meant the difference between life and death. I felt I had no right to be so generously cared for in the midst of such abject need.

Despite all this, a visit to India surges with excitement, the more so for my wife and myself as we saw the sacrificial work of our people in hospitals, dispensaries, clinics, schools, homes and hostels. In Calcutta, the Governor insisted that we be accompanied wherever we travelled by an armed guard. If rifles were not really necessary, the uniformed detachment in its official van certainly made an authoritative passage for us through the clogged traffic. Curious and fateful events had been happening in a section of the city we were to visit. The guard lined up, guns at the ready, as we walked from the car, across the road and in to our Behala Girls' Home. If life was grisly in the neighbourhood, inside the home it was like heaven. The place was spotless, the girls attractively dressed and the whole environment permeated with contentment and happiness. If such standards were possible here, why not throughout the area, throughout the city? Funds would be a first requirement, and astronomical sums would be needed to effect any noticeable improvement. But more than money would be needed. The same kind of dedication to a high purpose that motivated the officers in charge of the home would be essential. How to generate that kind of commitment must be the sharpest of all challenges to India's legislators and the public-spirited leaders of the nation.

Over-population and poverty tailgate each other in a threatening spiral. Both are problems of incredible magnitude and affect Salvationists like all others. A helpful session with officers had occupied the morning at a Northern India centre, and lunch was being taken in the home of the divisional commander. Suddenly, the meal was interrupted by an officer calling for the urgent presence of the territorial commander, a highly-respected Indian officer holding the rank of Commissioner. The request was stammered out breathlessly, indicating that serious trouble was developing. The Commissioner left at once and, on returning, explained what had happened. Salvation Army officer doctors and nurses had attempted to follow our session with a family-planning lecture for women. No sooner had the lecture begun, however, than irate husbands had stormed the hall and extracted their wives, so deeply ingrained are traditional mores. If a large family ensures the economic safety of aging parents one can understand birth-control teaching being resented as an invasion of privacy and an unwanted threat to parental finances.

In another state we were being driven to our appointment by the United Nations representative for the area and, as we approached, were surprised to see some three hundred officers squatting on the ground blocking our entrance. A spokesman said that unless some practical help could be given they would be forced to go "on strike." The territorial commander travelling with us was sure that subversive voices had been preaching to the officers who normally were totally loyal. For them, such action was alarmingly out of character. Intuitively I realized that authority must be maintained, though my heart ached for these men and women who were serving where drought after drought had brought indescribable hardship. Not a green leaf of anything edible had survived, and the price of any available food was high out of reach. I said that all must attend the planned session. If they did, I would meet them afterwards for discussion. All did attend, but the gathering was as unpliable as any experienced.

Immediately afterwards we met, and I listened again to their spokesman. Deepening sympathy for their cause softened my concern about the irregular protest. I explained that I could not do for them what could not be done for the thousands of other officers throughout India. But, thanks to a generous benefactor who, prior to the tour had made a substantial donation to be applied wherever I personally thought it would be beneficial, I could, *ex gratia,* make a small grant in view of the unusual deprivation they had suffered. The bonus was a pittance, but the fact that their plight had been recognized and immediately helped, melted away all further dissent. In the afternoon session there was such a ready rededication to continued faithfulness, however unfavourable the circumstances, that one was almost grateful for the tensions of the morning.

When I think of India I think of the word, "bifurcation." This botanical term, meaning "a division into two branches," had become a byword in the jargon of politics, the desire for secession and autonomy of states and within states springing frequently out of caste, language, geography and power struggles. Pressures for bifurcation within the Army were not unknown. In Southern India, by a series of quite natural appointments over a period of years, a situation developed in which, in the administration at Trivandrum, a centre of Malayalam population, the majority of senior officers were Tamils. It was finally seen to be necessary, in 1970, to "bifurcate" and to create a south-western and a south-eastern territory with headquarters in Trivandrum and Nagercoil respectively, the latter headquarters later being relocated in Tirunelveli.

Eight years later something of the same sort happened in the north when a territorial headquarters was established in the federal capital of New Delhi. The north-eastern India territory was "bifurcated" and the eastern India territory was created to give more helpful supervision from

Calcutta to the immense work in Mizoram, the borders of which were usually open only to the Mizo peoples.

Always I marvelled at the extensive preparations made for the enormous rallies at which we spoke throughout India. Giant pandals decorated with flowers and tapestries sheltered thousands of fervent worshippers from the burning sun or the evening winds. Nights in certain parts of India can be penetratingly cold. At Dhariwal, dressed in tropical uniform, I shivered throughout an evening meeting while the congregation huddled comfortably in their blankets. Afraid of catching a cold, I hurried to the staff house of a nearby mill which had been put at our disposal. To my pleasurable surprise I discovered that there was an abundant supply of hot water for a bath. I was so anxious to feel warm again that I did not bother to orientate myself to the unfamiliar surroundings but made straight for the bath. No sooner had I slid my shivering body into the comforting water than the lights went out, power cuts being fairly frequent. I should have been prepared. Instead, I had to prowl through unknown rooms and corridors hoping to come across the bedroom in which my belongings had been placed. One more lesson in the necessity always for foresight!

Few sights can be more inspiring than to see twelve thousand people gathered for a religious service on an Indian evening. At Ahmenabad, seated and standing, there were people as far as the eye could see, the whole scene latticed by fluorescent strip lighting that seemed to shine more brightly as the night darkened. And everywhere in India, the welcomes were spectacular. We rode into towns on the most imaginative of floats and, in one instance, sailed into the town on the bridge of a massive representation of a ship. Always there were flowers. Often we were so heavily garlanded that I had to assure the crowds that underneath all the blossoms there really were visitors who had come to be with them, to learn to know them, and to talk to them of the salvation to be found in Christ. Enthusiasm and sincerity went slightly awry in one telegram welcoming us to south-eastern India. The sender had obviously resorted to a pre-worded social greeting adorned with chiming bells, bursting flowers and a pair of amorous doves. It read: "Hearty congratulations on the new arrival!"

At the gates of the village of Puthencruz, in Kerala, there was a unique welcome. A dense crowd was gathered around a beautifully caparisoned elephant. I was invited to approach the animal and speak to it. I did so with a degree of reserve, but was urged by the crowd to "Get closer! Get closer!" I threw caution to the breeze, and as I stood before the elephant its trunk slowly unrolled from somewhere behind its bulk. In it was a magnificent bouquet of flowers which, with remarkable gentleness, the elephant "handed" to me. After this unusual welcome we climbed the hill to see a leper colony where not only adults were treated, but where the presence of leprous children made a walk through the wards a heart-rending exercise. I thought of the pioneering Colonel Wm. A. Noble, MD., FACS., FICS., a Salvationist doctor eager to expand the Army's ministry of healing, standing one day with nothing but empty land before him and saying, "This is where a leper colony will be." Now, I saw so much where once was nothing.

Erratic plane and train schedules were no deterrent to ceremonial welcomes. Why should these good people deny themselves of sleep and shelter in order to make my wife and me feel at home? Such thoughts were uppermost when the night express from Madras steamed into Bapatla at 4.30 a.m. A first streak of light in the eastern sky was too weak to dismiss the darkness. Our coach was near the end of the train, and where it stopped there was no platform. We were lowered to the ground, kind hands taking special care of my wife, far from well, but insisting on continuing the tour. A heavy grey mist gave a fuzzy outline to scores of oil lamps, flaming torches and waving flashlights. Before the train pulled away we were wreathed with garlands and breathing the wet perfume of flowers whose freshness had been preserved in cold water until the moment of requirement.

Suddenly, the scene exploded in colour and sound. As the locomotive's whistle split the silence, musical instruments of many kinds began their serenade, a fusillade of shots rang out and fireworks burst into the sky. Rose petals from a dozen baskets carried by charming girls in traditional dress were showered on us as we climbed into the car that brought up the rear of the procession to our hospital, leprosy settlement and vocational institute. Marchers alongside held lamps illuminating the staunchly smiling but very white face of a very sick wife. But neither the languorous hour, the after-effects of a benumbing train journey, nor drooping feelings of fatigue or illness could lessen our appreciation of such pageantry, and the memory of it will not be erased by the passing years.

On reflection, our work in India deserved more time, thought and concern than I gave it. My wife and I felt we could identify with the Indian people, and as my respect for India's ancient wisdom multiplied so did my understanding of its problems. Having inaugurated an annual conference of territorial commanders, I must hope that they, in their formulating of evangelical battle plans, will bring to reality some of my dreams for the nation to which, by tradition, St. Thomas, with his doubts of Christ's divinity long gone, came to found seven churches at Malabar and died a martyr at Madras.

A first visit to the border city of Amritsar has already been mentioned. On our second visit to this centre of the Sikh religion arrangements were made for us to visit the Golden Temple, an island of gleaming domes and pinnacles reflecting themselves in a large sacred pool, the Amrita Saras (Pool of Immortality) from which the city derives its name. Disciples of an entirely different faith, our feet nevertheless were carefully washed and stockinged by an attendant before entering the temple precincts. Time did not allow us to accept the leading priest's cordial invitation to take a meal with him, but as we pottered through the amazing structure Booth-Tucker's witness came to mind. Here in this Dharamsala in August, 1885, he made history by preaching the Christian gospel.

* * *

Only forty miles from Amritsar lies Pakistan, its imposed border with India having divided not only differing faiths but also families, Salvationists among them. When a small group of officers saw our party off, they stood waving good-bye on one side of a white line while another group of officers stood on the opposite side of a white line to greet us. Thirty or forty metres separated them. Two officers who had once worked together spotted each other on opposite sides of the border. They waved energetically at each other and shouted greetings, not having seen one another for many years. Even now, a handshake was impossible and a brotherly embrace something that belonged to a lengthening past. In my pocket I carried greetings from officers to brothers, sisters and other relatives with whom contact was infrequent. Whatever their necessity, closed borders are symbols of lost trust.

Whenever I see or hear the name Pakistan two pictures come immediately to mind. One was a morning scene, early in the day before the onslaught of heat and high humidity. The air was still fresh, the traffic not yet fully awakened and the streets almost empty. Already, outside one of the Army's dispensaries, a long queue of patients had formed, some rolled into human balls inside the blankets that had warmed them through the night; others, erect but half-asleep, bodies vertical but heads nodding; still others pacing nervously around the courtyard; and still others, anxious mothers feeding skeletal babies from an obviously ungenerous supply. With the arrival of the Salvation Army nurse and the flinging back of the dispensary doors dawn became day. Nothing specially remarkable about the scene I have told myself many times since. The world knows hundreds of such queues, and that particular dispensary is only one of many opened at dawn by many dedicated nurses. Yet somehow that scene mirrored all similar scenes. The lines of pain on those patients' faces bespoke the pain of all humanity. In the thought of dawn and the promise of relief; of dawn and dedication; of dawn and new hope, there was something indescribably comforting, seeing that with the pills or the injection there would be a quiet reference to the Great Physician.

If one vignette had to do with dawn, the other had to do with dusk. A mammoth afternoon gathering had been conducted at Sheikhupura, some miles from Lahore. Salvationists from surrounding villages had assembled with their welcome signs identifying their points of origin. The crowd, with its banners and bright clothing, was a riot of colour, as though the frugality of life could be blotted out by splashes of red, and the lack of proper housing be washed away with streams of yellow. A wisp of a girl, tiny for her eight years, sang in perfect English Canada's national song, "O Canada, we stand on guard for thee!" while standing throughout at a full salute.

The meeting over, it was back to the villages; for some, a walk of many miles. On both sides of the road families filed slowly along, children clutching at their mothers' saris or carrying on their heads the baskets which earlier had been filled with the day's necessities. Dusk was already enfolding the marching, singing groups. In the brief twilight I saw the other scene which etched itself into the memory—little groups of adults, squatting in the deep ditches at the side of the road, their identifying placard stuck into the soft earth like some "Vote for So-and-so" sign at election time in a western land, or a "House for sale" sign common to all the world. Near the signs, the little groups were praying, all heads but one bowed and hidden in crossed hands. Only the face of the petitioner of the moment was lifted towards heaven, strikingly serene and, to us as we drove by, soundlessly earnest. For these ditch-congregations the rally had not ended, would never end. For them the earthen banks were cathedral walls and the moistening grass a chancel carpet.

* * *

Zechariah's prophecy concerning the day of the Lord, "At evening time it shall be light," stirs a remembrance of the most beautiful sunsets in the world, seen as one stands on the seashore at Colombo, Sri Lanka, and watches the sun go down over the Indian Ocean. Daylight pursues the crimson sun as it moves towards the horizon. Across the expanse of sea the light lingers, and one is caught by surprise when turning the gaze back to land to see that everything is already wrapped in heavy darkness. Sri Lanka, formerly Ceylon, and named by early Moorish traders "Serendip" (from which comes our word, "serendipity"—the gift for making fortunate discoveries by accident), is unquestionably the pearl of the Indian Ocean.

On our second visit we found Sri Lanka a difficult destination to reach. Trouble began at London's Heathrow airport. A strike had grounded all the planes of the airline with which we were booked to fly. A dance of indecision followed. Flitting from one airline desk to another, sifting possibilities, we finally accepted advice to proceed to Paris, hopefully to make a connection for Colombo. The wintry weather of London and Paris was bearable, but, shuffled on to Amsterdam, again hoping to make the connection that Paris could not provide, we ran into some of the Netherlands's bitterest winter with deep snow and freezing temperatures. Here there was the possibility of a connection, but at an hour no official seemed able to forecast. We were then taken to a suburban hotel which, unfortunately, was no warmer inside than out. By this time all members of our party were shivering and well on their way to a cold, or worse. To make the best of a refrigerating situation, my wife wrapped herself in the bed covers and fell asleep. Hardly had she done so than a loud knock preceded an announcement that a bus would be leaving in ten minutes for the airport and for an eight-hour flight with an airline whose name we had not heard of before.

When we flew into Sri Lanka and its overpowering heat the congress welcome meeting was over. Alas, we were still in heavy serge uniforms, with no sign of the luggage containing everything that might make tropical living more comfortable. There was to be a further endurance test. A meeting was scheduled to be held in Kandy in the central highlands, seventy-two miles inland, where the altitude meant lower temperatures. Enroute we stopped to watch a trio of elephants lazing in the river beside the highway. The mahouts quickly urged the animals up the bank and on to the roadway in the hope that their tricks would be rewarded with a few cents. We had been forewarned to make a contribution. The alternative was to be deluged with a giant spurt of muddy water from the trunk of one of the elephants in response to an annoyed master's signal. It was worth the few coins to see the performance and to remain clean.

The visit to Kandy was filled with excitement. A troupe of the famous, silver-ornamented Kandy dancers, their incredibly acrobatic turns, twists and somersaults in no way interfering with their music-making, led us to the university auditorium to which the public had come for a meeting. Trinity College's historic association with the pioneer Salvationist, Colonel Weerasooriya, whose cry, "The cross is the attraction!" was often quoted by William Booth, was not lost on us. But coming down from the heights of Kandy in the midnight hours to the sea-level heat and humidity of Colombo was the final assault. In the car my wife's distress was painfully apparent. The doctor's diagnosis was severe pneumonia. Though every possible helpful arrangement was made, the remainder of the tour for my wife was a struggle, stoically faced, but resulting in a chronic complaint which, in the coinage of lessened health, is for her part of the price of dedication.

The chairman of the Army's advisory board in Colombo, Mr. Mallory Wijesinghe, a barrister trained at London's Inns of Court, and whose father-in-law had been the last governor of Ceylon prior to the country's independence as a republic, shared a dream with the territorial commander, Commissioner Eva Burrows, in which I found myself actively involved. A three-phase development scheme was to include a new social institution, a new headquarters building and a multi-storied commercial edifice. The latter's profitability would, it was thought, make the Army's work in Sri Lanka self-supporting. Thanks to the generosity of certain parts of the world, the first two phases were accomplished, but sufficient gift or loan capital could not be found for the commercial undertaking; the clouds of recession were already darkening the financial skies of the western world. On his frequent visits to London the chairman would call at International Headquarters to assure the administration that hope had not died. The majestic sun that nightly painted the Indian Ocean with such breathtaking beauty inevitably rose again each morning. The day of achievement, said this unflagging friend, would also dawn.

No officer who has the opportunity of attending a session of the invaluable South Asia college for officers will regret, I feel certain, that I decided that this stepping-stone experience should take place in the birthplace of serendipity.

* * *

"General," said the president of the Burma council of churches, one of the speakers at a luncheon tendered in Rangoon to our party, "do you think that Salvationists around the world sometimes forget their little Army here in Burma?" With relief I heard him add, "But you have remembered the forgotten Army!" My thirty-six hour visit, the first ever possible by an international leader, barely justified the speaker's compliment. The work in this single-party socialist republic, largely Buddhist, has been prayerfully and practically remembered since its inception in 1915 despite the vicissitudes—enemy occupation, the dissolution of all democratic institutions, martial law, economic tribulations and insurgency—through which the country has passed. The miracle is that the work has survived at all, since the appointment of badly-needed expatriate reinforcements to aid the devoted but hard-pressed nationals has been impossible for many years.

Though bordered by Bangladesh, India, China, Laos and Thailand, Burma, according to a recent publication, "looks more into itself, gilding and regilding its pagodas, clinging to its Buddhism, turning away from corrupting outside influences, vainly trying to build a country proof against its big neighbours." This probably explains the protracted, detailed and rather exasperating formalities, even with the helpful presence of an embassy official, that had to be completed before admittance to the country was granted. A "closed" society imposes strict regulations on all who enter or leave. All currency is declared and the visitor is provided with a columnar form on which the debits and credits of all transactions, hotel bills, meals and so on, must be recorded while in the country. The balance must be as accurate at departure as on arrival. Nor are the restrictions only to do with money and personal belongings. Other forms requiring a signature are undertakings not to convene any public meeting or to preach.

Major Saratha Perieswami, whose position is uniquely described as Liaison Officer, emerges as the heroine of the work's survival, though she would be the first to protest that there are others. Solveig Smith in her book, *By Love Compelled,* mentions at least one other. "Of the drama of the intervening war-time years," says the authoress, "there is little on record. We know that Adjutant Saw Kedoe, deprived of his uniform ... and without a shirt to put on, had the Army crest tattooed on one shoulder and the Army flag on the other. A permanent witness to whom he belonged!" There are no tattoo marks, as such, on the person of Major Perieswami, but hardship and problem have worn crevices into her face and forehead, and self-denial has reduced her frame to the sparest necessity for housing the unquenchable fire of dedication that burns within. She is not unlike Mother Teresa in appearance and is fully her counterpart in sacrificial service.

Our first surprise as we approached the heart of the city of Rangoon was to see a building, newly-painted white, standing out from all others in its gleaming redecoration. "That," said the Major with pride, "is the headquarters." The under-secretary travelling with us, aware of shortages, paint among them, asked the inevitable question: "But, Major, where did you get the paint?" "That," she replied, "is something that International Headquarters will never know." Ours was the laughter of congratulation.

A public meeting being out of the question, a "birthday party" brought together the Salvationist family and its many friends. I never did discover whose birthday it actually was. There was an immense cake, but it bore words of welcome and made no mention of any birthday, past or to come. During the proceedings I welcomed into the Home League a new member, 89-years of age, who sang with a gusto that belied her years a song of greeting. The climax came when a young accountant and his charming wife stood under the Army flag and were commissioned as officers. Educationally the two were well equipped. Burma has one of the highest literacy levels of all oriental lands. Unfortunately, every attempt to get the couple to a training college outside the country had failed. Both spoke English as well as their own polytonic, mono-syllabic language, and would have benefited by the experience. To conclude the commissioning the crowd sang the Founder's song, and the new lieutenants, both of whom had grown up in Salvation Army children's homes, were roundly applauded. Some 180 Burmese children are today in similar care.

Times had changed since Kipling's verses, "On the Road to Mandalay," first transported their readers to a romantic interior of Burma. But when I visited the homes for unwanted boys and girls I saw little misses who could easily compete with Kipling's ideal of "A neater, sweeter maiden in a cleaner, greener land." What, I wondered, would life have been for these children without the compassion that enfolded them? It was disturbing to contemplate where they might otherwise have been. At the boys' home I listened to the band. The white uniforms of the instrumentalists were impeccable; the instruments were almost unplayable. How musical sound could be coaxed through piston-less valves remains puzzling, but the throbbing bass of an archaic sousaphone was a pleasant surprise despite the bell's battered circumference. I was invited to conduct, and we chose the hymn-tune, "Onward, Christian Soldiers." The sound did not flow like the Irrawaddy, but conductor and instrumentalists finished their presentation together—as much a triumph for me as for the musicians.

CHAPTER 24

"... Through All The Earth."

My boyhood reading was liberally sprinkled with stories of South America's vast pampas, swift horses and the adventures of the hardiest of cattle-raising gauchos in a wild, new continent. Later, I came to know that hardiness is a necessary element in the character of all Salvation Army workers in South America, without which there is no survival. Whether one can have a proper conception of Latin American countries without actually having visited them is doubtful. Even when visited, one has to guard against drawing superficial conclusions. Sao Paulo, Brazil, looks like a New York and a Chicago rolled into one. With its towering buildings, arterial underpasses, its multitudes of darting Volkswagens, its colourful mosaic pavements and elegant shops, and its magnificent residential areas the city is overwhelming. Overwhelming also are the shanty towns that cling to the city's periphery. Here, cardboard replaces chrome, and uncleared brush replaces ornamental gardens. But the extremes only reinforce the impression of the city's varied immensity. We arrived late in this metropolis. Brazilian dignitaries and Salvationists had waited patiently in the airport lobby where, despite there being hardly enough room to breathe because of the throngs of people, a space had been cleared. Fifty singers, one for each year of service in Brazil, burst into a golden jubilee song while representatives of city and state read and presented parchments of welcome.

I had not expected to hear in Brazil band music of such technical excellence, but the congress band played with surprising competence Eric Ball's

"Songs of the Morning." Perhaps it should have been spelled, "mourning," not because of any fault in the musical presentation, but because later in the gathering there happened an embarrassment which I will always recall uncomfortably. In order to salute the territory on its golden jubilee I had had a special flag prepared in London. The territorial commander, the late Commissioner Joseph Dex, thought that the presentation should be a special feature, and it was arranged that, at a proper moment, a curtain would rise to reveal the flag. When the flag was completely displayed, instead of the cheers I expected, there was dead silence. Alas, the wording on the flag was in Spanish and not in Portuguese, the language of Brazil. So much for someone's knowledge of geography!

The variety of endeavours into which compassionate service has taken the Army was newly appreciated when visiting the industrial training centre, *Lar das Flores* ("Blossom Home"), at Suzano, where some two hundred children, orphans or discards from broken homes, are cared for. Trades such as printing and farming are taught, but it was the carpentry shop that impressed me most. Under qualified instructors boys were manufacturing doors of every shape and size, from tiny louvred doors for cupboards to immense, ornate doors for the presidential residence. Making doors was opening a door to a productive life which would otherwise have been denied to these unfortunate youngsters. Many of Brazil's achieving artisans today are graduates of this amazing centre.

Our second arrival in Sao Paulo, seven years after, had a dramatic touch. Though his travel documents had been checked in London prior to departure, a new regulation made Commissioner Norman Marshall's documentation incomplete. To our dismay and his chagrin this member of our party was marched off and placed under house arrest in an airport hotel while we moved on to fulfill the schedule of appointments. Unless his stay could be approved officially by four o'clock that afternoon the Commissioner would have to return to London by the next plane. Ten minutes before the time expired his stay was agreed. If a New Testament Rhoda forgot to open the gate in her gladness at seeing the Apostle Peter following his miraculous release from Herod Agrippa's prison, there was equal gladness when the Commissioner arrived during the congress welcome meeting and walked to the platform. No "ex-prisoner" ever got a more rousing reception.

* * *

When our visit to Argentina was announced, I was invited to a luncheon at the Argentinian embassy in London and introduced to the leading staff. Every assistance was given in making arrangements, so that when we arrived in Buenos Aires we had the help and companionship of Dr. Roberto R. Bravo, a theologian serving in the department of religious affairs. In this city in 1890 four Salvation Army officers, none of whom spoke Spanish, began the Army's work in Latin America. From this most pleasant city, which has had its full share of unpleasant times, the work spread to six South American nations.

In a country under military rule, a high-ranking officer is usually appointed to head each ministry; in Argentina the department of worship falls under the ministry of foreign affairs. I found it a peculiar experience to be discussing religious matters with a senior military officer, and asked myself why? Under the gold braid and rows of service ribbons was a personable, even jovial, individual with a sensitivity concerning spiritual matters. The uniform, however, left me in no doubt that it was the wearer's responsibility to draw the line that all communions and denominations in Argentina must toe.

We called upon the editor-in-chief of one of the leading daily newspapers. He, and his father before him, had championed the Army's cause and helped in whatever ways were possible. Seated in his unpretentious office, he noticed that I was staring at the windows behind and above him, and explained that what I saw were actually bullet holes. The feelings of some extremists had run high over a stand taken by the paper on some subject, and the death of the editor seemed to be the way of retaliation. Mercifully, the bullets had missed their mark, and the editor said he was leaving the windows as they were. The bullet holes would remind him that if it were necessary to speak out for justice and truth he must always have the courage to do so.

I do not know how my place of accommodation in Buenos Aires became known, but each time I entered the hotel women beseiged me with requests to intercede with government authorities on behalf of their husbands, sons and brothers who were among "the disappeared ones." In broken English, and holding out photographs, they tearfully asked if I could find out the whereabouts of their loved ones. These were frustrating encounters because of my utter helplessness. When I mentioned the subject delicately to certain government officials I was asked to believe that the mysterious disappearance of any citizen was part of a troubled past which ought to be forgotten. Did they, I now wonder, have some intuition that before long a new day and a new order would usher in a less-troubled future?

* * *

We flew to Montevideo, the capital of Uruguay, where, in between a series of appointments and a public meeting, I walked along the long promenade looking out to where the River Plate meets the South Atlantic, scene of the dramatic scuttling of the *Graf Spee* in the early days of World War II. On that bright afternoon, with the waterfront crowded with holiday-makers, it was almost impossible for the mind to conjure up the grim scene in which the naval giants of two nations were locked in battle. Yet, when the event happened, the attention of the whole world was focussed on it. The peaceful view now stretching before me was, I ruminated, far more desirable. So was the view I had of "El Atardecer," the Army's home for the aged. In a choice setting, this accommodation for the elderly must rank among the best for its attractiveness and quality of service. The leading businessmen I met insisted that it was the best. They also reminded me that when the noted British explorer, Sir Ernest Shackleton, died at South Georgia Island in January, 1922, the authorities asked if his body might rest in an Army building in Montevideo. Shackleton, as a junior officer, had sailed with Scott when the *Discovery* made its historic voyage to the Antarctic in 1901. He later led other expeditions, in 1909 coming within ninety-seven miles of the South Pole while members of his party reached the South Magnetic Pole and the summit of Mount Erebus. Among the belongings accompanying Sir Ernest's body was his Bible. In many places it was underlined, certain verses being doubly underlined in blue and red ink. One such was verse 10 of Psalm 139, "... Thy right hand shall hold me."

* * *

Chile, when visited for the seventieth anniversary congress, was also under military rule. I was received by the president, General Augusto

Pinochet, impressively uniformed in cream and gold. Our conversation centred on the subject of freedom of religion in the country. The president's reserve thawed as he assured me that such liberty was the right of every citizen. He suggested that I should walk through the parks of Santiago and see the various denominational groups holding their services without any official surveillance or interruption. On the Sunday afternoon I did so. There were many groups, some small, others larger. Strangely, only the Army's service had a large congregation surrounding it. Here, the communion rail of the church, the Mercy-Seat of the Salvation Army, was a drum; not laid on its side, but standing as if ready for the drummer's next beat. Four pieces of carpet were quickly and quietly laid around it to form a square on which many seekers knelt while being counselled. "A square of prayer," rhymed in my mind.

The president said he greatly admired the Army's social action and, in a way, had emulated it. The wife of each military general appointed in charge of a ministry had been given specific responsibilities, one to supervise the care of the aged, another to work on behalf of the homeless, another to see that all possible was being done for needy children. He indicated that it was the government's pleasure to have issued a postage stamp commemorating the Army's seventy years in Chile, and, during our stay in Santiago, the minister of communications, with his aides, came to our territorial headquarters and, in a pleasing ceremony, presented an advance edition of the stamp. My interview with the president was well covered by the press.

Chileans are among the warmest-hearted people I met. Their love of country positively glows when they sing their national anthem, surely one of the most dramatic—and longest!—of all national songs. It is a slice of grand opera, replete with brilliant fanfares and stirring climaxes. The military general appointed to accompany us and render any necessary courtesies was not the only one who, in our meetings, when the anthem was played and sung, stood at ramrod attention. All Chileans, it seemed to me, are devoted patriots.

A zonal conference in Santiago de Chile brought together leaders from Central and South America and the Caribbean. Separated by thousands of miles, and with budgets that demanded austere living and the most economical administration, the territories and their leaders were virtually in isolation from each other. From Sao Paulo in Brazil to

Buenos Aires in Argentina is 1200-miles "as the crow flies"; from Sao Paulo to the Chilean capital is some 1600-miles. To journey from Sao Paulo to Mexico City one faces a flight of some 3500-miles, and it is even farther to Kingston, Jamaica. We convened in a charming Roman Catholic conference centre, its gardens shaded with trellised vines and with bright sunshine warming the days. An enormous, alabaster moon shone at night. Conferences have to be reckoned not only in man-hours contributed, but in travel and accommodation costs, and delegates knew of my abhorrence of conferences that had no issue. They determined to turn the time to good account. From early morning until well past the hour when nearby villagers had retired, the problems of the lands that had given birth to liberation theology, and where converts were many but recruits fewer because of the Army's non-sacramental position, were earnestly discussed. Time was given to discover how Spanish-language materials could be jointly prepared and shared in order to save money and multiply effectiveness. An annual meeting of the leaders of the Latin American countries was approved in order that mutuality of effort might be stimulated.

An abundance of the fruit for which Chile is noted graced every meal, wholesome in content and cheerfully served by the women of the centre. At the end of the conference I was asked if I would thank the Mother Superior and the sisters for their hospitality. I readily agreed, and awaited the arrival of the stately, be-wimpled woman to whom I should make my remarks. I was jarred into sudden speech when it was pointed out that Mother Superior and members of her order were already in the room, and waiting. I had not expected the reverend mother and her colleagues to be dressed in jeans and sweaters. Throughout the week they had ministered in humility with "the grace of service," minus the slightest show of religious authority.

* * *

It was midnight when we flew into La Paz, Bolivia. Due to the high altitude, some 14,000-feet, we literally staggered from the airliner with its pressurized cabin to the terminal, the highest in the world. One actually gasps for breath until there is some degree of acclimatization, but we tried to walk smartly across the tarmac as sounds of singing filled the misty air. La Paz ("The Pot") is well-named. The city sits in a hollow, surrounded by mountains. Its streets are peopled by women wearing bowler hats and carrying children on their backs and men in typical, brightly-coloured toques.

In the pulsating public meeting we met again the quartette which, with its native songs, had created great enthusiasm among the crowds attending the 1978 international centenary congress in London. When I admitted Lieut-Colonel Jorge Nery to the Order of the Founder the gathering almost went out of control. For twenty-six years, until the time of retirement, the Colonel and his wife had directed the Army's affairs in Bolivia and had seen it grow to an entity with its own training college and a network of busy social services. Officers who work in the remote parts of this country merit the laurel wreath of gratitude. The quality of their teaching could be seen, for example, in the music-making of a group of young people from one of our homes. With confidence and competence they provided music with flutes, traditional pipes and guitars. Playing with the ensemble was a blind and deaf lad who had so responded to tuition that he was now an accomplished teacher of the accordion.

* * *

Fellow-passengers deplaning with us in Mexico City must have thought they had arrived in time for fiesta. Outside the terminal, late at night, were crowds of uniformed Salvationists, young and old in national costumes, and with a band providing spirited music. *El Ejército de Salvacion* was in good heart and determined so to convince the airport throngs. The welcome, shortly after, of Mexico's president, Jose Lopez Portillo, was no less encouraging. With the country's crushing troubles on his mind he could have been forgiven had he been far less affable. Described by one international publication as "an active intellectual," who governed "more like a monarch than a democratic leader," I found him outspokenly concerned that the Army's work, valued, he said, by both government and the people, should go forward.

That the country was passing through an economically stormy period could be gauged from the graffiti daubed wherever it would attract notice. It is evidently regarded as a public right to paint political slogans wherever the eye falls on the walls of public, commercial and educational buildings. So many noble buildings at the university were disfigured in this manner. But if the modern is despoiled, the historic is respected. At Tectihuacan, the centuries-worn pyramids comprising the "City of the Gods," with no policing in sight, are protected by the innate awe of the visitors. Walking among the amazing ruins we pondered the life and times of an ancient people and their strange forms of worship. What would the Toltecs—who had worshipped the moon within these, to them, holy acres—have thought could they have forseen that in the year of our Lord, 1969, a man would walk on the face of their sacred moon?

Normally street processions are not allowed in this most populous of all the world's major cities, nor are churchmen permitted to wear religious garb in public. Special authority having been given I was able to review the marching forces led by the visiting, red-jacketed Texas divisional band. At the monument to Benito Juarez, the revered emancipator of the Mexican people, a huge crowd gathered thinking, I suspected, that the purpose of the gathering was political. Preaching and praying was not allowed, but I was authorized to give "an oration." It was a priceless opportunity to speak of The Salvation Army as an international religious and social service movement, and of its message, which is more important than the movement and its ministry. The crowd listened intently. At the end, with Latin fervour, someone shouted into the microphone: "Viva Mexico!" ("Long live Mexico!"), and the crowd, with hands in the air, responded, "Viva Mexico!"

"Viva Juarez!", bellowed the cheer-leader, and the throng answered, "Viva Juarez!"

"Viva El Ejército de Salvacion!" Again there was a mighty shout, "Viva El Ejército de Salvacion!" Had the Army ever before been so wildly cheered by a non-Salvationist crowd?

Then, with fervour fully maintained, the voice cried, "Viva El General Arnold Brown!" The crowd, arms flung high, roared its response, "Viva El General Arnold Brown!" I could only say, "Amen!" It was a generous gesture of good will; but how many of the cheering thousands, I wondered, had ever heard of Arnold Brown, and why should they wish him long life? For that moment, and many others, Mexico will always be gratefully remembered.

* * *

In February, 1976, the world's attention was focussed on Guatemala. Millions who did not know the country's location on the map, knew through the media that one of the most devastating earthquakes of the last century had resulted in shocking losses of life and the obliteration of entire towns. Except for a brief, early period the Army had not served in Guatemala, but at the request of a burdened government sent in a relief team. It was assigned to a town called Tecpan, sixty miles inland from Guatemala City (country and capital share the same name) and 7,500-feet up in the mountains. A concrete block-making machine was shipped in and the men of the area taught how to operate it. Ash from nearby volcanoes provided the main ingredient for the building blocks. Under professional supervision five hundred and forty homes were erected. Built to new standards the houses would be virtually impervious to any earthquake shock.

Two motorcycle policemen escorted our party from Guatemala City to Tecpan, speeding faster and faster up the rising mountain roads while drivers in the convoy nervously attempted to keep up with them. For the villagers it was a triumphal occasion. They waited outside the town hall where the mayor and councillors, with elaborate ceremony, adorned me with an apron denoting my authority as "head man of the village," a rare honour. Then followed what, in the style of Britain's monarch, has become known as a "walkabout." Houses had been festooned with yellow, red and blue bunting. Fireworks heralded our arrival at each street, and rifle shots punctuated the music of strolling instrumentalists. The walkabout ended at the village fountain, built in the shape of The Salvation Army's crest and painted in the Army's colours. Here, where water is drawn and the women meet for the exchange of news, is a permanent, functional reminder of the Army's practical interest in them.

That evening heavy rain soaked the village but did not dampen the enthusiasm of the villagers. In the neat, new Salvation Army hall every available space on chairs and on the floor was occupied. Outside, the rest of the villagers stood unmoving in the teeming rain while the service of thanksgiving proceeded, a service which included the dedication of the infant child of the young officer couple, the first appointees to this new charge.

If it took an earthquake to bring the Army to Guatemala, it would now take more than an earthquake to dislodge it from the people's affection. Deplaning in the capital city we were greeted by an expert group of marimba players rendering "O Boundless Salvation." The mayor, Colonel Abundio Maldonado, spoke glowingly of the Army's assistance in establishing an alcoholic treatment centre in addition to other appreciated services. The secretary for foreign affairs, with whom we had discussion, felt that soon Guatemala must discontinue receiving aid from other nations, and must work out its own salvation. Three years had passed since the death-dealing earthquake. The calamity was now history. Perhaps so, but I was confident that the succour that had flowed towards Tecpan and its people in their hour of darkness and desperate need would never be forgotten.

* * *

The Costa Rican people, like ourselves, made the most of our brief stay, the first visit of a General in twenty-five years. Construction crews had worked overtime and feverishly through the preceding eight months to complete the rehabilitation centre for chronic alcoholics which I was officially to open. Situated in the beautiful mountainous area of Concepcion de Tres Rios, my first glimpse of the finished project made me gasp with surprise and the private secretary with me to whistle in astonishment at its spaciousness and modern amenities. Its size reflected the extent of the need that had brought it into being; Costa Rican authorities described alcoholism as the country's most serious social problems. With dulling regularity I had heard the same lamentation in country after country. In one land where the Army maintains a large network of hostels for men, a survey had indicated that 75% of all those sheltered had problems related to alcohol abuse. Major and Mrs. Bernard Smith who had pioneered the work in Costa Rica seven years before, and whose energy and compassion had already made a rehabilitation centre in San Jose irreplaceable, saw hope maturing as the new facility, surely among the finest of its kind, came into being.

Great help had been provided by Dr. J.B.A. Kessler, chairman of the Army's advisory board, in whose home, set in lush tropical surroundings, we stayed. In the humid evening, the air filled with what to me were strange sounds, all of which could immediately be identified by the doctor and his wife, ways and means of rendering aid to neighbouring, suffering Nicaraguans were discussed. If that night we seemed to be on the edge of nowhere, we were reminded of the real world and its compactness when the interesting fact emerged that the doctor had been born in a house only steps away from where we were living in Beckenham, Kent. I had passed his birthplace innumerable times.

* * *

Contrasts in Salvation Army life and service are frequently encountered and are often vivid. Leaving Atlanta, Georgia, and the Golden Jubilee Congress with its thousands of delegates, massed musical aggregations and splendid buildings, and arriving in Panama with its handful of devoted officers and soldiers, could well serve as an illustration. At the Panama Temple Corps torrid heat and saturating humidity failed to restrain spiritual enthusiasm. Overjoyed at being able to welcome international visitors, a woman Salvationist concluded her spirited words of greeting by seizing the corps flag and marching with it around the hall, the congregation entering into the demonstration with lusty singing. Soon, it seemed, the building itself was swaying with excitement. Flag officers around the world know that when a flag is mounted care must be taken when meeting obstructions. But on this jubilant occasion, and with this unpracticed, temporary flag-sergeant, things were different. I saw it coming—or going!—as the flag crashed into one of the new lighting fixtures and splinters of glass fell to the floor. The collision caused the intrepid female to change course suddenly and, as the flag swirled about her, the metal crest at the top of the pole plunged into the air-conditioning machinery which, with a spurt of sparks, came to an untimely end. The episode left our heroine undaunted, the congregation exhausted with joy, and "her beloved General" murmuring the encomium given centuries before to one whose contribution was worthy of emulation: "She hath done what she could!"

In the control tower of the Miraflores Locks, some of the mechanical mysteries of the Panama Canal were learned. Great ships were passing through the locks as we looked down on their upper decks. Only the pressure of one man's hand on a single lever was needed to set in motion the movement of waters that could noiselessly lift or lower the huge vessels. Regulations prevented the courteous controller from allowing us actually to operate the machinery, but he asked that I put my hand on the all-important lever and, for an instant, consider, as he put it, "the frailty and force of a human hand." I did so, but reflected also on the unseen forces without which hand and lever would be ineffective.

* * *

Work in the Caribbean embraces a number of island countries and, in area, constitutes one of the largest territories in the Salvation Army world, "two thirds of it," the late Commissioner Wm. Chamberlain used to delight in saying, "under water." Direction is given from Kingston, Jamaica, where one can participate in some of the most inspiring meetings to be experienced anywhere. During one visit we faced from the platform a large banner of greeting stretched across the back of the hall. With much amusement we noted that the sign-writer had changed our name from Brown to Green. Though we decided not to mention the mutation, the Roman Catholic Archbishop, the Most Reverend Samuel Carter, who was present, drew on it to the crowd's enjoyment for his welcoming remarks. "We rejoice," he said, "that we have Mrs. 'Green' with us. You see, if she were a 'Brown' she could be at home with her babies like other brown Jamaican mothers."

There was always satisfaction in returning to the school for the blind in Kingston, a facility I had opened when Chief of the Staff, and at which ceremony we met for the first time His Excellency, the Governor-General of Jamaica, Sir Florizel Glasspole. He was then minister of education. The Army has no firmer or more respected friend. During the turbulent days through which Jamaica was passing Sir Florizel remained a symbol of strength and hope for his people. We saw for ourselves something of the absence of law and order when through the crowds leaving one of the congress meetings a group of young men, organized like a plague of locusts, snatched handbags and wallets and were gone before the bewildered losers could collect themselves. Returning late at night to our hotel I gently reminded our driver that we had run through two red traffic lights. He made no apology. "At this time of night," he said, "there are no stops. To stop is to invite trouble." As we slid through another red light he added, "You may not mind being shot, but that's not for me."

With characteristic West Indian cheerfulness, despite difficulties and deprivations, the proclamation of the Gospel and the care of the needy never slackened. Human need always has its touching side. A 93-year-old woman, living alone in a slum area, made a pathetic appeal for "all I need—two tablespoons of sugar to sweeten my tea." None had been available for weeks. Officers were no strangers to gunfire, holdups, breaking and entering, and other kinds of violence and crime. But nothing could affect the joyous congregational singing in which West Indians excel, nor the sense of prospect as I commissioned fourteen new officers, the first time a General had been privileged so to do in that part of the world.

In Barbados it was "crop-over" time. The sugar harvest was in and it was the moment, so congress organizers felt, for "a harvest of souls." They were not disappointed. It was a gladdening experience to see the simplicity of a child in the sincerity of an adult as crowds of choice spirits sought spiritual refreshment and moved nearer to God in dedication. To Bridgetown came delegates from Trinidad, Tobago, Grenada, Antigua, St. Vincent, Guyana, Suriname and St. Lucia. From St. John's, Antigua, came thirteen bandsmen, models of discipline and astonishingly expert musicians. How often in London's Trafalgar Square had Salvation Army bands played near the base of Nelson's column. But around an older Nelson's column, erected in the centre of Bridgetown in 1807, the same praiseful music was played by Antigua's capable "thirteen."

There were pleas to visit all the Caribbean countries. The spirit was willing but schedules were inflexible and the years of possibility too few. There were two visits, however, which dug deeply into our emotions, one to Haiti and the other to Cuba. Of all "the crowded ways of life" none to me were more thronged than the streets of Haiti's capital, Port au Prince. Passage through the dense crowds was hazardous. Our driver gave full weight to the horn and almost full weight to the accelerator. Somehow, the sea of humanity parted just in time to allow us through and immediately after closed in behind us. "What if someone is knocked down?" I asked. "Then there is a visit to the police station and a small payment to be made," replied the driver. "And what if someone is killed?"

I asked. "Then there is a visit to the police station and a somewhat larger payment to be made." I did not know whether the driver was exaggerating in the smallness of the payments he mentioned. Perhaps he was, but obviously, and regrettably, life was all too cheap.

We were comfortably hosted in a hotel bearing the name *Sans Souci* (Without Care). Haiti, unfortunately, is crushed with cares as a visit to any one of our clinics quickly confirms. The constantly multiplying population multiplies the need for proper food, medical treatment, housing, education and employment. At the request of the Canadian International Development Agency which, with the Army, had made funds available for its construction, I went to Fond-des-Negres to open a new day-school accommodating some twelve hundred fortunate children. Hundreds who could not be enrolled could only look longingly at the outside walls and enviously at the schoolrooms within. In the seventeen other day-schools, educational work means not only teaching, but feeding three thousand pupils a day.

Government ministers, we observed, were given strong security. When the minister of education arrived he was accompanied by a platoon of armed guards. The woman officer in charge of our work, missionary extraordinary, certificated pilot and restless pioneer, had trained a little group of instrumentalists who began proceedings by playing the Haitian national anthem while the country's flag was raised at a corner of the roof of the building. At the first notes, the military officer gave orders to "Present arms!" and he himself came to a full salute. There was another flag to be raised, and the captain had decided she would perform this ceremony herself. As she slowly hoisted the Salvation Army flag above the school tears of joy over the accomplishment streamed down her cheeks. To accompany the flag-raising, the captain's little band, as planned, began the tune, "There is joy in The Salvation Army." At the first notes, the platoon commander again ordered arms to be presented and once more he stood rigidly at the salute until the song had ended. According to the girl captain the salute was neither ill-timed or misplaced; hers was a flag for all nations, she said, and the song was a universal anthem.

* * *

Not until almost the last tense minute did our visas for Cuba come to hand, though embassy officials in London were courteous and helpful. At the time, entry was possible only from Kingston, Jamaica, Mexico City or Toronto, Canada. Travelling from Kingston meant that we could have the company of the then territorial commander, Colonel (now Commissioner) Orval Taylor, and his wife, Cuba being in their area of responsibility. Met by the chief of protocol in Havana, immigration and customs formalities were quickly completed. In the airport crowd, Russian military officers, smartly and colourfully uniformed, were obviously perplexed while trying to identify our uniforms and insignia.

A journalist recently described a visit to Cuba as "a ride in a time machine going backwards." Automobile styles recall earlier decades. The divisional commander's car, of Canadian make, had chugged its way beyond two or three normal lives. Every few blocks, we discovered, there was a tantalizing emergency stop. A fender had to be banged back into position, or the engine hood kept levitating. Buildings also showed signs of deterioration, but the streets were litter-less and boulevards were constantly being manicured. There were no blatant signs of poverty, and for this, credit where credit is due. Troops of children wearing gold-coloured shorts or skirts, white shirts or blouses and the red tie or scarf of membership in "the pioneers" were everywhere. Government officials made arrangements for our party to visit one of the several "Children's Palaces" on the island. School children are brought to one of these palaces, impressive in both architecture and amenities, once a year for a period in residence. If the child is interested in dentistry, he can spend his days in a modern surgery, handling the instruments and learning about teeth and their care. In an uptodate television studio young people were operating costly equipment, others were script-writing, and still others were learning how to act before the cameras. There was a large attendance in laboratories devoted to the history and possibilities of space exploration. Everything we saw emphasized the government's concern to shape the mind and destiny of the country's next generation of leadership.

Our people, necessarily, had to be concerned about the present generation's aged and infirm. The elderly may not be part of any programmed future, but their need of accommodation and care is immediate. If refinements are lacking, the old people's home we visited is flooded with compassion. A growing roster of residents meant encroachment on the limited quarters of the officer couple and their three children. As newcomers arrived, the family's apartment shrank until, for them, all of life is lived virtually in one room.

The reader's own knowledge of current affairs will put into perspective the serious significance of our meeting with the twenty-five officers and cadets. Through the island's period of separation and silence, so far as most of the world was concerned, the work had gone on due to the fidelity of this group whose one aim had been to serve God and their fellow Cubans. A translator, hired for the session, failed to appear, but the day was saved when the private secretary, Major John Bate, who had served in Chile and Spain, stepped in to recall his seldom-used Spanish. An expected accompanist also defaulted. Again, the private secretary filled in, moving from pianoforte to platform as needed. These improvisations in no way lessened the devotional intensity of the gathering. I experienced some of the most chaotic inner feelings of my life during this session: frustration in knowing that the provision of any reinforcements for the company before me was impossible; sadness that I could give no encouragement to any who held hopes for a transfer to other areas of work so that they might follow the relatives who had preceded them; admiration for the dedication that had kept the officers at their posts when all subsidies had disappeared and International Headquarters was beyond contact; and, above all, gratitude for the reality that "In Christ there is no East or West ... no South or North." In moments of solitude I still hear the group singing, "*No tengo temor*," while in English we sang with them, "No, never alone, He promised He never would leave me ..." The words of Christ, "Lo, I am with you always" swept across that sacred session with undeniable veracity. In a life situation such as is known by these officers there are no idle or meaningless gestures. As the meeting concluded, the entire group moved to the front of the hall. Each one present clutched the flag, symbol of the Gospel's universality, and sang again their pledge of faithfulness to Christ's cause, "All my days and all my hours ...," however uncertain the future might be.

Two public gatherings were held, one in the cathedral and the other in a Presbyterian church, both of which were crowded. For these occasions a translator was found, but the private secretary's help at the keyboard was again a necessity. On the order of service for the cathedral gathering I noted the item, "Timbrel Display." What kind of a "display" could it possibly be? This was not the United Kingdom or Australia where the musical management of the tambourine has become a fine art. When announced, a young girl of fourteen wearing a white blouse with blue "S's" on the lapels, denoting her junior soldiership, stood in front of the high altar. To background music provided by a recording she presented her "display," and then stole back into the shadowy cloisters. As we left the cathedral Bishop Gonzalez embraced me. With moist eyes, eyes that reflected the heroism of his Christian cross-bearing, he commented on the little girl's timbrel playing. "I've seen her play before," he said, "and always I find myself deeply moved. Tonight, when I saw her in front of the altar, before this crowded congregation, I thanked God that He still has His Miriams who play the music of victory and praise to His honour and glory."

CHAPTER 25

"The Golden Cord Close-binding"

The inclusive term, "Australasia," by which non-Antipodeans usually mean Australia and New Zealand was, I had learned, as little accepted by New Zealanders as it would be by Australians if the designation were "Zealandasia." The term, "Australasia," appears to have been introduced by Charles de Brosses in his *Histoire des Navigations aux Terres Australes"* published in 1756, as a vaguely defined geographical description of Australia, New Zealand, New Guinea, New Britain and certain lesser islands in their immediate vicinity. The Prime Minister of New Zealand, the Rt. Hon. Robert Muldoon, gave abundant evidence during our courtesy call of his respect for the Army, but also let me know in forthright language that the term, "Australasia," was out, and that its replacement, "Oceania," was in. For this there were justifications. Trading areas and political relationships had created a new sphere of common interests. Perhaps the presence of Commissioner Harry Williams, at the time international secretary for the Americas and *Australasia,* may have caused the prime minister to question the segmenting of our administration. New Zealand's economy, he emphasized, was more closely linked with Japan than Europe and with other Far East countries than with the United Kingdom. The difficulties of distance had yielded to the conveniences of proximity. Perhaps Mr. Muldoon does not yet know that his mini-lecture led to an almost immediate revision in our administration; "Australasia" was detached from the Americas and became part of "The South Pacific and Far East" section of the overseas department at International Headquarters. (The "Far East" designation has since been replaced by "East Asia.")

The strength of the Army in New Zealand is remarkable when it is remembered that the national population is just over three million. In the State Opera House in Wellington, both the prime minister and the leader of the opposition, the Hon. Wm. Rowling, united in welcoming delegates and international visitors to the territory's 95th annual congress. Both men impressed me by the easy manner in which they gained the attention and response of the congregation. The leader of the opposition spoke seriously of the need to pass on to the next generation the highest standards of morality, of human dignity and responsibility. At that moment none knew that when he and his wife reached home tragedy would have claimed the life of their seventeen-year-old daughter. Salvationists entered intensely into the family's sorrow. In this gathering I repaid a long-standing debt, and handed to the territorial commander, Commissioner Lawrence Smith, a Bank of England draft in the amount of 200 Pounds as repayment of money sent in 1882 by a Miss Arabella Valepy, of Dunedin, to William Booth, to meet the cost of sending pioneer officers to New Zealand.

In the montage of memories gathered in New Zealand one sees and hears again the marriage of lovely Maori melodies to beautifully intricate timbrel displays, and senses again the sweeping passion of the late Major Condon's selection, "Easter Glory," played by the Wellington City Band while scenes depicting the Crucifixion and Resurrection were rear-projected on a large screen. In Christchurch, meetings were held in the new, world-famous city hall. The first of many seekers at the altar was a woman who, knowing nothing of The Salvation Army or its use of the auditorium, had come to view the magnificent architecture and had decided to stay for the meeting.

New Zealand's natural beauty could be seen from the small flying-boat which ferried us to Rotoroa, the Army's island treatment centre for alcoholics. I could see no traces of the disastrous fire which earlier had resulted in the loss of several buildings. All had been replaced. Like its sister island-centre of Kuron, off the Swedish coast, where similar rehabilitative work is pursued, Rotoroa sparkled with its attractive facilities and atmosphere of achievement. If St. Theresa of Avila could silence a scandalized visitor who saw the holy woman happily eating a well-cooked bird with the rejoinder, "There is a time for partridge and a time for penance," I may be forgiven for mentioning that at Rotoroa I had the finest fish dinner I can remember, the fresh-caught product of the seas which wash the island's shores. If there was food for the body, there was abundant nourishment also for one's faith. Scores of men, once shackled by alcoholism, had found here the liberating efficacy of Divine grace. The amphibious craft arriving for our return journey swooped gracefully on to the water but, as it waddled on to the beach, nose-dived into the sand. Upended, it looked as if its career, and our return journey to the mainland, was over. But with effort and expertise the damage was righted and we flew back safely as the late afternoon sunshine gilded the choppy waters and verdant coastline.

* * *

Returning to Australia in 1980 for the national centenary congress in Adelaide, already described, my wife and I felt no strangeness. Our appreciation of the continent's vastness and vitality and of its rugged Salvationism was born two years before when a lengthy tour began in Western Australia. We arrived on the heels of a tornado for the first congress conducted for twenty-two years, by a General in Perth, the beautiful capital city, and delegates were welcomed by an unusual "Call to Celebration" banner consisting of 11,450 paper flowers, all made by one man officer. Here we stayed in the Army's modern Railton Hotel. I recalled a visit paid to my office at International Headquarters by Commissioner Railton's granddaughter, Dame Ruth Railton, and her husband, the newspaper publisher, Cecil King. Dame Ruth related how she and her husband, while walking through the streets of Perth, had come across the building bearing her family name. They had entered to enquire about its ownership. Its excellent amenities, Dame Ruth said, were in startling contrast to the spartan conditions in which her pioneering Salvationist grandfather had felt most comfortable, and she doubted that he would have been excessively gratified over such a commemoration.

One of the happiest and most eager groups of young people encountered during my career invited me to take breakfast with them in the Morley Citadel, a converted honey factory. Like others, I had heard of "the Australian breakfast," but imagination paled in the light of reality. Never before, I told the young people, had I eaten "fried zeppelins." The sausages were the largest I had ever seen alongside bacon and eggs.

The premier of Western Australia, Sir Charles Court, invited me to his office. He told me of his early days as a bandsman in The Salvation Army, but modestly refrained from revealing that he eventually became Australia's national champion cornet soloist. I mentioned to the premier that when it came to champions I was also familiar with the achievements of his daughter, Margaret, internationally-known as a tennis star. On one occasion at Perth, accompaniments to the congregational singing were provided not by a band but by a competent orchestra of Salvationist-musicians. When congregation and orchestra united, an "oratorio" effect resulted, and I could almost imagine myself in London's Royal Festival Hall once again listening to Bach's "Matthew" Passion. The Western Australia congress, so successful in attendances and so rich in spiritual results, concluded with a brilliant festival in the university's cathedral-like Winthrop Hall, last used by the Army during a visit of General Evangeline Booth in 1935.

The long succession of congresses in Australia and New Zealand are for the Army's leader perhaps the most demanding of all his overseas campaigns. For my wife and I the marathon included gatherings in Wellington, Perth, Melbourne, Sydney and Brisbane, with a series of Easter meetings in Christchurch, as well as visits to Tasmania and Papua-New Guinea. Some of our predecessors had found the physical challenge too heavy, and we accepted advice to spread the visit. Australians, however, want their money's worth, and before the tour ended the number of events was well past the three hundred mark. In few parts of the world are public leaders so closely affiliated with the Army's aims as Australia and New Zealand. In Melbourne, the Governor of Victoria, Sir Henry Winneke, received me not only in his official capacity but as long-time chief patron of the Red Shield appeal. In conversation with the premier of the state, the Hon. Richard Hamer, the speaker of the house and members of the cabinet with whom Commissioner Arthur Linnett and I lunched, I realized again that our light was not "under a bushel." We are under closer observation than we think. One of my table companions who felt that "the Army works miracles" was surprised at my rejoinder that the "miraculous" belongs to God and that we only work.

If there is such a thing as pardonable pride I experienced it in Melbourne when marching Salvationists, for an hour and a half, passed the saluting base. I gave the Army salute, forefinger pointing to Heaven, as forty-seven bands encouraged their groups to follow a lively step. Five thousand Salvationists and friends made the best of an unsuitable building for the public meetings. Congenial surroundings are always an advantage, but the fervour, the uninhibited singing and the eagerness to enter into new commitment to the cause of Christ proved that drabness matters little to those who want to "worship in spirit and in truth."

One of the most crowded days of our leadership was spent in Hobart, Tasmania, where William Booth made his first landfall when coming to this part of the world. In conversation with His Excellency, Sir Stanley Burbury, the Governor asked if the General's Trust were still functioning. The question took me by surprise. Not many within the Army itself were aware of the trust's existence. Shortly before his death, Booth had sugested to his son, Bramwell, that a trust be set up from which allowances for future Generals could be met. This would free the international leader from dependence upon Army funds and, since disbursements would be under the aegis of the Charity Commissioners, probity would be ensured. I told Sir Stanley that he appeared to have a most intimate knowledge of Salvation Army affairs. This led him to say that as a young lawyer he had acted for a client who was challenging the terms of an estate from which the Army was to benefit. The testator, a devout Christian and philanthropist, had offered to finance William Booth's growing work provided certain changes were made in the Army's doctrines. Booth resisted the proposal, preferring to go without the aid which would have been exceedingly substantial and much needed. The admirer did, however, make a bequest to the Army which later came to be part of the corpus of the General's Trust. Contested in court, the submission was made that the money would not go to the poor, but would actually find its way to "the idle rich." His Excellency told me that he lost the case. The judge, to use Sir Stanley's phrase, "laughed me out of court." I was able to tell the governor that the trust, established in 1913, was still active, but that it had long since proved inadequate of itself, despite wise management, to meet even the modest needs of the incumbent, so drastically had the purchasing power of money diminished through the years.

Sydney's famed opera house, an architectural wonder, rises grandly like a multi-plumed bird out of the waters of the harbour. Salvation Army instrumental and vocal music filled the reaches of its acoustically perfect auditorium during congress gatherings from which—an all-too-infrequent problem!—crowds were turned away. While the city hall was overfilled with all standing room occupied, massed bands with their hundreds of instrumentalists had to take possession of the nearby cathedral square. Statistics matter little in the realm of the spirit, but the number who publicly sought more of the blessing of God upon their lives during the Sydney meetings was so large as to leave us freshly marvelling at the effectiveness of the Holy Spirit's ministry.

The congress gatherings were overshadowed with sadness for my wife. The territorial commander, Commissioner Leslie Pindred, had recently lost his partner. She was the officer to whom my wife, when commissioned, was appointed, and together they commanded two corps. The great affection in which each held the other would have had special fulfilment had a reunion been possible after forty years of separate activity in various parts of the world.

Just prior to our arrival in lovely Queensland, the "Sunshine State," the premier had ruled against the holding of public processions and demonstrations, for reasons I did not come to know. When we reached Brisbane for our "Celebration of Faith," newspapers were commenting, tongue in cheek, on the arrest of clergymen who had whistled hymns while marching in protest against the decree. There was no interference, however, with our congress marches which gave colour and martial sound to a city bathed in brilliant sunshine. Whatever restrictions on marching the streets had affected early-day, or present, Salvationists, not once in the whole of my life had I personally encountered any such restraint. In those countries where public demonstrations are frequently used to incite disorder I had made it a point to explain to the head of state that when Salvationists announce the Gospel in the outdoors it is an act of peace designed to lead men and women to the best of all moral and spiritual values. Whatever their inner thoughts, no national leader I met argued against the Biblical assertion that "righteousness exalteth a nation."

In Brisbane we were left in no doubt as to one of Australia's great occupations, sheep farming. As an introduction to their demonstration, the youth of Queensland enjoyed singing, "Click go the shears," while on stage a live sheep was dexterously sheared by a young Salvationist.

* * *

Salvation Army work in Papua-New Guinea had not reached the quarter-century mark when, with Commissioner Leo. Ward, I made a visit to Port Moresby. From the prime minister, Sir Julius Chan, came expressions of the highest appreciation concerning the rapid development of the work which includes maternal and child welfare clinics in the highlands, hostel and welfare centres, and a vocational training centre. The acronym, SALT, very much in evidence, puzzled me. The world at that moment was interested in the current Strategic Arms Limitation Treaty, but in what way, I wondered, could the Army be related to its discussion? The acronym, I shortly discovered, stood rather for Salvation Army Leaders' Training, vitally important to this remote part of the world perched off the north-east tip of continental Australia. The programme was designed to fit young Papuans for the prominent places they must occupy in the days to come.

The prime minister told me that in Papua-New Guinea more than seven hundred languages are spoken in addition to English and Melanesian pidgin, forty percent of all the world's languages. Official broadcasts are made in some one hundred different languages each day! It is to the credit of officer-nurses that, in order properly to minister to the inhabitants, they learn the language of a village which may not be understood even in the next community. To one such, who had spent twenty-three years as a nurse and evangelist in remote areas, I presented a certificate of recognition, a ridiculously small recompense for the devotion with which her skills had been rendered. She, however, insisted that the recognition was undeserved. "Blessed are the meek!"

The miraculous development of the work was further understood when I commissioned six nationals as Salvation Army officers and opened a newly-erected headquarters at Boroko. A huge outdoor welcome gathering filled the Koki Hostel basketball court and crowded the slopes around it. Twelve corps groups appeared in differing regional costumes. Garishly painted "warriors," who in music and motion brought the past to life, stood side by side with immaculately uniformed

Salvationists. Billows of laughter and shouts of joy filled the hot night air and echoed in the tropical darkness. A colourful but Christless past had yielded to a Christian present for these hundreds upon hundreds of dark-skinned people whose smiles were unfailing and whose sincerity was touching. A number of Salvationists are leading the race towards high literacy. In Papua-New Guinea I heard some of the most eloquently convincing testimonies to the transforming grace of Christ.

* * *

Indonesia is a necklace of nearly fourteen thousand islands, all but a thousand of which are inhabited. At the time of our visit strongly Muslim political leaders were crusading against the presence of "foreign missionaries." They were contending that all who represented other than Islam should be expelled within two years. Implemented, this would adversely affect our extensive work, but I was assured by the official responsible for religious affairs in East Java that the Army's contribution to the well-being of the people was its own warrant for the work's continuance. Following events in Jakarta and Bandung a delayed flight brought us to Surabaya. Descending from the plane we were met by a contingent of Salvationists, one of whom was dressed in a grey uniform of a different style. We learned why; not only was he the treasurer of one of the Surabaya corps, but he was also chief medical officer of the Royal Indonesian Navy.

From a Salvation Army standpoint, Indonesia is a perennial pioneering process, and in many remote areas villagers are still pleading for the Army's presence. The fairly recent thrust into Central Celebes involved grave hardship on the part of the missionaries, and in a few instances almost fanatical persecution. But many of the villagers were desperately anxious for the Kingdom of God to come "on earth." Women and children hauled buckets of sand and gravel from distant river beds to the site of new buildings. Men carried sheets of galvanized iron on their backs along dangerous mountain trails in order to make their places of worship strong and lovely. One man trekked hundreds of miles to a city to watch chairs being made. He returned and, with primitive tools, made scores of them so that school children would have something to sit on. In North Celebes the wife of an officer appointed in charge of a new children's home was herself one of the small children picked up from the street when Surabaya was burning during the revolution which followed enemy occupation. At the general hospital in Surabaya rooms and corridors were crowded with patients. In six other general and maternity hospitals, in branch hospitals and many clinics, in some eighty day-schools and at a teacher training college the work goes on. The name of The Salvation Army is widely known. Curiously, in all Indonesian languages, it is the same: *Bala Keselamatan.*

If we felt the heat more here than in other tropical countries a rest period had been arranged so we might regather ourselves before proceeding to Japan. We were to relax in Denpasar on the dreamlike isle of Bali, theme of so many romantic songs. The plane was late, and the automobile in which we left the airport appeared to be travelling away from, rather than to, the beach resort where we were to stay. It was! In the dark, suddenly we were surrounded by shouting and singing youngsters from one of our children's homes. Their exuberance cancelled our weariness, and soon a happy meeting was in progress. At the end we made to leave, but were informed that we were to share a typical Indonesian meal. The children were to have dinner with their "father and mother" from London; not often did "the parents" walk beside the palms of Jalan Cokroaminoto and into their home. The preparations and the dining took time. Midnight was not far off when our party arrived at the hotel, a fairyland of lights set in luxurious gardens. No effort had been spared to make our stay enjoyable. Nowhere had we seen so beautiful a floral arrangement of welcome as graced our room. Stationery, napkins, matches, all were stamped with our names in gold. And, as though arranged for our personal enjoyment, through the windows we could watch the spectacular festivities following a Balinese wedding. But the schedule was relentless. In the dark of the next morning we drove to the airport. Only from the window of the departing plane as dawn broke did we catch our one view of Bali. Below were the indescribable beaches, the lush green and masses of floral colour, all the beauties we had hoped to see. "Adieu, intermission! Farewell, Bali!"

* * *

At the main entrance to the royal palace in Tokyo I was left alone with a frock-coated interpreter, pleasant in manner and efficient in his profession. Together we walked the long corridors that led to the audience chamber. If simplicity begets elegance, then the surroundings were extraordinarily charming. When presented to His Imperial Majesty, Emperor Hirohito, one picture occupied my mind—that of a man who, with consummate courage, had offered himself at the end of World War II in expiation for his people's aggression. This was the emperor who had renounced his divinity before a nation that had regarded him as a deity, yet in his courteous humanity the Divine spark of personal dignity was impressively present. The regality remained. I did not have to explain The Salvation Army to him, and His Majesty's references to it were based on more than a pre-audience briefing. The royal family had assisted the Army's work through the years. What is now Booth Hospital, at Suganami, was once a royal establishment given to the Army for its work.

Despite the fact that the Emperor spoke to me only in Japanese, with translation the conversation flowed easily. His Majesty showed few signs of advancing years. More in the manner of professor than emperor, he pressed me to say what my plans were for the Army's advancement and for what reasons they had been conceived. I felt like a doctoral candidate defending his dissertation. What paths, I wondered, would the conversation have taken had Commissioner Gunpei Yamamuro (the Army's first Japanese leader) been in my place? Yamamuro was fond of quoting a proverb: "The peach and the apricot trees never speak, but there is always a path leading to them." Although the trees are silent, their blossoms are so beautiful that people want to see them. The path towards the trees is therefore always well defined. What were for me the trees? What were for me the paths? These were His Majesty's questions. I left the audience gratefully aware that I had been permitted to converse with one of the consequential, if enigmatic, figures of the twentieth century. When I stepped from the portico of the palace on to the gravelled path, translator and equerry bowed low in farewell. Retired Commissioner Shinichi Yoshida pointed gleefully to his watch and said triumphantly, "Thirty-eight minutes. Good! Audiences with His Imperial Majesty are usually much, much shorter." For me, thirty-eight minutes was not long enough.

Prominent on a wall in our home is a black and white wash painting of Mount Fuji, its conical peak ringed with white cloud. The picture is more valued because it is the artistry of a 94-year-old corps sergeant-major who wanted us always to remember Japan and our fellow-Salvationists. At the base of Mount Fuji, which has towering symbolism for the Japanese, we met all our Far East leaders in conference. Day after day we watched the sun bathe the pinnacle in varied degrees of light and colour. Could there be a better backdrop for an official conference photograph? But at the appointed time there was no Mount Fuji. It had melted into a cocoon of clouds. Japanese Salvationists, however, are more constant. A small, influential force in the country, *Kyu-sei-gun* seeks to keep spiritual considerations before the people of this highly-industrialized nation. Despite the amazing technological developments of their fellows, Japanese Salvationists have not lost the art of personally communicating the Good News of the Gospel. While outdoor meetings are in progress, individual Salvationists speak to those who appear needy and hopeless. "Captures" are brought into the meeting. Sitting with them, Salvationists explain the Gospel and, finally, accompany them to the altar as they kneel in surrender to God's will for them. Near the front of the congregation during our first visit sat Mrs. Masayoshi Ohira with her fully-uniformed Salvationist woman companion. Not long afterwards, Mrs. Ohira took her place as wife of the prime minister whose short term in office, was, regrettably followed by an early death.

A year later my wife and I were again in Japan, this time for congress gatherings. Again, royal interest was shown in our visit. We were invited to an audience with Crown Prince Akihito and Crown Princess Michiko. We were about to bow our way into the royal presence when, with Western courtesy, the Crown Prince and Princess advanced towards us, hands outstretched in welcome. Several members of the royal entourage joined us around a large, low, round table. No interpreter was necessary. The royal couple were completely at home in English, though the Crown Prince complimented Colonel (now Commissioner) Rightmire, the territorial commander, on his fluent use of Japanese. Like the emperor, the Crown Prince was well informed concerning the Army's services, but in one direction he differed from his father. While his Imperial Majesty had wanted to know my plans for the international operations of the Army, the Crown Prince was much more concerned about what was being done in Japan, and with what new developments might be expected in his own country. While we talked, the Crown Princess drew my wife aside. She spoke as mother to mother about the coming of age of her eldest son, of the responsibilities he would be expected to carry, and of the problems that teen-agers struggle with in present-day society. She asked that her family be remembered in our prayers, an assurance that my wife readily gave.

All our appointments and interviews, indeed all arrangements during our stay in the Land of the Rising Sun, were marked by courteous briskness. In our meeting with the governor of Tokyo, Shunichi Suzuki, there was no haste, yet not a moment was wasted. The presentation of the city's medal reflected an understanding of the Army's mission, but it was presented with a gentle crispness that indicated respect for my time as well as the governor's. Briskness characterized our journey on the famed bullet train. For precision, our timetable matched that of the railway itself: "Greeted by station-master at 8.05 a.m.; tea in his office, 8.08 a.m.; escorted to platform at 8.15 a.m.; board train 8.18 a.m.; train departs 8.20 a.m." The stationmaster, in gold-braided uniform and wearing white gloves, marched us between two armed guards to the exact place where we would enter the coach and take our reserved seats. He bowed, briskly, as the express slipped out of the station on its fast run to Kyoto.

The strictures of precision were fewer at the reception tendered by the Canadian ambassador, His Excellency Bruce I. Rankin, at which opportunity was made to meet a number of leading figures in Japanese life. Many were interested in the fact that new worship centre was being opened in our Kyose complex, a spiritual "heart" for the diverse humanitarian work being rendered. That the Army's work could not function without a spiritual "heart" could not have been more eloquently expressed than by Bishop Ichiro Kikawada, in Osaka, and by the president of the International Christian University in Tokyo, Dr. Hideyasu Malagawa. During the congress a mini-pageant, "One Seed Multiplies," was presented. Japanese Salvationists believe this to be eminently true in the spiritual realm, and everything I saw confirmed that they are diligent sowers of the Gospel seed. So close an affinity do I feel with the Japanese that, to their joy, my first word to the congregation during my last visit to Tokyo was the cry of the father to his family when entering his house after a day's labour — "I'm home again!"

* * *

Another recollection should be added here. Geographically, perhaps, the memory should be among those associated with the United States, but the episode happened while flying the polar route from Tokyo to London. The airline had just introduced a new feature, sleeping berths, and a friend had met the surcharge in order that my wife and I might arrive at International Headquarters somewhat rested after the exhausting Far East tour, and more ready for the heavy schedule of events to come. The benefit of the berths was only partial. Awakened all too soon by the hostess, we were, she said, now landing at Anchorage, Alaska. In the light of dawn everything was ice blue. Mother Nature's cold hand had the whole marvellous scene in her grip. Only the towering, snow-covered mountains of the Aleutian Range, with nearby Mt. McKinley, its peaks the highest points in North America, appeared unflinching. We shivered as we hurried into the terminal and its warmth. Escorted to a private room we found it filled with welcoming officers. The servicing of the aircraft allowed enough time for a hymn of thanksgiving, for a period of prayer, for the sharing of organizational news and for the expression of some devotional thoughts. The miracle of modern transportation had made possible, between Japan and the United Kingdom, a pre-breakfast officers' council session in Alaska strengthening both faith and fraternity.

* * *

Meetings in Hong Kong permitted us to share in the fiftieth anniversary of our work in the crown colony, work which had burgeoned expansively and with great rapidity. In the limited area of Hong Kong, Kowloon and the New Territories, with a population of more than six-million, the Army maintains some eighty centres of work. Kindergarten, elementary, secondary and special schooling is provided for almost ten thousand pupils. Institutions in their service cover the whole spectrum of social need. The governor of Hong Kong, the highly-esteemed Sir Murray MacLehose, impressed me as a formidable personality. Perhaps his great height compared with my own had something to do with it. He had definite ideas as to how things should run in the colony to which Her Majesty The Queen had appointed him, and a clear way of stating them. He was afraid that the Army was expanding its social services too fast and too far. It was the only time I heard this kind of observation anywhere in the world. Obviously, the governor wanted no duplication or overlapping by service organizations. He came as near as a ferry ride across the harbour to reprimanding our advisory board chairman, Mr. W.R.A. Wylie, over the too-swift multiplication of our facilities, and suggested that there should be a period of consolidation. Mr. Wylie's riposte would have pleased William Booth. Said Wylie, "The Army must do *something* when it sees a need."

The governor, soon to retire, was keenly interested in what was being done for the refugees flooding into Hong Kong from Vietnam and mainland China. His interest matched my own. By Royal Auxiliary Air Force helicopter I was flown to the Lantau island prison of Chi Ma Wan. The director of Her Majesty's prisons sat beside me. In his accent I could hear my father speaking, and to the official's pleasure I immediately identified his home city as Liverpool. We landed outside the gates of the centre where detainees were provided by the Army with every possible form of supportive care. The prisoners had awaited my coming with interest, and with oriental cleverness a colourful sign of welcome had been made out of bits of waste paper and hung across the iron gates. It was not easy to look unfalteringly into the eyes of disappointed men and women whose hopes of a better life in a new environment had been washed away as they stepped from the border river into the arms of the police, or drained away with their last ounce of physical strength as the mountain climb ended in custody. In the camp were Chinese who had tried vainly to enter Hong Kong purporting to be Vietnamese. Here credentials were being examined. Once identified as Chinese they would be deported. If there was frustration in the eyes of the Chinese, the eyes of the Vietnamese reflected the nightmare of a harrowing sea voyage, shot with hunger and illness, that had brought them to the government dockyard and reception centre in Kowloon. Yet for them there was some hope of permanent resettlement in a third country, an experience for which our workers were trying to prepare them as adequately as possible.

I saw a letter written in limited English by a young Vietnamese inmate. In part it said: "Today, in this beautiful blooming season, we, more than three hundred children in Chi Ma Wan Vietnamese refugee camp, truly pay our respects to your Army. We will surely never forget the great grant sent us from Jesus Christ. We are the next generation of the human race. Unfortunately, hostility pushed our lives to tragedy and melancholy. God has had mercy on us. He sent you angels who brought us warmth and happiness."

Hong Kong's young Salvationists are talented singers and clever instrumentalists. In a demonstration given by the young people a united song was announced. A tiny boy, with one of the largest bass drums I had seen, began a drumming display which signalled the singing entrance from the back of the auditorium of two hundred little boys and girls, all in school uniforms bearing the Army crest. Each held high a miniature Salvation Army flag and, while waving it enthusiastically, sang in splendid English, "There's only one Flag for me." The audience was captivated. I experienced that rare tingling of excitement that belongs to life's special moments. What a Christian witness these Chinese children could make in their own generation if their feet stay in the ways of righteousness! What a witness is already being made by adult Salvationists, I thought, as I "inspected" the troops, more than a thousand of them, three times the strength of Gideon's Old Testament army, drawn up in parade formation in the searing heat of a brilliant Sunday afternoon.

* * *

Citizens of Taiwan, the Free Republic of China, celebrated the "Double Ten" (the 10th of October), their national day, during our stay in Taipei. Chinese lanterns were everywhere. Holiday-makers flew their soaring kites high in the blue sky. Momentarily we might have wondered where we really were when a tartan-clad piper welcomed us to the capital city with a rendition of "Amazing Grace," while vivacious young timbrellists added an international Salvation Army touch. Taiwan, formerly Formosa, is a newer expression of our work, begun only fifteen years prior to our visit. Our stay was short, but long enough; we met all the officers of the island in council, participated in an ecumenical rally and, at a luncheon meeting, spoke to two hundred leading personalities in the fields of government and religion. For the public meeting a group from Taichung travelled 150-miles to sing a version of the 23rd Psalm, accompanying themselves on traditional Chinese instruments. Timeless truth. Ancient sounds.

The premier of Taiwan, Sun Yun-Suan, and his minister of the interior, Chi Chuang-Huan, were as generous in their appreciation of the Army as they were burning in their hopes for the future of their nation. I learned of those yearnings in more detail at a private meeting of influence-makers who asked that in my world travels I should put forward the case for Taiwan's legitimacy. Echoes of Quebec! Once more I described the Army's non-political stance, but assured the company that it was all-important for me to know the aspirations of the peoples whom we served. Taiwan's development is so astonishing that one could almost accept the confidence with which the notion was advanced that mainland China should move into the twenty-first century under the government of Taiwan. Remembering that the People's Republic of China would soon register its population at one billion two hundred million, and that the Free Republic of China, based in Taiwan, numbers only 17-million; and, noting also, that mainland China is the third largest country in the world as against Taiwan's island area of only 14,000 square miles, one wonders if the political expectations of certain Taiwanese are the "stuff of dreams." Those who spoke to me passionately believe that more than one historic change has begun with a dream.

* * *

Unity in diversity could not be more observable than when Salvationists of several races and cultures met for meetings in Singapore. The central corps hall is unique with its pagoda-like roofs and the grim gargoyles that look down quizzically from the frieze inside. The people enjoyed the facetious remark that never before had I seen former leaders so memorialized. They knew, as I did, that our work in Singapore and Malaysia had been directed by a succession of devoted and highly-capable officers and that God had remarkably blessed their labours.

Our only journey aboard the supersonic Concorde clipped many hours from the flight time, London to Singapore, and permitted us to crowd in a number of important interviews as well as public meetings, a lecture to cadets in training, and council sessions with officers who came from all parts of the command, Penang, Malacca, Ipoh, Sarawak and Kuala Lumpur. On arrival I was greeted by Dr. Eee Peng Liang, chairman of Singapore's council of social services, with whom I had corresponded. His friendship and influence is gratefully remembered by all who have met him. By his arrangement we rode from the steps of the Concorde to the terminal in the most opulent mini-bus I have seen, the interior being reminiscent of the finest American railway club car with its deep carpets and reclining, revolving seats. Some say that Singapore is the cleanest city in the world. I have not seen them all, but with Havana, Cuba, as a close rival, it would appear to be so. In this cleanest of all cities open-air meetings are not permitted, but Salvationists make their evangelical outreach in whatever ways are open to them.

I should like to have discussed this with the prime minister, Mr. Lee Kuan Yew, but a meeting was not possible. I was told that he followed a rule of not conferring with any religious leaders. Quite apart from his religious or political beliefs, the prime minister gained my admiration whenever we saw him interviewed on television during his fairly frequent visits to London. He communicated compellingly with his strong personality and superb management of the English language. We were received instead by the president, Dr. Benjamin Henry Sheares. An eminent obstetrician, he had delivered the infants of several Salvation Army officers and, because of this, had followed their careers with particular interest. Dignified but frail, the president spoke with difficulty, almost in a whisper, due to the affliction that would soon end his life. His hoarseness caused our own voices to lower, and a soft hush settled over the interview when the president spoke simply and beautifully of "the things of the heart."

During my last call at Singapore the positive results of faithful missionary endeavour were eloquently demonstrated. I presented to a congregation that overflowed the temple-like hall Major Margaret Burns, a diminutive Canadian, now retired, who had served in Singapore for many years. She had been awarded the Certificate in Recognition of Exceptional Service for work which, in its selfless, and possibly reckless, pursuit of the spiritual and material well-being of the needy, was rendered with total humility. With others, she had been interned in the notorious Changi prison camp during the war, but this harsh experience had in no way reduced her affection for the place or the people. Now advanced in years, she had lived for the day of return. When it came, I saw her surrounded by well-dressed women who had arrived in their privately owned cars. They had loaded the Major with flowers and fruit, and were embracing her, several of them with tears of joy. These were the girls for whom she had cared in the home she had managed. Some were from desperate backgrounds; others had been nameless when taken into care as infants. Most had now made creditable places for themselves in life and in society. If I did not see the prime minister, I saw in this vignette something which would have greatly pleased him.

* * *

The expansion of the Christian church in South Korea during recent years is overwhelming. In a country where until 1910 Confucianism was the official religion, Christianity is now described as "the most active religion in Korea," and some of the largest churches and congregations in the world are located in this divided land. During enemy occupation the Army knew severe persecution, but the voice of prayer was never silenced though martyrdom was the bitter glory of Major Noh Yong Soo and perhaps others. Today the work is described as going forward "by leaps and bounds." If an earlier Seoul Boys' Band had been marched into oblivion by enemy soldiers, the final end still a mystery, its reborn successor had earned its plaudits internationally. Londoners who had heard the band's excellence at Wembley, the Royal Albert Hall and at Selfridge's, will have a warm thought for South Korea and its people. The surging spirit of praise and prayer in this land has found impressive expression in music. I was correctly reported as saying that "the singing moved my wife and myself to the highest heaven."

Korean Christians treasure the gift of prayer. It is not a sphere in which one cares to make comparisons, but in no other country can one sense such earnestness in prayer. I was surrounded by it when speaking to an all-party national assembly prayer breakfast in the parliament buildings. I was informed that among Christian people and in almost every church, and certainly in every Salvation Army hall, people meet at 4.30 a.m. or 5.00 a.m. every morning, summer and winter alike, to pray. For Koreans, prayer is intensely personal. Their conversation with God is intimate and refreshing. Often, each person present prays out loud for himself or herself, disregarding all others in the room. In the large gatherings we attended scores came forward to the altar and prayed aloud in this fashion. At first, to the Western ear and mind, it seems to contradict reverence, but only at first. This is not a show. There is no extremism, only an uninhibited outpouring of thanksgiving and petition. The praying crescendos then falls away like surf throwing itself landwards and expending itself on the beaches. Again and again the waves of prayer return to gather themselves for another climax. Some petitioners are mumbling; others are shouting; a few are silent; some are singing; but sincerity has all firmly in its grasp. One must accept that this fervency in prayer is the secret of the Army's astonishing progress. New corps are continually being opened—forty within four years—and congregations are regularly seeding new ones. Because the Spirit is at work, the outflow of compassion shows itself in social services of the highest order. There are five hundred orphanages in South Korea. Two Salvation Army homes were named among the year's "top ten." They were described by the government as "model institutions."

The work has been blessed with gifted Korean and expatriate leadership. The two Korean commissioners who supported me, Chun Yong Sup and Kim Hai Duk, were men of deep spirituality and uncommon acumen. A nine-storey office building had been erected in downtown Seoul, the income from which would help to make the work throughout the country more self-supporting. Koreans are imaginative, and perfectionists, when it comes to ceremonial occasions. I was given white gloves to wear when unveiling the three huge characters, vertically displayed on a prominent wall of impressive edifice, which spell out "The Salvation Army" in Korean—*Koo Sei Kun*. Thanksgiving to God for the success of the venture was expressed, and I then pulled away the long bunting that had veiled the lettering. As it fell away, a flight of doves fluttered skywards. A celebratory luncheon was taken in bright sunshine on the open roof beside the Korean and Salvation Army flags streaming stiffly in the breeze. From this vantage point one could see the city with its energetic millions. Hours later, not one of those millions was to be seen. A periodic alert had sent the crowds scurrying to appointed shelters. The streets were cleared for crawling tanks and speeding armoured vehicles. Even where prayer is made, where Christianity flowers and national prosperity increases, threatening forces are never far away.

* * *

If the welcome at Manila's international airport was one of the least spectacular of our Far East arrivals there was a reason. Public assemblies at places like airports are not permitted. But at the hotel where we were to stay the management had no such prohibitions. Filling the driveway to the entrance were hundreds of smiling, singing, flag-waving Salvationists making sure, in the white glare of television lights, that the visiting international leaders, and the new command leaders, Lieut-Colonel and Mrs. Arne Cedarvall, whom we were to install, were convinced that they were welcome.

I was gladdened by the youthfulness of our forces in the Philippines. Trim, eager, wholesomely attractive, young Filipino Salvationists hold shining promise for the future since dedication crowns all other of their qualities. They used their considerable talent skilfully at an open-air evangelistic festival in the Rizal Park amphitheatre, holding the attention of thousands of workers and their families enjoying the evening breeze at the close of a fiercely hot day. Interspersing songs accompanied by the rhythmic beat of thousands of clapping hands were simple, direct testimonies to a personal experience of Christ. The words of witness were applauded as vigorously as the musical items. On either side of the stage were the flags of the republic and the Army. Both employ the colours yellow, red and blue, and this gave me opportunity to comment on the spiritual symbolism of our flag, to restate the purposes of our movement, and to speak of the individual's need of the saving grace of Christ.

Though Salvationists are a minority in the country's religious community, they are determined that their light should not be hid. Attracting attention, my wife and I headed a Sunday morning procession in a horse-drawn conveyance. Alighting, we saluted the cheerful force that marched by us into the large Roman Catholic auditorium loaned for the day, the one suitable building available. I was greeted by His Eminence himself who took huge pleasure in confirming that his name, as I had read, is Cardinal Sin. He added that Divine grace had changed his nature, if not his name. He asked that his sacred premises be "filled with hallelujahs." They were!

* * *

Can affection be more graciously displayed than in Hawaii? "Aloha" permeates all of life. Late at night, my wife and I stood encircled by those whom I called "the golden people" while, with arms linked and swaying gently, they sang again and again, "Aloha oe" ("Farewell to thee"), refusing to let us go and pleading with us to return quickly. Hawaiian Salvationists carefully preserve the grass and bamboo hut in which Robert Louis Stevenson, engineer, barrister and notable author, completed the manuscript of "The Master of Ballantrae," and which is now part of the Army's Waoli tea-room to which come visitors from all parts of the world.

For the Hawaiian Christian the exquisite beauty of the islands is a special manifestation of God's handiwork. Two prayers they use make this pleasingly plain:

> *We bless Thee, O God, Designer and tailor of trees, Who hast blessed our islands with trees wherein we find shade from noonday heat, cover under which men can talk, and forms that lift us to nobility. So cause us to grow with the fullness of a monkeypod, the straightness of a royal palm and the gentleness of a jacaranda in bloom. Amen.*

> *Keep me a listener in the world of music, O God, so that I hear the ocean drumming on its floor, tradewinds plucking tunes from trees, and cardinals saluting another morning. Amen.*

CHAPTER 26

The Final Year

During my final year in office I did not want to be what in political terminology is known as "a lame duck." Some colleagues were unfamiliar with the term, though its meaning could fairly easily be guessed. According to the 20th Amendment, following a national election in the United States of America, a final session of the old legislature usually lasted from December to March during which a president, vice-president and the members who had failed to win re-election were necessarily ineffective "lame ducks." I was sure that my unknown successor would not expect the administrative machinery to decelerate, leaving an accumulation of unresolved matters; nor would he appreciate a total absence of forward planning to which he could add his own emphases. To pad quietly through the terminal months was against my nature and intention. As it was, I would be retiring at a younger age than any of my predecessors. Good leaders around the world, when seeking decisions, should not be fobbed off with such delaying phrases as, "This must wait for my successor ...," "I do not wish to prejudge the next administration's view ..." In the matter of senior appointments, for example, important preliminary steps always have to be taken, in some instances a year or more ahead in order to avoid later confusion. A number of such appointments were in the offing, all the more difficult to plan since not until the High Council made its choice would it be known who my successor would be, or what moves in territorial or other commands would necessarily flow from his taking office.

With appreciation I record that throughout the final year I was given total, undiminishing support by the Army's leaders. They made it obvious that they, too, wanted the Army's direction to proceed progressively, even though certain of them must have realized that changes resulting from the High Council's deliberations might involve them personally. The corporate aim, in a word, was normalcy. As it transpired, the last months in office, in respect of stress, were for me the most abnormal of all, due, particularly, to concluding negotiations with the World Council of Churches concerning The Salvation Army's relationship (details of which were related in Chapter 18), and to a television broadcast which, on the evening of May 26, 1981, propelled the Army in the United Kingdom into undeserved notoriety. The guns of criticism delivered a massive broadside.

That Tuesday night, for millions of viewers, one of Britain's independent television companies aired a documentary film which purported to be a careful investigation into the management of our hostels for men. A free-lance team had produced the programme as one of a series of *exposés* which, it was virtuously asserted, would awaken the nation to the gross misapplication of its tax and charity pounds, and would force the subjects of the film to "put their houses in order." On these grounds, those watching the film were treated to some sensational viewing.

Members of the team, in accordance with the Army's usual practice, had been given the open-door treatment. Arrangements had been made for them to visit wherever they wished and to question whomever they wanted. It was not long, however, before the team's curious methods aroused speculation on the part of several hostel managers as to what the film-makers were really after. It began to emerge that a one-sided, critical picture was the objective. Interrogation was often convoluted in order to confuse the answerer. One manager's comments were played off against another's, with no allowance for differences in locality, type of accommodation, or even the kind of men being served. Managers were alarmed to see problem individuals whom the Army was sheltering deliberately chosen for filming while their muddled voices were recorded. One man, portrayed as "an authority" on hostel living, was filmed with briefcase under arm and Tower Bridge impressively in the background. He was led skilfully to speak negatively of the sixteen years he had been accommodated in hostels. Why he had for so long used such facilities was an unasked question. Britain's television viewers that night could not know that the man had three times been a patient in the Army's alcoholic centre, and that same morning, probably aware of the airing of the programme that evening, had simply disappeared from the centre.

The team turned its attention to the way in which the hostels were financed, and that particular year's appeal envelope, they thought, provided them with lively ammunition. It stated that 14% of the appeal income would be directed to the maintenance of social services in the United Kingdom. This was the detonator for which the investigators were looking. Managers and the departmental head were on record as saying, quite sensibly, that buildings, amenities and services could be greatly improved if more money was available. Why, then, the interviewers queried, should a meagre 14% be allocated to social work when many donors thought all of the appeal income was for such services? What was not understood was that from the annual appeal many other services, including the social work carried on in several hundred corps and community centres throughout the country, were also supported. The crucial but ignored point was that the budget requirements of the social services were completely met from a variety of sources, only one of which was the allocation from the annual appeal. In fact, additional funds were continually being found for capital needs, several new hostels having been erected within the past decade. The film, nonetheless, focussed on some of the oldest hostels and ones most in need of refurbishing or replacement. For the film-makers' purposes the annual appeal percentage figure was dramatically valuable, and not even the explanations of the Army's chancellor to a chartered accountant employed by the team succeeded in adjusting the producers' views.

There were unpleasant side issues. Reports reached us that members of the team, in the rôle of "exposers," were making slanderous remarks in public about the Army. Some who heard the adverse comments were shocked and annoyed and complained to various authorities. At this point I asked if the team would meet me. It was an uncomfortable session. I gave as my reason for the meeting the wish to gain some idea of the team's integrity. Of the Army's integrity I had no doubts. When I brought up the subject of the team's propagandizing against the Army it was shrugged off as inconsequential. Every effort was made by the team to impress me concerning their honourable motivation; all they wanted was more and better accommodation for the homeless. I asked them to remember that the Army was the largest charitable provider of accommodation for the homeless in the United Kingdom, and that for more than ninety years it had struggled to do something about the problem despite limited personnel and finance. If the team had discovered remediable circumstances, why had they not reported them to us, or to government authorities, rather than producing a documentary which could detract, instead of assist, the good work already being done? The commercial aspect of the undertaking was, I felt, all too apparent, and I suggested that if there really was personal anxiety for the well-being of the more than eight thousand who slept under the Army's roof every night in Great Britain, I would employ the members of the team for six months at their present rate of income to work in various hostels. The proposal was dismissed in silence.

As the conference concluded, the team concentrated on securing agreement to my being filmed while answering allegations of inefficient and heartless management. One of the team had posed as a tramp and, by testing beyond normal limits the patience of admitting staffs (most of whom were themselves men with problems and receiving help), and in some instances the managers, had elicited controversial comment. I insisted that posing as an unemployed wanderer was a deception, and that when it was done to secure sensational material for monetary gain the stratagem was all the more unworthy. The team contended that it was following in the footsteps of William Booth who had also explored the doss houses of his day. His only aim, I pointed out, was to help the inmates, and he did not pose as any other than himself.

Almost immediately my wife and I were leaving for centenary congress gatherings in Paris. Other international appointments stretched out through succeeding weeks. There was no possibility of a filming session before the date on which the broadcast was scheduled. I proposed that if the team had unanswered questions I would provide written answers by return. The confrontation ended perfunctorily. I was not reassured. The film, I suspected, was already edited to near completion, and I feared the worst. The questions arrived the same day. The next morning the answers were delivered by hand. When the film was telecast it was evident that the question and answer procedure had been an empty exercise. Instead, my photograph appeared with commentary indicating that I had been "too busy" to defend the Army's position or to answer the allegations.

This led to the most painful aspect of the broadcast's aftermath. Many dedicated Salvationists knowing nothing of the actual circumstances were bitterly disappointed that I had not participated in order to set the record straight. I could not blame them. They were the ones who, the morning after the presentation, had to face their colleagues in office or college, or their workmates in shop and factory. As the episode recedes into the past I still salute the courage of those who unflinchingly went into public houses and leisure centres the following Saturday night to sell copies of *The War Cry* despite the furore created by the broadcast and the for-and-against references filling the newspaper columns.

From some source it had been learned that the team intended to make the most of their investment of time and thought. There was to be a book published in the current "book of the film" style. At this point, letters went to the head of the broadcasting company expressing the Army's doubts as to the accuracy of the film, and to the intended publisher asking that before any printing the facts be checked. The publisher replied that no manuscript had been submitted and that there could be no comment until it was. The broadcasting company assured us that opportunity would be given to preview the film, but would not promise any changes. A letter to the Independent Broadcasting Authority elicited an acknowledgement that read more on the side of the broadcasting company and far less impartially than one would have expected from an "independent" body.

The director of features at the broadcasting company arranged for the Chief of the Staff with other officers to see the film near the date of airing. At this screening the blow fell. Despite the director's prediction that the film would be regarded as "balanced" by the British public, the officers realized that its impact would be harmful to the Army's cause, upsetting to fellow-Salvationists and a test of allegiance for many whose trust in the movement's work had been demonstrated practically through the years. The film opened with an appeal for funds being made by His Grace the Duke of Westminster. To this, the Chief of the Staff objected. His Grace had worked assiduously to bring the appeal to a successful conclusion, and to associate him with such a distorted report was discourteously unfair. It was agreed that the scene should be deleted. It was. But when the programme was released the scene had simply been replaced with one equally malapropos, that of the Lord Mayor of London making a similar appeal during the same ceremony in which the Duke had participated.

The preview unveiled the shabbiness with which the programme had been threaded together. Four former officers who had left the ranks, one of them many years before, were interviewed. None had ever managed a men's hostel. Their participation was a sad exhibition of mingled self-justification and arrogance, all the sadder when, after reading the files concerning the four, I knew the reasons for their severance. Active officers had wanted to participate positively in the film. One, once an unemployed itinerant, had been rescued from despair in one of the hostels. Now a manager, he was told, "Your story's not the kind we're after." A far different production would have resulted if, as well as the four ex-officers, four who were actively and joyously engaged in the work, despite its burdens and hazards, had been permitted to comment.

One particular hostel came in for heavy criticism even though local authorities and the Army had found large sums of money with which to improve the amenities. The film mentioned the large number of men—more than four hundred—housed in this hostel and then showed a propped-up bath-tub, stained with the oxidation of the years which, it was implied, had to serve the bathing needs of all the residents. What was not said was that the men used showers, and that nearby there were many of them, more than sufficient for the needs of the institution, and all functioning daily. Committing so small a detail to paper may seem picayune, but the power of such a distortion to destroy goodwill is enormous, and so is the problem of counteracting its damage.

On the day of the broadcast I sent a letter to the editor of *The Times* which appeared the next morning:

> From the General of The Salvation Army.
>
> Sir, It is not the practice of Salvationists to spring to their own defence in answer to criticism; that would deflect from their basic task of unceasing warfare against evil. This is as true of modern as of past detractors.
>
> Following the airing by ATV, planned for tonight, of the documentary, *For God's Sake, Care!*, a preliminary version of which we have seen, the public may want to know the facts, and are entitled to expect us to state our case.
>
> The Salvation Army is a movement for Christian evangelism taking the Gospel to the unchurched. It is not concerned only with the provision of food, clothing or shelter, but with the totality of human need. We must

minister to the whole man. When we run hostels, homes for the elderly or for children, trace missing relatives or deliver soup and rolls to men "kipping" under the bridges, it is done in that context.

Our aim is not simply to ameliorate but to assist Divine grace in changing the life-style and raising the hopes of the downtrodden and dispossessed.

When people complain of a mistaken emphasis and demand more resources for social work and less for religion they are making a distinction that Salvationists do not recognize and cannot accept. Every attempt to influence the wayward to reform or the footloose to settle is social work in anybody's language, but its aim, unimposed on the recipient, yet hoped for by the providing, is spiritual.

On the allegations against our hostel managers made in the programme, I have no doubt that our managers are able to spot a "phoney." Men bearing concealed cameras and tape recorders are about as indistinguishable in a room full of hostel dwellers as a hooded klansman in a village choir. Experienced hostel managers invariably recognize a person in genuine need. In today's welfare state those honestly without the price of a bed are few and far between. It is part of the task of our staff to identify the needy and render the assistance they really want, not only of a material kind.

If the film's allegations of physical violence are sustained, and I am far from accepting them at present, then we may have to reconsider our long-standing policy of using unemployed residents as staff in our hostels. The effect of such a policy change would be a loss of jobs and, taken together with the theoretician's present penchant for small hostels, would quickly lead to a substantial reduction in the number of hostel beds.

If the state or commercial market were able to make up the loss, we would rejoice. Our hostel programme, begun as an emergency service, has continued for 90 years. It is arguable that it has fulfilled its purpose, but the thousands of men, and alas of women too, requiring shelter as well as those sleeping rough, do not encourage us to believe that we can yet relax our efforts.

International Headquarters,
The Salvation Army,
London, EC4

Yours sincerely,
(Sgd.) Arnold Brown
General

There was a favourable response, but not all television viewers read *The Times* and the spotlight continued to shine on the subject for some weeks. Meanwhile, three things happened. An internal review of the services given by the hostels was instituted. Every criticism advanced by the film was scrupulously investigated. Concurrently, efforts were made to discover who had interested the producers in the plight of the homeless, and why The Salvation Army had been chosen as the *béte noir.*

Enquiries led to a pressure group crusading for more hostels of smaller size, each to accommodate not more than thirty persons. The group's financial statement revealed that its chief source of income came from two government departments, and that its expenditures were devoted mainly to salaries and publicity. It seemed curious that government departments should be subsidizing a pressure group whose aims could only be realized by massive government spending, and at a time when the maintenance of existing social services was taxing the national treasury to the limit.

With Commissioner Anna Hannevik, leader of the social services in the United Kingdom, I saw the minister of one of the two departments and explained that we also were in favour of smaller hostels and a more personal relationship with the residents. Our new complexes, varying in size, had "clustered" accommodation providing for the man who could live entirely on his own, for those who needed partial care, and for those who required total support or treatment for problems of one kind or another. The viability of the small hostel was discussed. It was our opinion that "circumstances alter cases," and that, depending on locality, type of accommodation needed, and the stripe of person requiring care, the number accommodated should not be arbitrarily fixed but intelligently calculated in the light of finances available. The minister confirmed what I had often felt—that the Army, being closer to the problem than most, should more often speak authoritatively to the government on such matters. My comment that the Army would, if the government wished, close its hostels and turn its attention to other forms of service, was received with consternation. As we left, we were plied with words of encouragement to continue the work.

The pressure group had had the active support of a member of parliament known for his espousal of good causes and an almost fanatical opposition to anything that multiplied the unhappy lot of the underprivileged. For this he was to be commended. As part of the group's crusade this member, immediately following the telecast, called for a government enquiry into the Army's management and financing of the hostels. This provoked a reaction at Westminster which he had not expected. Unbeknown to us, a substantial number of members, of various parties, immediately signed a motion lauding the Army's ministry and asking that the broadcasting company be directed to give the Army equal time for reply. A number of members felt it would be useful, should their constituents raise the matter, to have heard the Army's side, and I was invited to speak to a private meeting of members and answer questions. The member associated with the pressure group sat directly opposite me and, once the meeting was called to order, set out to cross-examine me. The exchanges were not without asperity, but I felt that the facts, as I stated them, were being heard and weighed. The questioning member was eventually reminded that he had dominated the proceedings for too long and that others had questions to ask. With this, the voluble member excused himself and left. A comprehensive report covering the allegations and our findings, together with a financial statement showing in detail the operation of our social services, was distributed to all members of the House, and the meeting ended with plenty of good wishes. I walked out of the committee room in the House of Commons, through St. Stephen's Gate, and into the London twilight. The early evening traffic swirled around Parliament Square. Westminster Abbey, backlighted from the western sky, stood solidly impressive. Churchill, from his commanding statue down the road, seemed to be saying for my benefit, "We shall fight ... we shall never surrender!"

The third outcome was the registering of a complaint by the production team with the Advertising Council. It was alleged that the wording on our appeal envelope was misleading. But when the Council rendered its decision we were found not wilfully to have misled the public, and all appeal materials for the following year were given full, advance approval. The team's attention nevertheless persisted. As complainants, they had early notice of the Advertising Council's decision, and immediately released an item to the press which appeared to vindicate their action. The story had an early death.

As the weeks went by the public's attitude towards the Army, expressed in correspondence, through the media and by donation of funds, swung increasingly in its favour. The "silent majority" began to speak supportively. Not far ahead would be the Christmas appeal and, thereafter, in the month of February, another national appeal. These would reveal the practical feelings of the British public. I, myself, would be gone from the scene, but no-one would await the returns with more concern and hope. In the language of the Book of Proverbs that hope was not deferred, nor was the heart made sick. Both appeals were generously supported.

Traditionally in the mind of the British public the General is part of the United Kingdom scene. Every General has lived in London, not Geneva or Washington, and though he (or she) may preside over the international affairs of the Army he is also, under law, the fiduciary head of the Army in Great Britain. Perhaps it is because of this that British journalists do not feel they are dealing with the most reponsible sources unless they interview the General or the Chief of the Staff. In a way this is understandable, particularly if the matter concerns the social services which do not answer to the British Commissioner but to the Chief of the Staff, the General being the senior officer of the social work trust under which the services are rendered. Invitations to state functions are also directed, first of all, to the General—a throwback, one presumes, to the days of William and Bramwell Booth. And certainly the Salvationists of Britain regard the General as very much one of their own. Like other Salvationists he is on the roll of a corps and takes his place in the congregation when he is not travelling.

This perhaps explains how I personally became so involved in the upset caused by the broadcast. It also explains why a group of local officers (lay leaders), greatly concerned about the effects of the televised programme, bypassed all intermediate levels of leadership and asked to see me personally. They represented a large body of concern, but were completely reassured when the whole story was told. Subsequently, at their request, the Chief of the Staff, the British Commissioner and myself met a large group of local officers. Once again the details were related. I was stirred by the way in which these men and women who invest so much of their life in the movement, drawing from it spiritual uplift and a sense of fellowship but nothing whatever in a material way, regarded the matter as their own.

The group selected three of their number to visit the broadcasting company and register their feelings with the highest authority. This they did, and won the promise of air-time for a Salvation Army programme by which the balance might be restored. Out of the gathering came also strong confirmation that the soldiery, while grateful recipients of any public encouragement and praise, did not expect its officers, unsupportedly, to protect the Army from the detractor's devices. In 1891 it was the violence of a 7000-strong Eastbourne mob; an harassment, however, that was local and directed against Salvationists themselves.

In 1981 it was an attempt by the power of television to discredit the Army nationally in the minds of millions. But, as in earlier years when public opposition took much less subtle forms, the ability to "close ranks" was just as immediate and just as determined.

CHAPTER 27

The Laden Caravans

As retirement approached reflection increased. I scribbled the words: "In retrospect I see a train / Of caravans go by; / Laden, they move across life's way / Towards a sunset sky." Some of the caravans, as I viewed them, were crammed with unspoken thoughts, unrealized hopes, uncompleted projects and unfulfilled dreams. Others were overloaded with privileges that life had brought, chief among them the joy of announcing what R. L. Stevenson described as "this bracing Gospel" in hostels and hospitals, in prisons and at street-corners, in tabernacles, chapels, cathedrals and abbeys, and in scores of stadia and amphitheatres around the world.

In the preaching art I confess to having felt less confident as the years unrolled. Was it because the sublimity of the message is beyond human comprehension? As experience increased it was more clearly understood that the glory of the Gospel deserves the eloquence of angels. Yet something must be said to a disillusioned, weary and hope-less world, and I saw sufficient response to the Good News to encourage, as well as to demand, a faithful and frequent retelling of it. George Herbert, Cambridge University's public orator at 27-years of age, and at 37-years of age an ordinand, gave us in 17th-century language what surely are among the most compelling lines ever written about the proclamation and the proclaimer of the Gospel:

Lord, how can man preach thy eternal word?
He is a brittle crazie glasse:

Yet in thy temple thou dost him afford
This glorious and transcendent place,
To be a window, through thy grace.

If the preacher bears, rather than forbears, this onerous obligation, his declaring of Biblical truth will "not return ... void." In the knapsack of the Salvation soldier there must always be his guide-book, the Bible. In recent decades the Salvationist has seen his Bible, his uniform and his flag burned or otherwise destroyed. Yet the Word of Truth has lingered in his heart. While suffering in detention camps, estranged behind iron or bamboo curtains, whole Gospels have been recalled from memory and written out by hand. It is upon this Book of books that the certainty of The Salvation Army's message rests. For the Salvationist, and all others, the Bible cannot be equated with *Time* or *Newsweek*. The news magazines may "fill us in" concerning current events. The Bible alone will "fill us" with the principles and precepts that make more than news—that make individuals who rise to their highest God-given potential.

The countless opportunities for dipping into the inexhaustible well of Scripture and ladling out its reviving waters to the parched in spirit led to the highest privilege of all, that of seeing large numbers, in circumstances of infinite variety, accepting as personal Saviour the One who continually offers the Water of Life to those who "thirst after righteousness." Often painfully aware of my limitations and spiritual failures, I marvelled that an unworthy vessel could serve Divine purposes. But it was the word I spoke—the "thus saith the Lord"—that mattered, not the tongue that uttered it. It was the Divine grace that the word conveyed that counted rather than any grace of phrase.

It has been a standard question of the media, put to me in Hausa, Korean, Melanese-pidgin, svenska and a score of other languages: "What changes, as leader, are you making?" I had answered cautiously at the beginning. ("Let not him that girdeth on his harness boast himself as he that putteth it off."—1 Kings 20: 11) Now, doffing the armour of office, a new restraint against the predicting of changes is sensed. The shape of the battle is never the same for very long. The commander-in-chief must devise the strategy and employ the tactics that guarantee victory, and none but he knows all the facts. What I realized for myself when in office, I must allow for my successors.

But some things must not change. The twin thrusts of The Salvation Army are irreplaceably the proclamation of the Good News of Salvation in Christ and the determination, as far as possible, to bind up the world's wounds and salve its sorrows. If the movement is to validate its Divine mandate these dual aims must be pursued whatever changes come in structure and methodology. Moving with the times does not mean that proven values fall out of date. Love for God and man, one vertical, the other horizontal, each different in degree and demonstration but the same in sincerity, is an obligation upon all who call themselves Salvationists. The spiritual and material needs of man are linked in every aspect of his existence and the Salvationist, under God, must minister to both.

Changes will come. They started early in the Army's history and have continued ever since. Adaptation to the inevitable shifts in the social, economic and political nature of nations will be ensured by generous applications of "sanctified originality"—the newest way of doing the old, effective things. I do not fear for any lack of this precious element if there is reliance for inspiration on the Holy Spirit. His illuminating guidance is frequently unpredictable, inevitably wise and always issuing in new accomplishments that glorify God and ennoble His people. If the movement remains "under the shadow of the Almighty" it need never follow the brontosaurus into fossilized extinction! As ordinary people called to an extraordinary task, Salvationists must be both simple and sophisticated; simple enough in their approach with the Gospel that the simplest can understand, and sophisticated to the degree that they are aware of the world of science and technology which surrounds them. I bristle every time I hear someone use the phrase, "the post-Christian era." It is not a post-Christian era, I tell myself, while *I* am still a Christian. In fact, there are evidences that the "remnant in Israel" is much larger than many suppose. For this "remnant" the overwhelming task is to reach the homeless mind and the alien heart.

If I refuse to admit that this is a post-Christian era, I have to admit that it is a dangerous one. Danger arises for the Army when, through any neglect of its interior life, the critical faculty is lost and, as a movement, it risks being engulfed by the prevailing culture. Against such a hazard unity is strength. The internationality of the Army, binding the ligaments of its many parts, gives the movement's anatomy toughness. In a day when, on the one hand, Christians are discovering a new unity of spirit and, on the other hand, the historic churches are struggling toward a much more difficult to achieve organic union, the one-ness of the Army, operating in eighty-six countries and bracketing an infinite variety of peoples, is nothing short of miraculous. In recent years this one-ness has been subjected to many stresses, and perhaps the end is not yet. Nationalism which has split empires and federations, and tribalism which establishes boundaries within colour blocks, do not exempt the Army in their assertiveness. But the intention must persist that The Salvation Army will remain a world movement with a world message and a world responsibility, because it is one Salvation Army looking to one Lord and Saviour whose exaltation and service is the one task it longs to fulfil.

Perhaps some hearers tired of my repeated declaration that the front-line of The Salvation Army must always run through the agony of the world. But the repetition flowed from a deep belief that only in this way could the movement fulfil its Divine commission. Though facilities are increasingly modern, officers more highly certificated, and a wide variety of disciplines are now at the disposal of God in His regenerative work, the Army's milieu is "within a yard of Hell." Carpeted halls need not be foreign to the drunkard's vomit. The Army's cleverest musician can be the most passionate evangelist. Gutters and back-alleys must remain part of the Army's territory, and marching the main streets we must not forget it.

A few lines earlier I stated that in a spiritual sense this era is a dangerous one. It is also dangerous in the everyday meaning of the word. Towards the end of my incumbency regard for the personal safety of world religious leaders became a matter of serious concern. The attempt on the life of Pope John Paul II emphasized the fact that danger had become a vocational hazard, not only for pontiffs, but for lesser mortals who also might be the victims of "the sizeable sickness of our times." To suggest that a Salvation Army General might have to wear a bullet-proof vest seems preposterous. Common-sense points out, however, that a disgruntled individual, whose mental balance has been displaced by the weight of frustration or life's cruelties, may feel that he can only restore that balance by eliminating the head of the body which he thinks has laid on him the last straw of humiliation. In several of the countries I visited men and women of God had been wounded, tortured and murdered. Occasionally I wondered if I would have their capacity to rise above physical threat, and could only hope that with Divine assistance I might be able to do so. As it was, I was providentially spared such testing. Many of those who looked to me as leader ran a thousand risks in their daily service. For their sakes I could not, and did not, in any way spare myself—minus a bullet-proof vest!

The privilege of leadership would be no privilege at all if it were not for the commitment of "the led." Those who comprise our global Army are the salt of the earth. To have had some responsibility for them, and to have been acknowledged by them with respect and even affection, has been a privilege worth any occasional rocking of the organizational caravan. If the caravans in my train bore identification, like the goods carriages that make up the world's freight trains, one would undoubtedly be labelled *Fellowship*. This caravan, I'm afraid, exceeds the allowed weight limit. I have known fabulous riches of comradeship and contact. To leave one's home and family for My sake, said Jesus, is to cross the threshold of many homes and be embraced as a member by many families. For my wife and myself this promise of Jesus has been redeemed time after time. I am utterly defeated in trying to describe the familial spirit that binds Salvationists together, for "familial" it genuinely is. "Blest be the tie that binds our hearts in Christian love." I sometimes wonder if the clergy read their *Crockford's* with the same feeling of relationship to those listed as do we when leafing through a *Disposition of Forces*. Salvationists, as the New Testament writer to the Romans expects Christians to be, are "given to hospitality." The Shunemite woman's chamber with "a bed, and a table, and a stool, and a candlestick" would often have sufficed in our travels. But Salvationist hospitality, and that of a multitude of friends, seems to go beyond the necessities. To our numerous hosts we can only echo the prophet Elisha's words to the widow of Shunem, "Thou hast been careful for us with all this care," and add our heartfelt thanks. Not for the prodigal son only has there been the fatted calf.

Nor by any means was I an Atlas carrying the Army world alone. Good colleagues were legion. Those who shared the load were countless. Always there was the loving, empathetic help of a wife whose own caravans jogged alongside mine. Let no mistake be made. The wife of the international leader of The Salvation Army needs to be a special person. Not only must she bend "the sympathetic ear" when there is no one else to whom the leader can talk, but she has her own large army on the distaff side to inspire, and this she must do in between the tours and campaigns which, if anything, demand more of the woman than the man. If the "hands of Moses were steady until the going down of the sun" because of Aaron's and Hur's devotion, mine have been made so by the upholding of many. In the culminating appointment, loyal Chiefs of the Staff and an Advisory Council with its collective wisdom were backed up by concerned leadership at International, territorial and command headquarters throughout the world. The small personal staffs that worked closely with me every day displayed dedication, competence and often great resourcefulness. Their names are indelibly written in our memory and wreathed with gratitude and affection.

The eschatological words of our Lord, "Pray ye that your flight be not in the winter," had present and practical import in respect of our farewell to London, England, and our return to Canada. As we moved through the long sequence of private and public farewell occasions the December weather hardened. Crowded retirement gatherings in Glasgow's stately city hall, in the massive town hall at Leeds with its fifth largest pipe organ in Europe, in Westminster Chapel where, as a youth, I had listened spellbound to the expositions of Dr. Campbell Morgan, and in the familiar, domed Westminster Central Hall in London were suffused with the warmth of goodwill and good wishes while outside Britain was shivering through one of its coldest and stormiest winters. The Living Bible (Ecclesiastes 5: 20) provided my text for these leave-takings: "To enjoy your work and to accept your lot in life—that is indeed a gift from God. The person who does that will not need to look back with sorrow on his past, for God gives him joy." That joy was unaffected by the three-day delay of our flight while Britishers shook themselves loose from the weather's icy paralysis and we remained stranded in an airport hotel where my retirement birthday, the 68th, was celebrated. If only I had been born in June! It was still winter when we flew in to Toronto, but the sunny welcome of family and friends banished all thoughts of inconvenience or snowy blast. We were home again, and in time for Christmas.

The churches correspondent of *The Yorkshire Post,* Michael Brown, once asked me how I would like my epitaph to read. I reminded him that few people devise their own. A true epitaph is not a distillation into a few choice words of one's self-evaluation. Rather, it is, in a form of words, how those who have known an individual well wish to remember him and to have him remembered. Perhaps the safest procedure is to add nothing to the calendar record of birth and death, leaving all estimations of worth or weakness to the mercy of God. The interviewer, however, was insistent, and anyone poring through the files of that established journal can read that, with considerable reluctance, I said that the epitaph might be couched in such words as: "He did his work well and with a great love for the task." There would be more of hope than assurance in such an inscription, though the hope is passionately held. What is certain is that the work to which my wife and I were called—freighted with joy, overflowing with sacred opportunities and productive of an abundance of undeserved rewards—is one for which, because of its nature and eternal consequences, one's best is all too little.

Thankfully, that is all God requires.

L'Envoi ...

AS YET UNTOLD

(From Prince George to Vancouver involved a long south-eastward flight over the Canadian Rockies. As we neared our destination all that could be seen from the window of the plane was a vast sea of cloud, across which a reddening sun flung great washes of colour. The cloud-expanse was unbroken save for the upthrust peaks of a few mountain giants which seemed, somehow, to be pinnacle-peering at the majestic view that was ours. I remembered suddenly that those mountains were rooted on earth —more than four miles below.)

The everlasting peaks are there,
  And what an angel's view I share;
An Arctic waste of carpet cloud
  The timeless pinnacles enshroud;
    Unending ice-cap of the sky,
    (Or is it ocean-foam flung high?)
    And through this wonder-world of winds
          Go I.

The everlasting peaks are there,
  And what angelic thoughts I share!
My earth-shod soul shall surely rise
  By faith and pinnacle the skies,
    Eternal vistas to behold,
    Where grace and glory will unfold,
    So near to God, delights as yet
          Untold.

— A.B.

Appendix

NOMINATION SPEECH

(Members of the High Council who accept the nomination for the office of General are required to address their fellow Councillors before the balloting begins. The following is the speech, reprinted from *The Officer,* delivered prior to my election.—A.B.)

Mr. President, officers and fellow-members of the 1977 High Council:

If I came to this place, and for this same purpose, three years ago, with great trepidation, that trepidation, I must confess, is increased as I stand before the Lord, and all of you, at this moment. When I reflect on how uncertainties and upheavals have multiplied in the world in so short a space of time, it is impossible that anyone nominated for leadership of a world movement like ours could fail to ask himself, "Who is sufficient for these things?"

But what I also said three years ago, I repeat. I stand here again without spiritual fear. I may be gravely concerned about much that is happening in the world, and I am; but that anxiety does not overshadow my confidence in our Lord and Master who, in His own good time, will bring all things under His rule.

I realize that it is not so much what a man says in a solemn moment like this that weighs so seriously in the mind of a High Council, as what that man has been saying throughout his whole life. The promises he may make here are important, but they are no more important than the promises he has kept throughout his officership. It is nearly forty-three years since I closed my office desk and set my face toward what I believed to be my life's work. Through the whole of that time, the Divine grace which saved and sanctified me has sustained me. It is to that Divine grace that I must look as trustingly in the future as I have been assisted by it in the past.

It is that same Divine grace which enables me, at this moment, to view these proceedings as a spiritual exercise set apart from all ordinary electoral motives. We all feel the deep solemnity of this hour. We are all aware of the world-wide challenge which confronts us and, at the same time, of the boundless opportunities which are opening up to men and women who have faith in God and love for Christ. As much as any in this chamber, I am aware of my limitations and my inadequacies. Because of this, I must testify in Paul's words to the Corinthians, as rendered by Moffatt, that "I possess this treasure in a frail vessel of earth to show that the transcending power belongs to God, not to myself" (2 Corinthians 4: 7). The frailty of this vessel is humbly and regretfully acknowledged, but I am convinced that "the transcending power" of God is sufficient for our Army and for the continuance of its effective work and witness in the world. A "transcending power" that will bring in an Eternal Kingdom is surely a power upon which any leader and, indeed, the Army as a whole, can rely.

I beg leave of the Council to repeat some of the things I said here three years ago, but perhaps in a different form. I see the General's task in this way:

1. *The General's lead must, above all, be spiritual.*

If the emphasis has been upon evangelism, it must still be upon evangelism. That emphasis must be renewed; it must press more heavily upon every one of us. Therefore, as I see it, the next General, whoever he may be, must take the lead in sacrifice, in devotion and in soul-winning endeavour.

2. *He must call Salvationists to a renewed emphasis upon our doctrine.*

It seems to me that our doctrine needs to be made alive again in the consciousness and witness of our people. I do not look upon this "faith once delivered" unto the saints as merely an interesting collection of truths which we must only protect and defend. I think of our faith as knowledge, as conviction, as challenge, as a moral and spiritual dynamic that should be as intelligible as it is undauntable. It will be the task of the General, by every means possible, to make real and vital to this generation the beliefs so fervently held and taught by our great founders.

3. *He must see to it that wherever and whenever possible administration will be streamlined.*

We do not want a movement whose superstructure threatens its equilibrium. I am all for finding the swiftest and most efficient ways of meeting the avalanche of demands—legal, governmental, financial—that flow in upon the Army in these days. But our officers must remain as free as possible to "preach the acceptable year of the Lord ... to heal the broken-hearted." The leader must encourage the most intelligent overhauling of our systems, so that our structures will be such as will properly serve the Army's soul-winning purposes. There can be no justification for them beyond that.

4. *He must be a General for youth.*

In many parts of the world today's generation of Salvationist youth is displaying a recapturing of the selfless, evangelistic daring of their grandfathers and their great-grandfathers. They are writing songs that will outlive us all. They are crusading for Christ through new forms of expression and appeal and, in this respect, I have a feeling that the end is not yet. Our international leader, by all means at his disposal, must multiply this priceless asset in order conscientiously to discharge his undertaking to both the present and the future.

5. *He must ensure the enlargement of "the female ministry."*

The record will confirm the seriousness I place upon the preservation of this distinctive feature of Salvation Army life. In a day when so many movements are groping towards an equality of recognition, an equality of opportunity and responsibility for women and men, the lead given to the world by The Salvation Army must not be lost. Need I say more on this subject? It is perhaps one that has passed beyond discussion, and requires courageous implementation.

6. *He must speed the progress of the Army in the developing countries.*

The command of Jesus, "Go ye into all the world and preach the gospel to every creature" is one which the Army has not evaded. I see the General as one who has a direct administrative interest in missionary territories motivated by a strong missionary love. In this sphere of Army service there is, I believe, abundant room for creative initiative, for new things to be done in new ways, so that Christ, the hope of the world, may be lifted up to new visibility, to wider acceptance, and to new glory.

7. *He must increase the place of our soldiery.*

For the Army, the term "sanctified manpower" means not only officers but soldiers. Our Salvationists take their religion to the office and the factory. They can bring back to the Army a knowledge of the world and its needs, of the people and their perplexities. There is a vast number of Salvationists who, while delighting in our traditional forms of participation and service, are eagerly awaiting the clarion call to the making of new and adventurous kinds of participation. Few aspects of a General's work could be more important to the future than this.

8. *He must arouse Salvationists to the desperate need for officer reinforcements.*

Nothing more securely links the present of The Salvation Army to its future, or determines the passion and effectiveness of that future, than the recruitment and training of its officers. We praise God for the increased number of candidates in many parts of the Army world, but more must yet be done to make officers and soldiers alike realize not only the need, but also their responsibility to try and meet it. The availability of sanctified men and women is the great need for today and for tomorrow, and I would expect the General to give the strongest possible emphasis to this end.

9. *He must be committed to the principle of one Salvation Army.*

All of us feel that the Army is a precious possession of God. It was Divinely brought into being. It has been Divinely nurtured. It has been Divinely favoured. This implies, to me, a sacred obligation to preserve, as far as is humanly possible, its oneness of spirit. I believe the Army to be a world movement with a world message and a world responsibility. I could not be party to bringing in any kind of federation of autonomous Salvation Armies, and I would pray for the wisdom to frustrate any secular pressures that would seek to force this upon us. I believe that the Army should demonstrate in itself the unifying power of the Word it proclaims. It should be *one* Salvation Army because it looks to *one* Lord and Saviour, whose exaltation and service is the *one* task it longs to fulfil.

Finally, I believe that the powers of the General's office are not so much *invested* in him, which is the legal (and perhaps the weakest) part of his authority, as they are *entrusted* to him by a loving and loyal people and, therefore, may not be used by him in the least degree as his own prescriptive right. I understand completely that the General's authority is not in the power decreed by any Deed, but in his humble and constant reliance upon God in the closest fellowship and cooperation with our officers and soldiers. In 2 Corinthians 10: 18 (New English Bible), Paul says it not only for himself, but for us all, "Not the man who recommends himself, but the man whom the Lord recommends—he and he alone is to be accepted."